The Other Side of Zen

BUDDHISMS

A PRINCETON UNIVERSITY PRESS SERIES

Edited by Stephen F. Teiser

———————

The Other Side of Zen: A Social History of Sōtō Zen Buddhism in Tokugawa Japan,
by Duncan Ryūken Williams

Relics of the Buddha,
by John S. Strong

Becoming the Buddha: The Ritual of Image Consecration in Thailand,
by Donald K. Swearer

The Impact of Buddhism on Chinese Material Culture,
by John Kieschnick

The Power of Denial: Buddhism, Purity, and Gender,
by Bernard Faure

Neither Monk nor Layman: Clerical Marriage in Modern Japanese Buddhism,
by Richard M. Jaffe

Buddhist Learning and Textual Practice in Eighteenth-Century Lankan Monastic Culture,
by Anne M. Blackburn

The Red Thread: Buddhist Approaches to Sexuality,
by Bernard Faure

The Other Side of Zen

A SOCIAL HISTORY OF SŌTŌ ZEN
BUDDHISM IN TOKUGAWA JAPAN

DUNCAN RYŪKEN WILLIAMS

PRINCETON UNIVERSITY PRESS

PRINCETON AND OXFORD

Published by Princeton University Press, 41 William Street, Princeton, New Jersey 08540

In the United Kingdom: Princeton University Press, 3 Market Place, Woodstock, Oxfordshire OX20 1SY

LIBRARY OF CONGRESS CATALOGING-IN-PUBLICATION DATA
Williams, Duncan Ryūken, 1969–
    The other side of Zen : a social history of Sōtō Zen Buddhism in Tokugawa Japan / Duncan Ryūken Williams.
      p.   cm.   — (Buddhisms : Princeton University Press series)
    Includes bibliographical references and index.
    ISBN 0-691-11928-7 (cloth : alk. paper)
    1. Sōtōshū—Social aspects. I. Title: Social history of Sōtō Zen. II. Title: Buddhism in Tokugawa Japan. III. Title. IV. Buddhisms.
    BQ9412.6 W55 2005
    294.3'927—dc22   2004044339

British Library Cataloging-in-Publication Data is available

This book has been composed in Sabon

Printed on acid-free paper. ∞

pup.princeton.edu

Printed in the United States of America

10 9 8 7 6 5 4 3

ISBN 13: 978-0-691-14429-0

CONTENTS

FIGURES AND TABLES

FIGURES

TABLES

ACKNOWLEDGMENTS

THE CAUSES AND CONDITIONS that give rise to a book are innumerable, but I would like to express my gratitude to at least some of the people who helped me produce this manuscript. As a graduate student at Harvard University, I was launched onto the scholar's path by Masatoshi Nagatomi, while Helen Hardacre directed the doctoral dissertation on which much of this book is based. Whatever contribution my research might make to the field, I owe the greatest debt to these two distinguished scholars of Buddhist studies and the study of Japanese religions, respectively. My training in the study of Japanese Buddhism was enriched by Masatoshi Nagatomi's encouragement to investigate the topic within the broader world of East Asian Buddhism. He instilled in me a concern for placing the study of Buddhism within cultural contexts while never losing sight of the Buddhist tradition as a whole. Helen Hardacre taught me the importance of setting my studies on Zen within a sociohistorical framework so as to connect the study of religion to society. She encouraged me to learn how to read Tokugawa-period handwritten materials, which allowed me to investigate temple and local history archives throughout Japan. With extraordinary patience and compassion, these two teachers shaped not only my research, but also my entire outlook as a scholar.

Since the bulk of the research for this book was conducted in Japan, I must mention several individuals who assisted me during the summers of 1993–97 as well as the more extended dissertation research period of 1998–2000 and postdoctoral work during 2002–3. I was fortunate to receive the guidance of two scholars who shared their wisdom, unpublished documents, and invitation to attend seminars and field research trips. Tamamuro Fumio of Meiji University, a pioneer in the study of Tokugawa-period religions, helped me to understand Sōtō Zen Buddhism in the context of early modern Japanese religious history by encouraging me to focus on the lives of ordinary temple priests, temple economics, and quantitative data. He accompanied me on numerous trips to Eiheiji and Noto Sōjiji temples and to innumerable local history archives. Hirose Ryōkō of Komazawa University, a leading researcher of medieval and early modern Sōtō Zen history, advised me to think about the Sōtō tradition in the context of local society, patronage patterns, and regional administration. He also accompanied me on research trips to Eiheiji Temple and provided me access to the documents held at the Sōtōshū Bunkazai Chōsa Iinkai at Komazawa University.

A number of scholars, including Andō Yoshinori, Itō Katsumi, Kōdate Naomi, Matsuoka Takashi, Ōwada Kōichi, Sakai Tatsurō, Tsutsumi Kunihiko, Umezawa Fumiko, and Watanabe Shōei, also helped me recognize the significance of popular tales, narrative literature, and the cults of local deities for my study. Many institutes and temples also supported my research in Japan by freely sharing original documents in their possession. They include the Atsugishishi Hensan Shitsu, Etoki Kenkyūkai, Hakone Chōritsu Kyōdo Shiryōkan, Higashiurashi Hensan Shitsu, Komazawa University Library, Sōtōshū Shūmuchō (headquarter offices, Bunkazai Chōsa Iinkai, Jinken Yōgo Suishin Honbu, and Sōtōshū Sōgō Kenkyū Center), as well as individual temples and their priests: Chōjuin (Shinohara Eiichi), Jizōji (Asai Senryō), Kenkon'in (Shimada Taizen), and Senryūji (Sugawara Shōei). Thanks are also due to the many individuals who helped me read and transcribe these manuscripts, including Hiromoto Shōko, Inoue Asako, Kuroda Hiroshi, Marufuji Tomoko, Minagawa Gikō, Tanaka Hiroshi, and Yamamoto Akiko.

Studies in Japan were further enhanced through affiliations with the Faculty of Comparative Culture at Sophia University in 1997–98 and with the History Department (which kindly provided a research office) at Komazawa University during 1998–2000 and 2002–3. At Komazawa University, many professors helped me receive access to the university's large collection of materials on Sōtō Zen, including Kumamoto Einin, Nara Kōmei, Ōtani Tetsuo, and Sasaki Kōkan. The fellows of the Shūgaku Kenkyū Bumon of the Sōtōshū Sōgō Kenkyū Center at Komazawa University received me warmly and patiently answered my numerous questions. Particular thanks go to Aki Eibun, Hareyama Shun'ei, Hirako Yasuhiro, Ikegami Kōyō, Ishijima Shōyū, Itō Yoshihisa, Kaneko Shūgen, Kirino Kōgaku, Matsuda Yōji, Shimomura Kakudō, and Yokoi Kyōshō.

Although errors of interpretation or translation in this book are mine alone, the research and writing proceeded smoothly because of the insightful comments and critiques of many people who read chapters or the entire manuscript. During the dissertation writing stage, Harold Bolitho and Charles Hallisey constantly advised me to reflect on the significance of the project for the fields of Japanese and Buddhist studies, respectively. Their encouragement from the early stages helped me imagine ways in which this study might be of interest to non-Sōtō Zen specialists. Other Harvard professors who assisted me throughout my graduate career included Diana Eck, Christopher Queen, and Lawrence Sullivan. Helpful suggestions also came from researchers at other universities, including Barbara Ambros, Andrew Bernstein, William Bodiford, Steve Covell, Richard Gardner, Hank Glassman, Steven Heine, Hiromi Maeda, Mark Mullins, David and Diane Riggs, Kate Nakai, Paul Swanson, Mary Evelyn Tucker, and Alex Vesey. Proofreaders helped me with the writing, including Victoria James, Paula Maute, Beth Miller, and Debra Robbins. Finally, the three anonymous reviewers for Princeton University Press provided insightful commentary that helped me reflect on the broader themes of the volume. Special thanks goes to one reviewer in particular who provided an exhaustive and meticulous list of corrections.

The publication process would have been impossible to navigate without the kindness, patience, and editorial insight of Stephen Teiser, the general editor of the "Buddhisms" series, and my editor and copy editor at Princeton University Press, Fred Appel and Anita O'Brien, respectively. An earlier version of chapter 3 was published as "Funerary Zen: Sōtō Zen Death Management in Tokugawa Japan," in *Death Rituals and the Afterlife in Japanese Buddhism*, ed. Jacqueline Stone and Mariko Walter (University of Hawai'i Press, 2004), and chapter 5 as "How Dōshō's Medicine Saved Dōgen: Medicine, Dōshō'an, and Edo-Period Dōgen Biographies," in *Chan Buddhism in Ritual Context*, ed. Bernard Faure (Routledge Curzon Press, 2003). I am grateful to the editorial boards of these presses for permission to print revised versions of those pieces.

This book was written during my time at Trinity College and at the University of California, Irvine. My colleagues in the International Studies Program at Trinity and the East Asian Languages and Literatures Department at the University of California at Irvine were most supportive and provided me with the time to complete this manuscript. Many thanks to Trinity's Nicole Reichenbach for her work as my research assistant.

I would also like to acknowledge the institutes and fellowships that made this research possible financially: the Atsumi International Scholarship Foundation, Bukkyō Dendō Kyōkai, Harvard Center for the Study of World Religions, Japan Society for the Promotion of Science, Harvard Edwin O. Reischauer Institute of Japanese Studies, Andrew Mellon Foundation, Rocky Foundation, and Yokohama Zenkōji Scholarship.

Finally, boundless gratitude is due to the people closest to me—my Zen teacher and my family. Ogasawara Ryūgen, abbot of Kōtakuji Temple, has guided my Sōtō Zen priestly life while I simultaneously walked the scholarly path. My parents, Stephen and Tsutae Williams, have been my steadfast supporters from the earliest times, providing me with opportunities to pursue my dreams. Assistance on the Japanese materials from my mother and on the writing in English from my father reflects their long-standing efforts to educate me bilingually and biculturally. And last, but certainly not least, I owe my deepest gratitude to my wife and best friend, Barbara Ambros, who not only gave me refreshing scholarly advice when I came home with writer's block, but also supported the whole experience of putting together this book through all the highs and lows, day in, day out. Endless bows.

This book is dedicated to my late brother, Nigel Williams, an inspirational human being.

THE MODIFIED HEPBURN SYSTEM is used for the romanization of Japanese terms. Apostrophes are used only in rare cases to prevent misunderstanding with similar transliteration or to designate discrete syllables after "n" (as in on'aratamechō). Commonly used Japanese and Sanskrit terms and place names do not bear diacritical marks, nor are they italicized.

Japanese names are rendered in Japanese order—surname followed by given name, except for individuals who have chosen to adopt the Western style. Temple names that include the suffix *ji, tera, dera, in,* or *an* (meaning monastery, temple, subtemple, or hermitage) or shrine names that include the suffix *jinja, gū,* or *miya* (meaning shrine) are retained as inherent to the name. English explanatory words such as temple or shrine are added, despite the redundancy, for the convenience of the reader. The same principle has been applied to Japanese villages, towns, and cities.

In providing dates, years are given according to the Gregorian calendar except when part of a translated text. However, months and days are given according to the Japanese lunar calendar system, for example, "twenty-seventh day of the first month."

Sanskrit terms follow the conventional system of transliteration, while the pinyin system is used for Chinese terms. When referring to the Taishō canon, the abbreviation "T" will be followed by the volume number, page, and register (a, b, or c).

ABBREVIATIONS: REFERENCE WORKS AND JOURNALS

DNBZ   *Dai Nihon bukkyō zensho.* 151 vols. Tokyo: Bussho kankōkai, 1911–22.

DTG   *Dōryōson teito gojun junshakuki.* Edited by Itō Dōgaku, Chishō Misawa, and Shōei Watanabe. Minami Ashigara: Daiyūzan Saijōji, 1986.

EJTS   *Edo jidai tōmon seiyō.* Edited by Yokozeki Ryōin. Tokyo: Bukkyōsha, 1938.

HIBK   *Hokkaidō indogaku bukkyōgaku kenkyū kiyō.* Sapporo: Hokkaidō University.

IB   *Indotetsugaku bukkyōgaku.* Hokkaidō: Hokkaidō Indotetsugaku bukkyō gakkai.

IBK   *Indogaku bukkyōgaku kenkyū kiyō.* Tokyo: Tokyo University.

KDBK   *Komazawa daigaku bukkyōgakubu kenkyū kiyō.* Tokyo: Komazawa University.

KDBN   *Komazawa daigaku daigakuin bukkyōgaku kenkyūkai nenpō.* Tokyo: Komazawa University.

KDBR   *Komazawa daigaku bukkyōgakubu ronshū*. Tokyo: Komazawa University.

KDZN   *Komazawa daigaku zen kenkyūsho nenpō*. Tokyo: Komazawa University.

MAS   *Minami Ashigara shishi*. 8 vols. Minami Ashigara: Minami Ashigara, 1985–99.

MZZK   *Manji zoku zōkyō (Nihon zoku zōkyō)*. 151 vols. Taipei: Chūgoku bukkyōkai, 1946.

SBCM   *Sōtōshū bunkazai chōsa mokuroku kaidaishū 3, 4, 5, 6*. Edited by Sōtōshū Bunkazai Chōsa Iinkai. Tokyo: Sōtōshū shūmuchō, 1996–2003.

SK   *Sōtōshū komonjo*. Edited by Ōkubo Dōshū. 3 vols. Tokyo: Chikuma shobō, 1972.

SKK   *Sōtōshū kenkyūin kenkyū kiyō*. Tokyo: Sōtōshū shūmuchō.

SKKK   *Sōtōshū kenkyūin kenkyūsei kenkyū kiyō*. Tokyo: Sōtōshū shūmuchō.

SSCM   *Sōtōshū shūhō chōsa mokuroku kaidaishū 1, 2*. Edited by Sōtōshū Shūhō Chōsa Iinkai. Tokyo: Sōtōshū shūmuchō, 1991–94.

SZ   *Sōtōshū zensho*. Edited by Sōtōshū Zensho Kankōkai. 1929–35. Re-ed. 18 vols. Tokyo: Sōtōshū shūmuchō, 1970–73.

SZD   *Shinpen Zengaku daijiten*. Edited by Komazawa Daigaku Zengaku Daijiten Hensanjo. Tokyo: Taishukan shoten, 2003.

T   *Taishō shinshū daizōkyō*. 85 vols. Edited by Takakusu Junjirō and Watanabe Kaigyoku. Tokyo: Taishō issaikyō kankōkai, 1924–34.

ZSZ   *Zoku Sōtōshū zensho*. Edited by Sōtōshū zensho kankōkai. 10 vols. Tokyo: Sōtōshū shūmuchō, 1974–77.

MISCELLANEOUS

attr.   attributed
Ch.   Chinese
d.   died
esp.   especially
Jpn.   Japanese
n.d.   no date
n.p.   no publisher
Skt.   Sanskrit

Toward a Social History of Sōtō Zen

UNTIL THE 1980s, scholars of Japanese Zen Buddhism in the West almost always focused on three major approaches to Zen. Zen was taken as a form of mysticism, as an Eastern philosophy, or as a part of Japanese culture. Examining meditation, the philosophical writings of well-known Zen masters, or "expressions of high culture" such as the Zen garden or the tea ceremony, these scholars tended to isolate the Zen Buddhist tradition from both its sociohistorical context and the broader Japanese religious landscape in which it was embedded. Zen was portrayed as a pure and timeless truth, untainted by the social and political institutions of medieval and early modern Japan. Furthermore, both popular and academic writing about all three major Japanese Zen schools—Sōtō, Rinzai, Ōbaku—presented Zen as a unique tradition, set apart from other Japanese Buddhist and non-Buddhist religious traditions. In the case of the Sōtō Zen school, the subject of this book, such scholarship advanced the understanding of Zen philosophy, poetics, or meditation but failed to illuminate how the Zen school participated in the broader social and religious landscape of late medieval and early modern Japan. Edwin O. Reischauer, the well-known Japanologist, was one of the first critics of these approaches. He stated in 1981, "It is ironic that Zen philosophy, which is commonly characterized as being beyond words, has inspired millions of words in English print, whereas Zen institutions, though vastly important in many aspects of medieval Japanese civilization and in no way beyond description in words, have drawn so few."[1] During the past twenty years, a small but significant scholarly response to Reischauer's criticism has emerged in the West. These scholars, based on the postwar research of Japanese historians of the Zen school, have begun to examine the establishment and development of Zen Buddhism in Japan as a social and political institution.[2]

Following this newer scholarly lineage, this book uses the work of these scholars to address the question of how Sōtō Zen managed to grow from only several thousand temples in the early sixteenth century to 17,548 temples by the early eighteenth century and become the single largest school of Buddhism in Japan.[3] The answer to this question cannot be found in the writings of the sect's founder Dōgen (1200–1253), or in what is often presumed to be the sect's primary activity, Zen meditation. Instead, the enormous growth of Sōtō Zen temples must be explained by an exploration of the broader political and religious life of the late medieval and early modern periods as well as the social role played by Buddhist temples in the ordinary layperson's life.

During early modern (1600–1867) Japan, also known as the Tokugawa or Edo period, the Sōtō Zen sect was in certain respects distinct from other Buddhist sects. Despite these doctrinal, ritual, and organizational characteristics, Sōtō Zen at the same time fully participated in, and indeed helped to create, a common or transsectarian religious culture that characterized early modern Japanese Buddhism. The key to the growth of Sōtō Zen lay in its ability to maintain the sect's distinctiveness and nonsectarianism simultaneously. For instance, while priests promoted the unique power of Sōtō Zen's healing practices and funerals, those same priests also knew that for Sōtō Zen temples to be accepted in local society, they needed to incorporate local deities, beliefs, and customs, as well as participate in the emerging, common Buddhist culture of early modern Japan. Although many historians of Japanese Zen Buddhism have highlighted the distinctive aspect of the school, such as meditation and kōan practice, the tremendous growth of Sōtō Zen cannot be explained without equal attention to the ritual life of temples, which, if anything, deemphasized sectarianism. Especially from the perspective of ordinary village parishioners, the skill of the Sōtō Zen priest in adapting local funerary customs, incorporating local deities at the village temple, or fulfilling such social needs as healing the sick and praying for rain played a far more significant role in attracting followers than Sōtō Zen's distinctive teachings or practices.

Although the mid-Tokugawa period saw the emergence of the so-called sect restoration movement that promoted a form of sectarian orthodoxy and orthopraxy, neither the study of Dōgen's texts nor the practice of Zen meditation took place at any more than a tiny percentage of the roughly 17,500 Sōtō Zen temples during the eighteenth century. A few elite monks of the period may have imagined a return to the original teachings and practices of the founder, but the lived religion of the vast majority of Sōtō Zen temple priests and their parishioners centered around practical benefits to life in this world (genze riyaku) and the management of the spirits of the dead in the world beyond (raise kuyō).[4] Practical Buddhism, which offered benefits in this world, and funerary Buddhism, which offered benefits for the world beyond, became the two major pillars of Tokugawa-period transsectarian Buddhist religious life for ordinary parishioners.

When examined from this perspective, the Zen priest's main activities, which typically were praying for rain, healing the sick, or performing exorcistic and funerary rites, illuminate a different side of Zen. This book's focus on "the other side of Zen" is much like Barbara Ruch's concept of "the other side of culture" found in her study of medieval Japan, in which she argues for recovering "the texture and contours of the daily life of the great majority of medieval men and women."[5] As in Ruch's study, I deliberately highlight some aspects of Zen while downplaying others. For instance, I have made a conscious decision not to profile the lives and writings of certain relatively well-known Sōtō Zen masters of the Tokugawa period, such as Manzan Dōhaku or Menzan Zuihō, important figures in the so-called sect-restoration movement of the early eighteenth century, who in recent years have received attention for their contributions to doctrinal studies and their attempts to create a Sōtō Zen orthodoxy and orthopraxy.[6] Although these two monks appear in this book, I have left it up to other scholars to discuss their place in the development of Sōtō Zen in the Tokugawa period because such monks, however great their impact on monastic training temples, had limited impact on practices at the vast majority of temples: the prayer and parish temples.

While not eliminating these monks from my discourse, I have "decentered" them from my account of Tokugawa-period Sōtō Zen history. Instead of focusing on the "great masters," this book reveals the religious life of mid-level or typical Sōtō Zen priests and the ordinary people who came into contact with them, a counterbalance to the customary approach to the study of Japanese Zen Buddhism, in which "unique," "great," or "exceptional" Zen monks have represented the entire tradition. I discuss the "great monks" primarily for contrastive purposes, to reveal the ritual and mental universes of the majority of Zen monks and their lay followers, though avoiding an overly simplistic dichotomy of "popular" versus "elite" Buddhism.

The truth is that the well-known "orthodox" Zen monks of the Tokugawa period were paradoxically marginal, in the sense that their rhetoric of orthodoxy and orthopraxy had surprisingly little to do with the actual practices of most Sōtō Zen temples. In fact, as this book will demonstrate, the vast majority of ordinary Sōtō Zen monks and laypeople never practiced Zen meditation, never engaged in iconoclastic acts of the Ch'an/Zen masters (as described in hagiographical literature), never solved *kōans*, never raked Zen gardens, never sought mystical meditative states, and never read Dōgen's writings. While some Tokugawa-period monks and some modern scholars may have construed such activities as true Zen, this study asks not what Sōtō Zen ideally ought to have been, but what Sōtō Zen actually was, as lived by ordinary priests and laypeople.

By deemphasizing the "great monks," I am not making the error of trying to recover a Zen discourse of the margins and pass it off as the mainstream.[7] This study's articulation of the Zen Buddhism of the "middle," which is neither the "great monks" nor an oppressed marginal group, focuses on the vast majority of ordinary Sōtō Zen priests and laypeople as a new type of social history of Buddhism. As James Obelkevich noted in an early social history of popular religiosity within the Christian tradition, "The older genre [of ecclesiastical history] has traditionally been occupied with the clergy, with the churches' institutional machinery, and with 'pure' theology. . . . The result [of new studies on popular religion], even when the explicit concern is with church and clergy, is not so much ecclesiastical history as a variety of social history—a social and cultural history of religion."[8]

A social history of this kind necessarily involves the study of "popular religion," a concept laden with problems. In this book, I use the term in some contexts to mean a "common religion" shared by all members of the Bud-

dhist priesthood and laity, and at other times to refer to a religious life that
was at odds with the orthodoxies and orthopraxies advocated by the so-
called great monks.[9] This "common religion" included not only the beliefs
and practices shared by Sōtō Zen laypeople and clergy, but in many respects
also the aspects of religious life common across Japanese religions. Ian
Reader, for example, has attributed the growth of Sōtō Zen to its use of "the
common currency of Japanese religion rather than the restricted currency of
monasticism."[10] The complex interplay of customs, beliefs, and rituals
shared across the spectrum of Japanese religions, such as healing or funerary rituals, often served as the common denominator that bound priest to
layperson, as well as members of different sects in the same village. However, popular religion also generated tensions, contradictions, and beliefs
that were at odds with the orthodoxies of the headquarter temples or with
governmental policies on religion. This book thus explores both the conti-
nuities and disjunctions of popular Sōtō Zen within Tokugawa society. An
examination of why this topic has not received adequate scholarly investigation leads us to explore new sources and employ new methods to uncover
early modern Sōtō Zen Buddhism.

New Sources in the Study of Early Modern Sōtō Zen

New sources uncovered by researchers in the past twenty-five years have expanded our ability to imagine various aspects of Tokugawa-period Sōtō Zen
Buddhism. Valuable manuscripts—including temple logbooks, prayer and
funerary manuals, letters to and from village officials as well as the government's Office of Temple and Shrines, death registries, miracle tales of popular Buddhist deities, secret initiation papers, villagers' diaries, fund-raising
donor lists, and sales records of talismans—were unearthed in the 1970s
when local governments and Buddhist temples started creating archives to
house documents such as these.

Recent English-language studies on material culture and Buddhism, such
as Gregory Schopen's *Bones, Stones, and Buddhist Monks: Collected Papers
on the Archaeology, Epigraphy, and Texts of Monastic Buddhism in India*
and *Buddhist Monks and Business Matters: Some More Papers on Monastic Buddhism in India*, and John Kieschnick's *The Impact of Buddhism on
Chinese Material Culture*, have also provided models for those of us working on the historical study of "Buddhism on the ground."[11] The material
record in Japan has been expanded to include collections of nonliterary
sources such as roadside stone inscriptions left by pilgrims, talismans left in
thatched rooftops, and cemetery tombstones. These historical materials
were initially surveyed by local and prefectural governments, which began
to collect and microfilm such artifacts from temples and shrines or private
family collections for the purpose of publishing local histories. Beginning in
the 1970s, in every region of Japan down to the smallest of villages, local

governments established historical archives for the purpose of publishing local history. Especially during the late 1980s and into the 1990s, with the cooperation of shrines and temples (which held some of the best data for local history), a rich trove of manuscripts was assembled, microfilmed, and cataloged.[12] Although only a very small portion of these handwritten documents have been transcribed into printed form, several million manuscripts have been collected from Sōtō Zen temples alone. While most Western scholars of Japanese Buddhism rarely avail themselves of these archives, I have made a point of using both handwritten manuscripts and printed transcriptions as they most clearly reveal the daily activities of priests and lay parishioners.

Local governments hoping to establish a special place in history for their town or city contributed to new research by scholars of Japanese Zen history who were interested in exploring the development of Zen temples at the local or regional level. Suzuki Taizan's 1942 work, *Zenshū no chihō hatten* (The Regional Development of the Zen School), had been the sole reference work on the spread of Zen in local society during the medieval period.[13] But with growing scholarly interest in local history, the late 1980s and 1990s produced a number of seminal book-length studies on local Zen. These included Hirose Ryōkō's *Zenshū chihō tenkaishi no kenkyū* (1988), Hanuki Masai's *Chūsei Zenrin seiritsushi no kenkyū* (1993), Harada Masatoshi's *Nihon chūsei no Zenshū to shakai* (1998), and in English, William Bodiford's *Sōtō Zen in Medieval Japan* (1993).[14] In addition to these books, articles on the spread of Zen and local society have been featured in Japanese university, local history, and religious studies journals.[15]

Local history projects also inspired a number of priests of Sōtō Zen temples to research and publish their own temple histories. Furthermore, starting in the mid-1980s and continuing into the 1990s, larger temples began to assemble teams of local historians and university professors to sort through their manuscripts. In the case of the Sōtō school, noted scholars such as Hirose Ryōkō, Ishikawa Rikizan, and Tamamuro Fumio adopted the techniques used by local historians to catalog the thousands of manuscripts held at individual temples.[16] These techniques included cataloging manuscripts by theme (such as temple-government relations, temple founding legends, temple economics, and parishioner registers), number coding each document, and using special envelopes for their preservation. The basic methodology for such archival preservation and cataloging came from the experience of an earlier generation's techniques for sorting early modern political and legal documents. The resultant temple histories, which were often published to coincide with an anniversary of the temple's establishment or the founding monk's death, included such materials as documents on the temple's first patron, land deeds from feudal lords or the Tokugawa government, the founding legend of the temple, and information on the temple's abbots and parishioners, cultural treasures, and the relationship of that temple to other temples.[17]

Individual temples' efforts have taken place in tandem with two major sectwide projects to catalog temple manuscripts: (1) the Zenshū Chihōshi Kenkyūkai's cataloging of 12,470 documents in five volumes from 1978 to 1998,[18] and (2) the ongoing project of the Sōtōshū Bunkazai Chōsa Iinkai (Committee on Surveying Sōtō School Cultural Assets), which has thus far cataloged nearly fifty thousand documents, which have been serialized in the Sōtō school's official periodical, *Shūhō*, since 1981.[19] This study draws on hundreds of manuscripts from both the Zenshū Chihōshi Kenkyūkai and the Sōtōshū Bunkazai Chōsa Iinkai archives, many of which have never been studied before by either Japanese or Western researchers.

TOKUGAWA BUDDHISM

The large quantity of new sources makes a more detailed study of Tokugawa-period Sōtō Zen possible, and, more significantly, the increasing variety of materials enables the writing of an entirely new type of social history. Most archives of Sōtō Zen temple manuscripts have tended to focus on older medieval manuscripts, especially anything by Dōgen (such as copies of the *Shōbōgenzō*), philosophically oriented texts such as commentaries on Zen Master Tōzan's "five ranks," and other Zen masters' "recorded sayings" (*goroku*). On the other hand, materials related to a temple's founding (patronage or legends), ritual activity (manuals or logbooks), economics (landholdings or fund-raising drives), relationships with its parishioners (parishioner registers or letters regarding legal disputes), as well as popular literature and art (miracle tales of Buddhist deities or mandalas) have also been more comprehensively cataloged since the mid-1980s. This variety is particularly evident with Tokugawa-period materials, which number roughly ten times their medieval equivalent. Temple fires, time- and weather-damaged paper, the nature of record keeping, and other factors have contributed to the relative paucity of extant medieval sources. Even within the Tokugawa period, more manuscripts are available later in the period. While the study of medieval Japanese Buddhism suffers in part because of a paucity and lack of variety of sources, the study of Tokugawa-period Buddhism can be made difficult simply by the sheer volume of manuscripts available.

Despite this abundance of sources, scholars of Japanese Buddhism have generally ignored the Tokugawa period and have focused instead on medieval Buddhism. This can be attributed, in part, to the thesis of the degeneration of Buddhism during the Edo period (*Edo bukkyō darakuron*) advanced by the influential historian of Japanese Buddhism, Tsuji Zennosuke, who viewed Buddhism during the Edo or Tokugawa period as corrupt and in decline and thus unworthy of serious scholarly attention.[20] This book, in contrast, will demonstrate that Tokugawa Buddhism was as full of vitality during the Tokugawa period as in any previous era, if not more so. As suggested by a recent study of Buddhism in Song China, another period until recently marked as an age of Buddhist decline, we must critically examine the characterization of later periods as being in decline when contrasted with an earlier "golden age" of Buddhism.[21]

While it is true that Tokugawa Buddhism cannot be characterized as a golden age in terms of the development of new schools of Buddhist thought, it was a period that saw the unprecedented expansion of Buddhist institutions in Japanese society. This institutional growth of Buddhism came about due to the government's establishment of a mandatory parishioner system in which every Japanese family was required to register and maintain membership at a Buddhist temple (*danka seido*). This allegiance to Buddhism of virtually the entire populace, even if it were at times only nominal and customary, was unprecedented in Japanese history.

The power to mandate allegiance to the Buddhist religion was derived from a larger system of authority in which the new shōgunal government, established by Tokugawa Ieyasu (1542–1616), stood at the head of a pyramidal structure of authority that extended from the center to the farthest corners of Japan. In terms of the administrative of Buddhism, the new Tokugawa government's Office of Temples and Shrines oversaw the so-called head temple and branch temple system (*honmatsu seido*). Each Buddhist sect designated a headquarter temple that was approved by the government. With the headquarter temple at the top of a pyramid, all temples in Japan were linked through a hierarchical network of head and branch temples to the sectarian headquarter. This relationship was originally formed by links between a Buddhist teacher's temple (head temple) and his disciples' temples (branch temples). This linkage between two generations of temples formed the basis for regarding a particular temple as being hierarchically superior to another. Under the Tokugawa regime, informal lineage-based ties became formalized, and even temples that had no lineage ties were sometimes arbitrarily placed in head and branch temple relationships. This system consolidated sectarian hierarchies for all Buddhist temples by the early eighteenth century as the government increasingly exerted its control over Buddhist institutions. At the same time, as we shall see in chapter 2, power relations between the government and headquarter temples, between head temples and branch temples, or between temples and their parishioners were never one-sided; instead they were often negotiated and sometimes inverted in an ongoing and dynamic process.[22] The major structural features of Tokugawa Buddhism thus developed out of a secular need for control, but they also served to create a nation of Buddhists for the first time and to establish nationwide sectarian institutions that persisted into the modern period.[23]

Although studies on Tokugawa Buddhism have dramatically increased in the past twenty years, this field remains relatively unexplored compared with the study of medieval Buddhism and other religious movements of the Tokugawa period such as Neo-Confucianism, "Shintō" and nativism (Kokugaku), early Christianity (Kirishitan), or the so-called new religions

CHAPTER 1

that emerged at the end of the Tokugawa period.[24] Recent Japanese research on Tokugawa Buddhism focuses on particular temples, sects, monks, or Buddhist deities and challenges the notion that Buddhism was in decline. Reflecting the Japanese trend, Western scholars have also begun to give attention to the Tokugawa period through new book-length publications and a surge in doctoral-level research.

The Sōtō Zen school, however, has been curiously understudied. Even though it was one of the largest Buddhist schools during the Tokugawa period, book-length research on Buddhist traditions has mainly focused on the Jōdo, Jōdo Shin, and Nichiren schools because of the efforts of a few prolific scholars who have concentrated on those sects.[25] Although my decision to focus on one sect (Sōtō Zen) was based on its significance as the largest sect of Buddhism, and the fact that covering more than one tradition of Tokugawa Buddhism would have been too unwieldy, there are drawbacks to any sect-specific research. During the Tokugawa period, the government tried to organize Buddhist schools by distinct sects, but sectarian lines were like semipermeable membranes through which the ideas and practices of various sects readily crossed. Especially in the case of Sōtō Zen, the influences of esoteric Buddhism, Shugendō, "Shintō," mountain cults, and Onmyōdō were particularly striking, as they shared—and sometimes accused each other of stealing—ritual practices (see chapter 3). The medieval "esotericization" (*mikkyōka*) of Sōtō Zen continued well into the Tokugawa period with mutual influences among this wide range of groups.[26] With this intermingling in mind, this book examines both the Sōtō Zen sect's distinctive practices and its nonsectarian participation in the broader currents of the Tokugawa period's religious landscape.

THE OTHER SIDE OF ZEN: A NEW APPROACH TO THE STUDY OF ZEN

This book consists of six chapters on the social contexts of Sōtō Zen's growth during the Tokugawa period. Chapter 2 begins with an examination of the Buddhist parish temple (*dankadera*). In the case of Sōtō Zen, by the mid-Tokugawa period more than 95 percent of all its temples functioned as parish temples where parishioner funerals and memorial services constituted the primary ritual activity of the temple. Zen Buddhism, despite its image in the West of freewheeling, aniconic Zen masters, did not operate in a political and legal vacuum. Indeed, a key force in the growth of Sōtō Zen was its skillful alliance and cooperation with political authorities of the Tokugawa government (*bakufu*), as well as at the regional and local levels in the establishment of these parish temples. Unlike the Jōdo Shin and Nichiren schools, certain subgroups within which faced persecution from authorities, Sōtō Zen temples were at the forefront of the implementation of the state's religious and social policies of control through the establishment of parish temples in every region of Japan. What began initially as a government policy based on the fear of subversive elements in the religious community, especially the numerically small but influential Christians, became by the 1630s a method for monitoring the entire Japanese populace through the system of parishioner temple-registration (*tera-uke seido*). The role of Sōtō Zen parish temples in the implementation of this system of governmental tracking of the population through temple-registration is examined in chapter 2, along with the development of a comprehensive system of parish membership at such temples. Parish members had both ritual and financial obligations to these temples, such as participation in funerary and memorial rites and the financial support of the parish priest and temple maintenance. Such obligations were placed on the heads of households who represented the family unit. These affiliations continued generation after generation, binding parishioner families to a particular sect's temple and providing a new legal basis by which Sōtō Zen—and any sect able to attract large numbers of new parishioners—was able to maintain its growing number of temples.

However, the practice of funerals and memorial services for deceased relatives cannot simply be reduced to a response to a government directive but must also be thought of as part of a deep human need for ritualizing death. Chapter 3 is a study of "funerary Zen," a reference to *Funerary Buddhism*, the title of Tamamuro Taijō's classic book on Japanese Buddhism and its association with death management.[27] A Sōtō Zen–specific rite such as providing a deceased parishioner with a priestly ordination at the funeral appealed to parishioners because it purportedly enabled the deceased to immediately attain Buddhahood. At the same time, the popular notion in Buddhist and local religious culture that the dead required a more lengthy period of rites than simply a funeral played an equally important role in shaping Sōtō Zen funerary practices. The transsectarian and localized aspects of funerary Zen is illustrated through two topics: women's damnation into the so-called Blood Pool Hell because of the "pollution" associated with menstrual blood, and the Thirteen Buddha Memorial Rites, which continued at intervals over a period of thirty-three years. In both cases, the transsectarian Buddhist ideology of karma overrode Sōtō Zen-specific beliefs of immediate salvation at death, which led a dead person's spirit through a series of rites to a more gradual ascendance to Buddhahood, or (as was more commonly believed) to family ancestorhood. Chapter 3 argues that this flexibility of the Sōtō Zen priests, who permitted wide-ranging local variation in the coexistence of both the logic of the funeral proper and the management of the dead over time, was precisely what made funerary Zen a key element in the growth of the Sōtō Zen school in various provinces.

Although funerary rituals oriented toward the afterlife (*raise kuyō*) played a major role in the development of Sōtō Zen Buddhism, nearly as important to its vitality were practices that provided practical benefits in the present world (*genze riyaku*). Chapter 4 explores the world of Sōtō Zen prayer temples, which were populated with local deities and rowdy pilgrims, and charismatic lay leaders who flourished during the latter half of the Tokugawa period. This chapter provides a detailed study of the Daiyūzan Saijōji Temple, a prototypical prayer temple and one of the so-called three great Sōtō Zen prayer temples (*sandai kitō jiin* or *sandai kigan-sho*), and examines how it provided "this-worldly" benefits. Drawing on often overlooked sources such as temple logbooks, pilgrims' diaries, road-side stonemarkers, local legends, and minutes of pilgrimage confraternity meetings, a colorful picture of this major Sōtō Zen temple emerges. This picture includes festivals particular to this temple that incorporate local Shintō *kami* and esoteric Buddhist rituals and pilgrim groups that congregated at the site to collect potent talismans and medicine. The success of this prayer temple stems from its careful balance of specifically Sōtō Zen aspects of the temple (its founder Ryōan's legendary powers gained through meditation, and the transformation of his disciple, Dōryō, into a powerful *tengu* deity) and its incorporation of local deities and esoteric Buddhist practices.

Although most prayer temples offered a wide range of practical benefits, such as rainmaking, the protection of fishermen at sea, or financial success, one of the most popular benefits offered by Sōtō Zen was the prevention and healing of illnesses. Chapter 5 presents two detailed studies: of a herbal medicine manufactured at a Sōtō Zen-affiliated pharmacy in Kyoto (Dōs-hōan) and of a bodhisattva cult of Jizō faith healing at a Sōtō Zen temple in Edo (Kōganji). These case studies not only provide a sense of the role of Sōtō Zen institutions in Tokugawa-period medical practices but also illustrate how medical practices shaped the character of the Zen school. The herbal medicine (Gedokuen) produced at the Kyoto pharmacy, which had an exclusive contract with the Sōtō sect, was sold both directly to temples and to high-ranking monks who visited Kyoto. This popular medicine, which according to an early Tokugawa-period text was purportedly sanctioned by Dōgen, gave Sōtō Zen temples an attractive alternative to other herbal medicines sold by other sects, such as Daranisuke, the well-known stomach medicine promoted by the itinerant priests of Mount Kōya. These medicines appealed to the vast majority of Japanese villagers who did not have access to the expensive doctors of the major cities. The healing offered by Sōtō Zen temples was not limited to the sale of medicines but extended to faith in Buddhist deities housed at Zen temples. Kōganji Temple, commonly referred to as Togenuki Jizō, popularized the cult of the "Splinter-Removing" Jizō, whose talismans were produced at the temple and were ingested or ritually cast into a river or the sea as a prayer to the bodhisattva for healing. In a period of rampant epidemics, when a person's sickness was believed to have been caused by angry spirits or their bad karma in a previous life, magico-religious therapeutics such as these played a significant role in the social arena of a Sōtō Zen temple.

Through the study of these kinds of prayer temples and parish temples, this book proposes a three-part explanation for the exponential growth of the Sōtō Zen school by the mid-Tokugawa period, namely, the ability of

Sōtō Zen priests to attend to the needs of both the dead (*raise kuyō*) and the living (*genze riyaku*) while successfully negotiating Tokugawa government directives. To arrive at this conclusion, Buddhism is treated first and foremost as a religion (a complex of institutions, doctrines, and rituals), not a philosophy.[28] "Lived religion," in contrast to a timeless philosophy, compels us to examine the interrelations among religious and political institutions, doctrines, and rituals mediated through the religious lives of actual persons. Especially since we now have a breadth of sources, including popular literature, ritual manuals, villagers' diaries, government records, and stone markers, we must make the attempt to integrate the triad of ideas, institutions, and ritual. In this sense, this book prioritizes the study of Buddhists, rather than Buddhism. To be more precise, it is a study of people's lives in addition to the ideas that inform them.

However, the people at the center of this study are not the extraordinary or exalted monks recorded in the annals of Zen history. More often than not, in the field of Zen Buddhism, accounts of great Zen masters and their doctrines have often been strung together and then published as "the history of Zen"—an approach rightly critiqued by John McRae as the "string of pearls' fallacy." Without reference to nonmonastic institutions and popular practices, these studies masquerade as full representations of Zen history. This book examines the other side of Zen—the lives of ordinary clerics and laypeople—the "little people" as the Annalists would put it.[29] Just as the Annalists challenged traditional historical studies in Europe, this research challenges some of the traditional perspectives in the study of Buddhism and Japanese religions, aiming to shift our attention from an exclusive focus on outstanding, exceptional religious individuals and their ideologies to the daily practices of the majority of ordinary Japanese Buddhists. I am not suggesting that doctrinal dimensions of religion, or its exemplary figures, are of no importance, but rather that we question our tendency to place them at the center of what constitutes the Buddhist tradition. The individuals who searched for and experienced extraordinary spiritual insights and developed highly sophisticated philosophical doctrines must be noted. But to suggest that they or their doctrinal formulations are central to the Buddhist religion, or that the broader social contexts in which they existed is irrelevant, is to seriously misconstrue not only the Sōtō Zen tradition, but perhaps Buddhist tradition in general.

Especially in the case of Tokugawa Sōtō Zen, there is a major disjuncture between the doctrines, rituals, and institutions that constituted the mainstream practices of the sect and what the great monks of the day considered as orthodox. This book attempts to demonstrate that the Zen tradition was far more complicated, contradictory, and tension-filled than previously described. And yet, this is not a study simply replacing a focus on an elite tradition with a celebration of everything that it is not. Robert Sharf, in his recent study of Chinese Buddhism, correctly warns against a total dismissal of the elite monks in the writing of a more popular social history: "attention to popular practice should not serve as an excuse to ignore the products of the elite tradition altogether."[30] Instead of ignoring the elite tradition, I have attempted to put it in perspective. By focusing on the faith and practices of the vast majority of Sōtō Zen adherents, previously understudied popular apocryphal texts are highlighted, without denying the importance of the Buddhist scriptures of the elite tradition. What the gaze over to the other side of Zen permits is a recognition that most Tokugawa-period Sōtō Zen Buddhists saw Zen meditation not as a practice expressing Buddhahood or an aspect of monastic training, but as a technique for deriving esoteric powers to save those in distress.

I have left to a future scholar the difficult task of writing a history of Zen in which the gaps between previous understandings of the tradition and what is presented in this book are thoroughly resolved, giving a coherency to the sect. Part of the difficulty in writing a history of Zen in which highly complex doctrinal theories (such as Tung-shan's "five ranks" or Dōgen's theories of "being-time") might be interwoven with themes such as salvation from the Blood Pool Hell or the worship of healing bodhisattvas as part of one field of religious practice is that, in many respects, they fail to form a whole. Of course, when an integrated landscape of Sōtō Zen life comes into view, such as the esoteric power of a prayer temple's popular festival deriving from monastic discipline (chapter 4) or the efficacy of a herbal medicine coming from its association with Dōgen (chapter 5), it is duly highlighted to show how the Buddhist worlds of elite and popular shared a seamless reality. But at the same time, the real success of the medieval and early modern Sōtō Zen school lay in the fact that most of its priests ignored contradictions and lived in multiple universes of praxis without ever having to explain or integrate the whole. This book attempts to reveal a more disorderly and incoherent world of Zen from the one we more commonly know—the other side of Zen.

Registering the Family, Memorializing the Ancestors: The Zen Temple and the Parishioner Household

ALTHOUGH TODAY'S POPULAR IMAGE of a Zen priest envisages a serene person deep in meditation, the vast majority of Tokugawa-period Zen priests rarely practiced meditation. Excluding the meditation practice required at specialized monastic training centers, most Zen priests spent their energies on various ritual practices oriented toward their lay patrons. This chapter takes up the development of parish temples (alternately *dannadera, dankadera,* or *bodaiji*), which constituted more than 95 percent of Sōtō Zen temples and comprised the primary arena for the religious life of ordinary Zen priests and lay Zen Buddhists. Temples of this type, which became the economic and organizational backbone of all the major Buddhist sects, served as the ritual center for death rites for generations of parishioners. Here, priests performed funerary and memorial services, issued posthumous names and memorial tablets for the home altar, and provided the land for family gravestones. In addition, new Tokugawa government directives issued in the early seventeenth century banning "heretical" religions such as Christianity established strict edicts mandating parish temple membership for every Japanese. This state-backed authority gave sects with strong ties to the Tokugawa government and local domainal officials an edge in expanding themselves during the early years of the Tokugawa period.[1]

To comprehend the rapid growth of Sōtō Zen in the Tokugawa period—indeed, the formation of all sects—we must understand the new temple-parishioner relationship that developed within the context of both the temples' desire for a stable economic base (as vested in its hereditary parish members) and the Tokugawa bakufu's desire for control over both the temples and the populace. We begin this study with a rather scandalous incident from 1786 when a Sōtō Zen priest used his authority to pressure a female parishioner into engaging in sexual relations. The following excerpt of a letter from Towa, a female member of Chōsenji Temple (a Sōtō Zen temple in Sagami Province) to the head of Seigen'in Temple (a higher-ranking temple in the same province) describes a complicated three-year affair that she had with the abbot, Tetsumei.[2]

> Tetsumei, the abbot of my family temple, Chōsenji Temple, had been coming by my home from time to time asking me to fix his robes. It was on one of these occasions that he made advances toward me, but I rejected them because he was a priest. . . . As time went on, the temple had to put together its Registry of Religious Affiliation. The priest Tetsumei visited my house and told me that if I didn't

have sexual relations with him, he would not place his seal on our family's name in the registry. He pointed out that this would cause a lot of trouble for my husband Matabee, and making various other threats, he pressed me to be intimate with him. Without choice, as a thoughtless woman, I had relations with him on numerous occasions from roughly three years ago. . . . Since Tetsumei promised me that if the villagers learned about the affair, he would either take me in as his mistress or escape the village with me, this relationship dragged on. . . .

Since my husband Matabee worked in the next village, I was usually concerned about strangers coming by during the night. However, when Tetsumei and I were secretly having an affair one evening, the two of us were blissfully unaware of someone coughing at the front door. To our surprise, it was Matabee. I greeted my husband as if nothing had happened and sent Tetsumei on his way. . . . Having witnessed this affair between Tetsumei and me, my husband declared that he wanted to see both of us severely punished. However, because Tetsumei was the head of our family temple, Matabee decided not to report on the monk since that would not only be looked down upon in the community, but would also insult our ancestors. Instead, Matabee slapped me, shouting, "I will divorce you," among other things. Someone who heard this commotion came into the house and calmed Matabee down. Later that evening, he returned to his workplace. . . . Once night had fallen, I went to the temple and quietly slipped into Tetsumei's sleeping quarters to discuss the situation. I asked him once again to break things off, but Tetsumei replied that despite Matabee's discovery, and even if the affair came out into the open, he would continue to love me. Tetsumei then promised that we would be forever together even if we had to commit double suicide. Given this, the affair continued.

However, one evening when Tetsumei was over at my house, my husband Matabee caught us again. When he realized he was discovered, Tetsumei ran out of the house. . . . Not able to overlook the affair this time, Matabee went to the temple and told Tetsumei about his intentions to divorce me. . . . Having been abandoned by my husband and not being able to return to my own parents' home, the only option I could see was to go through with the promise Tetsumei had made about us committing double suicide. On the third of the eighth month, I took a knife from my house and headed to the village official's house to report what I was about to do, before heading off to Chōsenji Temple. I confronted Tetsumei and reminded him of his promise, edging closer to him with the knife. He ran off. . . . I have had my matchmaker sign his name and place his seal along with mine to end this letter. Please bring in Tetsumei for questioning and upon finding out the truth, I would be grateful if you would restore my good name.

The seventh day of the eighth month, Tenmei 6 (1786)
Seals of Towa and Shichirōuemon the Matchmaker

Although there are indications that Towa may have had some affection for Tetsumei at certain points in the affair, the letter depicts this Zen priest as someone who abused his position of authority to force a parishioner to engage in sexual relations with him. He not only made heavy-handed threats but was deceptive and cowardly when confronted by both Towa and her husband. According to Towa, the single most important factor in her getting involved with Tetsumei was his threat to withhold the temple's seal from her family's name in the Registry of Religious Affiliation. What was the Registry of Religious Affiliation, and why was the priest's threat to withhold the temple seal on this document so effective? An examination of the history of this type of registry, mandated by the Tokugawa government for every parish temple, will illuminate the ways in which Buddhist sects managed to solidify their parish membership.

Furthermore, Towa's husband did not report the priest's behavior the first time he discovered the affair because he did not want to embarrass his family/parish temple priest, as that would insult his ancestors. What was the significance of the family/parish temple priest, and why would claims against him affect one's ancestors? With the light shed on the role of the parish priest at Sōtō Zen temples, the central place of such priests in maintaining order among both the living parishioners and their dead ancestors will become clear. Within this context, I will also discuss the ritual and financial obligations of parishioners to the temple, with a particular focus on the assignment of posthumous ordination names. Finally, I will trace the story of the Towa-Tetsumei incident to its conclusion, including the priest's side of the story, which ultimately led to villagewide threats of mass defections from the parish temple over Towa's poor treatment. This and similar incidents detailed below led to a gradual weakening of temple control over its parishioners during the latter half of the Tokugawa period.

Indeed, the theme of the gradual strengthening and weakening of control within the socioreligious landscape of Tokugawa Japan is central to understanding the establishment of a pyramid-like hierarchy of relationships between the central government (bakufu) and the domains, the government and the temples, the head temples and branch temples, and the parish temples and their parishioners. To understand the growth of Sōtō Zen, and Buddhism more broadly, we must first examine the historical conditions that allowed for the establishment of socioreligious authority under the Tokugawa shōgunate.

THE ANTI-CHRISTIAN CAMPAIGN

The Registry of Religious Affiliation—from which Tetsumei threatened to withhold his seal—and other temple-registration documents required by law had their roots in the anti-Christian campaigns and ordinances of 1613–14. Christianity, which had achieved a foothold in certain regions during the sixteenth century through the efforts of Portuguese and Spanish missionaries, was increasingly seen by the new Tokugawa regime as a subversive force and a threat to its hegemony.[3] Indeed, the first edicts against Christianity were issued before the establishment of the Tokugawa government under Toyotomi Hideyoshi in 1587.[4] The threat of Christianity, as seen from the perspective of those who attempted to gain control over the country, lay partly in its Biblical teachings that seemed counter to Japan's established religious traditions, but principally in the issue of Christian loyalty owed to God and to the pope over Japan's secular authority.[5] This general suspicion that Christians could not be loyal members of the new order, in addition to a series of incidents involving apparent Christian backing of antigovernment forces,[6] led the Tokugawa regime to issue the Order to Expel the Missionaries (*Bateren tsuihōrei*) in the twelfth month of 1613, banning and expelling the Jesuit *bateren* (padres or missionary fathers).[7] In the following year, Christianity was forbidden to all Japanese.

Ieyasu, the first Tokugawa shōgun, had ordered all nonrepentant Christians (i.e., those who would not "return" to Buddhism) to be exiled to Tsugaru (Mutsu Province), and later to be expelled to the Philippines. Léon Pagès reported in 1869 that many former Christians had reverted to Buddhism in the Kokura Domain in Kyūshū, some under threats from domainal authorities that Christian women would be sold into brothels.[8] To check that no Christians remained, the bakufu ordered the first Investigations of Christians (*Kirishitan aratame*) to be conducted by each domain. Areas with high a concentration of Christians, such as Kyoto and Kokura, were the first to respond with detailed reports on the situation.[9] The government then ordered investigations to check the religious inclinations of suspected Christians. Each domain was mandated to send this investigation to the bakufu to account for all the "fallen Christians" or Christians who had reverted to Buddhism (*korobi Kirishitan*).[10] One investigation included house checks for suspicious Christian objects of worship carried out on 127 individuals, revealing that while 57 of them were in the clear, 70 had crosses, rosaries and prints, medallions, or small statues of Christ and Mary. Upon completion of such an investigation, "former Christians" had to be certified as upstanding Buddhists, which was done through a Certification of "Toppled-Over" Status (*Korobi shōmon*) attested to by a Buddhist temple priest and local village officials. For example, in the Shimoge District, the peasants Jōchin, Mitsuemon, Sōgorō, and Sasuke first submitted documents saying that they were no longer Christians. Their letters were then appended with two certificates, one from the village's Sōtō Zen temple, Jufukuji, and another from village authorities verifying that the peasants' statements were true and that they were now parishioners of Jufukuji Temple.[11] This type of certification, in which the temple and village officials shared responsibility for ascertaining and vouching for the status and identity of former Christians under their jurisdiction, served as the prototype for later temple registration certificates such as the one onto which Towa, the female parishioner cited above, needed the priest Tetsumei to place his seal.

Sōtō Zen temples, like other Buddhist temples, profited from the growth in parishioners resulting from the government-sponsored forced "reversion" to Buddhism. Indeed, compared with other sects, Sōtō Zen was the most able and willing to respond rapidly to local daimyō and bakufu campaigns by making former Christians into parishioners of hitherto small Sōtō Zen temples. For example, in the case of former Christians in Hayami District (Kokura Domain), an area with one of the highest concentrations of former Christians (in 1614, 786 individuals out of a total population of roughly 1,209), 658 people (84 percent) became parishioners of the Sōtō Zen temple Kōzen'in (Yufuin Village).[12] The conversion of entire Christian villages to the Sōtō Zen sect was not infrequent.

For example, consider the activities of the Sōtō Zen monk Suzuki Shōsan (1579–1655),[13] who helped to establish many temples in the Amakusa region of Kyūshū.[14] Formerly a warrior, a retainer of the Tokugawa family, he became a monk in 1621 and served as the first abbot of Onshinji, a Sōtō Zen temple built by his younger brother, Suzuki Shigenari (1588–1653), in the Tokugawa stronghold of Mikawa Province. With his younger brother's support, he raised funds from local lords to build other Sōtō Zen temples that served as parish temples. Shōsan had a strong vision of a new country founded on Buddhist principles and wrote a stinging critique of Christianity, the *Attack against Christianity* (*Ha Kirishitan*), which was published in woodblock print form after his death in 1662.[15] Especially after the peasant-Christian rebellion in Shimabara (Kyūshū Island) during 1637–38, which resulted in tens of thousands of government and rebel casualties, the bakufu and daimyō intensified Buddhist temple efforts to investigate and further tighten their ban on Christians.[16] The heads of the decapitated Christians were hung on the perimeters of Hara Castle, gruesome demonstrations of the consequences of disobeying the government's new religious policies. With the designation of Shimabara and Amakusa as special bakufu territories, Suzuki Shigenari led the anti-Christian campaign in Amakusa as the new magistrate of the region. It was during 1642–49 that Shigenari implemented a policy, with bakufu approval, to build new temples or rebuild old ones to keep hidden Christians in check and to promote Buddhism. In 1642 Shigenari asked his older brother, Shōsan, to come to Amakusa to help stabilize the Christian situation through the promotion of Buddhism. Over a period of three years, Shōsan established thirty-two new Sōtō Zen temples, at which he left handwritten copies of his *Attack against Christianity*. This document was instrumental in the government policy of control in areas with large Christian populations.[17] Shōsan's disciples continued to monitor subversive religious activity in the Kyūshū region based at the region's newly established head temples: Tōkōji and Kokushōji (Sōtō Zen), and Enshōji and Sōenji (Jōdo). With permission from local authorities, Sōtō Zen priests actively participated in the anti-Christian campaign, in part to gain parishioners for their new temples.[18]

Starting in 1638, further efforts to weed out any remaining Christians were conducted through a government system of rewards whereby anyone who reported the whereabouts of a Christian would receive between thirty and fifty silver coins; the report of a lay "brother" (*iruman*) would fetch one hundred coins, and any Catholic priest (*bateren*), two hundred coins.[19] The same office of the Nagasaki commissioner to which Suzuki Shōsan had connections was instrumental in the adoption of another method to uncover suspected Christians: the *fumi-e* (picture to step on). Scholars of Japanese Christianity still dispute the origins of the *fumi-e*,[20] but there is a consensus that between 1620 and 1669 the practice of forcing suspected Christians to step on an image of Jesus or Mary (the earliest versions were sacred icons, some hand-drawn images and others woodblock prints) was organized at the office of the Nagasaki commissioner.[21] In 1669 this office commissioned twenty copperplate *fumi-e*, which were more durable and could be used to test the faith of a large number of people, especially in all the domains of Kyūshū Island where, on specified days, all members of the nonsamurai classes were required to step on the image to prove that they were not Christians.[22] This practice continued until 1858 when it was officially abandoned.

The search for Christians was further institutionalized with a new system of certifying every Japanese as a non-Christian and, simultaneously, as an upstanding Buddhist. The first surveys of Christians, beginning in 1614, were followed by a more extensive one ordered by the bakufu in 1659 in which not only the parish temple, but the *goningumi* (a unit of five households sharing mutual responsibility) were required to attest to the fact that no one in their group was a Christian.[23] Certificates of temple registration (*tera-uke shōmon*) issued to Buddhist parishioners guaranteed the non-Christian status of the certificate. By 1671 the practice of temple investigation and registration had become near universal.[24]

Consequently, during the first half of the seventeenth century the vast majority of Japanese people, who had not previously had an affiliation with a particular temple, became potential parishioners. While religious faith may have influenced the decision to affiliate with a particular sect's temple for a small percentage of people, factors such as geographic proximity, social loyalties, and the priests' ability to perform funerary rites tended to weigh more heavily than belief in one or another set of Buddhist teachings. The Sōtō Zen school was quicker than others to recognize these factors, and thus during 1620–50 it built thousands of new temples or upgraded existing facilities, tightened its connections with daimyō and lower-ranking lords, and promoted its ability to perform funerals and services for parish members and their ancestors.

While the vast majority of Sōtō Zen temples were constructed during 1540–1650,[25] early founding dates are often unreliable because temples naturally tried to make it seem as if they were older than they really were, often attributing their founding to a teacher or even "grand-teacher" of the actual founder.[26] Furthermore, for the thousands of Sōtō Zen temples that have a sixteenth-century founding date, the "temples" were really nothing more than small chapels, often housing a Buddhist deity, and did not have a resident priest until a Sōtō Zen priest decided to make the facility his residence. In many cases, it was not until the implementation of the seventeenth-century temple-registration system and the adoption of new parishioners that small chapels transformed into what we now imagine a temple to be, with a main gate, several halls, and a graveyard.

THE TEMPLE-REGISTRATION SYSTEM

Although this practice of mandatory temple registration of all community members, regardless of their suspected Christian affiliation, became near universal in the 1670s, the first examples of temple registration can be found as early as the tenth month of 1635, a few months after the bakufu ordered the areas directly under its control to undertake such a registration.[27] Since pockets of resistance to the bakufu, the 1637–38 Shimabara rebellion being one, continued into the 1630s, it is not surprising that the areas most closely linked with the Tokugawa family and government, and the regions with the largest Christian population, would respond most rapidly to the government directive.[28] Indeed, one of the earliest known responses to the bakufu order was from a Sōtō Zen temple, Sōgen'in (Ōba Village, Sagami Province), in which the abbot of the temple reported to the village head that his parishioners were faithful Buddhist followers and not Christians.[29] Village headmen collected and submitted such certificates to domain officials in standardized form as the Registry Investigating People's Religious Affiliation (*Shūshi ninbetsu aratamechō*). I have discussed elsewhere the explosion in parishioner certification in the following thirty years, as increasing numbers of Sōtō Zen members were officially registered and a more comprehensive temple-registration system was put into place and detailed information, such as ages, became the norm for family entries.[30]

The next step in the universalization of the temple-registration system came in the fourth month of 1669 when the bakufu banned the Nichiren Fuju Fuse sect.[31] In addition to Christians, the only other religion banned and targeted throughout Japan was this sect of the Nichiren school, which refused to either receive (*fuju*) donations from members of any other sect of Buddhism or give (*fuse*) to anyone outside their strict interpretation of Nichiren Buddhism.[32] Though several daimyō also targeted other "heretical" religions such as the Ikkō (Jōdo Shin) school in Satsuma Domain,[33] this order banning the Fuju Fuse sect meant that temple registration certificates now had to include a pronouncement that the individuals were neither Christians nor Nichiren Fuju Fuse members. At Sōgen'in, which was the first temple in Japan to respond to this bakufu order, the new certification style was developed later in the same month. For example, for the registration of one Jirōbee and his family, the following certificate was issued:

THE CERTIFICATION OF A PARISHIONER

Jirōbee (plus his wife and children) of Hatori Village have been parishioners of the Zen temple, Sōgen'in Temple, generation after generation. In accordance with the directive, they are neither Christians nor members of the Fuju Fuse sect. If there is any doubt about their following these outlawed teachings, I will go to any lengths to dispel them. This [document] has been written just in case there are any questions in the future. Fourth month of 1669; Certified by Sōgen'in Zen Temple of Ōba Village, Sagami Province (a branch temple of Sōseiji Temple, Odawara City, Sagami Province); Further certified by: Hatori Village Head, Hachirōemon; To: Naruse Gozaemon; Note: There is not a single mistake in the above, (signed and sealed) Naruse Gozaemon.[34]

This new style of temple certification, which was based on the bakufu's fear of the subversive potential of both Christianity and the Nichiren Fuju Fuse, was adopted as the standard by all Buddhist temples. Although the Buddhist temple held primary responsibility for monitoring and reporting on its parishioners to the village head, each village head had to gather these certificates so that reports, called the Registry of Religious Affiliation (*shūmon aratamechō*), also known as the *shūmon ninbetsuchō*, the *shūshi aratamechō*, or, less commonly, the *kasū ninbetsu aratamechō*, could be compiled.[35] As with the example of Jirōbee above, the temple sent the certificate to the village headman, who in turn forwarded it for approval to the local magistrate (Naruse Gozaemon) and on to the office in charge of religious inspection, the Shūmon aratameyaku, established by the bakufu in 1640. Since the data on each individual would pass through ever higher levels of authority, up to the bakufu itself, requiring verification each step of the way, the temple-registration system served as one of the basic methods for the bakufu to monitor the populace and maintain order during the Tokugawa period. As Robert Sakai has observed, "by the early nineteenth century religious proscription had become a minor part of a major policy for social control."[36] This function of temple registration—to collect basic data on individuals for the government's monitoring efforts—tended to de-emphasize religious faith as the determining factor of temple affiliation. Instead, geographic proximity to a given village temple carried greater weight in determining sect affiliation. Because the Sōtō Zen school established more than seventeen thousand temples (albeit many small in size) in thousands of villages throughout Japan, rather than concentrating on a few large or prestigious temples in the major cities, it capitalized on the government demand that every villager be legally affiliated with a temple.

A typical register compiled at the village level (by either the village head or the *goningumi*)[37] included a preamble, which eventually became standardized to include the statement that there was not a single Christian in the village; if a former Christian or relative lived there, a note was added.[38] This was followed by a family-by-family directory describing the head of the family (his age and relatives), his place of residence (and, if different, his place of birth), and the name of his parish temple. For example, one of the oldest such registries, the 1665 *Sagami no kuni Ashigara Kamigun Chitsushimamura shūmon ninbetsu aratamechō*, included the following entry for a village headman named Bun'eemon and his family, who were parish members at the Sōtō Zen temple Jumyōji.[39]

> Zen Sect: Bun'eemon (Village Headman, age 64)—Place of Birth (Suruga Province); Official Place of Residence (Onkuri Tanaka Village, Suruga Province); Parish Temple: (Jumyōji Temple, Matarame Village)
>
> Zen Sect: Wife (age 59) [seal]—Place of Birth (Sagami Province); Official Place of Residence (Chitsushima Village, Western Sagami Province); Parish Temple: Jumyōji Temple, Matarame Village)
>
> Zen Sect: Son, Gonzaemon (age 37)—Place of Birth (Suruga Province); Official Place of Residence (Chitsushima Village, Western Sagami Province); Parish Temple: (Jumyōji Temple, Matarame Village)
>
> Zen Sect: Son, Shirōbee (age 29) [seal]—Place of Birth (Suruga Province); Official Place of Residence (Chitsushima Village, Western Sagami Province); Parish Temple: (Jumyōji Temple, Matarame Village)
>
> Hokke (i.e., Nichiren) Sect: Wife's Mother, Myōfuku (age 85)—Place of Birth (Sagami Province); Official Place of Residence (Chitsushima Village, Western Sagami Province); Parish Temple: (Myōkyōji Temple, Chahata Town, Odawara Domain)
>
> Total: Five people (three men, two women)[40]

What we can tell from this entry is that Bun'eemon served as the Chitsushima Village (Sagami Province) headman even though he was originally from Suruga Province (where his two sons were also born). He married into this family (which was not of sufficient high status to have a family name) based in Sagami Province, which must have originally had some connection to the Nichiren school (which is why the elderly mother-in-law was able to remain a member of the Nichiren temple Myōkyōji).[41] However, since Bun'eemon was affiliated with the Sōtō Zen school, this family would henceforth retain that sect's affiliation. In other words, with the exception of those marrying out of their family and thus out of the family's lineage, the registration system expected families to maintain whatever sect affiliation the head of their household had chosen or, later, whatever sect affiliation the family had "traditionally" been.

This type of religious registry continued to be compiled in virtually every village in Japan until 1872, when the last such survey, commonly referred to as the *Jinshin koseki*, was carried out under the new Meiji government.[42] The system of temple registration also continued until 1871, when the new *Kosekihō* (Family Registration Law) came into effect, making it mandatory for citizens to register directly with the government instead of at the temple. Thus for the duration of the entire Tokugawa period, this practice of temple registration legally obligated parishioners to maintain their membership at their parish temple under the threat of being branded a "heretic," which continued to have meaning even as the possibility of Christian subversion of the government disappeared. This was because government persecution of "heretical religions" (*jashūmon*) continued into the eighteenth and nineteenth centuries with death sentences and torture for those found guilty of unorthodox beliefs.[43] Temple parishioners' fear of being branded Christian was heightened because of the legal discrimination against and ostracism of those who were merely descendents of Christians. The surveillance of former Christians went hand in hand with the monitoring of descendents of Christians (up to three generations for women and five generations for men).[44] For example, the bakufu reissued the order to all domains to survey former Christians and their descendents in 1687. This directive included the provision that, "if a person who was formerly a Christian dies, the corpse should be packed with salt [i.e., for preservation] so that the Commissioner Overseeing Christianity can check the body."[45] Even though an individual may have had strong faith in Buddhism, the taint of being associated with Christianity or a descendent of Christians meant that neither a proper nor a timely funeral would be held, since at times the corpse of a suspected Christian was preserved in salt for up to a month until an investigation into whether the corpse showed any signs of Christian worship or sympathy was concluded. While living, such people were registered every half year at the temple in a special register (*Kirishitan ruizoku koseki*), and at death they were often excluded from burial in temple grounds, being buried in the mountains instead.[46] Tamamuro has estimated that in 1688 there were probably about fifteen to sixteen thousand such descendents of Christians throughout Japan.[47] This fear of being branded Christian, and the knowledge that such an association would affect living relatives as well as future descendents, consolidated the membership of the parish temple in Tokugawa Japan. The priest held complete discretion regarding the identification of parishioners in good stead. This coercive aspect of the temple-registration and parish temple system was the driving force of the Towa-Tetsumei incident previously cited, wherein the Sōtō Zen priest threatened Towa that he would not certify her family as non-Christians and warned of the trouble it would cause her husband if she would not have sexual relations with him.

The temple-registration system began as a means to monitor suspected Christians, with the temple guaranteeing that those registered as parish members either were not Christians or were no longer Christians. Yet as this registration process was expanded to include all Japanese, it strengthened the establishment of the local parish temple. The coercive, and later customary, aspect of this system, however, was one of the key elements that consolidated the temple-parishioner relationship. After the Sōtō Zen school was successful in attracting numerous parish households to its temples by the midseventeenth century, it was able to retain this membership generation after generation through a set of ritual and economic obligations that bound the parish household to each of its nearly 17,500 parish temples.

The Household and Family Parish Temples

Although the primary legal obligation of each parish member to his or her temple was the periodic registration to certify that the household was not affiliated with any of the "heretical religions," parishioners also had a set of generally observed economic and ritual obligations to the temple. Indeed, the various Japanese terms for "parishioner" (*dan'notsu*, *danna*, or *danka*) originally had strong economic connotations, as they are derived from the Sanskrit term *dāna* (giving/donating/generosity) and were used in the medieval period to refer to major temple donors.[48] However, in the Tokugawa period, while *dan'notsu* (or *dai dan'notsu*)[49] continued this primary meaning, the term *danna* started to refer to parish temple members in general, whether they were major donors or not. This was in part due to the expansion of the temple-registration system that required all Japanese (not just wealthy patrons) to be considered not as temple sponsors per se, but as certified non-Christian temple members with financial and ritual obligations.

Furthermore, this temple membership was not an individual affair, but rather the unit of religious affiliation of the "household" (*ie*), an increasingly widespread unit of social organization that had its roots in the medieval period.[50] Thus from the mid-Tokugawa period onward, the term *danka* (though used interchangeably with *danna*)—which includes the Chinese character for "household"—became the dominant term for parish households whose affiliation was passed down hereditarily. Thus once a family registered at a particular temple, the connection to that temple continued for successive generations, during which sect changes were virtually impossible.[51] For the Tokugawa bakufu and the head temples of each sect, the term used for this type of parish temple was *dannadera* or *dankadera*, reflecting the reality that the vast majority (more than 95 percent) of all temples in Japan were financially dependent on their members, as opposed to the government, wealthy individual sponsors, pious pilgrims, or tax-free arable land.

From the perspective of village-level government, parish temples functioned primarily as an administrative channel through which to monitor its subjects. In contrast, for each household, the main benefits of membership were the security of being certified as a non-Christian and the funerary and ongoing memorial services that temples provided for all the members of their family, from the ancestors to future generations. In this sense, the parish temple became virtually synonymous with a funerary temple. Indeed, while the government and the head temples employed the terms *dannadera* or *dankadera*, parish members themselves rarely used these terms, but often referred to their parish temple as a *bodaiji* or a family memorial temple, a term rooted in the medieval period.[52]

As Buddhist funerary and ancestral rites for ordinary people developed in this expanding network of parish temples, these rituals were no longer privately negotiated family affairs, as in the medieval period, but became a part of an overarching system that tied the parish households to the temples and the temples to the state. As Buddhist temples were mandated to perform funerary services, which for most people had previously been performed by the family or with the cooperation of itinerant priests or other villagers, Buddhist sects had to respond quickly to this new role. And while it was the duty of the Buddhist temple to perform these services for each household, parishioners were also under legal obligation to attend these rituals and pay for them. In a document that looked like a government decree but was composed by Buddhist priests, dated the fifth month of 1613, the Definitive Regulations for Parish Members of the Sect (*Gojōmoku shūmon danna ukeai no okite*), the following parishioner obligations are laid out:

> 1. Those who do not support the temple should not be allowed to be a parishioner.
> 2. Even if one is a leading parish member, all parishioners are duty-bound to visit the temple on the following occasions: the sect founder's memorial day, the Buddha's memorial day, the summer ancestral festival, the vernal and autumnal equinoctial services, and the memorial days of one's ancestors. If [this it not observed], the temple's seal will be withdrawn from the Registry of Religious Affiliation unless urgent reasons are reported to the office of religious affairs.
> 3. On the memorial day of one's ancestors, one must invite the priest over to the house and treat him generously. If one attempts to perform a funeral by oneself or asks anyone other than one's parish temple priest, that will be taken as a sign of belief in heretical religions and will be reported. Further, one must make donations to the temple in accordance with one's standing. In temple construction and repairs, one must financially support the temples. Ancestral rites shall not be done at temples of other sects. One must obey what the temples say.[53]

What this text emphasized to parishioners was their obligations for ritual attendance (funerals first and foremost, but also regular temple and ancestral rites) and financial support. Whether it be to pay for rituals or temple construction, it is clear that parishioners were not simply being asked but were obligated to support their parish temple. Not to do so was to risk being branded a heretic. The regulations were well known to parishioners of all Buddhist schools because they were read aloud by the abbot at major temple festivals (the Buddha's and founder's memorial days, for instance) and were recited and memorized by children at temple schools (*terakoya*). Indeed, many Sōtō Zen temples still hold copies of this document.

Though this stress on the financial obligation may seem overdone, the scale of the physical construction of many of the sect's temples that took place after 1620 suggests that these directives succeeded in soliciting ever greater funds for parish temples.[54] The social penalties for not fulfilling the ritual and financial obligations were heavy. While the threat of being branded a Christian had less coercive power as time progressed, the general rule was that a household that refused to ritually and financially participate to the temple's satisfaction would be temporarily taken off the Registry of

Religious Affiliation. Without the temple certification, all household individuals were "off register" (*chō-hazure*) and written up in what was called the Registry of Nonhumans (*Hinin-koseki*). Those categorized as "nonhumans" (*hinin*) faced discrimination in everyday life as well as in funerary rites. It was this harsh reality that the priest Tetsumei hinted at when he threatened not to place his seal in the Registry of Religious Affiliation if Towa refused sexual relations with him. To avoid the fate of being treated worse than those of the lowest social status, virtually everyone fulfilled their obligations to the parish temple. For those who did not donate money or labor to the temple, a ten-year sentence of being "off register" resulted. To get put back on the regular temple-registration list required a written apology promising never again to disobey the temple, naming a guarantor who would vouch for the household, and offering to make a back payment on all dues and handing over an extra punitive fee.[55]

However, there were not only social and monetary penalties. Sōtō Zen priests warned of the spiritual penalties of not attending to memorial services and temple donations. In the well-known collection of morality tales, the *Inga monogatari* (1658–59), by the Sōtō Zen priest Suzuki Shōsan (discussed earlier), a severely ill man is told that his illness was caused by his negligence of parish temple affairs.

> There was a retired Hakusan mountain ascetic living in Ōtsuka Village (in Edo) named Zenzaemon. He took in his elder brother's son as his adopted son but died shortly thereafter, in 1632. The elder brother went to Edo to get some temporary work, but when he returned to the village, he also died. So the adopted son took over as the head of the household. However, this son didn't have faith and never held memorial services for Zenzaemon. In was then that the son started to become frail and very ill. On the seventh day of the eleventh month of 1645, the son's mother came over and said the following, "Return all the household items that we gave to you [when you were adopted in our family]! You've received the karma of hungry ghosts getting so frail and ill because you didn't properly observe the memorial services for our family ancestors." She continued, "You must count them one by one and return all the hoes, spades, and garments." Astonished at hearing this, the son asked the [Sōtō Zen] monk Honshū to perform memorial services [for his ancestors]. Honshū went to the temple to recite sutras all day before returning to the son's house, saying, "Come at once to the temple with a donation." After doing this, the sick son recovered completely.[56]

Suzuki Shōsan's story highlights the activity of one of his disciples, San'ei Honshū, who was well known as a Sōtō Zen figure who could appease angry ghosts. In this story, Honshū was called upon by a negligent son, whose mother told him that his misfortune stemmed from his lack of attention to his ancestors. The priest recited sutras on behalf of the ancestors, and the son was cured after he made a financial donation to the temple. Here, the message of the Sōtō Zen priest is clear: misfortune will befall those who do not fulfill their ritual and financial obligations to Buddhist temples. In this case, the spiritual misfortune of turning into a hungry ghost was conflated with the son's enfeebled body, which could not absorb food.

Reflecting the emergent merchant culture in the Tokugawa period, the well-known phrase popularized during this era, *jigoku no sata mo zeni shidai* (even hell's affairs hinge on money), pointed to the "costs" even in the afterlife. The notion of heading off misfortune in the world hereafter through financial contributions to the temple was most evident in the purchase of posthumous ordination names (*kaimyō*), which were assigned to the deceased at all Buddhist temples. Just as the social status of the living was affected by the rapidly developing money culture, the posthumous name reflected the individual's social and economic status in both this world and the next.

COSTS OF BUDDHAHOOD: POSTHUMOUS NAMES AND SOCIAL DISCRIMINATION

George Smith, a visiting Anglican bishop from Hong Kong, described the inscriptions of temple gravestones in his book *Ten Weeks in Japan*, published in 1861: "A close inspection of these family mausoleums, with their areas swept and surrounded by rows of upright monuments, gives a favourable impression of their regard of the dead. . . . The inscriptions bore the posthumous names given by the priests to those persons whose surviving friends deemed it worthwhile to invite sacerdotal offices at the funeral and to expend the customary fees on the Buddhist temples."[57] Smith correctly observed that temple tombstones did not bear the given name of the deceased family member but a special posthumous name bestowed by a Buddhist priest who had received some form of payment. The term *kaimyō* is used here in its broad Tokugawa-period sense to mean the posthumous name given to a parishioner by the parish temple abbot at the funeral. The original meaning of the term was a spiritual "name" (*myō*) written with two Chinese characters, given to those, whether monastic or lay, who had agreed to abide by a set of Buddhist precepts (*kai*).[58] In the medieval period, and among other Buddhist sects as well, the term *kaimyō* (lit. "precept name") was interchangeable with the term *hōmyō* or *hōgō* (lit. "Dharma name"), which was also written with two Chinese characters.

However, in the context of the parish temple system during the Tokugawa period, *kaimyō* began to be used by parishioners to refer almost exclusively to the posthumous names given to deceased family members, while *hōmyō* tended to be used for monastics (although Sōtō Zen priests continued to use these terms interchangeably). Furthermore, although the kaimyō, strictly speaking, referred only to the two-character precept name, as posthumous names became more elaborate in the Tokugawa period (with names comprised of four or more Chinese characters), it became common to refer to the entire string of characters as the kaimyō.[59] This posthumous name given at the time of the funeral acquired increasing significance both spiritually, as a guarantee of an esteemed afterlife, and socioeconomically, forging an important link between the parish temple priest and the family.

The practice of bestowing kaimyō on lay people began during the medieval period, not within the context of the funeral, but during precept ordination ceremonies (jukai-e). Hirose Ryōkō has demonstrated that the growth of the medieval Sōtō Zen school during this period owed much to the practice of bestowing kaimyō at mass precept ordination ceremonies held over several days involving hundreds or even thousands of lay ordainees.[60] Such events were attractive not only because of the bestowal of the kaimyō, but because each participant received a *kechimyaku*, a special Zen lineage chart linking the newly ordained precept holder through the unbroken lineage of Zen successors all the way back to Śākyamuni Buddha. Medieval records studied by Hirose show that a segment of the lay ordainees participated in multiple mass ordination ceremonies without discouragement from the priests. The attraction of such events probably lay in the popular belief that the more Zen lineage charts one collected, the more talismanic protection one would receive, and that increased participation at temple events on holy days increased one's chances of salvation in the afterlife.[61] This association of posthumous names and Zen lineage charts with other-worldly salvation probably shifted the emphasis from bestowing posthumous names at funerals rather than at precept ordination ceremonies.

Indeed, in 1551 a Christian missionary observer, Cosmo de Torres, described the Zen lineage chart inscribed with the deceased's posthumous name as "an identification document, for which people pay a lot of money, to go to the other world."[62] In other words, to have a posthumous name linked to the lineage of the Buddha assured one of passage to heaven and, according to Torres, had the talismanic power to prevent evil from disturbing the holder of the document in his or her journey in the afterlife. Perhaps he described it in such terms because of the medieval Christian linkage of donations to the Church and salvation in the afterlife—the notion, as Le Goff has put it, of a "'passport' to the hereafter."[63] While medieval Christians may have bought their passport to heaven by leaving money to the Church in their wills, and Chinese Buddhists achieved the same through paying off guards in the other world,[64] Tokugawa-period Buddhists assured their place in the heavenly realms by paying for their posthumous names. In other words, although Sōtō Zen priests may have understood the posthumous name as first and foremost a precept name enabling the dead to join the Buddhist order, for laypeople, the same name had a different significance: assurance that the deceased would properly turn into a revered "ancestor" and have a place in the heavenly realms.[65]

The posthumous name was significant not only because of the assurances of a secure place in the other world, but also in its social meaning for this world. The permanently assigned name was not only engraved on tombstones and written into the Zen lineage chart, but engraved onto one's memorial tablet (*ihai*) and inscribed into one's family register (*kakochō*, lit. the register of the past; William Bodiford's translation is "necrology"). Family honor required obtaining the best possible name for the deceased. The selling of posthumous names, with its elaborate ranking of titles, became a major source of revenue of Buddhist temples of all sects by the beginning of the seventeenth century.[66]

The full posthumous name was most commonly thought of as having two parts, with designated uses of Chinese characters to distinguish men and women of the same rank: (1) the precept/Dharma name itself (*kaimyō/hōmyō*), and (2) a suffix rank name (*igō*), which was thought to denote the depth of the person's faith in Buddhism. In addition, if the person was of a high social standing, a prefix was added by employing a specially designated title, most often reserved for daimyō and other high-ranking families. The general hierarchy of names was as follows:[67]

Prefix Titles for Persons of High Social Standing
Rank 1: Ingō (two characters plus the character "In")[68] plus Dōgō (two characters)
Rank 2: Dōgō (two characters specific to the Zen sect, also called *azana*)
Part 1: Precept (*Kaimyō*) or Dharma (*Hōmyō*) Name (Two characters, also called *imina*)
Part 2: Suffix Rank Name (*Igō*)
For Those With Prefix Titles
Rank 1: Daizenjōmon (Male) or Daizenjōni (Female)
Rank 2: Daikoji (Male) or Shōdaishi (Female)
For Ordinary Parishioners
Rank 1: Koji (Male) or Daishi (Female)
Rank 2: Shinji (Male) or Shinnyo (Female)
Rank 3a: Zenjōmon (Male) or Zenjōni (Female) [above 20 years old]
Rank 3b: Zenmon (Male) or Zen'ni (Female) [usually below 20, but not a child]
For Children
Age 4–14: Dōji (Boy) or Dōjo (Girl)
Age 2–3: Gaiji (Boy) or Gaijo (Girl)
Age up to 1: Eiji (Boy) or Eijo (Girl)

In other words, it was not the two-character precept/Dharma name itself that was ranked, but rather (with the exception of children) the assignment of the prefix and suffix characters that suggested a hierarchy in the afterlife. Although the high-rank titles were supposedly assigned to indicate the depth of faith in Buddhism, and thus confirm the abundance of good karma that would result in a better afterlife, such an assessment of faith could not be divorced from monetary donations to temples, especially if the donor was of a high social standing. For example, the *ingō* prefix was meant to be assigned to those who demonstrated their faith in Buddhism by contributing the funds to build a temple building (*in*). In other words, ranks were determined not by faith alone, but by the amount of money donated and also the social standing an individual held during his or her lifetime.

The ability of money to override matters of faith or social standing was a chief characteristic of the increasingly money-driven Tokugawa society. Although the official stance of the Sōtō Zen school established that peasants could not be awarded the high-ranking Koji (Male) or Daishi (Female) suffix titles, rich peasant families who had the means to make substantial donations to the temple did receive such titles to honor their ancestors.[69] Indeed, some temples posted prices for the various ranks or sent price lists to parish members so that they would know the going rate of posthumous names.[70] Death was not the great equalizer in the eyes of Buddhists in the Tokugawa period. Instead monetary contributions, in effect, determined the social hierarchy of this world and also determined one's fate in the next.

A small but influential circle of Sōtō Zen monks denounced the tendency to charge parishioners for assigning high-ranking posthumous names. In 1730, for instance, Kakumon of Sūshinji Temple recorded a warning from the influential temple Daitōin to all temples in its lineage: "Posthumous name ranks of 'Koji,' 'Daishi,' or 'Anju' should not be easily given out to someone without merit."[71] The well-known Menzan Zuihō also criticized secret transmission manuals (*kirigami*) of all kinds, including one titled *Ihai daiji danshi* (The Secret Manual on the Great Matter of the Ancestral Tablets), which detailed the methods of determining posthumous names.[72] But for the most part such warnings went unheeded, and the general trend during the Tokugawa period was toward the increased commercialization of posthumous names.[73]

While the stress on monetary contributions for a better posthumous name was meant to assure a better afterlife for a deceased member of the household, it also reflected the prestige of the family members still in this world. A high-ranking and well-chosen set of Chinese characters for an ancestor was a point of pride, especially as by the 1640s it was customary for such names to appear on the gravestones and memorial tablets of parishioners. By the late seventeenth century, after the temple-registration system was fully in place, it also became standard to write the posthumous names in the registry of the deceased.[74] Hirose Ryōkō, in his study of 13,250 posthumous names inscribed in such registries at four Sōtō Zen temples, showed that in northern Kantō, this practice had become widespread by the 1660s.[75] This registry was used as a tool for both ritual life and social management, as the deceased person's posthumous name, death date, and occasionally secular name and age at death was listed under a particular day, used by the temple abbot to schedule memorial services. The rank of the posthumous name would also remind the abbot of how much to charge per memorial service (the higher the rank, the higher the fees).[76]

At the same time, these registries were also used as a tool for social management and discrimination.[77] As noted in the case of the abbot Tetsumei pressuring his parishioner Towa, without an abbot's seal at the time of temple registration, an entire household could be taken off register and written up in a separate Registry of Nonhumans, or be assigned clearly discriminatory posthumous names in the regular registries to identify such people. If a family failed to make adequate financial contributions to the temple (taken as a sign that one was disloyal to Buddhism and therefore a suspected Christian or Nichiren Fuju Fuse believer), they risked being relegated to the category of nonhuman a term that originally referred to a class of people in Japanese society associated with animal butchery, tanning, and other "polluted" work and therefore considered outcasts (eta-hinin).[78] Others relegated to this separate register were former Christians (for up to five generations), criminals, homeless people, lepers, and the disabled.[79]

In other words, Tokugawa-period social outcasts were treated as such by Buddhist temples as well. Although Buddhist priests were not the cause of their social marginalization and discrimination, by placing such people off register, they gave a semi-official sanction to the isolation of special groups of people. Just as with the case of leprosy (which will be discussed in chapter 5), the ideology that lumped the disparate outcast groups together was twofold. It maintained that those considered potentially threatening to the Tokugawa order (for example, Christians, criminals, homeless people, or those who did not contribute enough to their parish temple) needed to be kept in check and should receive discriminatory and harsh treatment. Furthermore, those who were born into an outcast group (eta-hinin, lepers, the disabled) had to accept discrimination because their condition was understood to be the result of bad karma accumulated in a previous lifetime. For example, the Sōtō Zen sect used the Ten Fates Preached by the Buddha (Bussetsu jūrai), to promote the beliefs that a short life was caused by killing animals in a previous life (which was obviously directed toward eta-hinin, many of whom worked as butchers or tanners); that illness was caused by ritual impurity in a previous life, with leprosy being the archetype of such "illness"; that poverty was the result of a failure to donate to the Buddhist priesthood in a previous life, a warning to those who did not meet their financial obligations to the parish temple; and that disabilities resulted from violating the precepts.[80] This was, in fact, the widely accepted interpretation of karma during the Tokugawa period, in which a person's present social and economic well-being was believed to be determined by the karma accumulated in a previous life.[81]

Sōtō Zen priests did more than justify discrimination with ideology and passively record outcasts in special registries. They performed discriminatory rituals and bestowed discriminatory posthumous names on outcasts as a public act.[82] For both the outcasts and the mentally disabled, the style of the funeral service and the treatment of the corpse were clearly marked as different from the regular style.[83] The abbot did not directly participate in such a person's funeral, which meant that the Zen lineage chart was never given to an outcast member of the temple.[84] Further, because association with outcasts, who were considered polluted, was deemed a cause of bad karma, special talismans were given to relatives and villagers to protect them from deceased outcasts.[85] The earliest extant records of how to perform such discriminatory rituals date back to 1630, which exponentially increased during the course of the Tokugawa period.[86]

The posthumous names bestowed by priests on outcasts were also distinctive.[87] Some discriminatory posthumous names (*sabetsu kaimyō*) were assigned based on the use of distinctive Chinese characters:

1. Use of "outcast," *sendara* or *senda*, derived from the Sanskrit *candala* or *shuda*, derived from the Sanskrit *śudra* (the lowest of the four castes)[88]
2. Use of "servant," *boku* (male: *bokunan*, female: *bokujo*), or "leather worker," *kaku*, which referred to outcast occupations (m: *kakumon*, f: *kakunyo*)
3. Use of "beast," *chiku*, which implied "nonhuman"

These characters used to compose posthumous names clearly identified the deceased as an outcast either in the temple register or on the family gravestones. In other cases, the reference would be more subtle, with a telltale character or part of a character added or dropped.[89]

Such discriminatory names increased during the first half of the eighteenth century,[90] but certain families, previously assigned such names generation after generation, bought their way out of the outcast status (though only in regard to the temple registries and gravestones), a practice that began in the late eighteenth century. In 1778, for example, at the Sōtō Zen temple Chōfukuji (Maruko Village, Shinshū Province), a certain Matsuemon, who was upset because his parents had received the discriminatory posthumous name "boku" (servant), donated a warehouse to the temple in order to have the name changed. In fact, most parishioners of Chōfukuji were former Jōdo Shin believers (the sect with the highest numbers of outcast members) who became Sōtō Zen parishioners at the beginning of the temple-registration system.[91] Although the Sōtō Zen sect did not have a particularly large concentration of members of the outcast community, the sect had a disproportionately large number of temple registries that included discriminatory names. Further, based on a 1983 survey, the Sōtō Zen sect had the highest number of discriminatory registries (5,600 Sōtō Zen, 1,771 Jōdo, 254 Tendai, and 40 Kōya Shingon) as well as gravestones with such names inscribed (1,911 Sōtō Zen, 231 Jōdo, 12 Shingon, and 10 Tendai).[92]

While discriminatory practices at Sōtō Zen temples reflected the social reality of Tokugawa society, it is clear that the sect also played a role in reinforcing such discrimination, both socially in this world and spiritually in the next. In some sense, these discriminatory ways of dealing with social outcasts (whether administratively, socially, or ritually) helped to define practices for "regular" parishioners and their dead. By setting funerary ritual standards for ordinary parishioners through the designation of discriminatory rites for outcasts, and by setting standards for parishioner obligations to the temple (especially financial obligations) by threatening omission from the regular temple registry, Sōtō Zen priests managed to maintain a steady membership in their parish temples. And yet, despite the power that was seemingly in the hands of the priests, parishioners starting from the mid-Tokugawa period found ways to weaken the parish temple's control over them and gain some decision-making power in temple affairs.

CHALLENGES TO TEMPLE AUTHORITY FROM PARISHIONERS

The force of bakufu law behind the temple-registration system, the forged decrees regarding parishioner responsibility toward the temple, the legends about becoming a hungry ghost if ancestral memorial services were not properly observed, and the fear of various types of social discrimination all served to reinforce the parish temple priest's authority over the membership. However, the absolute power of local temple priests of all sects began to be challenged from both above (the bakufu) and below (the parishioners).[93] It started slowly in the latter half of the seventeenth century and gained momentum toward the end of the eighteenth and into the nineteenth century.

This chapter began with an account of the three-year affair between Towa and the abbot of Chōsenji Temple, Tetsumei, but without revealing the conclusion of this incident. Towa, in a letter to Seigen'in Temple (Chōsenji's head temple) dated the eighth month of 1786, had accused Tetsumei of forcing her into sexual relations by threatening to withhold his seal from the Registry of Religious Affiliation. Although her husband had discovered the affair, Tetsumei, in his formal response to Seigen'in Temple's inquiries, steadfastly denied any relationship in a letter sent later in the same month:[94]

> Regarding the accusations of an affair between Matabee's wife and I (who all live under the authority of Matsudaira Magodayū in [Hayakawa Village]) which was forwarded by Matabee, I have no recollection of such a thing. Therefore, having been accused of such a thing, I went to the village office to deny the allegations. I am writing this to you to let you know that I took this step. Eighth month, 1786[95]

Though adultery was punishable by death and Tetsumei ultimately admitted to the affair, the sequence of events that followed reflects both the strength of the Buddhist parish temple and a gradual weakening of the temple priest's absolute power over his parishioners.[96] First, the other Sōtō Zen temples in the surrounding villages jointly submitted two letters requesting that the head temple take pity on Tetsumei and let the branch temples work out a discreet agreement with Towa and her husband that would not involve the head temple, lest it come to the attention of the bakufu's Office of Temple and Shrines. Second, since the rumors of this affair had spread like wildfire to Chōsenji Temple's parishioners, a secret agreement was being negotiated that called for compensation of Towa and Matabee on condition that the parishioners not press the issue any further.

The negotiations broke down when the villagers heard rumors that the priest Tetsumei had been boasting that he could get away with a simple charge of "neglect and guiltless self-indulgence" because he would pay off the head temple. This created an uproar among even the parishioners closest to their parish temple, who threatened to end their affiliation with Chōsenji Temple. Despite knowing the severe penalties of not obeying the parish temple, on the seventeenth of the eleventh month, 1786, the parishioners discussed their options at a village official's residence. The head temple had no choice but to demand a letter of apology from Tetsumei admitting to what he had done. However, while such a gesture might have been enough in an earlier stage of the Tokugawa period, some parishioners, sensing their power, demanded that Tetsumei be removed from the abbotship of Chōsenji Temple or otherwise face a mass desertion of the membership. One of the parishioners, Shinzō, detailed his reasons:

> The personal character of Tetsumei is exactly as described in the letter originally sent to you (the head temple, Seigen'in) from Towa. Although you have shown mercy to Tetsumei and decided to solve this matter privately in the village, we have also heard rumors that temple representatives have gone to Yamamoto Senji [the matchmaker] with money to solve this quietly. How is it possible that we could trust a man of such character with the abbotship of our family temple, which means he is in charge of memorial rites for our parents and ancestors? Eventually, we too will have our funerals conducted by this man. This is completely unacceptable for we will be the butt of jokes. Even if we ignored what others thought of us, we [would nevertheless] absolutely refuse to accept him [in this position].[97]

In the end, the head temple removed Tetsumei from the abbotship of Chōsenji Temple. Although I have not been able to ascertain Tetsumei's activities following this incident, since his punishment was simply removal from the abbotship of this particular temple and not defrocking, he may well have been assigned to an abbotship at a Sōtō Zen temple in a different region. Perhaps Tetsumei's lack of contrition caused even his staunchest allies to abandon their support, or perhaps fear at the head temple of an embarrassing full-scale investigation by the Office of Temples and Shrines made his removal possible. Although this incident was obviously an extreme case, it is one of an increasing number of challenges made by parishioners to their parish temples by the latter half of the eighteenth century. As I have discussed elsewhere, the power of the local villages to influence Sōtō Zen temples has been a longstanding theme in the spread of the sect in rural Japan.[98] Especially with certain temples having a high turnover rate of abbots due to the so-called rotating abbot system, the ability of the wealthier lay temple "officers" (the *danka sōdai*) to dictate the way in which parish temples were managed increased during the latter half of the Tokugawa period.[99] However much the socioreligious structures favored priestly authority in the first half of the period, the latent power of the local villagers to demand that temples respond to their needs asserted itself when opportunity arose.

The absolute authority enjoyed by local temple priests was also curbed from a different direction by regulations issued periodically by the bakufu. The first such directive dates to 1665 when four members of the bakufu's Council of Elders issued the *Jōjō*, a five-point directive to all temples.[100] These regulations included the prohibition of expensive Buddhist ceremonies that burdened parishioners. Though the directive was not consistently implemented, it reflects bakufu officials' concerns at the growing power of local temple priests over their parishioners and marks the beginning of a series of regulations from the top down to curb that power.

For example, sixty years later, the official bakufu record, the *Tokugawa jikki*, details new directives—the 1722 *Shoshū matsuji okite*—issued by the head temples of each sect to the branch temples to curb temple abuses of power.[101] Citing the laxity of local temple monks, these directives list problems such as priests holding parties at temples and discriminating against parishioners who could not afford high fees. The directives of the Sōtō sect, in particular, concerned the exorbitant showering of money, food, and gifts on the temples and priests. The amount of food at post–memorial service dinners was regulated (one soup dish and three side dishes maximum), and the serving of alcohol to priests on such occasions was prohibited. Obligations for parishioners were also lightened by decreasing the number of mandatory temple visits and lowering the value of required parishioner gifts to the temple. The repeated issuance of these regulations, however, reflects the fact that local temples routinely ignored the warnings.[102]

The Towa-Tetsumei incident came in the midst of such shifts in the power dynamics between temples and parishioners. In another incident that, amazingly, involved the same Chōkokuji Temple a mere twenty-three years after Tetsumei's dismissal, parishioners exerted their collective authority once again to dismiss an Sōtō Zen abbot. This time, the entire parish signed a letter dated the twenty-fifth of the sixth month, 1819, outlining fourteen points that they found objectionable about the abbot named Gyokutan and demanded his removal.

- When someone dies and needs a funeral, he demands exorbitant fees.
- For memorial services held at a parishioner's home, he extravagantly comes to even a poor house with both a young attendant priest and another attendant [to charge more money].
- For memorial services held at the temple, even if most arrangements are made by the relatives, if the donations are low he gets angry and orders them out.
- When we have to make offerings, he insists on 200 *mon* cash, two *shō* of rice, and vegetables.[103]
- In cases of aborted or miscarried children, or infants that died in childbirth, he charges one *ryō* two *bu*, which is far too expensive for poor households.
- For the memorial services [from the first to the thirty-third year], he demands that we pay the prices that he writes on a signboard hung at the temple.
- Even if a baby dies before the "seventh day" [when it becomes fully human], he

performs a full-fledged funeral and demands that annual memorial services be held.

- One of the parishioners, Hikoemon, was severely beaten by the abbot and is still suffering.
- There are always actors at the temple and they hold their play rehearsals there. In addition, the abbot often leaves the temple and goes out to other people's residences to play around at night.
- Calling her an "old laundry woman," he has a young woman living with him.
- He hides fish in the temple's food containers [though he is supposed to be vegetarian].
- He takes money from the parishioners and uses it to visit prostitutes.
- Inviting shadow puppeteers to the temple, he holds drinking parties with young women.[104]
- He roams the village uncontrollably, going after young women and trampling any young man that gets in his way.[105]

Obviously fearing the power of the abbot to retaliate against anyone opposing him, this letter, sent to the head temple, was signed by all the parishioners in what is called the *karakasa renpanjō* style; that is, a ring of seals at the end of the letter that made it impossible to single out a leader or instigator. Since ordinary letters were signed with clear indications of social rank (a higher-ranking person in a village would put his seal above others, for example), this way of signing the document both precluded the abbot from taking revenge on any one individual and also demonstrated the solidarity of the parishioners' demand that he be dismissed. A similar letter was sent the next day to further detail Gyokutan's bad character. It accused him of, among other things, impregnating the villager Goröemon's daughter, which resulted in an abortion on the twentieth of the fifth month. He had paid her for sex, all of which was arranged by Bun'eemon's wife, with whom the abbot had also been having an affair for some time, which prompted Bun'eemon to divorce his wife. Here, the expectations of parishioners are clear. They wanted the parish priest to (1) perform funerals and memorial services, but not with undue extravagance and at inflated prices, (2) show consideration for a family's circumstances (being poor or having lost a young child), and (3) refrain from philandering, drinking parties, and other forms of "playing around." Ultimately, the head temple of Seigen'in agreed with the parishioners, and in the following month, Gyokutan was dismissed as abbot of Chōkokuji Temple.

While these incidents did not cause any parishioners to annul their temple membership, the complaints and subsequent punishments reflected the growing power of parishioners to influence their parish temple. While the parish temple system started to transform itself during the Tokugawa period, the overall stability it provided, in the form of political stability for the bakufu and economic stability for the Buddhist temples, enabled it to remain the overriding framework for Sōtō Zen as well as other sects. While the Sōtō Zen hierarchy allowed parishioners to make occasional demands regarding alterations to ritual or abbotship changes, it firmly opposed all attempts of parishioners to quit the temple or change sect affiliations. The growth in the number of temples and parishioners enjoyed by Sōtō Zen in the first half of the seventeenth century could only be sustained if each of its 17,500 temples retained its membership—and with it, the steady income the members generated.

A case that went all the way up to the Office of Temples and Shrines in Edo illustrates the Sōtō Zen leadership's overriding concern to maintain temple membership. A high-ranking official of the Kumamoto Domain, Tanaka Sahei, was a parishioner of Zenjōji Temple, a Sōtō Zen temple located adjacent to Kumamoto Castle.[106] In 1737 he fell terribly ill. Though doctors tried to cure him and Sōtō Zen priests performed prayers for him, his illness did not subside until he met Myōonbō, a priest of the Nichiren sect affiliated with the large Honmyōji Temple (Hōdo District, Nakao Village). Through what Tanaka considered the miraculous intervention of Myōonbō, he was apparently cured immediately. Wanting to become a parishioner of Honmyōji Temple out of gratitude to Myōonbō and due to his newfound faith in Nichiren sect teachings, on twenty-third of the sixth month, 1737, he sent a request to Zenjōji Temple to give him permission to quit his temple so that he could join the nearby Nichiren temple. This request was immediately declined, so Tanaka wrote a second letter proposing a compromise: he would, as an individual, leave the Sōtō Zen temple, but his family (as represented by his adopted son who would represent the future family lineage) would remain parishioners at Zenjōji Temple. The Sōtō Zen temple abbot responded:

> In regard to the request to change sect and temple affiliation, given that our temple did nothing wrong, it is not clear whether the problem lies in our sect's teachings, the temple, or its abbot. There has been no special reason given for leaving our temple. Though it may seem reasonable to the individual to simply change his sect or temple, if this individual leaves during my tenure as the abbot of the temple, it will trouble me greatly because this individual's family has had a long and distinguished connection to our temple as parishioners. . . . The meaning of being a temple parishioner involves not only receiving a funeral and incense-offerings [memorial services] at the temple, but also receiving the temple certificate showing that one is not a member of an evil sect. Therefore, it should not be possible for one to change sect affiliation with such impunity.[107]

The Nichiren temple, Honmyōji, responded with its own letter to the Office of Temples and Shrines arguing that the religious faith of the individual, not his familial sect affiliation, should be the central factor in determining a parishioner's temple affiliation. Despite this appeal, which referred to the government's own directives that allowed for sect change, the government sided with the Sōtō Zen temple's claims that sect affiliation changes should not easily be granted for heads of families. In a harsh ruling, Tanaka Sahei was stripped of his secular title and put under temporary house arrest. What the conclusion to this case reveals is the government's fear of setting precedents on individual choice regarding a parish temple or sect based on factors such as religious faith. For the Sōtō Zen temple, the idea of the stability of its temple membership and maintenance of the status quo overrode the particulars of individual religious choice.

Once parishioners came into the Sōtō Zen fold in the late sixteenth and early seventeenth centuries, the temple registration and parish temple systems served as mechanisms through which this stable membership could be retained generation after generation. Though these systems began initially as a way to control Christians and other potentially threatening religious groups, they expanded to include virtually the entire populace. Ordinary parishioners were obligated to their parish temple both ritually and financially not as individuals, but as members of the household (ie), which continued its hereditary membership for the purpose of memorializing ancestors.

The development of practices such as the assignment of posthumous names and the creation of family genealogies within the temple's ancestral registers bound parishioner households to the temples, not necessarily out of religious faith, but through social pressure. This coercive aspect of temple membership, initially created and spread by Sōtō Zen priests who were affiliated with the anti-Christian campaign, was just as important to the establishment of the sect as was its appealing ritual practices. As the Tetsumei and Gyokutan incidents illustrate, the position of the parishioners vis-à-vis the priesthood involved a complex negotiation of power. Ultimately, however, the economic necessity of a stable membership for the temples and an orderly tracking of the population for the political authorities rendered it nearly impossible for parishioners to switch sects. This parish system was especially advantageous to sects like Sōtō Zen, which managed to secure large numbers of parish members in the early part of the 1600s. Sōtō Zen parish temples, which comprised the vast majority of the sect's network of temples, thus served as the ritual and economic backbone of the Tokugawa-period Sōtō Zen institution. With parish temple authority inextricably linked to political authority, "funerary Zen"—to be discussed in the next chapter—had a powerful institutional setting within which it could be practiced.

Funerary Zen: Managing the Dead in the World Beyond

"FUNERARY ZEN" EMERGED as a combination of Chinese Chan/Zen, esoteric, and Pure Land Buddhist, and localized death ritual practices in the late medieval and early modern periods. Although funerary practices found an institutional base in the Tokugawa government's temple-registration policy and the subsequent demand for parish temples, the practice of funerals and memorial services for deceased relatives cannot simply be understood as a response to a government directive but must also be seen as part of a deep human need for ritualizing death.

Death rituals were the central practice at Sōtō Zen parish temples. In addition to the funeral proper, Zen priests performed memorial rites at intervals for a period of thirty-three years following a death. Large festivals for the dead, such as the summer Obon Festival for the ancestors or the Segaki Festival for hungry ghosts, were important events in the temple's annual ritual calendar. Services were also performed for "hungry ghosts," "the ancestors," and women and children who had died during childbirth, thus universalizing funerary Buddhism in Japan by the seventeenth century. This chapter describes the historical development of this funerary Zen and shows how it was intimately tied to the growth of the Sōtō Zen school during the Tokugawa period.

THE FUNERAL: MANAGING THE RECENTLY DECEASED

In *Ten Weeks in Japan*, the visiting Anglican bishop George Smith correctly observed a fairly typical process of handling an ordinary villager's death during the latter half of the Tokugawa period:

> When death has visited a Japanese family, the relatives of the deceased despatch [*sic*] a messenger to some Budhist [*sic*] temple to fetch a priest, who visits the dwelling and performs certain rites over the corpse. . . . After the departure of the priest, the relatives cause the dead body to be washed with warm water, and make the necessary preparations for placing it in the round circular coffin or tub in which the corpse is deposited. . . . It is then left for a period of one to four days in the house, during which time the priest (if the family be in good circumstances and able to pay a fee of an *itzebu* [usually romanized as *ichibu* or "one bu" worth of currency] or less) returns to the house and resumes his prayers and incantations,

reciting some Budhist office with the customary beating of hollow sounding-board and the tinkling of a bell in measured time of stroke.[1]

Although Smith could not understand the symbolic nature of this rite, he correctly guessed that the time between the moment of death and the completion of the funeral required the intervention of a Buddhist priest. Ordinarily, before the arrival of the priest, the body would have already been cleaned with warm water by a family member or a close friend and placed into a coffin dressed in a set of fresh clothes.[2] At the wake itself, Sōtō Zen priests would recite mantras in front of the deceased, including the *Taiya nenju* (Prayer on the Eve of the Funeral), which involved a brief address to the deceased, who had become an "enlightened spirit" gone (or "returned") to "the ocean of eternal tranquility." The priest(s) would then recite the names of the Ten Buddhas and various sutras, the merit of this act being transferred to the deceased.[3] The role of the priest at the wake was limited to this brief service, which laid the groundwork for the more elaborate and important funeral proper. The immediate family played a more important role during the period prior to the funeral, taking care of both the deceased and visitors to the house. On the night of the wake, for example, family members would spend the entire night with the deceased. In some regions, a relative would actually share the same futon with the deceased, who would be placed in his or her bed one last time.

Depending on regional, rather than sectarian customs, the funeral proper would then be held at either the family's house or at the temple.[4] In either case, the time from death until the funeral marked the first of three charged phases in the Buddhist management of the dead (the funeral, the forty-ninth day, and thirty-third year after death). Sōtō Zen Buddhists in the Tokugawa period followed this process common to all Buddhist sects in which the recently deceased person was both ritually purified (from the commonly held pre-Buddhist notion of the pollution of the corpse) and deified in various ways as an "enlightened spirit" (*kakurei*), a resident of a Buddhist heaven or pure land, a "Buddha" (*hotoke*), or an ancestor (*senzo*). This shared ritual culture is what Tamamuro Taijō had termed "funerary Buddhism" (*sōshiki bukkyō*), the title of his classic work on the subject.[5] Sōtō Zen priests both participated in and helped shape this common Buddhist culture of managing the dead, but funerary Zen also had a number of unique characteristics.

The interaction between elements peculiar to the Sōtō Zen funerary approach and the cosmological and ritual aspects common to Japanese Buddhism as a whole was a dynamic process that allowed the sect to embed itself into local village life, which also had its own unique funerary customs. At times, Sōtō Zen, generic Buddhist, and local beliefs and practices toward death were in conflict, producing contradictory goals and rituals.[6] But in the main, the Sōtō Zen tradition accepted a multiplicity of practices and a division of labor in funerary practices in which the household (living relatives) was obligated to observe rituals that would transform the deceased into an ancestor. The temple was responsible for enlightening the dead, saving them from the lower realms of existence, and sending them to a Buddha land, and the community was in charge of neutralizing the pollution of the dead, which affected the larger community. The ability of Sōtō Zen priests to participate actively in the broader funerary culture at the local level while still imprinting a unique Zen mark on funerary rites was the key to its acceptance at the village level.

The Japanese Zen funeral first developed during the medieval period was based on Chinese Chan monastic regulations (*shingi*), such as the 1103 *Chanyuan qinggui* (Jpn. *Zennen shingi*), which detail the procedures for monastic funerals.[7] The Japanese Sōtō Zen founder, Dōgen, did not include funerary procedures in his ritual repertoire, so it was not until the third-generation monk Gikai's death in 1309 that the first Sōtō Zen funeral was conducted under Chinese Chan monastic regulations.[8] The first Japanese Sōtō Zen monastic regulations, which included a section on how to perform funerals, was the *Keizan shingi*.[9] This text would become one of several manuals aimed at standardizing monastic procedures in the Tokugawa period. It retained the basic Chinese Chan monastic funeral style, although it dropped some of the Pure Land elements and added new rituals for memorializing the lay dead.[10]

In this earliest-known Japanese Sōtō Zen example of a standardized memorial verse for the layperson, two striking aspects appear: the use of the word "enlightened spirit" (*kakurei*) to refer to the dead, who was imagined to reside on the banks of nirvana, and the scant difference between lay and monastic merit-transfer invocations. The term *kakurei*, while rarely used by ordinary villagers of the Tokugawa period, was a standard term employed by Sōtō Zen priests (especially in secret ritual initiation papers) to refer to those who had undergone Zen funerary rites. Indeed, from the point of view of the Zen priest, the purpose of the Zen funeral was to "deliver" or "return" (depending one one's interpretation) the deceased to an "enlightened" state. While Pure Land imagery is not completely absent from later monastic texts, and almost always present in lay interpretations of the afterlife, official Sōtō Zen manuals tend to refer to the enlightened spirit as residing in heavenly states such as the banks of nirvana, in a generic Buddha's realm, or in a vast, tranquil ocean of equanimity. However, these images competed with the more popular Japanese Buddhist visions of the afterlife, which included both heavens (Amida's Pure Land, Miroku's paradise, sacred mountains) and hell-like realms (the hungry ghost realm or the various hells). The ability of the Sōtō Zen tradition to allow both types of imagery to coexist, without ever fully integrating them, was one reason for their early success not only in promoting their brand of funerary Zen, but in setting the ritual framework for other sects to copy. Sōtō Zen priests, who often incorporated esoteric Buddhist and Onmyōdō funerary practices, even fought a lawsuit that went all the way to the Office of Temples and Shrines with some *yamabushi*, who had accused the Sōtō Zen priests of stealing their rites (each sect often borrowed elements of funerary rites from each other).[11] Although in this sense, Sōtō Zen funerary rites were woven together with materials from Chinese Chan, Japanese esoteric, and local folk traditions, their distinctive aspect was the posthumous priestly ordination of the layperson. Starting from the mid- to late fifteenth century, the performance of lay funerals was a crucial element in the spread of Sōtō Zen in rural Japan, especially in combination with the establishment of the parish temple system in the early Tokugawa period.[12]

Motsugo Sasō: Priestly Ordination for the Lay Dead

Though the first specifically lay funeral ritual was created in the mid-Meiji period, one of the most significant characteristics of the Tokugawa-period Zen funeral was the ordination of a deceased layperson as a priest so that the monastic funeral could be performed.[13] Indeed, this practice of ordaining the lay dead as Zen priests was one of the very few elements of Sōtō Zen funerals that was standardized by the early Tokugawa period, crossing Zen lineage and regional boundaries.

While the Sōtō sect's funerary rites were similar to those of other sects of Japanese Buddhism of the time, one striking and unique aspect of the Zen funeral was the posthumous granting of the priestly precepts (*motsugo sasō*) and a special Zen lineage chart (*kechimyaku*) to the lay dead so that the dead person would be enlightened and saved through a special posthumous ordination. As William Bodiford has noted, "This ritual enabled the monastic last rites of China to serve laypeople in Japan."[14] In other words, one of the important transformations in medieval Japanese Zen was the adaptation of the Chinese Chan monastic funeral for Japanese lay patrons such that a monastic funeral could be performed for the lay dead who would be ordained into the monastic order, albeit posthumously.[15] Although the monastic funeral was originally imported from China, this Japanese Zen practice of posthumous ordination of the lay dead allowed laypeople access to elaborate monastic rituals that ushered them into the Buddha's realm.

After consecrating the immediate vicinity of the body, the ceremony to ordain the deceased layperson as a Zen priest would begin by washing and outfitting the corpse with a new robe. According to the secret initiation manual for the posthumous ordination ritual, the *Motsugo sasō jukai shiki*, "For the newly dead, give the person a tonsure. The precept teacher should provide the dead with a robe, a bowing mat, a begging bowl, the Three Refuges, the Three Pure Precepts, and the Ten Grave Precepts. The precept teacher should take the place of the deceased to receive these items."[16] In other words, the officiant shaved the layperson's hair (today, this is generally only symbolically observed as a small clump of hair is removed) to represent acceptance into the priesthood. The deceased was also presented with all the necessary items of a Zen priest: a robe, a mat, and a begging bowl. Furthermore, the basic moral precepts—the sixteen articles consisting of the Three Refuges, Three Pure Precepts, and Ten Grave Precepts—were administered to the dead person. Here, a priest took the place of the deceased, who was obviously unable to answer affirmatively to the question of whether he or she would vow to keep the precepts. William Bodiford notes one explanation of how the dead could receive these precepts, as described in *Motsugo jukai sahō*:

> How can one posthumously become a monk?
> *Answer*: "Neither saying 'No' nor 'Yes'"
> A Phrase?
>   "No self appearance; no human appearance."
> Explain [its meaning].
> *Answer*: "When [something has] absolutely no appearance, it can become anything."
> *Teacher*: "But why does it become a monk?"
> *Answer*: "Not saying 'No' and 'Yes' is truly to become a monk (*shukke*)."
> A phrase?
>   "The sagely and the ordinary know of themselves [who they are]." [17]

This *kōan*-like dialogue is based on the idea that the inability of the dead to answer "yes" or "no" was proof that they were indeed enlightened, reminding one of the well-known episode of Vimalakirti's "thunderous silence." Though such nuanced understanding of posthumous ordination may not have been widespread among either monks or laypeople, it does point to the more general notion that the state of being dead was equal to the state of being a Buddha (*hotoke*). Indeed, one manual explicitly stated the precept ordination's power to immediately transform the dead into a Buddha:

> When ignorant men receive the Bodhisattva Precepts, the dust [that covers their spirit] immediately disappears and finally the spiritual light burgeons forth. This is why it is said that when beings receive the Buddhist Precepts, they immediately achieve the rank of Buddha, a rank identical to that of the Buddhas of great awakening. This is what it really means to receive [the title of] son of the Buddha. [18]

The posthumous priestly ordination was connected both to this notion of immediate enlightenment and to a kind of initiatory function of funerals. Through ordination, the dead person was initiated into the Sōtō Zen lineage in a narrow sense but at the same time was initiated as a "son of the Buddha." In other words, the dead entered into the Buddha family, the world of the Buddha.

This entering into the Buddhist family lineage through posthumous ordination, combined with the power of the priest magically to send the dead into the other world, tended to demonstrate the immediate efficacy of the Zen funeral to provide salvation. The idea of salvation (*jōbutsu*) literally meant to "become a Buddha," but the term was often used simply to mean a deliverance from the sufferings of this world and the hells (i.e., to be delivered to a higher realm, often imagined to be a Buddhist heaven or pure land). The priest's power was further symbolized in the ritual bestowal on the dead of a special Zen lineage chart. This chart (*kechimyaku*) linked the newly ordained precept holder through the unbroken lineage of Zen successors all the way back to Śakyamuni Buddha.[19] Bernard Faure has written about the meaning of receiving the *kechimyaku*:

> The lineage diagrams thus became magical talismans in which the name of the cleric or layperson was connected to those of past Buddhas by a red line, symbol of the blood (and spirit) lineage to which he or she was attaching him- or herself. Awakening is no longer the *sine qua non* for transmission; on the contrary, it is ritual initiation that becomes the performative act par excellence, the symbolic realization of awakening recorded by the *kechimyaku*. For people participating in this ritual, the moral content of the Precepts was less important than the magical transformation of karma that it was supposed to achieve.[20]

Upon ordination, the dead (or the living, if the ordination ceremony was held while alive), would receive a special Dharma name or precept name, as discussed in chapter 2. This name was written into a space at the bottom of a lineage chart. Sometimes written with ink made from the abbot's blood, this document would often be placed in the coffin of the deceased to accompany them on their journey to the world beyond.[21] Although the Zen lineage chart was originally handed down from master to disciple as proof of Dharma succession, the efficacy of bestowing the document on the dead to erase evil karma and deliver them to a higher realm seems to have been promoted by Sōtō priests by the early Tokugawa period.[22]

Indeed, it was not just the ordinary dead, but spirits symbolizing unfortunate fates in the afterlife—ghosts, dragon girls, snakes—that also seemed immediately to benefit from the bestowal of the Zen lineage chart. In a Tokugawa-period legend, Zen Master Dōgen was credited with using a Zen lineage chart to save a woman who had turned into a wandering ghost:

> The feudal lord of Echizen Province, a certain Eihei, had a concubine. Once when Eihei was traveling, his wife took the opportunity to drown his concubine in a nearby pond and thus killed her. The dead concubine's spirit came upon a traveling monk and told him of her sufferings in the world beyond. She then gave him one part of a red sleeve. Hearing about this, Eihei thought to turn his living quarters into a temple so that her spirit could be saved. He invited Dōgen to his temple and the Zen Master bestowed a Zen lineage chart on the woman's spirit and she was liberated. With this, Eihei decided to become a monk and later became the founder of Eiheiji Temple.[23]

This folk account of the origins of Eiheiji Temple never appeared in the older Dōgen biographies such as the *Kenzeiki* because it ignored some basic facts, such as the Echizen feudal lord being from the Hatano family and Dōgen being the founder of Eiheiji Temple. However, the theme of salvation through the bestowal of the precepts and the Zen lineage chart was so central to Sōtō Zen efforts to demonstrate their priests' powers of magical salvation of those suffering in the world beyond that this legend of Dōgen's salvation of the concubine's spirit eventually made its way into the nineteenth-century Dōgen pictorial narratives (*eden*) and biographies such as the *Teiho Kenzeiki zue*.[24]

Sometimes such ghosts returned in a vengeful manner, but the Sōtō Zen lineage chart apparently had the power to appease these angry spirits as well. One example appears in the seventeenth-century popular collection of morality tales, the *Inga monogatari* (by the Sōtō Zen monk Suzuki Shōsan):

A PERSON WHO TURNED INTO AN ANGRY GHOST BECAUSE
HE WAS KILLED FOR NO REASON

A man named Abe killed his manservant for no reason. The manservant's spirit took the shape of a snake. Like a vengeful ghost, this spirit bothered everyone in the Abe family. So in 1646, the Abe family called on the [Sōtō Zen] monk San'ei to help. The monk broke down a shrine, cleared some trees, deposited a Zen lineage chart into the ground, and set up a small wooden *stūpa*. [All became well] after he conducted rites [at this site] for seven days.[25]

Although tales of visits from ghosts from the world beyond to harass the living or request help did not exclusively feature Sōtō Zen priests (Jōdo priests and Tōzan shugen *yamabushi* often appear in these legends as well), as Tsutsumi Kunihiko has noted, Sōtō Zen priests were featured in a disproportionately large number of such legends.[26]

Another motif in such salvation stories is ghosts or other spirits leaving behind evidence that could substantiate the fact that they had been saved by a monk. The ghost of the concubine whom Dōgen had saved left behind a single sleeve of the flowing "ghost robe" that was commonly imagined to be worn by ghosts. Similarly, the ghost of the feudal lord Hatano Yoshishige, whom Dōgen, in a different legend, saved with a Zen lineage chart left behind a sleeve. While Eiheiji Temple never deigned to exhibit such otherworld objects, several Sōtō Zen temples throughout Japan, as well as a few from other sects, exhibited ghost sleeves in an effort to demonstrate to laypeople the power of their monks.[27] Enjōji Temple (Hanamaki City, Iwate Prefecture), for example, periodically exhibited the sleeve of a certain Shikauchi Hyōbu, who allegedly became a ghost after his death because his descendants did not respect his last wishes that a Sakyamuni statue be donated to the temple. Fuzan, the abbot of Sōseiji Temple in the mid-Tokugawa period, saved the ghost, and its sleeve was kept as evidence of salvation at Enjōji Temple, a branch temple of Sōseiji.[28] A similar ghost's sleeve piece can also be found at Gankōji Temple (Ehime Prefecture), and an illustrated scroll of such a sleeve can be found at Tokushōji Temple (Niigata Prefecture).[29]

Sōtō Zen temples, along with some other sects' temples, displayed such mementos from the world beyond as proof of the power of their ability to manage and save the dead. A list of Tokuunji Temple (Tōjō Village, Hiroshima Prefecture) treasures compiled in 1862 included demon and goblin horns as evidence left by these otherworldly creatures attesting to their salvation. These treasures would occasionally be exhibited for lay believers through public displays on certain days of the year.[30] Other temples held such mementos as animal claws and teeth (allegedly from beings saved from their animal form), dragon scales (from dragon girls who were saved), or crab shells (from crabs defeated by Zen masters in Dharma combat).[31] The basic message seems to have been that if Sōtō Zen priests could have saved such lowly beings through the bestowal of precepts and the Zen lineage chart, that power could also be transferred to ordinary human beings to achieve postmortem spiritual liberation. The combined power of the posthumous monastic ordination and the Zen lineage chart gave the sect a valuable tool in recruiting potential parishioners as they displayed the unique power of bestowing salvation via their funerary ritual. By broadening the appeal of Buddhist funerals to all classes of society in a way that downplayed karmic merit, the Sōtō Zen sect found a way to tie monastic powers with a powerful and quick method of salvation in the funeral rite. Yet, as the sect began to develop the full range of rituals to manage the dead, the Zen funeral by itself proved insufficient to garner the kind of broad-based appeal necessary to solidly establish the sect in local society. To do that, Sōtō Zen would need to draw also on commonly accepted notions of the afterlife that went counter to the notion of immediate salvation.

The Long Journey to Become a Buddha-Ancestor

When a person dies and is given a Buddhist funeral in Japan, it is customary for most people to refer to the deceased as *hotoke* or, more honorifically, *hotoke-sama*. The Sino-Japanese character used to represent the term *hotoke* is also read *butsu* or "buddha." In other words, the Sino-Japanese character that means buddha [*butsu*] is also given the native Japanese reading *hotoke*. And yet, while people will speak of a deceased person as having "become a *hotoke*," they do not say that he has "become a buddha [*butsu*]." This difference in usage arises since the term "buddha" originally meant "someone who has awakened to ultimate truth," and not merely a deceased individual.[32]

As the anthropologist Sasaki Kōkan suggested, one of the features of Japanese Buddhism has been the use of the Sino-Japanese character for the Buddha to refer to the dead. Ambiguities such as the use of this term *hotoke* allowed the Sōtō Zen sect to maintain that the dead became Buddhas and yet still retained the characteristics of a spirit that needed management. If the "logic of Buddhahood" functioned within the funeral rite, a parallel "logic of spirit taming" shaped other posthumous rites.

The notion that dead spirits remained in a state of pollution and instability, needing appeasement and taming, existed prior to the advent of Buddhism in Japan and continued to hold considerable sway in the common religious imagination of Tokugawa-period people.[33] While ordinary people believed that some spirits easily found tranquility and a new residence (mountaintops being a common resting place), many spirits were thought to be unstable and even dangerous if appropriate ritual action was not taken to appease them or ward them off.[34] Thus the need for priestly intervention. Buddhist priests incorporated indigenous, pre-Buddhist ideas of the unstable spirit that had not yet departed for the underworld with the Buddhist idea of a period of a dead person's "intermediate existence." By the late medieval period this had created a pervasive belief that funerary rites functioned to purify the dead and to provide for their welfare, but also to escape harm from those spirits prone to attack or possess the living, or to cause calamities or epidemics.[35] Thus a major concern of Buddhist priests came to include managing unstable, unruly, or wrathful spirits by appeasing them through music and dance, driving them away with bonfires, or containing them.[36] Through these rituals, people hoped to placate the spirits so that they would be transformed into either benign ancestors or guardian spirits who could protect the family or the village. This belief had pervaded the Japanese religious landscape by the late medieval period and therefore oriented people toward death rituals that would be performed over a lengthy period of time until the spirits had stabilized. This discrepant logic, seemingly in conflict with the immediate salvation of the Zen funeral, nonetheless had to coexist alongside it within the framework of funerary Zen.

The multivalence of death was succinctly captured in the term *hotoke*, mentioned above, which could "signify variously buddha, ancestral spirit, and spirit of the dead."[37] Although scholars disagree as to why and when the term came into usage to refer to the dead, and dispute the original meaning of "buddha," by the Tokugawa period the doctrinal meaning of the term to refer to an enlightened person overlapped with the popular meaning referring to the dead.[38] So while the rhetoric of Zen priests focused on the fact that their funerals would send the deceased into "the land of the Buddha," and enable them to "achieve the same state as the Buddha," or "join the Buddha's family," they simultaneously performed a wide range of posthumous rites premised on the fact that the "spirit" also needed to be cared for over time. Although some scholars have argued that Sōtō Zen priests simply "accommodated superstitious folk beliefs," in fact, they helped to promote the very idea of needing protracted funerary rituals.

The length of time needed for continued sutra readings and other rituals for the dead was determined by the goal of postfuneral rituals for the dead: to transform them into Buddhas and/or ancestors. The logic behind memorial rites, generally called *tsuizen kuyō*, evolved from both folk beliefs about commemorating ancestors and Buddhist ideas about the spirits of the dead. The folk belief was that the spirit required time to settle down from the upheaval of death and rid itself from death's pollution. The Buddhist belief was that the spirit needed time and merit (produced either by one's own disciplines or dedicated by someone else) to cancel the heavy weight of bad karma that the deceased had accumulated. On the one hand, then, the goal of such funerary rites was to help the dead spirit settle down and become purified through the ritual intercession of the living, which transformed the polluted body into a venerated ancestor. On the other hand, not only was the goal to help the dead join the collective ancestral body of the household, but, through the cancellation of karma, the deceased (often dwelling in the hungry ghosts or hell realms) could transform into the body of the Buddha or, at least, into a resident of the higher of the six realms in Buddhist cosmology.[39]

THE TEN KINGS AND THE THIRTEEN BUDDHAS

Buddhist memorial and ancestral rites took their most developed form in an elaborate series of memorial rites called the Thirteen Buddha Rites (*jūsan butsuji*), which constituted the most common death ritual observed at Sōtō Zen temples during the Tokugawa period. The rites of the Thirteen Buddhas (*jūsanbutsu*) had their roots in the Chinese Buddhist belief in the Ten Kings (*jūō*). Chinese Buddhist apocryphal texts, such as the *Shiwang shengqijing* (Jpn. *Jūō shōshichikyō*), detailed the seven rituals that the descendants of the deceased needed to perform during the first forty-nine days after death (the traditional number of days needed for rebirth) so that the deceased might escape punishment in hell and be reborn in the heavenly realms.[40] In addition to these rituals, the belief in the Ten Kings required propitiatory rituals to be performed for each one of the Ten Kings that guarded the hell realms. The basic theory involved performing rites to the "protective Buddhas" who, being the "original source" of the Ten Kings, could influence the outcome of their judgment favorably and save the deceased from hell's sufferings. These ten memorial rites for the dead, based on the belief in the Ten Kings as developed in Japanese apocryphal sutras such as the *Jizō jūōkyō* and *Jūō santansho*, later became a standard part of funerary rites in the Shingon, Tendai, Zen (both Rinzai and Sōtō), Jōdo, and Nichiren traditions.[41]

In the case of Sōtō Zen, the Ten Kings and Ten Buddhas belief seems to have developed only after the time of the well-known priest Tsūgen Jakurei (1322–91), who conducted such rituals according to his "recorded sayings." Paintings depicting the Ten Kings sitting in judgment over the dead were used for ritual or didactic purposes at the old New Year celebration (the sixteenth of the first month) or during the Obon Festival in the summer, which were times of the year that the ancestral spirits were thought to return to this world. Enomoto Chika's study of Ten Kings paintings at temples in the Murayama region of Yamagata Prefecture reveals that during the Tokugawa period, people in that region hoped to achieve salvation for their ancestors by praying in front of such paintings.[42] It is likely that rites centering on appeasing the Ten Kings took place both when ancestral spirits were thought most likely to be present as well as on set dates commemorating a person's death.

While conforming to the basic idea of performing periodic rituals to the Ten Kings and their corresponding Buddhas or bodhisattvas, during the Kamakura period Japanese Buddhists added three extra rites (the rites of the seventh, thirteenth, and thirty-third years) and three extra corresponding Buddhas, totaling thirteen Buddha rites.[43] Though the notion of the Ten Kings did not completely disappear, by the middle of the Tokugawa period the Thirteen Buddha series of rites became standard at most Buddhist temples, including Sōtō Zen temples. Indeed, completing the full cycle of the thirty-three year memorial service for one's ancestors became a major theme at Sōtō Zen parish temples that promoted the idea that it took thirty-three years for the spirit to come to term into a new rebirth.[44]

In one example from the late Tokugawa period, the abbot of Chōjuin Temple (Shimousa Province) related to a family why the full set of the Thirteen Buddha Rites was necessary to prevent their recently deceased head of household from falling into the hells, or at least lessen his suffering in the world beyond. The abbot explained that the fourteenth-day rite was necessary, for example, because the hell king of that day (Shokō-ō) had related to him the following:

> The [deceased] is suffering and crying because of the evil acts he committed toward his wife during his life. However, his death did him no good because the inheritance he left had become a source of contention among the children. Having left behind such unfilial children, it was inevitable that he would fall into hell. However, if a memorial service were held [on that day], it would serve as a mysterious method to save him.[45]

The family paid for the necessary ceremony only to be told by the abbot on the twenty-first day that the next hell king was ready to throw the man into hell, but if the children donated the fees for the memorial service that day, there was still a chance that their father could be saved. Next, the family was told that they needed to pay for the thirty-fifth-day memorial service because on this day, the deceased would be tied up in front of King Enma with a mirror placed in front of him to reflect his past evil karma. The elaborateness of the memorial service, explained the abbot, would determine whether the deceased would go to a Buddha land, go to a heaven, return as a human, or be sent on to the next hell king. The abbot continued offering this type of rationale for three years as the deceased was allegedly sent from one hell king's judgment to another, not only because of the his heavy karmic weight, but also because the living descendants' karma was not sufficiently good to bring ultimate relief to the deceased until all the rites of the Thirteen Buddhas were completed.

Despite the logic of the funeral (immediate salvation through the priest's power to send the deceased into the company of the Buddhas), a different kind of logic was at work with these ancestral memorial services held at the same temple. Sōtō Zen priests first had to damn the dead to a lower realm of existence before they could gradually, over a thirty-three-year period, erase the karma that weighed down the dead spirit.

Within the Thirteen Buddha Rites, the forty-ninth day and the thirty-third year were particularly charged with meaning. Until the forty-ninth day after death, the dead spirit existed in a liminal state.[46] Because the spirit was thought to leave his or her house for either the family grave or another world on the forty-ninth day, this was a crucial period when the pollution of death was lifted.[47] The forty-ninth day (though, as in the case of the Chōjuin Temple case above, sometimes the thirty-fifth day) represented the juncture at which the fate of the dead person was determined, thus making it a particularly heightened moment in Buddhist death management. Furthermore, the day marked a sense of closure for the living, who during that period (the minimum socially accepted time of mourning, though in certain regions mourning lasted for up to a full year) observed special customs. Based on the idea that the family was also affected by the pollution of the corpse, customs such as using salt for purification after the funeral or refraining from marriage during the following year became commonplace.[48]

The third and final significant moment in the Buddhist management of the dead came in the thirty-third year after the death.[49] In the Sōtō Zen tradition, the practice of performing the full set of rites up to the thirty-third year appears to have become standard by the mid-Tokugawa period, as seen in Manzan's *Nenki saitenkō* and in the scroll paintings of the Thirteen Buddhas hung in temples for ritual use.[50] In esoteric Buddhist traditions, the thirty-three years also symbolized the length of time the deceased in the earth's womb took to mature and be reborn as a Buddha.[51]

After thirty-three years of rituals, the dead person was supposed to have become, in Buddhist parlance, fully liberated and have gone to a Buddha land, or become a Buddha. Within the context of ancestral worship, the thirty-third year also signified the moment when a dead person was transformed into a full-fledged ancestor of the household. Stephen Teiser, in discussing the gradual transformation of a deceased individual into an ancestor in China, described the purpose of ancestral rites as "to effect the passage of the dead from the status of a recently deceased, threatening ghost to that of a stable, pure, and venerated ancestor."[52] In Japan, in contrast to China, the ancestor was also conflated with the notion of a *kami*, prompting Robert Smith to note that the thirty-third year marked a transition from "a buddha to god."[53] Furthermore, as suggested by the practice of removing the memorial tablet of the ancestor—alternately throwing it away, placing it on the kami-altar (*kamidana*), or taking it back to the Buddhist temple—the thirty-third year removed the autonomy of the individual deceased spirit, as the personality had merged with the collective of household "ancestors" (*senzo*). Robert Smith has described this whole process as one where the deceased person's "spirit is ritually and symbolically purified and elevated; it passes gradually from the stage of immediate association with the corpse, which is thought to be both dangerous and polluting, to the moment when its loses its individual identity and enters the realm of the generalized ancestral spirits, essentially purified and benign."[54] Just as in the world of the living, where the household (and not the individual) was the basic religious unit in the Tokugawa period, the dead could not retain their individuality for too long either.

The Sōtō Zen priest's explanation above, that the weight of karma was so heavy that it required ritual action for thirty-three years, can also be understood as a response to the living relative's hope that ancestors, who may have fallen into a state of suffering, could benefit from this-world intercession. As Jacques Le Goff suggested in regard to the Christian tradition, "From the earliest centuries of the Church, Christians, as funeral inscriptions reveal, hoped that a dead man's fate was not definitively sealed at his demise, and that the prayers and the offerings—that is, the intercession—of the living could help dead sinners escape Hell, or, at least, benefit from less harsh treatment."[55] Similarly, the Sōtō Zen priest acted as a mediator between the living and the dead, and between this world and the next, resulting in a fluid world of multiple, and sometimes contradictory, funerary practices.

THE *BLOOD POOL HELL SUTRA*: WOMEN'S DAMNATION AND SALVATION

One of the most striking examples of priestly mediation and intervention on behalf of its parishioners in the afterlife was the emergent belief that Sōtō Zen priests could save women from a particularly gruesome hell, the Blood Pool Hell (*chi no ike jigoku*), through developing faith in a Buddhist scripture, the *Ketsubonkyō* (Chin. *Xuepenjing*, or the *Blood Pool Hell Sutra*).[56] The origins of the transmission to Japan of this apocryphal sutra, a very short, 420-character text composed in medieval China, is debated among scholars.[57] This is in part because each sect and group that propagated this text claimed to have been the first to obtain the scripture from a Chinese monk or through miraculous intervention. In the case of the Sōtō Zen sect, Shōsenji Temple in Shimousa Province, which became a major center for the cult of the *Ketsubonkyō* during the Tokugawa period, claimed that in 1417 the bodhisattva Jizō miraculously deposited the text in some marshes near the temple.

According to a 1730 temple document explaining how the scripture first appeared in Japan, a nun, who had been suffering in the Blood Pool Hell, possessed a young girl so that she could use the girl's body to speak to the abbot of Shōsenji Temple about the horrors of this hell.[58] According to the text, which is translated in full as appendix A, the sufferings in this hell include, among other things, the following:

Six times a day we come out of the pool to drink blood. If we refuse to drink it because of its horridness, frightening demons come and torture us with metal rods
before we get thrown back into the blood pool, screaming to no avail. In the
blood pool, countless insect-like creatures with metal snouts come to pierce our
skin and worm into our flesh to suck our blood, before grinding into the bone to
feast on the marrow. There are no words that could describe this pain.

The dead nun explained to the Zen priest that to recite, copy, and worship
the *Ketsubonkyō* was the only method to free women enduring this terrible
ordeal. After this visitation, the priest had a dream of the bodhisattva Jizō,
who told him he would find the sutra in a marsh near the temple. The priest
then conducted a seven-day ritual of reciting and copying the sutra, which
apparently freed both the young girl from the possession and the nun from
the torments of the Blood Pool Hell.[59]

The nun had been properly ordained, but the text makes clear that all
women, regardless of their station in this world, inevitably fell into this
gruesome hell because of the evil karma accrued from their menstrual
blood, and that of childbirth, which was thought to soil sacred beings (nature kami as well as Buddhas and monks) after seeping into the water supply.[60] This belief in the damnation of all women to a specially reserved hell
was popularized by the Sōtō Zen sect and accompanied the notion that salvation from this fate was possible only if Buddhist priests and relatives of
the deceased women interceded by performing ritual activity connected with
the *Ketsubonkyō*, thereby petitioning Jizō for help. Just like the thirty-three-
year series of memorial services, the cult of the *Ketsubonkyō* within the Sōtō
Zen sect reveals two important tendencies within funerary Zen: the emphasis on gradual salvation premised on a damnation to the hell realms, and an
ever-growing universality of the ritualization of death that came to include
all women and children.

Although monks and nuns from other Buddhist traditions had been involved in the propagation of the *Ketsubonkyō* and its ideas—Kumano
bikuni[61] in the late medieval period, and Jōdo sect monks[62] in the early Tokugawa period—Sōtō Zen priests were among the most active proponents of
the sutra during the mid- to late Tokugawa period, with Shōsenji Temple,
along with Mt. Tateyama,[63] being major centers of *Ketsubonkyō*-related activity. Shōsenji Temple[64] promoted itself not only as the birthplace of the
sutra in Japan,[65] but also as the locus for women's salvation (a sign displayed
at the temple until 1970 proclaimed it to be a "Training Hall for Women's
Salvation").[66]

To highlight their ability to save women, the priests of Shōsenji and other
Sōtō Zen temples promoted the idea that women were absolutely incapable
of avoiding the Blood Pool Hell. To do this, they linked the salvific powers
of the sutra with the pervasive ideology of women's pollution in medieval
and early modern Japan. The following Dharma lecture given by the Sōtō

Zen priest Unrei Taizen (1752–1816) in 1804, in front of two thousand men and women at Jōanji Temple (Shima region, near Ise), makes clear the commonly held attitudes toward women:

> Recently, the abbot Senjō (currently residing in Ōmi Province), while he was the abbot of Daitakuji Temple in Shinshū Province, was in charge of the construction of a large bell for the temple. Several young men were busy with the foot bellows to make the copper bell, when a couple of young women of the village turned up at the construction site and asked for a turn in pressing the bellows. But when they tried to pour the molten copper into the bell mold, it turned into a solid block. Spectators, who had gathered in quite a number, gasped when they saw that it didn't pour out. The head bell maker's face turned white with worry. They decided to try again on another day, explaining to the abbot that the process was polluted by the presence of some women at the last attempt. Since this was why the bell wasn't able to be made the first time, the bell maker requested to the abbot that no women be allowed nearby during the second try. The abbot agreed, but when they started the process again, this time not even the fire would start, which meant that they could not pour any molten copper. Surprised, the head bell maker was at a total loss as to what to do.
>
> It was then that a monk appeared, telling the bell maker to search for a copy of the *Ketsubonkyō* and to place it into the bellows. He found a copy belonging to the abbot Senjō and did as he was told. The fire started immediately and the copper began to melt. The bell maker and everyone present jumped up in joy, and before long the bell was complete. When they looked at the final product, it was a grand bell without any flaws. Furthermore, it gave off a magnificent sound.
>
> "All of you, listen to me carefully. The terrible nature of women's pollution knows no bounds, and only the *Ketsubonkyō* can neutralize it. That we can receive the amazing benefit of this sutra today is a blessed thing indeed. For those who sincerely would like to receive this talisman, come and request it later today."[67]

The disruption of molding a Buddhist temple bell because of the polluting presence of women is a motif found in well-known Noh plays such as *Dōjōji*.[68] In this sermon, the Zen priest delivered a straightforward message: women are by nature polluted and, because of their pollution, offend all things pure and sacred, such as a temple bell. Shōsenji Temple, for instance, distributed *Ketsubonkyō*-related talismans to ward off women's pollution (see figure 1 for a Blood Pool Hell sutra cover and figure 2 for a Jizō talisman). This idea of women's pollution, especially in connection to blood, extended beyond the *Ketsubonkyō*. It was an ideology widely disseminated by Sōtō Zen priests that reflected and fueled the growing marginalization of women during the Tokugawa period.[69]

Within the Sōtō sect, secret transmission documents such as the 1810 *Ryūgi no daiji*, for example, recommended that during precept ordination ceremonies or any temple or shrine visit, all women should have on their selves a special talisman with a stamp of the Three Treasures (Buddha, Dharma,

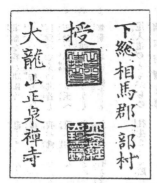

Figure 1. Cover of the
Blood Pool Hell Sutra
given during precept
ceremonies. Shōsenji
Temple, Abiko City.

Sangha), to avoid offending the Buddha and other deities with impure menstrual blood.[70] In addition, the text recommends two other talismans—one
to stop menstruation and the other to start it up again—for women to ingest
before and after a temple visit. The sect also sold other talismans to ward off
women's pollution, mainly featuring Ususama Myōō (Skt. Ucchuṣma, lit.
"garbage" or "leftovers"; also known as Mahābāla, lit. "great force"), an
Indian deity known for its capacity for devouring and thus purifying all
things, which was converted to Buddhism.[71] In the Japanese monastic Zen
tradition, Ususama stood as the guardian of the bathroom, but in nonmonastic circles he was known for his great powers of purification—for example, his ability to cleanse both men and women of sexual diseases was
particularly well-known (see fig. 3). In other words, though Sōtō priests
highlighted the power of the *Ketsubonkyō* to save women from hell, they
persuaded women of this by emphasizing their polluted nature that condemned them to the Blood Pool Hell in the next life. Salvation had damnation as its prerequisite.[72]

To prepare for this gendered salvation, women at Shōsenji Temple participated in a wide range of *Ketsubonkyō*-related ritual activities, ranging from
copying the sutra to placing it in coffins at funerals.[73] Achieving rebirth in a
Buddha land, or at least avoiding the Blood Pool Hell, seems to have been
the purpose of placing the *Ketsubonkyō* in a woman's coffin at the time of
her funeral or placing it in a grave of a female relative who did not receive
the sutra at the time of her death. Another ritual that involved the offering
of copies of the *Ketsubonkyō* at Shōsenji Temple was the river "hungry
ghost" ceremony.[74] The riverside ceremony involved setting up a wooden
Jizō image with a temporary altar. After recitation of the sutra, copies of the
text would be floated down the river for the welfare of all suffering beings,
but especially for women who had died in childbirth and for miscarried or
aborted children. To demonstrate symbolically the alleviation of suffering of
those in the Blood Pool Hell, the ritual participants would pour water onto
a piece of red cloth, suspended on four bamboo poles over the river, until the
red dye had washed out.[75]

Figure 2. Jizō talisman for women's salvation.
Shōsenji Temple, Abiko City.

In addition to the temple members, thousands of pilgrims visited this Sōtō
Zen center of the *Ketsubonkyō* cult and made donations to it from as far
away as Shinano and Mikawa provinces and Osaka and Kyoto cities by the
late Tokugawa period.[76] Furthermore, to justify the prominent place that the
Ketsubonkyō teachings were taking in the Sōtō sect compared with other
sects, a document from circa 1628 recounted a legend about the appearance
of a *Ketsubonkyō* text at Mt. Tiantong in China, where Dōgen had trained,
thus linking the sutra with the sect's founder.[77] Although this kind of ritualization of the afterlife was at odds with the rhetoric of immediate salvation
at the funeral, by the mid- to late Tokugawa period, the ideology of gradual
salvation became a central theme in funerary Zen.

Other important aspects of Tokugawa period funerary Zen were the inclusion of more classes of people for whom death management became necessary, and the expansion of ritual practices, such as special funerary rites
for women and children who had died during childbirth.[78] Rites such as
these were among the many "special circumstance" funerals for those who
had died particularly violent deaths, such as dying at sea or in a fire.[79] Beginning in the late sixteenth to early seventeenth century, priests wrote a

Figure 3. Ususama Myōō talisman for the purification of the body-mind and for the protection of women. Sōtōshū Shūmuchō, Tokyo.

large number of manuals on how to perform childbirth death rites, a topic not seen in medieval Sōtō Zen documents.[80] Childbirth deaths were frequent, and laypeople looked to priests to perform special rites for the dead women and their stillborn because of a popular belief that women who died in childbirth wandered as a ghost in the "intermediary stage" after death if the child and the mother were not "separated."[81] People thought that because such female ghosts were unable to achieve salvation, they would haunt the living and wreak havoc on local communities out of resentment. Most manuals of this genre therefore detailed rituals to separate the mother and child so that both would receive proper funerary attention. These included, for example, rites to determine the child's gender and to assign a proper posthumous name.[82] Using a magical formula, the priest would "give birth to the child" in the coffin by "expelling the fetus."[83] Though the monk Menzan Zuihō criticized this practice, this symbolic ritual separation of the mother and child meant that it was no longer necessary to physically extract the fetus by hand, thus providing a way for ordinary priests to avoid the impurity of blood and death.[84]

Children did not receive funerals as a general rule because children were not thought to be fully "human"—and so deserving of a funeral—until a certain age.[85] During the Tokugawa period, however, Sōtō Zen priests were part of the small but growing trend to provide children who died with special funerary rites and separate graves.[86] The idea of young children having spirits was also taken up in the context of government-ordered Buddhist preaching campaigns against infanticide, especially in the Tōhoku region. Sōtō Zen temples such as Shōonji in the Sendai Domain, under instructions from the Office of Temples and Shrines, took a central role in preaching campaigns at villages in the Higashiyama region aimed at warning peasants about the evils of infanticide.[87] Preaching manuals produced at other Sōtō Zen temples, such as Rinnōji and Kōkenji, noted the prevalence of infanticide in the Tōhoku region and emphasized the evil of killing children (their spirits would fall into hell as snakes) and the importance of having many children to counter the popular belief that more than one or two children would be an economic burden.[88] Graphic paintings of the tortures in hells reserved for women who committed infanticide can also be found from the early nineteenth century, attesting to the rising consciousness of religious injunctions against killing, and economically motivated governmental pressures to increase the Japanese population.[89] Here again, we can see a form of coordination between government policies and Buddhist sectarian interests to expand the ritualization of death to the entire Japanese population. As Sōtō Zen priests extended their funerary services to cover special circumstances or classes of persons, including women or children, the ritual repertory finally caught up with the impetus for universalizing funerals for every Japanese person.

But one should not simply assign the growth in funerary practices to Buddhist priests or government mandates. Indeed, many local death rituals and innovations came from villagers and local traditions that could not always be controlled or appropriated by either the government or Buddhist sects. For example, near Shōsenji Temple, in the greater Abiko/Tonegawa region, a heavy concentration of women's associations focused on rituals to avoid hell or painful childbirth as independent women's networks, and participated in the *Ketsubonkyō* cult separate from the temple proper.[90] For example, the Matsudokkō (Matsudo Association) was one such group centered on the cult of a local deity famous for ensuring safe childbirth, the Matsudo Daimyōjin enshrined at the Matsudo Shrine in Abiko Village. Matsudokkō women's associations made donations to both Shōsenji Temple and one of its branch temples, Hakusenji, as attested to by stone markers dating to as early as 1775.[91] Both temples enshrined statues of the life-prolonging Jizō for help in the next world, and at the same time the women of the association also requested Matsudo Daimyōjin to help in this world, especially with safe childbirth. Although Shōsenji Temple would have preferred a more exclusive relationship between believers in its *Ketsubonkyō* cult and the temple, they realized that most women in the region participated in multiple cults, held various views of the afterlife, and organized themselves independently of the temple into so-called associations or confraternities (*kō*). Within such all-women organizations, popular hymns, such as the *Ketsubonkyō wasan*, *Chi no ike jigoku* (Blood Pool Hell) *wasan*, and the *Nyonin ōjō* (Women's Salvation) *wasan*, were sung that merged various views of the afterlife, including those advocated by Shōsenji Temple.[92] One of the reasons that Shōsenji Temple became a major center of the *Ketsubonkyō* cult was that it managed to ground simultaneously the various themes associated with this cult—the special hell, women's pollution, the salvific powers of scripture and Buddhist deities, the importance of intervention by priests and relatives in the affairs of the afterlife—both in Sōtō Zen–specific legends and doctrines, as well as in ideas that dominated the local and transsectarian religious landscape.

The management of the dead through the Zen funeral and rites associated with the *Ketsubonkyō* exposes a fundamental disjuncture in the Zen funerary system. The Zen funeral's attraction, as suggested above, lay in the notion that through the intervention of the priest, the deceased could immediately attain a state equal to that of the Buddha. However, *Ketsubonkyō* rites, along with other aspects of death management, were based on the premise that the dead person had fallen into a realm of immense suffering (the hungry ghost or hell realms) and needed familial and priestly intervention. In other words, if the Zen priest had been successful in sending the dead person to a Buddha land at the funeral stage, there would be no need for the ancestral memorial services, held on a regular timetable for up to thirty-three years after death. One cynical view (given some support in chapter 2) is that Sōtō Zen priests simply multiplied the number of annual and memorial rites for the dead to force their parishioners to pay more money to the temple, thus securing a steady income base. However, it is also possible to understand this incongruence between funeral and other posthumous rites by recognizing that two parallel understandings of the afterlife—one specific to the Sōtō Zen sect, the other a more locally based transsectarian view—coexisted in funerary Zen without ever being fully integrated or explained.[93] This discrepant logic of Japanese Buddhist funerary rituals was not limited to the Sōtō Zen tradition, though the specifics of how such parallel logics were handled can reveal some sect-specificity.[94]

A major part of the appeal of Sōtō Zen funerary rites was the bestowal of the Zen lineage chart and the posthumous ordination at the funeral that immediately gave the deceased membership into the Buddha's lineage, or even Buddhahood itself. However, the more generic notion in Buddhist and local religious culture that the dead required a lengthier period of ritualization played an equally important role in funerary Zen. Whether it was women's damnation into the Blood Pool Hell or the Thirteen Buddha memorial rites, the heavy weight of karma explained the need for managing the dead through a more gradual ascendance to Buddhahood or ancestorhood. It was precisely the flexibility of Sōtō Zen priests, who permitted wide-ranging local variation in the coexistence of both the logic of the funeral proper and the management of the dead over time, that made "funerary Zen" a key factor in the growth of Sōtō Zen, embedding the sect into the fabric of ordinary people's religious life during the Tokugawa period.

CHAPTER 4

The Cult of Dōryō Daigongen: Daiyūzan and Sōtō Zen Prayer Temples

WHILE THE CREATION OF "FUNERARY ZEN" within the context of the Tokugawa bakufu's new religious policies certainly stands out as chief among the factors in the establishment of early modern Sōtō Zen, one must not conclude that Zen (or Buddhism) as a whole concerned itself solely with rituals for the other world.[1] To understand the vitality of Tokugawa Buddhism, it is also crucial to examine the many rituals and practices that temples provided to benefit life in this world. For a farmer, this might have meant prayers for rain; for a fisherman, prayers for safety at sea; and for a merchant, prayers for protection from theft or fire. For almost all segments of Tokugawa society, such practical benefits (*genze riyaku*) were sought at Shintō shrines and Buddhist prayer temples (*kitō jiin*) that featured the myriad kami, Buddhas, bodhisattva, and other members of the Buddhist pantheon noted for their prowess in the bestowal of this-worldly benefits. Sōtō Zen Buddhists participated in this culture of protection (from disaster, illness, theft) and benefits (wealth, large catches of fish, familial harmony), and the sect's prayer temples became some of the best known in Tokugawa Japan.

This chapter examines one such prayer temple, Daiyūzan Saijōji in Sagami Province, which featured a Zen monk-turned-*tengu* (goblin) as its main image of worship. Though our image of Zen often evokes a serene monastery, Daiyūzan became a major pilgrimage center bustling with pilgrims seeking prayers for a multitude of practical benefits. Neither a serene meditation center nor a temple dedicated to funerary rites, Daiyūzan was a prototypical prayer temple that defied simple categorization—a world inhabited by unique local deities, rowdy pilgrims, Zen priests, and charismatic lay leaders. The Sōtō Zen priests at Daiyūzan rarely engaged in meditation or death rites but spent their energies on esoteric Buddhist rituals, managing pilgrims, and selling talismans of the enshrined deity. Much like other prayer temples and sacred mountains that flourished in the Tokugawa-period boom in pilgrimage enabled by the newly developed highway systems, Daiyūzan's deity, Dōryō, drew thousands of visitors to the temple as well as to the public exhibitions of the deity's statue in the city of Edo. The text that follows is a translation of a letter reaching an understanding between Daiyūzan and some local village heads regarding a fight that occurred between drunk members of a lay association dedicated to Dōryō and local villagers during the parading of the Dōryō statue on its way to the city of Edo for a grand public viewing. The incident reflects the powerful energies that swirled around popular deities that brought this-worldly benefits to pilgrims, local villagers, and worshipers in Edo. The Sōtō Zen priests at Daiyūzan were put in an ambiguous position of needing popular lay support for its prayer temples, while simultaneously having to guard their authority and distance themselves from boisterous worshipers such as these.

NOTARIZED OUT-OF-COURT SETTLEMENT EXCHANGED
BETWEEN THE PARTIES INVOLVED[2]

Recently, a portable shrine [carrying the "spirit" of the deity Dōryō] from your temple left for Edo to be a part of the "public viewing" (kaichō) of Dōryō Gongen of Saijōji Temple in Sekimoto Village. This kaichō was to be held on the grounds of Chōkokuji Temple in the Shibuya district of Edo. On the sixteenth of the month, the portable shrine stopped at our village [Kano Village], when two men under your employ, Tetsugorō and Bunpachi, under the strong influence of alcohol, hurt Gonzaemon, Chūemon, Inosuke, Hikōemon, and Hikojirō.[3] The two were placed under arrest, and after questioning they testified that they had been drinking large quantities of sake. When their portable shrine had to slow down in the village, they had some sort of disagreement with the villagers that led the two to draw their swords and wound the five villagers. Your temple has accepted responsibility for this incident and since the five men are almost fully recovered, our village has accepted this out-of-court settlement.[4] We had a villagewide discussion and decided that since Tetsugorō and Bunpachi were simply drunk, the wounds to the five injured men were not life-threatening, and none of the injured bear grudges, we do not need to take this matter to court. All the people who signed below will not do anything to provoke ill feeling in the future. Just to be sure, we will exchange this notarized agreement for the future.

Twenty-eighth of the second month, 1819[5]

THE CONSTRUCTION OF A PRAYER TEMPLE

In 1819 a sixty-day public viewing (kaichō, "opening the curtain") of a normally hidden Buddhist statue from Daiyūzan Saijōji Temple was held at Chōkokuji Temple in Edo.[6] During the Tokugawa period, Daiyūzan was the largest Sōtō Zen temple in the Kantō region. Located in the station-town of Sekimoto (outskirts of present-day Minami Ashigara City), Daiyūzan was best known for its cult of Dōryō Daigongen (Dōryō, the Great Avatar), the protective deity of the mountain temple. A statue of Dōryō, transported by lay parishioners to Edo for public viewing, provoked the incident above.

As was common with the carrying of deities in portable shrines at festival times, a boisterous group enlivened by large amounts of alcohol (which was routinely offered to the deity) accompanied the Dōryō statue. This statue was usually displayed for public viewing at Daiyūzan only during the three annual "great festivals" (the "Taisai" held on the 27–28th of the first, fifth, and ninth months). While pilgrims flocked to Daiyūzan in the thousands on those three occasions, the temple also held three large *degaichō* (public viewing of the statue outside the temple grounds—in this case, in Edo) during the early modern period: 1784, 1819, and 1871. Although the worshipers of Dōryō caused the incident during the 1819 exhibition of the statue in Edo, the fact that it was a sacred festival where drunkenness might excuse normally prohibited behavior and the prestige of Daiyūzan seem to have mitigated any anger the injured villagers may have felt.[7]

Daiyūzan Saijōji Temple was founded by a well-known medieval Sōtō Zen monk, Ryōan Emyō (1337–1411)[8] in 1395.[9] In the latter part of the medieval period, Daiyūzan became the center of the so-called Ryōan-ha (Ryōan lineage), which dominated the Sōtō school in the Kantō region through the patronage of prominent families that rose and fell in the late medieval period, such as the Ōmori, the Ōta, and the powerful Odawara Hōjō.[10] By the mid-Tokugawa period, the temple, the third largest after the Sōtō Zen headquarter temples of Sōjiji and Eiheiji, oversaw approximately 3,800 branch temples, mainly in the Kantō region.

However, by the early Meiji period, Daiyūzan also came to be known as one of the "three great Sōtō Zen prayer temples" (*sandai kitō jiin* or *sandai kigansho*) along with Myōgonji and Zenpōji, or as one of the five great Sōtō prayer temples (*godai kitō jiin*),[11] which included, in addition to Daiyūzan, Toyokawa Myōgonji (Inari worship—Aichi Prefecture),[12] Zenpōji (Ryūjin worship—Yamagata Prefecture), Kashōzan Ryūgein (Tengu worship—Gunma Prefecture), and Kasuisai (Tengu worship—Shizuoka Prefecture). Its importance as a center of a major lineage tradition became overshadowed by its renown as a center for prayers for tangible, this-world benefits.

All five of the major Sōtō Zen prayer temples developed into major centers of prayer rituals that attracted large numbers of lay believers in the late Tokugawa and early Meiji periods. However, the worship of popular bodhisattvas and local deities, which formed the base of all prayer temples, had already begun during the medieval period when the sect spread into local communities, taking over small chapels of Jizō, Kannon, and Yakushi, among others, or temples without a resident priest, especially those formerly controlled by priests of the Tendai and Shingon schools or *yamabushi*, which meant that deities such as Fudō and Yakushi predominated. Indeed, by the Tokugawa period, deities such as Kannon, Yakushi, Jizō, and Amida were the most common images of worship in Sōtō Zen main halls.[13] Even the Sōtō Zen temple main halls that featured Śākyamuni Buddha, the sect's official image of worship, were often neglected by priests, parishioners, and pilgrims more interested in the side halls with the more popular bodhisattvas and local kami.

The ability of such deities to provide various types of tangible "this-world benefits" enabled Sōtō Zen temples to attract believers via priestly prayer rituals (*kitō*).[14] These rituals involved special recitations of sutras and *dhāraṇīs* or the disbursing of talismans for a good harvest, rain (*amagoi*),[15] or bountiful fish catches (*tairyō kigan*),[16] and for protection from danger at sea or from epidemic diseases. Although most temples included such prayers as a part of their annual ritual calendar or when asked, some temples during the Tokugawa period became so well known for the efficacy of prayers to the temple's deities that they came to be known as *kitō jiin* (prayer temples).[17]

At the center of Daiyūzan's rise as a Zen prayer temple was the cult of Dōryō. Shimazu Hamaomi noted in his 1814 pilgrim's diary, the *Hakone nikki*, "Going up from the 28-*chō*[18] stone marker, one can see the temple [Daiyūzan Saijōji] buildings which seem run down. . . . [But] if one climbs one more *chō*, there is the Dōryō Shrine, which, compared to the run-down temple buildings, is magnificent."[19] This observation suggests the relative prosperity of the Dōryō Shrine by the nineteenth century relative to the other temple buildings located at the center of the traditional Zen temple compound.

Dōryō (more formally Myōkaku Dōryō or Dōryō Daigongen) represents an interesting synthesis among Sōtō Zen, local kami traditions, and Shugendō.[20] Before becoming the protective kami of the temple, Dōryō was a disciple of Ryōan, though prior to meeting Ryōan he trained as a *shugenja* (mountain ascetic) at Miidera (head of the Tendai Jimon school) and served in 1348 as abbot of one of its subtemples, Konjōbō (later renamed Sagamibō).[21]

At Daiyūzan, Dōryō served in two important capacities during his eighteen years at the fledgling Zen monastery: the head cook (*tenzo*) and vice-administrator (*kansu*).[22] It was in the latter post in which he raised funds for the temple—combined with legends of his superhuman powers in preparing the grounds for the construction of the temple—that Dōryō gained a special place in the history of Daiyūzan. However, for the cult of Dōryō, which spread far beyond the temple grounds, his ability as a Zen monk foreshadowed his even greater abilities as a tengu. This transformation is said to have occurred on the twenty-eighth of the third month, 1411, following his master's death the previous day.[23] He is said to have assembled everyone in front of the temple's main hall and declared that with the master gone, his work as a monk was over, and henceforth he would ensure the safety of the temple. According to legend, his body was then engulfed in flames as he appeared transformed and stood on a white fox to promise a life free from illness and full of riches for those who sincerely worshiped him (see figures 4 and 5). He then flew and landed on a cedar tree in front of the main hall before taking flight toward the east, never to be seen as a monk again. From this instant on, Dōryō the Zen monk was transformed into Dōryō the tengu[24]—alive eternally and dwelling at the mountain as a protector of Ryōan's lineage of Zen and of the people living in the region surrounding the mountain temple.[25]

The Dōryō Festival

A tengu—often translated as a "long-nosed goblin"—has historically been associated in Japanese religions both with evil powers and with great

Figure 4. Dōryō scroll from
the late Tokugawa period.
Privately owned, Duncan
Williams.

beneficial powers.[26] One can find the roots of the concept of tengu in Chinese translations of Buddhist canonical literature, for example, the *Zhengfa nianchu jing* (Jpn. *Shōbō nenshokyō*; T 17, 721), in which the term *tiangou* (Jpn. *tengu*) refers to the Sanskrit term *ulka* (fire in the sky or a meteor).[27] The term also appeared in Chinese secular literature as a falling star that killed people or as the name of a star constellation. Somehow from the Chinese association of tengu with a celestial phenomenon, an association developed in Japanese medieval Shugendō between the tengu as a celestial winged being akin to the Indian garuda, and the tengu as a star that falls onto mountains and dwells there as an evil being. On the one hand, tengu tended to be associated with something awesome to be feared, or were regarded as evil beings of some sort (such as a wily bird spirit or a corrupt monk). On the other hand, the association of tengu with *yamabushi*

Figure 5. Statue of a tengu on route to Dōryō Shrine at Daiyūzan. Photo, Duncan Williams.

(mountain ascetics) added a different image of tengu as beings with special, superhuman powers.

Indeed, the Dōryō case suggests a conflation of the two images of the tengu as he was apparently quite an evil monk who, under Ryōan's Zen training, was able to redirect his enormous powers toward doing good.[28] It was in gratitude to Ryōan and the temple that Dōryō promised to provide benefits to those who believed in him and the institution of Daiyūzan.[29] His transformation into a tengu, rather than a standard Buddhist deity, reveals the similarities of the Dōryō cult with two other important Sōtō Zen prayer temples featuring mountain ascetic-type monks turning into local protective deities: Akibadera Temple (where the *shugen* practitioner, Akiba Sanjakubō, became a tengu while alive, turning into Akiba Sanjakubō Daigongen) and Kashōzan Ryūgein Temple (where Chūhō, the disciple of the founder of the temple, turned into a tengu protector).[30]

Because of the death of Ryōan and the transformation of Dōryō on the 27–28th of the third month, the 27–28th of each month became the center of Daiyūzan's ritual calendar. On those days each month the Dōryō Festival was celebrated, although the "Great Festival" (*taisai*) for Dōryō was held only three times a year (during the first, fifth, and ninth months). The highlight of the festival featured a rite called the Dōryō sairei or Dōryōsai (from the late 1860s, called the *Gokūshiki*).[31]

At this ritual, held as the darkness of the night enveloped the mountainside, priests offered specially prepared rice cooked with sacred waters and *azuki* beans to Dōryō in commemoration of his transformation into a tengu. Because Dōryō was a *tenzo* (chief monastery cook) during his days at Daiyūzan, the cooks of Daiyūzan (the main temple of Saijōji and the two subtemples of Daijiin and Hōon'in) offered purified rice at the Dōryō Shrine after climbing backward and masked up to the sacred area in total darkness. They spent the weeks prior to the ceremony observing strict vegetarianism and practiced climbing backward up and down the one hundred stone steps to the shrine while wearing a mask. These priests were joined by other groups: (1) the abbot of the temple, to whom they reported at the beginning and end of the offering; (2) the monks in charge of caring for the founder's hall who assisted them (their "eyes" while masked); and (3) the mountain ascetics who were on hand to lead the procession of ordinary monks. As this ceremony was performed, the regular monks recited sacred texts and blew conch horns at appointed moments but were essentially onlookers to a special esoteric ritual. The lay Dōryō pilgrimage association members were the other main group of onlookers who watched the ceremony from behind the rows of monks.[32]

While the practices of purification (bathing themselves, cleansing the wood used for cooking, and wearing white robes), recitation of esoteric *dhāraṇī*, accompanied by conch horns, and Zen meditation following the ritual were of utmost importance to the monks of Daiyūzan, for the vast majority of the worshipers assembled the display of the ordinarily hidden statue of the flame-engulfed Dōryō riding on a fox, and the handing out of talismans the following morning, were the highlights of the event. Although some pilgrims were accidental visitors to this display of the Dōryō statue, most visitors prepared for this major outing to Daiyūzan with plenty of *hannyatō* ("wisdom-water" or alcohol) and anticipation of a night of gambling until the morning ceremonies.[33] For the members of the Dōryō cult, the occasion of the Dōryō Festival was a night of esoteric ceremony and celebration followed by a morning of talismans and blessings, gained through viewing the sacred statue. The efforts of ordinary people to come into contact with this Zen monk-turned-tengu attest to the power and vitality of Sōtō Zen prayer temples that reveal a different side of the Sōtō Zen tradition from both the austere monasticism and funerary Zen.

The Tengu Talisman

Though the cult of Dōryō grew because of the vast array of benefits this deity was believed to provide (especially fire prevention and healing), the earliest evidence for its popularity outside of the temple's immediate vicinity lay in the rising demand for talismans printed from Daiyūzan's so-called Kongō Hōin (Diamond Treasure Seal) or Okanain[34] (Gold Seal, as it was more commonly called), which were handed out on the morning of the Dōryō Festival. According to the 1648 *Tōzan kaibyaku narabini kunin rōjin no kien*,[35] the seal that was used to make this talisman was discovered by two local deities, Iizawa and Yagurazawa Myōjin, who were disguised as elderly woodcutters while assisting Ryōan in the construction of the temple.[36] They came upon this sacred seal when Ryōan (or Dōryō, according to a modern variant) was digging a well for the temple and hit upon a metallic object. As the seal was removed from the ground, sacred water named Kongōsui (Diamond-Water) gushed out, providing an important resource for the water-deficient Daiyūzan.[37] Although today pilgrims and nearby residents take containers up to the Kongōsui Well to obtain what they say is the purest and most miraculous water around, during the Tokugawa period, this water source was off-limits to everyone but a few select monks assigned to provide offerings to Dōryō Shrine.

So while the water was not available to pilgrims, the Kongō Hōin or Okanain talismans were a different matter. The following regulations attest to their popularity by the mid-Tokugawa period:

Regulations for Making the Yūhō [Daiyūzan] Kongō Hōin Talisman

From olden times at Daiyūzan, the temple has given out one Kongō Hōin talisman per person on the twenty-seventh of each month in front of the founder's hall. However, recently we have heard that believers in this talisman of many benefits have been going on any given day to Daijiin and Hōon'in subtemples [of Daiyūzan] to receive as many talismans as they request. This violation of the tradition surely diminishes the power of the Kongō Hōin. Tenth month, 1741; If the Kongō Hōin is stamped and given out without following the rules, there will definitely be repercussions not only for Saijōji, the two subtemples, and the two administration temples, but for all the administrators and other monks who are associated [with Daiyūzan]. Eleventh month, 1764; From: Sōneiji abbot (Jūkan) and Ryūonji abbot (Tōgen); To: Saijōji, Daijiin, Hōon'in, Ten'ōin, and Daishōji.[38]

As this letter makes clear, Dōryō's talisman had grown in popularity by the mid-1700s, concurrent with the development of the pilgrimage to Daiyūzan. For the two head administrative temples of the Kantō region, Sōneiji and Ryūonji, to have gone out of their way to detail the specifications of when, where, and how many talismans were to be made—first in 1741 and again in 1764 when it was clear that the rules were not being followed[39]—the Kongō Hōin must have attracted increasing attention from pilgrims to Daiyūzan. For example, Mori Mozaemon records in his 1827 pilgrim's diary *Kōshin nikkichō* that he bought a Kongō Hōin talisman for seventy-two *mon* on the twelfth of the sixth month, showing again that the regulations were not being followed.[40] For some reason, Akutsu Shōemon notes in his 1848 pilgrim's diary *Shinrozan dōchūki* that he was able to purchase his talisman for less (twelve *mon*).[41] The popular writer Jippensha Ikku (1765–1839), in his 1822 *Dōryō gongen Hakone gongen nanayu meguri*, mentions fire and burglary prevention as the chief benefits of the Dōryō talisman.[42] The 1841 bakufu-sponsored regional survey of Sagami Province, the *Shinpen Sagami no kuni fudokikō*, describes the benefits of obtaining this talisman as "to avoid being infected during an epidemic and to escape robbers and wild animals when walking at night."[43] The use of the talisman to ward off diseases or treat illnesses, for example, continues to this day with the practice of placing the Kongō Hōin on the ailing part of the body.

The following 1821 story further illuminates how multifunctional the talisman was during the Tokugawa period:

> After drinking and making merry, a Yoshiwara prostitute and her customer went to bed. However, the prostitute turned her back to the man in the futon, saying that she had a stomachache. The customer then told her that it seemed strange that she suddenly had a stomachache, but that he had the famous Saijōji Okanain (Gold Seal) on him and this talisman should, if put on her stomach, cure her. However, instead of giving her the talisman, he gave her one gold coin. Putting the coin on her stomach, the prostitute said "I feel somewhat better now."[44]

Although this story is not about the healing powers of Daiyūzan's talisman but instead a funny story playing on the "gold" that can cure (the talisman) and the "gold" that can change a reluctant prostitute's mind (a gold coin), it does reveal the popular perception of the talisman. For the prostitute and her client to know that the "famous Saijōji Okanain" purportedly cured stomachaches, there must have been a general knowledge, at least in the city of Edo, that Daiyūzan talismans might be effective in treating ailments. While the cult of Dōryō was not limited to healing, the popularity of this talisman by the mid-1700s seems to mark the roots of the Tokugawa-period Dōryō boom. Of the late Tokugawa and early Meiji-period talismans that remain, Dōryō's powers as infused into these talismans apparently included protection against disasters, fires, illness, and family discord.[45]

THE DEVELOPMENT OF PILGRIMAGE ROUTES AND CONFRATERNITIES

How did word concerning Dōryō's powers spread so widely that by the end of the Tokugawa period, pilgrims to Daiyūzan traveled from near and far and even bribed priests for talismans? The answer lies in two new developments at Daiyūzan: first, the rise of the pilgrimage confraternities (kō) in the mid-1700s, and second, the promotion of Dōryō through public viewing of a normally hidden statue (kaichō) both at the temple and in the city of Edo.

Pilgrimage confraternities (known as kō, kōchū, or kōsha) historically developed as religious associations of devotees of a certain deity,[46] religious practice,[47] or famous shrine, temple, or sacred mountain.[48] Dōryō or Daiyūzan kō fits in both the first category (as a deity) and the third (as a pilgrimage site). Although Daiyūzan temple historians have claimed medieval origins for the popular Dōryō cult, the earliest evidence we have for the existence of the Dōryō kō is rather late in the Tokugawa period. Since these groups were administratively independent of Daiyūzan, the only written record about any Tokugawa-period kō held in Daiyūzan's archives is a hanging scroll from 1838 that records a donation of sixty-three thousand cedar tree saplings by the Shin Yoshiwara kō between 1765 and 1838.[49]

The emergence of these pilgrimage groups can also be traced from a different source: stone markers donated by kō to Daiyūzan. Although many of these markers have crumbled away with the passing of the years or have sunk into the ground, leaving only the very top visible, their reconstruction by a team of researchers from Minami Ashigara City has helped us recover the history of Daiyūzan's kō. Of the 434 pre–World War II stone markers found on both the mountain and the road to the mountain, 41 are from the Tokugawa period (see tables 1 and 2), the earliest from 1631.[50] Five Tokugawa-period stone markers were donated by pilgrimage confraternities to commemorate a gift to the temple from the kō or as a way of marking their presence at the temple.[51] The earliest of these was erected in 1782 by the Shin Yoshiwara kō, the same group mentioned above that donated cedar tree saplings to the temple. This group was based in the so-called Shin (New) Yoshiwara, the well-known pleasure district of Edo that moved to its "new" location near Asakusa in 1657 and was home to, at its peak, three to four thousand courtesans. The kō was headed by Kanshirō, the owner of the brothel Daikokuya, which was known around the time of the stone marker donation for its previous proprietor, Daikokuya Shōroku, who was the first

TABLE 1

Tokugawa-Period Stone Markers and Pilgrimage Confraternities at Daiyūzan

Year	Stone Marker No.	Donor	Origin	Donation
1782	18 ·	Shin Yoshiwara kō (65 names listed)	Edo	stone marker
1826	not listed	Gozen kō	Nishi Kaneda	Entsū Bridge
1864	36	Gojūashi kō (45 names listed)	Fujisawa	stone marker
1864	37	Seishin kōsha	Odawara	stone marker
1867	40	Wataritemawari kō	Edo	8,000 trees

Note: Adapted from Minami Ashigara Survey.

supervisory official (kenban) for the pleasure-quarters' geisha in 1779.[52] Another brothel owner, Shōzaburō of Suzukiya, is also listed on the stone marker as a donor. Sixty-three others were noted on the stone as fellow donors, but without their names we cannot be sure if this group referred to Yoshiwara brothel owners or the women who worked there.[53] In any case, combined with the above story of the Yoshiwara prostitute being "cured" with Daiyūzan's Okanain talisman, Daiyūzan must have been well known for people in this district of Edo.

The Shin Yoshiwara kō was the first of the growing number of Tokugawa-period pilgrimage confraternities. These, as the stone marker evidence suggests, really took off from the mid-1860s onward. Although the Shin Yoshi-

TABLE 2

Early Meiji Stone Markers and Pilgrimage Confraternities at Daiyūzan

Year	Stone Marker No.	Donor	Origin	Donation
1868	42	Shinryū kō	Shimousa	100 yen
1869	43	Shinjin kō	Bushū Nakahirai	10,000 trees
1871	48	Tokyo Kaiun kō (200 names listed)	Tokyo	stone marker
1874	49	Shinryū kō	Shimousa	100 yen
1874	50	Isshin kō	Tokyo	500 yen
1875	54	Sugi kō	Yoshikawa	25,000 trees
1877	58	Gokūme kō	Uraga (Sagami)	100 yen
1878	60 ·	Hirasaku kō	Miuragun (Sagami)	1,000 trees
1879	65	Kanagawachō kō	Kanagawa (Sagami)	100 yen
1880	69	Ryūhō kō (100 names listed)	Tsuchiya (Sagami)	100 yen
1880	70	Isshin kō	Tokyo	stone marker
1880	72	Gojuashi kō	Fujisawa	stone marker

Note: Adapted from Minami Ashigara Survey.

wara kō was unusually early, this does not mean that pilgrims were not visiting Daiyūzan before the 1860s, but rather that most pilgrims were not organized enough to leave traces of their existence. Indeed, the most likely scenario is a two-stage development of the pilgrimage to Daiyūzan. The first is a period spanning the late 1700s to 1860 during which pilgrimage groups to other sacred mountains developed an interest in Dōryō and informally visited Daiyūzan. A second stage can be seen from the mid-1860s to the present in which independent Dōryō pilgrimage associations come into existence—growing to between 350,000 and 400,000 kō pilgrims per year (a total of seven hundred thousand pilgrims if non-kō visitors are included).[54]

This first stage involved travelers to other sacred mountains, especially Mt. Ōyama and Mt. Fuji,[55] and to the hot springs at Hakone who paid their respects to Dōryō at Daiyūzan as a part of their itinerary. The bakufu regulated travel in the Tokugawa period so that pilgrims could not cross checkpoints without a letter from a local official.[56] Such permission was ordinarily granted for only one of two activities: visiting a shrine/temple on a pilgrimage or a hot spring for a cure. Therefore it is not surprising that those wanting to take a break from routine life would visit multiple sites of worship or combine visits to hot springs with those to shrines and temples. In the case of Daiyūzan, travel logbooks and diaries from 1803 to 1866 (see table 3) show that pilgrims came to worship Dōryō either before or after visiting Mt. Fuji, Mt. Ōyama, Ise Shrine, or the Hakone hot springs. The majority of these diaries were written by travelers whose primary purpose was not to visit Daiyūzan, but someplace else. Usually a trip to Daiyūzan made good sense both logistically (with an overnight stay at Daiyūzan's station town of Sekimoto) and religiously (to visit the Dōryō tengu).[57]

In the case of Mt. Fuji, whose pilgrimage associations grew so numerous that the bakufu banned them periodically (in 1775, 1795, and 1814), it would be quite natural for pilgrims from Edo City to pass through the station town of Sekimoto on their way to Fuji.[58] Especially if they took the Tōkaidō route, they could stay the night at the inns and pay their respects at Daiyūzan before traveling on.[59] These Mt. Fuji associations became the first mass group of pilgrims to visit Daiyūzan. One such Fuji kō traveler on an eight-day roundtrip journey from Edo noted that he worshiped at the Dōryō Shrine and ate dumplings at a Daiyūzan tea house before heading into the Ashigara Pass on the way to Mt. Fuji.[60] Despite the slight detour involved for Fuji kō pilgrims to stop by Daiyūzan, thousands of them made the trip because it was only a small diversion. Especially after the institution of a new policy at Mt. Fuji in the late eighteenth century that prohibited visitors from descending by a different route from the way by which they ascended, those using the Yoshida descent to the east to return to Edo had to walk through the Ashigara Pass.[61] Thus, it would be surprising if they did not stop at Daiyūzan, which bordered the pass.[62] If they followed this route back to Edo, they would also inevitably pass by Mt. Ōyama, also increasingly visited by Fuji kō members. Even today, a stone marker donated by a Fuji as-

TABLE 3
Pilgrimage to Daiyūzan as Seen in Tokugawa-Period Travel Diaries

Year	Name of Text	(Location Held)	Author	Travel Route Taken
1803	Fugaku seppu	(National Diet Library)	Wakuda Torajuku	Edo—Daiyūzan—Odawara—Mt. Fuji
1814	Hakone nikki	(Kanazawa Bunko)	Shimazu Hamaomi	Miura—Hakone—Daiyūzan
1817	Fujigane nikki	(National Diet Library)	unknown	Odawara—Daiyūzan—Mt. Fuji
1818	Hakone yokutōki	(Kanagawa Prefectural Kōbunshokan)	unknown	Hakone—Daiyūzan
1822	Dōryō gongen Hakone gongen nanayumeguri kikō bunsho	(Kanagawa Kenritsu Kyōdo Shiryōkan)	Jippensha Ikku	Daiyūzan—Hakone
1827	Kōshin nikkichō	(private—Nishigai Kenji)	Mori Mozaemon	Ōiso (Kanagawa Pref.)—Daiyūzan—Mt. Fuji
1828	Fuji zentei dōchū nikki	(Sanwa City Library)	Suzuki Matsuzō	Hachiōji—Mt. Fuji—Daiyūzan—Mt. Ōyama
1831	Fuji tozan nikki oboechō	(private—Nishigai Kenji)	Mori Mozaemon	Totsuka (Kanagawa Pref.)—Daiyūzan—Mt. Fuji—Machida—Mt. Ōyama
1833	Hakonezan nana onsen Enoshima Kamakura meguri	(National Diet Library)	Jippensha Ikku	Mishima (Shizuoka Pref.)—Hakone—Daiyūzan—Mt. Ōyama—Enoshima Benten—Kamakura
1838	Fuji Ōyama dochū zakki	(Kanagawa Kenritsu Kyōdo Shiryōkan)	a Fuchū villager	Fuchū (Yamanashi Pref.)—Mt. Fuji—Daiyūzan—Ōyama—Enoshima—Kamakura
1838	Gozanekitei kenbun zakki jō	(National Diet Library)	Rinkeibunbō Junki	Matsuda—Daiyūzan—Odawara
1839	Tamakushige futatsu ideyu michi no ki	(National Diet Library)	Hara Masaoki	Higanezan—Hakone—Daiyūzan
1848	Shinrozan dōchūki	(Fujino City Library)	Akutsu Shōemon	Odawara—Daiyūzan—Hakone—Ise Shrine
1850	Hakone Atami	(National Diet Library)	Kenzan	Daiyūzan—Hakone—Atami
1853	Ise sangū dōchū nikki oboechō	(National Diet Library)	Tachibana	Odawara—Daiyūzan—Hakone—Ise Shrine
1856	Saigoku dōchū nikkichō	(Unakami City Library)	unknown	Matsuda—Daiyūzan—Saigoku region
1859	Ise dōchū nikki tebikae	(Iwatsuki City Library)	unknown	Ise Shrine—Nara—Osaka—Konpira—Kyoto—Zenkōji—Daiyūzan
1866	Hakone kikō	(National Diet Library)	Ogawa Taidō	Hakone—Bentenzan—Daiyūzan

sociation, the Higashimaru kō, stands at the crossroads on the old Yagura (or Yagurazawa) trail indicating "On the left is the road to Mt. Ōyama and on the right, the road to the Dōryō Shrine."[63] Other stone markers indicating the way to Daiyūzan (see table 4) suggest that pilgrim groups and the villages cooperated to make the various routes more accessible with markers.[64]

Scholars such as Ōno Ichirō have discussed this practice of Fuji kō members passing back through Daiyūzan (from about 1831) because they believed that a trip to Mt. Fuji was only "half a trip" (kata mairi); in other words, members also needed to visit Mt. Ōyama to complete their pilgrimage.[65] The concept that both mountains needed to be visited as a set, according to Ōno and others, had its roots in two folk beliefs. The first is that Mt. Ōyama represented the male sex organ, while Mt. Fuji symbolized the female organ. The second idea was that the two mountains were mythologically joined as older and younger sisters. Although these ideas are intriguing, there is no evidence that the term "half a trip" was ever used in the Tokugawa period. The phenomenon of visiting Mt. Fuji and Mt. Ōyama as a set is likely due to a simple geographic fact that those returning to Edo from Mt. Fuji through the Ashigara Pass would have to trek past both Daiyūzan and Mt. Ōyama. The idea of "half a trip" was probably a later explanation of this practice.[66]

Sources from Mt. Ōyama also indicate that pilgrims visited these sites as a set. The earliest evidence at Mt. Ōyama is a prayer for the dedication of a small Dōryō Shrine on the mountain from 1777.[67] By 1831 a document titled Gosaireichū shoshūnō hikaechō held by the Ōyama pilgrim lodge, the Murayamabō, includes travel information of Ōyama kō members under the household's care.[68] The chronicler includes a section on 5 of the 214 groups that climbed Mt. Ōyama during that summer under Murayamabō's purview that also made a trip to Mt. Fuji. In addition, 2 groups appear under the entry "Came from Dōryō," suggesting that a small percentage of Ōyama kō members combined a trip to Daiyūzan with a trip to Mt. Ōyama. The growing popularity of Daiyūzan, then, was inextricably linked with the growing popularity of other pilgrimage destinations such as Mt. Ōyama, Mt. Fuji, and Hakone hot springs. As the Tokugawa-period pilgrimage boom expanded and the "culture of movement" developed, Sōtō Zen prayer temples such as Daiyūzan firmly embedded themselves into the larger religious landscape.[69]

LOCAL KAMI LEGENDS AND DAIYŪZAN

As if somehow to link Daiyūzan with the more famous pilgrimage site, Mt. Ōyama, legends tying the two sites together also began to appear in the Tokugawa period. The best-known legend attributed Ryōan's selection of Daiyūzan as a site for his Zen monastery to Ōyama Myōō, one of the major deities of Mt. Ōyama. In this story, Ryōan, returning to his native Sagami Province to look for a suitable site, was walking in the vicinity of the moun-

TABLE 4
Stone Markers on the Road to Daiyūzan

Year	Stone Marker No.	Location	Donor	Notes
1774	39	Hadano	Handani Sagoemon	Fudō Stone Relief (Saijōji is downstream)
1782	23	Kōzu	Shin Yoshiwara	Kō members of Yoshiwara (including Brothels)[a] and ten other unreadable establishments. Women donors[b] plus another joint kō (Yoshitokukō)
1787	21	Hiromachi	n/a	Batō Kanzeon Stone Relief (Saijōji Road on left)
1794	35	Hadano	Shin Yoshiwara	Brothel owners[c]
1806	40	Hadano	Unnamed kō	*Nenbutsu kuyō* Stone (Saijōji to right)
1817	36	Hadano	Unnamed kō	Marker dedicated to local kami, Kenrō Daichijin (Saijōji Road to left)
1844	6	Odawara	Odawara Village	Signpost to Dōryō Daigongen (to south)
1848	33	Mt. Ōyama	Okada Idayū and five other Ōyama *oshi*	Signpost to Dōryō Gongen
1867	19	Hiromachi	Reihai kō	Signpost to Saijōji Road (to left)
1884	17	Iizawa	Ishiwata Nakajirō	Signpost (Ōyama Road to left, Dōryō Shrine Road to right) by Fuji pilgrimage confraternity
1888	20	Hiromachi	Marufuji kō	Signpost (Sengo-kuhara to right, Doryō Shrine to left) by Fuji pilgrimage confraternity
n/a	7	Tsukahara	Harada Hisakichi	Signpost to Dōryō Shrine
n/a	44	Matsuda	n/a	Signpost to Saijōji (to left)

TABLE 4 (*cont.*)

Year	Stone Marker No.	Location	Donor	Notes
n/a	51	Yamakitachō	Fuji kō	Signpost to Dōryō (go down mountain road)
n/a	10	Sekimoto	n/a	Signpost of road to Daiyūzan Dōryō Daisatta
n/a	13	Minami Ashigara	Sugimoto	Signpost to Saijōji (to right)
n/a	48	Yamakitachō	n/a	Signpost to Dōryō Road (to left)

Note: Adapted from Ashigara Shidankai Survey.

[a] The brothels included Ryūzakiya, Nagasakiya, Kadoebiya, Daimonjiya, Shingawaya, Owariya, Inabenya, Shinfukudaya, Shinyorozuya, Bitchūya, Sanshūya, Kawachiya, Aizumiya, Yamatoya, Fukudaikokuya, Awaya, Koigiya, Tamaya, Tsuruyoshiya, Iseya, Yamadaya, Daikokuya, Ōsagamiya, and Fujimiya.

[b] Women donors included Tatsu (of Shinyorozuya), Katō Tomi, Ozawa Masu, Ōta Taka, Gotō Kane, Nao (of Daikokuya) and one unnamed geisha.

[c] The brothels included Daikokuya, Echizenya, Matsubaya, Wagokuya, Ebiya, Matsuya, Tawaraya, Sasaya, Takeya, Izumiya, Kanaya, Tamuraya, Ōgiya, Ōmiya, Surugaya, Muramatsuya, Ebisuya, Iseya.

tain when he came across a large gentleman who pointed to Daiyūzan. The gentleman served Ryōan as a guide and recruited people from the surrounding region help build the Zen temple. Later he revealed himself to be Ōyama Myōō, one of the deities at Mt. Ōyama. This story,[70] while not in early Daiyūzan founding legends, appears in several early Tokugawa-period Ryōan biographies linking the two mountains (see table 5).[71]

Another Tokugawa-period legend makes the Daiyūzan-Ōyama connection even more explicit. An entry from the 1721 *Kōgen Daitsū zenji sengoshū* by Daitsū Takushū, a monk whose teacher served as the fourteenth Daiyūzan abbot, includes the following:

According to temple lore, it is said that the Yūhō [Daiyūzan] monk Dōryō was a "transformation body" of Sekison Daigongen, and during Zen Master Ryōan's abbotship at Yūhō, Sekison turned himself into a monk to guard the Dharma lineage. From a long time ago, a large rock blocked the way in a corridor at the temple. The monks didn't know quite what to do with it, so they called on some workers to remove it. But when the workers came, the monk Dōryō said, "Stop, stop, I will do it." He picked up the rock with both hands and threw it out of the way. He grinned and left without a trace. Since then, the rock has been placed in a sacred area and worshiped as a protective deity of the Dharma lineage.[72]

TABLE 5
Legends of Daiyūzan

	A	B	C	D	E	F	G	H
Daiyūzan Texts								
Tōzan kaibyaku narabini kunin rôjin no kien (1648)	x			x	x	x		
Saijōji utsushi tozanyū kyūmeiji (1724)		x						
Ryūtaiji rinjū nikkan (1723–34)		x						
Daiyūzan Saijōji gokaisan engi (1737)	x		x	x	x	x		
Saijōji engi wasan (late Edo period)	x	x	x				x	
Monk Biographies								
Enpō dentōroku (1678)								
Nichiiki tōjō shosoden (1693)			x	x				
Honchō kōsōden (1702)								
Nihon tōjō rentōroku (1727)			x	x				
Secular Texts								
Hōjō godai jikki (1615–24)							x	
Shinpen Sagami no kuni fūdokikō (1841)							x	x

Note: The letters heading the table columns refer to the following legends:
A. Ryōan led by eagle
B. Ryōan led by Ōyama Myōō
C. Iizawa/Yagura Myōjin become Ryōan disciples
D. Nine kami promise to protect temple
E. Hakone Gongen provides water
F. Iizawa/Yagura Myōjin provide the Kongōsui
G. Mishima Myōjin provides the Kongōsui
H. Dōryō

Today, this large rock (the *ittekiseki*) in front of the founder's hall is encircled with a sacred rope. For local residents of Sagami Province, it would have been easy to connect a legend involving Dōryō and a rock with Sekison Daigongen (the great "rock" deity enshrined at Mt. Ōyama's Afuri Shrine). The claim in the legend was that Dōryō was actually the Mt. Ōyama deity Sekison, who transformed himself into a monk to support and protect Daiyūzan. These legends connecting Mt. Ōyama and Daiyūzan must have developed in tandem with the increasing number of pilgrims visiting both sites as priests from the two locations realized the advantage of linking their sites with other popular pilgrimage destinations.

The motif of local deities supporting and protecting Daiyūzan seems to have been a deliberate strategy of the temple to adapt itself to the local religious culture, on the one hand, while at the same time asserting its superiority over local deities. Indeed, this type of incorporation of local kami into the Sōtō Zen lineage through precept giving or Dharma teaching is not limited to Daiyūzan but is a long-standing theme within the Sōtō Zen tradition, sometimes called *shinjin kedo*. These deities would, in return, protect the temple that stood within its tutelary domain or provide resources such as water or hot springs; in other words, local non-Buddhist deities give back something concrete in gratitude for being allowed into the Buddhist fold.[73] This process exemplified the power of the Sōtō Zen priests, who would receive not only the spiritual and material protection of the local deities, but also the patronage of the local populace impressed by their command of the deities.

The earliest extant temple history, the *Tōzan kaibyaku narabini kunin rōjin no kien* compiled by Kōkoku Eishun in 1648,[74] included a number of legend cycles telling how local and translocal deities supported and protected Daiyūzan. First, according to the temple history, two local deities, Iizawa Myōjin (the tutelary kami of Iizawa, the village at the foot of Daiyūzan) and Yagura [or Yagurazawa] Myōjin (the tutelary kami of eighteen villages in northern Ashigara region),[75] came to Daiyūzan disguised as old men to study the Dharma under Ryōan. Becoming convinced of Ryōan's greatness after a night of questions and answers in the Zen master's quarters, the two deities lent their powers to the expansion of the new Zen temple.[76] These two deities discovered both the Kongōsui water source and the talisman seal while digging a well, providing the temple with an important natural resource as well as the magical Kongō Hōin talisman. Furthermore, according to the founding legend of the Sanmen Daikokuden (the Three-Faced Daikoku Hall), a shrine located to the west of the main temple compound, the three kami (joined as one in the form of Daikokuten) were protective deities who pledged to provide the temple with other natural resources: Iizawa Myōjin—rice, Yagura Myōjin—firewood, Hakone Gongen—water.[77] This meant that local villagers who took care of the shrines dedicated to Iizawa and Yagura Myōjin provided Daiyūzan with offerings of rice and firewood.[78] The incorporation of local deities into the Zen fold, then, involved not only the establishment of a relationship between Zen Buddhist figures and local deities, but the practical involvement of local residents in the transformation of a sacred mountain into a sacred mountain-cum-Zen temple.

Another legendary association of Daiyūzan with a popular pilgrimage destination can be found in the legend of *Tōzan kaibyaku narabini kunin rōjin no kien*, in which water is provided to Daiyūzan by Hakone Gongen, the tutelary kami of Hakone, a well-known hot spring to the southwest of the temple. In the guise of an old man, Hakone Gongen visited Ryōan during the winter of 1394 for ten days, during which time the kami received the Buddhist precepts and a Zen lineage chart. The legend informs us that the kami, having learned of Daiyūzan's water shortage, funneled water from Lake Ashinoko at Hakone to Daiyūzan through an underground waterway. This water came to be known as the Gongensui.

As with Mt. Ōyama, it was not simply the legends, but actual travel to both sites, a combination of visits to hot springs and temples/shrines, that became increasingly popular in the Tokugawa period.[79] Travel guides explicitly making the link, such as Jippensha Ikku's 1822 *Dōryō gongen Hakone gongen nanayu meguri kikō bunsho*, and small Tokugawa-period shrines dedicated to Hakone Gongen at Daiyūzan are indicators of this phenomenon.[80] A Hakone hot spring traveler, Hara Masaoki, in his 1839 *Tamakushige futatsu ideyu michi no ki*, provides a description of his travels to Daiyūzan:

> I was told by the innkeeper that "Past the Myōjindake is a temple, Saijōji. Enshrined there is Dōryō Gongen, who is even visited by people from Edo. Though it is a six *ri* walk from Odawara, if one goes another three *ri* past this mountain, the view is beautiful." So I thought I must go today. So together with a guide, I left the inn at the hour of the snake and arrived in Miyagino Village after a while and took a rest at a house selling vegetables. . . . We finally arrived in front of the shrine. Dōryō was once a Saijōji monk who mysteriously turned into a tengu and has ever since been worshiped as an avatar (*gongen*). If one worships him sincerely, prayers will come true, and so many pilgrims visit the place. The buildings look as though they have much work done on them by specialist carpenters. There are many donations visible, including masks of large and small tengu.[81]

In other words, even casual visitors like Hara Masaoki found the time to visit Daiyūzan's Dōryō Shrine because of its reputation as an important site that ought not be missed—even if only for the gorgeous view. Although his main travel purpose was to visit Hakone hot springs, by the 1830s there must have been sufficient promotion of Daiyūzan in the Sagami region that a traveler like Hara would feel obliged at least to take a look.[82]

INDEPENDENT CONFRATERNITIES: OCCUPATIONAL AND CHARISMATIC KŌ

The link between local deities and Daiyūzan, as well as the growing number of pilgrims, enhanced the temple's prominence in the religious topography of Sagami Province. This first phase of the Dōryō cult and Daiyūzan pilgrimage (during which it was dependent on Mt. Fuji and Ōyama pilgrims) was followed in the late Tokugawa period by new Dōryō-centered, independent pilgrimage associations. While groups associated with Mt. Fuji and Mt. Ōyama tended to visit Daiyūzan during certain seasons when they were on pilgrimage anyway, especially the summer mountain season, the independent pilgrimage groups timed their visits to Daiyūzan to coincide with the monthly Dōryō Festival (with particular emphasis on the occasions of the Great Festivals).[83] This second-phase kō development centered around two new types of organizations: occupational kō and kō lead by charismatic leaders.

The Shin Yoshiwara kō, discussed above as the first independent Dōryō kō, was the model for the new kō organized around occupations, Shin

Yoshiwara being organized around both the district after which it was named and the brothels located there. During the late Tokugawa and early Meiji periods, pilgrimage groups to Daiyūzan included groups of carpenters, firemen, fish market wholesalers (Uogashi kō and Kanzen kō), vegetable wholesalers (Abura kō, Takenoko kō, and Seika kō, who annually offered rape-seed oil, bamboo shoots, and fresh vegetables, respectively, to Daiyūzan), and shopkeepers (such as Sobashō kō or soba-noodle shop owners).[84] Especially for the firemen and fishermen, placing Dōryō talismans on their bodies gave them a sense of protection from fires and drowning.[85]

As with the kō visiting other sacred sites, Dōryō-centered kō were organized internally on three levels: (1) a group leader or co-leader, called the *kōmoto* (or a sendatsu), (2) group organizers, called *sewayakunin* (usually up to four, depending on the size of the group), and (3) the group's regular members, called *kōin*. With most of these occupation-based kō, the group leader and organizers collected monthly dues from the regular members and pooled the money so that a rotating group of members (sometimes chosen by lottery) could visit Daiyūzan on one of the festival days. This type of organizational structure is sometimes referred to as the *daisankō* system (a system to send a *daisan*, or a representative of the group, to the site). Nationwide, these type of kō were organized for pilgrimages to Mt. Fuji, Ise Shrine, and Kumano Shrine. This type of occupational or village-based Dōryō kō was very similar to those confraternities dedicated to Mt. Ōyama, Narita Fudō, Mt. Ontake, Akiba Shrine, and Kashima Shrine, all of which operated primarily in the Kantō region centered on locally, rather than nationally, famous pilgrimage sites.[86]

In contrast to these kō, which members joined to strengthen ties with other members of their profession or village rather than for strictly devotional purposes, in the late Tokugawa period there emerged kō led by charismatic leaders who emphasized strong devotional elements.[87] In the case of Dōryō kō, they were organized around a *kōmoto* or a sendatsu (a mountain ascetic who resided at Daiyūzan and guided pilgrims). These leaders had particularly strong religious experiences connected to Dōryō such as dreams, revelations, and spirit possessions, and the regular members of this "charismatic" type of kō were primarily interested in receiving the powers of Dōryō through their leader. Although most Daiyūzan sendatsu received their mountain ascetic training from other sacred mountains (for example, Mt. Ontake), these religious specialists were seen as charismatic individuals who could "channel" Dōryō's powers to kō members in the form of healing, counseling, and divinations, and they stood in contrast to regular *kōmoto*, whose functions were primarily administrative.[88] These charismatic leaders of the Dōryō cult brought the powers of the deity to the kō members, who lived mainly in Edo.

One such Tokugawa-period charismatic kō was the Isshin kō led by the Daiyūzan sendatsu Isshin Gyōja.[89] His group grew to several hundred by the end of the Tokugawa period and primarily attracted merchant-class Edoites such as fish market wholesalers from the Nihonbashi area and vegetable wholesalers from the Kanda Sudachō district. The main attraction was apparently the combination of Isshin's ability to receive revelations from Dōryō about what a kō member should do with his or her life and his power to perform esoteric rituals for this-worldly benefits, including healing. As Nakagawa Sugane has suggested, charismatic men and women, who claimed healing powers from possession by syncretic deities such as Inari, were the forerunners of "syncretistic new religions, not unlike Tenrikyō and Kurozumikyō, popular faiths that emerged in the late Tokugawa period and won great followings among the common people of central Japan."[90]

Isshin lived into the Meiji period, and in 1887 he healed a three-year-old girl, the daughter of prominent retailer Yamamoto Kinosuke, who had swallowed a small piece of metal that had become stuck in her throat. After performing esoteric rites to Dōryō, Isshin had the child drink down an Okanain talisman with some water, which allegedly saved the girl's life. Yamamoto Kinosuke, who eventually became head of the Isshin kō, made great efforts to promote the group even after Isshin's death because of his sense of gratitude to the charismatic leader. Since they had lost their leader who could easily communicate with Dōryō, Yamamoto first invited a Mt. Ontake ascetic known for his ability to communicate with Dōryō to join the group. Second, in 1902, he raised funds to rebuild the Inner Sanctuary (Oku-no-in), positioned about 350 stone steps above Dōryō's Shrine, where he also installed an Eleven-Faced Kannon (Jūichimen Kannon) to which Dōryō was said to have been devoted during his training at Miidera.[91]

Membership in the Isshin kō and similar kō led by other charismatic leaders grew to such a degree that buildings for the sole use of a particular kō were built on the mountain for their members' annual visits.[92] However, with many of these kō led by charismatic leaders, growth in membership came to a halt under the second-generation leaders who were not prone to possession by Dōryō and thus unable to perform divinations or perform healing miracles.[93]

IGAICHŌ AND DEGAICHŌ: TO REVEAL THE HIDDEN DŌRYŌ

Just as the sendatsu brought the cult of Dōryō to the people, the Tokugawa and early Meiji Dōryō kaichō (display of the ordinarily hidden deity) cited at the beginning of this chapter also fanned the growth of the cult. Although the Dōryō Festival on the twenty-eighth of each month served as an igaichō (statue display at the temple), on three occasions—1784, 1819, and 1871— degaichō (statue display outside temple grounds) were held in the city of Edo. By transporting the deity in a portable shrine, parading the statue along the route all the way to the Edo, and conducting advertising campaigns in the city, Daiyūzan and their associated kō were able to expose Dōryō to many more people than if they limited their displays and festivals to the mountain. These public displays were, in part, due to the fact that the journey up to the Dōryō Shrine was strenuous even for those in good health. That Dōryō was periodically transferred to the city of Edo meant many potential worshipers who could not visit Daiyūzan for health or other reasons would have a chance to participate in the cult.

Although several accounts of the practice of displaying a hidden Buddhist statue (*hibutsu*) in Kamakura or Kyoto exist prior to the Tokugawa period, kaichō was essentially a Tokugawa-period phenomenon, especially popular after the late seventeenth century.[94] And in terms of displays off temple grounds, it was also primarily an Edo City phenomenon, the first such display being held in 1676 when the famous Ishiyamadera Kannon came to the city.[95] These exhibits in Edo were held at various host temples (*shukudera*), the nonsectarian (though formally affiliated with the Jōdo sect) Ekōin Temple being the most popular site at which to display statues from around the country.[96] For the display of the Dōryō statue, Ekōin Temple, as the preeminent location for Edo City religious displays for all sects, was the preferred kaichō site (the display was held there two out of the three occasions).

The government granted permission to temples to hold these exhibitions in Edo so that the state coffers would not be depleted by constant requests for temple repairs.[97] Although fund-raising for temple rebuilding and expansion was certainly a major motivation for holding kaichō, the display was held for other reasons as well. Since the timing of the first exhibition, held in 1784 at Ekōin Temple, coincided with the start of kō activity at Daiyūzan, it appears that the temple was also attempting to boost the popularity of Dōryō in Edo.[98] In fact, Daiyūzan cited in its petition to the bakufu the request of lay believers of Dōryō that a kaichō be held in Edo to alleviate people's unease over both the Mt. Asama volcano eruption and the Tenmei-period famines.[99] The popularity of Dōryō in the city is supported by the fact that the temple was able to reach its financial goals early and was thus able to return the statue to Daiyūzan more than a week earlier than it had planned.[100] But two months after the exhibit, on the twentieth of the seventh month of 1784, a severe fire swept the temple grounds, destroying several of the main structures.[101]

One of the major impacts of this fire was the loss of the temple's prayer building, which was the ritual center for any prayer temple. Despite the financial success of the 1784 exhibit, due to the lack of funds prayers were held in a temporary hut for the next fourteen years. Because Daiyūzan hoped to restore all of the buildings by the four hundredth anniversary of Ryōan's death, the temple priests asked the Kantō-area administrative headquarters as well as bakufu officials for permission to conduct a fund-raising campaign at all of its 3,800 Ryōan-lineage branch temples. Although in its request the temple stressed the significance of Ryōan's anniversary and the fact that it had received permission from the local domainal lord, Ōkubo Aki, to raise funds, the bakufu rejected their request on three occasions

(1800, 1802, 1804) because of the financial burdens it would place on thousands of temples.[102] It was in this context that the temple planned a second exhibit in Edo, both as a temple rebuilding fund-raiser and to commemorate Ryōan.

This 1819 degaichō was held at Chōkokuji Temple in the Shibuya district of Edo.[103] The choice of Chōkokuji, a Sōtō Zen temple, over Ekōin was due to the financial situation at both the home and host temples. Chōkokuji, founded during the Tenna era (1681–83), featured a large Eleven-Faced Kannon statue said to have been made from the same tree as the famous Hasedera Kannon statues (in both Yamato and Sagami provinces).[104] Although the temple had tried to develop a kaichō tradition and fund-raising associations (*tanomoshikō*) to repay the costs of its Kannon statue, it had lost money each time it held an exhibition and was rebuked by its head temple, Daichūji (a branch temple of Daiyūzan). However, because of the success of the 1784 Dōryō degaichō, Chōkokuji Temple was extremely confident of recouping its losses with a display of Daiyūzan's tengu. A copy of a letter from Chōkokuji Temple to its head temple, Daichūji Temple, written to obtain permission to host Dōryō, claimed that it would host the Daiyūzan statue in full accordance with regular kaichō rules (suggesting that its previous Kannon kaichō had some irregularities) and that if the kaichō failed to make a profit, it would not ask Daichūji Temple for help.[105] With this kind of commitment, Daichūji Temple was able to convince Daiyūzan to hold its next kaichō at Chōkokuji Temple with the caveat that the funds raised would be shared between the two parties and kept within the Sōtō school, especially because one of Daiyūzan's objectives for this kaichō was to celebrate Ryōan's anniversary and consolidate alliances with the Ryōan lineage subtemples. The home temple's need to raise funds for the new construction and to commemorate Ryōan's anniversary, and the host temple's need to raise funds to clear debts incurred from previously mishandled kaichō, meshed to create the 1819 degaichō.

The exhibit at Chōkokuji Temple was a financial success as both temples worked diligently to ensure a successful outcome. One factor that contributed to its success, in contrast to the earlier 1784 event, was the active involvement of kō members who raised donations during the transportation of Dōryō from Daiyūzan to Edo.[106] Although the incident, in which kō members carrying the Dōryō portable shrine got into a fight with some villagers, was obviously not a part of their plan, the practice of kō members carrying the statue and parading it both in the villages along the route and in the city of Edo was a new strategy for spreading the word about Dōryō. While the dissemination of information through word-of-mouth and festive parading were the main ways in which kō members advertised the Dōryō kaichō, they also set up wooden bulletin boards announcing the events in Edo. Although the sizes of these billboards and their location were strictly regulated by the bakufu, this advertising method was a key to the success of the exhibits in Edo.[107]

The trend toward greater involvement of kō members in the Dōryō exhibits in Edo became even clearer in the final exhibit that took place in 1871 at Ekōin Temple.[108] Indeed, most of the planning for the event, which was the largest Dōryō exhibit, was organized by kō members rather than the temple.[109] In 1870 four leaders of the Yoyogi kō[110] appealed to Daiyūzan to allow the statue to be displayed in Edo to strengthen ties between lay believers and Dōryō.[111] When Daiyūzan replied positively, kō leaders and sendatsu from around Edo gathered for a meeting at Iseya Kahyōe's house on the eleventh of the eleventh month of 1870 and decided on Ekōin Temple as the preferred site for the exhibit. In contrast to the 1819 kaichō, which had the sect-specific agenda of celebrating Ryōan's anniversary by holding the exhibit at a Sōtō Zen temple, the lay leaders who organized the final exhibit of 1871 chose the less sectarian Ekōin Temple.[112]

By 1871 many Shintō-Buddhist syncretic temples began feeling the coming of destruction and financial ruin resulting from the new Meiji government's policy disfavoring Buddhism and separating Shintō-Buddhist combinative sites.[113] In the case of Daiyūzan, partly because Shintō priests were never involved with the management of the Dōryō Shrine, the Buddhist priests simply changed Dōryō's title from the Shintō-sounding "Daigongen" to the Buddhist "Daisatta" (*mahāsattva*).[114] This name change seems to have had little effect on the popularity of the 1871 exhibit, which was immensely successful. The parade, for instance, which started at Sengakuji Temple in Takanawa and ended at Ekōin Temple, lasted three days and had a circus-like atmosphere with clowns and acrobats providing entertainment. In addition to the kō members, kabuki actors, geisha, and worshipers in tengu masks joined the parade. This description of the event by Saitō Gesshin is confirmed by the 1871 *ukiyoe* (color prints) of the Dōryō exhibition illustrated by Utagawa Yoshimori, the second-generation Hiroshige print master, where amidst the crowds and the kō flags appear a miniature Dōryō shrine and a man in a bright red tengu mask.[115] Kō members' high level of preparation and organization for this event can also be gleaned from these prints. For example, the tengu fan designs on many of the participant's costumes reveal that much time and effort were put into this event and that it was not spontaneous, but a well-organized, affair. Indeed, the Meiji movement to separate Buddhism and Shintō inadvertently helped distinguish Dōryō as a deity (now functioning as a purely "Buddhist" deity) and his cult as an organization (with Dōryō kō becoming less dependent on Mt. Fuji kō), thus rendering Daiyūzan more viable as an independent cultic center. The cult of Dōryō at its peak, then, displayed a growing core of lay believers belonging to various types of pilgrimage confraternities outside the control of both the temple and other pilgrimage associations. This strong lay group that cooperated with, but was not under the direct control of, the Sōtō Zen priests is an important dimension of lay Buddhist religiosity during the late Tokugawa period.

DAIYŪGAN: DAIYŪZAN AND THE SALE OF MEDICINE

The late Tokugawa and early Meiji popularity of the Dōryō cult can finally also be seen in the rising sales of Daiyūgan, a medicine inspired by Dōryō and purportedly able to treat ailments such as diarrhea, coughs, and phlegm. The earliest extant record of the origins of this medicine is a 1841 letter written by a pharmacist, Nakamura Tōzō, to Daiyūzan, which reads:

> My ancestor [whose Dharma name is] Sōei Koji, during the Kyōhō era [i.e., 1716–35] made a pilgrimage to the mountain [i.e., Daiyūzan]. When he got there, Dōryō Gongen appeared to him in a dream and revealed to him the method for making the medicine Daiyūgan. Sōei then started to distribute this medicine to sincere believers who visited the [Dōryō] Shrine. Up until my generation, our family has been receiving your permission to sell [this medicine] at the mountain for which we are grateful. . . . If we can get your permission to continue as before, our entire family would be extremely grateful.
> From Tōzō and relatives, Tsukahara Village
> Fifth month, 1841
> To: Saijōji Temple administrative offices[116]

It appears that Dōryō gave Nakamura Tōzō's ancestor, Sōei Koji, the secret ingredients of a medicine called Daiyūgan in a vision in 1716, more than a hundred years before this letter was written. Sōei Koji was the Dharma name of Izumiya Sakuemon (who took the name Nakamura when he married into that family), a pharmacist based in Edo (Nihonbashi yonchōme). He became a devout believer in Dōryō when he married into the Nakamura family, who were parishioners of Daiyūzan's main subtemple, Tennōin. Having received Daiyūzan's permission to sell the medicine, Sakuemon must have made substantial profits from its sale medicine in the city of Edo because by 1720 he made a commitment to donate a very generous amount (three ryō) every year to Daiyūzan.[117]

However, the reason this letter was written was that during the previous year the Nakamura family and the temple had argued about the pharmacy's sales methods. Based in Tsukahara Village at the foothill of Daiyūzan (and no longer in Edo), the family had been rapidly expanding the sales of Daiyūgan in the late 1830s because they aggressively sold the medicine on temple grounds rather than in their pharmacy.[118] Having been at that time denied permission to sell the medicine on Daiyūzan's grounds any more, the family wrote to ask for the temple's approval once more. Their letter and other negotiations must have convinced the temple to reconsider, because a second letter was sent from the pharmacy outlining the conditions agreed to by the pharmacy and the temple for the medicine's sale, which included the following four points:

1. The pharmacy would have a space on the temple grounds to sell the medicine to pilgrims only on the occasions of the great festivals (i.e., three times a year).

2. The pharmacy would monitor the area between the Ryūmon and Entsū Bridges every morning and evening as a service to Daiyūzan.

3. The medicine would be available for sale at the pharmacy and the local magistrate and sold to other pharmacies only after careful consideration.

4. The pharmacy would donate a yearly sum to the temple.[119]

With these new rules in place, Daiyūgan became a popular purchase item for pilgrims to Daiyūzan, who had already begun to make visits to nearby Odawara for the well-known medicine Uirō.[120] Daiyūzan's medicine, produced from nineteen traditional Chinese herbs, was sold as a small red pill in packets of ten, after being produced in batches of 8,400 pills.[121] The packets came with a short explanation of the origins of the medicine:

> This mountain [Daiyūzan] is well known and respected by people as a sacred land of the Buddhas and kami where many miraculous things occur because it is protected by Dōryō Gongen. There is no doubt that this Daiyūgan has been given to us by Dōryō Gongen and thus has great divine powers. Believers should take this medicine, reading the above and believing in its sacred merits. Sōshū Sekimoto, Daiyūzan Saijōji, made with the "Diamond-Water" at Tsukahara Izumisai.

This "sacred medicine" came to rival the Kongō Hōin (Okanain) talisman by the Meiji period as a must-purchase item for pilgrims to Daiyūzan. Both the medicine and the talisman appeared to provide concrete proof of Dōryō's powers. In essence, the rise of Daiyūzan as a prayer temple providing this-world benefits was intimately tied to the temple's ability to package Dōryō's miraculous powers into sacred items that could be taken home.

The emergence of the cult of Dōryō during the Tokugawa period was thanks to both the rapid spread of new legends about the great powers of the deity and the physical movement of the cult. This included both pilgrimages to Daiyūzan and the "transportation" of the Dōryō cult to the surrounding regions through charismatic lay leaders and exhibitions in Edo. Different types of leadership structures oversaw different zones of Daiyūzan and the cult of Dōryō: (1) the Zen temple compound with its Sōtō Zen priests and Zen monastic training, (2) the Dōryō Shrine led by sendatsu and kō leaders with the occasional assistance from the Zen priests during the monthly Dōryō Festival, which included prayer rituals for this-worldly benefits, (3) the Sanmen Daikokuden in which local village headmen and Zen priests made offerings to local protective kami, and (4) the Dōryō cultic centers outside of Daiyūzan. This spatial differentiation of function and leadership helps to explain how complex Daiyūzan was and continues to be: a major Sōtō Zen administrative and monastic center as well as a lay-centered prayer temple. If one examines the history of the various temple structures, one can also see how the cult of Dōryō expanded from an almost invisible miniature stone Dōryō Shrine in 1672 to the appearance of a grand Dōryō Shrine by the late eighteenth century.[122] Indeed, the mid-Tokugawa period represented a turning point in Daiyūzan's history when it and so many other "prayer temples" were formed as cultic centers around a deity not found in the traditional Buddhist pantheon. This shift meant that prayer rituals overshadowed the temple's Zen monastic practice, so much so that in the Meiji period a special effort was made to rebuild the training monastery, which had become almost completely run down because donors ignored the temple in favor of the Dōryō Shrine.[123] In this regard, the cult of Dōryō was obviously a part of the Sōtō Zen tradition and yet, in many respects, it operated apart from it as well.

The combination of new pilgrimage routes, government policies limiting temple fund-raising, the emergence of lay organizations, and Daiyūzan's skill in adapting to the new religious landscape of the Tokugawa period all accelerated this development. Although most of the larger prayer temples within the Sōtō Zen school were founded in the medieval period, it was not until the mid- to late-Tokugawa period that conditions emerged for their development into popular, lay-oriented centers of worship. Among the many worldly benefits associated with Dōryō, the deity's ability to heal (as seen with both the Daiyūgan pill and the Kongō Hōin talisman) was one of the chief attractions for adherents from across sectarian boundaries. In the following chapter, this important theme of medicine and healing within the Sōtō Zen school will be examined in greater detail.

CHAPTER 5

Medicine and Faith Healing in the Sōtō Zen Tradition

THE LATE TOKUGAWA-PERIOD sale of the medicine Daiyūgan and its role in drawing pilgrims to the Sōtō Zen prayer temple Daiyūzan illuminates the importance of healing as a practical benefit that appealed to all classes of Tokugawa society. Tokugawa-period medical history has often been characterized by the emergence and introduction of new and more "rational" schools of neo-Confucian, nativist, and Western medical traditions. The majority of ordinary Japanese, however, were drawn to what some have pejoratively labeled "magical" or "superstitious" medicine sold by Buddhist temples. In fact, certain sacred medicines thought to be imbued with the power of the gods enjoyed a boom during the Tokugawa period. Their popularity was due in part to advertising, made possible by woodblock printing, and partly to an increase in long-distance travel. Despite important developments in pharmacopeia, surgery, and the professionalization of doctors, the crucial role of Buddhist priests in the sale of divinely sanctioned medicines and the public's strong faith in Buddhist deities for healing have been overlooked in most accounts of Japanese medical history. On the other hand, while Buddhism has often been broadly associated with healing and the alleviation of suffering, few studies examine concrete examples of Buddhist medicine or healing practices. This chapter details two Sōtō Zen case studies of a burgeoning Buddhist medical culture: the "Poison-Dispelling Pill," a herbal medicine produced at a Kyoto pharmacy and distributed nationwide by the Sōtō Zen sect, and the healing cult of the "Splinter-Removing Jizō," whose worship was centered on a Sōtō Zen temple in the city of Edo. These two examples provide a better sense of how Sōtō Zen Buddhist institutions participated in Tokugawa-period medical practices, and how medical practices shaped the character of Sōtō Zen Buddhism. As suggested previously, Sōtō Zen developed separate sect-specific religious practices, while simultaneously participating in a common Japanese religious culture. In the case of medical practices, this chapter will demonstrate how the herbal medicines produced at the Kyoto pharmacy unified and strengthened sect consciousness, as well as how the Jizō faith-healing cult enabled the Sōtō Zen sect to participate in practices of a transsectarian nature.

The following translated text introduces a segment of a one-page instruction sheet on how to take a medicine known as Gedokuen (or Gedoku), the "Poison-Dispelling Pill." Sent from Dōshōan, a pharmacy in

Kyoto, to Ryūsanji, a Sōtō Zen temple in Sagami Province, these instructions reveal how various Chinese herbal remedies were prepared and applied.

- For cuts, take some Gedoku in fine powdered form and lightly apply it to the wound. It is also fine to take a tablet[1] with water.
- For menstrual pains, mix 1 tablet of Gedoku into some freshly brewed hot water and drink it. Furthermore, for headaches, hot flashes, or faintness resulting from menstruation, 1 tablet of Gedoku should be mixed with 1 *bu* of the *senkyū* herb, 1 *bu*[2] of the *saiko* herb,[3] 1 *bu* of the *sanshishi* herb, and 1 *bu* of tree peony before taking it as above. Finally, if a woman has the symptoms of headaches and hearing loss, she should made some sap from some ground *sanshō* herb, mix it into some hot *miso* soup, before drinking it down with the Gedoku.
- For a cow unable to urinate, one can put the Gedoku tablet directly in its anus, or crush 5 pills into a powder, dissolve it in water, and make the cow drink it. If neither of these two methods works, one should mix 5 tablets with ground *miso* paste and give it to the cow, which will then mysteriously recover.

Purportedly able to cure anything from simple cuts to drowning, the power of this herbal medicine lay in its association with Dōgen, the founder of the Japanese Sōtō Zen sect, who was allegedly given the medicine by the daughter of the dragon king (in another variant account, a Japanese kami) during his visit to China. Traditional medieval hagiographies of Dōgen do not include this account, but during the Tokugawa period many versions of the origins of this sacred medicine appeared that linked this herbal pill to Dōgen. With both the Kyoto pharmacy and the Sōtō Zen sect able to benefit from sales of this popular medicine, the sacred origins of the pill was emphasized to highlight its ability to cure any ailment. This "Poison-Dispelling" (Gedoku) pill was purported able to cure all types of ailments because of the sacred and potent powers distilled into the medicine by Zen Buddhist priests. Not only did the pill allegedly cure all human ailments, the efficacy of this herbal medicine extended to birds and cows as well. This chapter begins with an examination of how this popular medicine came to be associated with the Sōtō Zen school and what role it played in the growth of the sect.

BUDDHIST MEDICINE AND DŌSHŌAN'S "POISON-DISPELLING" PILL

Most Japanese, even in the latter half of the nineteenth century, relied on Buddhist priests and healers other than physicians in times of illness. Despite the growing number of physicians, particularly in large urban centers such as Edo, Osaka, and Nagasaki, as George Smith, the visiting Anglican bishop from Hong Kong, observed, "Bonzes [Buddhist monks] are in greater request than the physicians."

The monotonous sounds of a Buddhist chaunt [sic] and beating of a hollow piece of wood, are frequently heard from the interior of a Japanese dwelling, in which some inmate of the household lies prostrate with fever or is afflicted with any other of the prevalent forms of sickness. . . . Charms and incantations performed by the priesthood are supposed to have their meritorious power; and the Bonzes are in greater request than the physicians. . . . On other occasions we discovered proofs of the popular mind in such cases being more impressed with the supernatural than with the physical remedies within their reach. A priest's gratuity is more willingly paid than a doctor's fee.[4]

Buddhism has always been a religion of healing. The motif of the Buddha as the great physician resolving all forms of physical and mental anguish is woven throughout its history despite the fact that early Buddhist monastic codes seems to have prohibited monks from practicing medicine.[5] In his well-known essay *Byō*, the Buddhologist Paul Demiéville classified Buddhist healing practices into three types: (1) religious therapeutics (good works, practices of worship, expiation, and meditation), (2) magical therapeutics (mantras, incantations, and esoteric ritual), and (3) medical therapeutics proper (dietetics, pharmacy, and surgery). He wrote, "The lines demarcating these three fields are not at all distinct. Where do 'religious' therapeutics stop? All of Buddhism is a single therapeutic."[6] This observation that the religious, magical, and medical therapeutics cannot be easily demarcated also holds true in the case of Buddhist healing practices in Japan during the Tokugawa period.

The history of Buddhist priest and temple involvement in medical practices in Japan began with the introduction of the religion from Korea and China.[7] Not only was faith in the healing powers of the new deities imported, but the palliative qualities of herbal medicines were also introduced at the same time. By the Tokugawa period, Buddhism had become part of competing and mutually reinforcing systems of healing in Japan. Indeed during the Tokugawa period, new production techniques and distribution methods of Buddhist-inspired medicine propelled Buddhist institutions to the forefront of the healing economy.

Historians have characterized Tokugawa-period medical practices as influenced by two new developments that overshadowed Buddhist-inspired medicine: (1) advances in Sino-Japanese medicinal treatment inspired by new schools of physicians connected to neo-Confucian and nativist schools in Kyoto and Edo, and (2) the school of "Dutch medicine" that entered Japan through Nagasaki and developed there and in the city of Edo.[8] Though these developments are significant if "newness" is the criterion for history, medicines and medical practices related to Buddhism that existed prior to the Tokugawa period not only continued to be popular among ordinary people but underwent new developments in both types and methods of distribution.[9] While Demiéville wrote that "all of Buddhism is a therapeutic," for the study of Tokugawa-period Japan we need to recognize that at least some of what is "therapeutic" is Buddhist.

I have written elsewhere on the intricate connection between Buddhism and the production of medicine in the Tokugawa period, and the link between the sale of medicine and the spread of the Sōtō Zen tradition is especially clear in the case of the herbal pill Gedokuen.[10] This medicine was linked with the healing efficacy of Buddhism through the following legend.

[The monk] Dōshō, tired from the long journey, fell terribly ill. [The Zen Master] Dōgen, worried about his condition, dabbled water on Dōshō's face. Dōgen then stood up on the bow of the boat and ordered the Eight Dragon Kings to listen: "[I am] the Japanese monk Dōgen, crossing the seas back to Japan. Surely there is no reason to permit such rough waves and winds which make us ill. Make the winds and waves calm down at once." After he shouted these words, the winds and the waves mysteriously subsided.

A dragon girl then emerged [from the sea]. "I am Princess Toyotama, the daughter of the Shagara Dragon King.[11] The Dragon Palace is one of the six realms where beings suffer the 'three heats,'[12] but during the era of Buddha, Monju bodhisattva visited the Dragon Palace with a copy of the *Lotus Sutra*. Because of the great merits [of the sutra], Ten'ō nyorai[13] predicted that an eight-year-old dragon girl would attain salvation [from the suffering world] in the future. Oh Dōgen, now that you have sailed here, [it is as if] a Buddha has come. I [purposely] stopped your boat at this spot because I hoped to have this karmic encounter. Please bestow a Zen lineage chart onto me." Thus spoke the dragon girl, tears streaming.

Feeling compassion, Dōgen gave her a scroll. This scroll was the first Zen lineage chart given to [a member of] the dragon family. It was then that the dragon princess took out some medicine from a lapis lazuli bowl. She gave it to Dōshō, who was near death, and he promptly recovered his health. Dōgen was amazed, prompting the dragon girl to explain, "This medicine came from the wizard, Ruri (Lapis Lazuli) of Wizard Mountain (Shinsenzan). On each of his visits to the Dragon Palace, he would leave this medicine in exchange [for things from the palace]. This medicine has now become a valued treasure of the Dragon Palace, which I will share with you because you shared the Dharma [with me]. On this piece of paper is the secret formula for the medicine, the Shinsen Gedoku Manbyōen (the Wizard Mountain 'poison-dispelling' pill). Please alleviate the ills and sufferings of all beings with it." Saying this, the dragon princess humbly presented [Dōgen] with a scroll. This was the origin of the Shinsen Gedoku medicine, which has been available from Eiheiji Temple ever since.

Dōgen and Dōshō became increasingly amazed [at what had unfolded] but turned toward the dragon girl and chanted, "May good fortune as infinite as the sea come to all sentient beings." At that, the bodhisattva Kannon appeared and the dragon girl was saved, first turning into a male. Miraculously, a single lotus petal emerged from the waves carrying the dragon [out of the water], surrounded by clouds that formed from the sea. Off they went, ascending above the clouds into the sky.[14]

This version of the legendary origins of the Shinsen Gedoku Manbyōen is one of several variant accounts that tied the miraculous herbal pill to Zen Master Dōgen and Dōshō, a fellow monk who purportedly accompanied him to China. This account, from the *Echizen no kuni Eiheiji kaisanki* of 1689, was performed as a puppet play as part of new genres of popular literature and drama called *sekkyōbushi* and *gidayūjōruri* that recounted Dōgen and other sect founders' lives through pictures and performance.[15] Just as with the theme of local deities bestowing gifts upon Sōtō Zen priests and temples after receiving the Dharma from them, the salvation of the dragon princess—a significant motif in Mahayana Buddhism—enabled the two monks to return to Japan with a medicine from the Dragon Palace that would henceforth be treasured in the human world.[16] As Lalou has pointed out, dragons are especially featured in pan-Buddhist literature as providers of healing techniques, while De Visser has noted that medieval Chinese texts claimed that there were more than three thousand types of medicine stored in the Dragon Palace.[17]

Although in this account Dōshō was ill and the medicine was offered by a dragon girl, in other variants the Zen Master Dōgen himself was the sick person and a Japanese deity, Inari, was the provider of the medicine. For example, Menzan Zuihō's well-known 1753 edition of Dōgen's biography, the *Teiho Eihei kaisan gyōjō Kenzeiki*, more simply known as the *Teiho Kenzeiki*, recounts the episode somewhat differently:

> Dōgen fell gravely ill on his way back from China but had no medicines that could be of use. Suddenly, an immortal appeared and gave Dōgen a herbal pill, after which he immediately became better. The master asked this deity to reveal its identity. The mysterious figure replied, "I am the Japanese kami Inari" and disappeared. The medicine became known as Gedokugan, which has been ever since been a part of the Dōshō family heritage. . . . Dōgen then told Dōshō that this rare and wondrous medicine had been bestowed on him by a true kami for the protection of the great Dharma, [and that] this medicine of many benefits should be distributed to temples so that they might spread the Dharma lineage.[18]

This story, which became the most popular account of the medicine's origins, was based on the earliest known version, the 1639 *Dōshōan keifu*, a family genealogy of Dōshō.[19] In this more detailed version, Dōgen was lying on the ground, his "body and mind about to leave him" when an old white-haired woman appeared out of thin air and offered a herbal pill to Dōgen's companion, Dōshō (an illustration of this scene is in the 1817 *Teiho kenzeiki zue*).[20] Taking the pill from Dōshō, the Zen master recovered almost immediately. Seeing Dōgen return from the brink of death, Dōshō pleaded with this mysterious person to reveal her identity and the formula for making this pill. She disappeared as suddenly as she had appeared, but not before uttering the formula for the medicine and informing the monk that she was the Japanese deity Inari in disguise.[21] We are also told that this herbal pill, Gedokugan (otherwise known as Gedokuen, or more formally as the Shinsen

Gedoku Manbyōen), later became a part of Dōshō's family heritage and that it was to become instrumental in the spread of the Sōtō Zen school.[22]

These two variants of the origins of the medicine reveal two important themes in the Sōtō Zen orientation toward this-world benefits. The first legend featuring the dragon girl can be understood as a part of the motif of deities providing this-world benefits, including medicines, in return for the sharing of the Buddhist teachings by a Zen priest. The second legend points to another enduring theme; namely, that of Japanese kami, such as Inari, appearing in times of need to protect Zen monks, representatives of the true Dharma in Japan. While the two legends differ in detail and emphasis, both Dōgen's and Dōshō's medicine are depicted as *manbyōyaku* (all-purpose medicine, literally "medicine [to cure] the ten thousand illnesses"). Unlike most Chinese herbal medicines, which targeted particular ailments or regions of the body, the class of medicines known as *manbyōyaku* was said to effect cures for any ailment if properly administered. The claims of universal efficacy often meant that these extraordinary medicines were tied to the miraculous powers of Buddhist, Taoist, or Shintō deities or saints. Gedokuen was no different, connected in one legend to the Japanese deity Inari and in another to the Taoist wizard/daughter of the dragon king.[23] The name of the medicine itself also suggests a strong connection to Buddhism. The Chinese character for poison (*doku*) used in Gedokuen is the same one used to express the three poisons (*sandoku*) of covetousness, anger, and delusion that characterize the *samsaric* world.[24] The medicine dissolves the poisons that afflict the physical body to effect a cure but also serves as an antidote to the larger affliction with the three poisons that hinder liberation.[25]

The motif of medical formulas being given during miraculous appearances or in dreams to priests and other faithful believers by Buddhist deities and saints is a longstanding one in the history of sacred medicines.[26] Dreams and miracles are realms of the extraordinary where new formulas and medicines can be imagined. One of the most famous of these "Buddhist medicines" selling in the city of Edo was Kintaien, another *manbyōyaku*. The formula for this sacred medicine came to an Ōbaku Zen monk, Ryōō, in a dream in which Gyōtei, the founder of Hizen Kōfukuji, appeared with a medicine pouch. During his days as a novice, Ryōō had undergone a very severe regimen of meditation and austerities with the result that he was almost always in pain. It was on one particularly painful night that Gyōtei instructed Ryōō in a dream on how to make Kintaien, the medicine in the pouch. The medicine apparently alleviated Ryōō's pain and inspired the monk to open what would become one of Edo's most famous pharmacies, Kangakuya, located in the Ueno Ikenohata Nakamichi district.[27]

Suzuki Akira has noted that the explosion in new medicines, especially during the early Tokugawa period, was inspired by visions of deities such as Yakushi, Jizō, or Kannon, who would reveal in dreams the formulas for the concoction of herbal medicines. It was precisely during this period that one also sees mass marketing methods used to promote the mysterious origins and efficacy of these Buddhist medicines.[28] Regardless of whether the formulas to Ryōō's Kintaien or Dōshō's Gedokuen actually appeared to them in dreams or not, the claim of the medicine's sacred origins meant that these new medicines could suddenly appear without having had the authorization of the orthodox medical establishment because dreams and visions of deities could not be verified.

Government regulations concerning the production and distribution of medicine also aided the emergence of such sacred medicines. For example, during the Genroku period (1688–1703), the Tokugawa bakufu issued new laws that took away exclusive rights to the production and distribution of medicine from clan and bakufu doctors. This resulted in a diffusion of the power to produce and distribute medicine, enabling pharmacies like Dōshōan to take full advantage of these new laws. The result of this law can be most clearly seen in the dramatic growth of pharmacies in the wholesale districts of Edo and Osaka.[29] In both these cities, these new venues for the sale of medicine clustered together, providing an intensely competitive market for new and specialty medicines.

It was not only pharmacies that provided new opportunities for the production and distribution of new types and increased volume of medicine. Buddhist temples and the Buddhist priesthood did not look idly on as the market for medicines expanded. Temples themselves became sites for the production and distribution of Buddhist-inspired medicines. Patients from around the country would make trips to temples and hospices run by temples that were known for curing specific ailments, such as hemorrhoids at the Nichiren temple Honshōji in Edo or lovesickness at Kongōshōji, a Shingon temple near Ise.[30] Conversely, traveling Buddhist priests such as the Kōya hijiri, affiliated with the Shingon Mt. Kōya, went out from their temples to make their rounds of village households much like the well-known traveling salesmen such as the Toyama no gyōshōnin.[31] Carrying talismans and the stomach medicine Daranisuke[32] from Mt. Kōya, by the mid-Edo period Kōya hijiri, for example, had developed a medicine-distribution network that reached areas as far away as Sagami Province.[33]

While bakufu officials opened up the production and distribution of medicines, they also tried to control and regulate medicine by passing new laws prohibiting dokuyaku (poisonous medicine) and niseyaku (imitation medicine). The sale of Buddhist-inspired medicines, such as Gedokuen, benefited from these regulations, because as long as the medicines did not actually poison anyone, these laws did not question a medicine's efficacy (especially if some form of faith in a deity was involved) and yet would guarantee a temple or a pharmacy like Dōshōan its patent on the medicine.

ADMINISTERING THE SACRED PILL

While Gedokuen was considered a cure-all medicine, and its efficacy attributed to sacred origins, there were specific instructions on how to administer the herb for different kinds of ailments. This suggests that rather than being simply a medicine taken on faith, Gedokuen was a part of a broader range of Chinese herbal medicines and as such required directives on how to take it.

A document sent from Dōshōan to Ryūsanji Temple, a Sōtō Zen temple in Sagami Province gives us an understanding of how this medicine was prepared and administered. This document, the *Shinsen gedoku manbyōen fukuyō no koto* cited at the beginning of this chapter and translated in full as appendix B, contains instructions on how to prepare Gedokuen to treat a wide variety of illnesses. Most entries describe ways to treat fairly routine types of ailments such as stomachaches, colds, headaches, faintness, scurvy, and gonorrhea, although more serious, life-threatening diseases such as malaria and smallpox are also mentioned. Typical entries include the following:

- For fatigue, take one tablet[34] of the Gedoku[35] and mix it with one *bu*[36] of the *nanten* leaf, one *bu* of aged tea leaves, one *bu* of incense, and a pinch of salt. For stomachaches, chest pains, constipation, or other stomach-related discomfort, use the same formula as above, but also add five *bu* of the herb *kumatsuzura*.[37]
- For influenza-related headaches, coughs, and phlegm, a mixture of eight *bu* of Gedoku along with one pill-size portion of ground beefsteak plant, one *bu* of dried orange peel, two *bu* of green tree bark, one slice of the white root of a scallion, and three ground ginger roots should be prepared. This same preparation should be taken by those infected during mid-winter cold epidemics or those with high fevers resulting from exposure to the wind.
- For gonorrhea, take five tablets of Gedoku and mix it in a large vat of water with a sprig of the *ikoko* tree cut thirty times, ten loquat leaves without the stems, two *bu* of corn, and three *bu* of licorice.[38]

With these routine ailments, the most common method of administering Gedokuen is to combine it in a ground form with other Chinese herbal medicine ingredients, and to drink it down with water, tea, or sake. The second way of administering Gedokuen is as a salve that is rubbed onto the afflicted area of the body. For example, in the entry under "chest worms," which could refer to a range of lung ailments, the instructions are, "For chest worms, one tablet of Gedoku should be mixed into water that has been slightly heated with steel and imbibed. In addition, a salve made from the same amount of Gedoku with mustard should be applied to the affected area."

The final section of this instruction manual lists specialized treatments for women and also for livestock. Menopause, postpartum pains, menstrual cramps, and leucorrhea have separate entries as "women's illnesses." Treatments for horses, cows, and birds using this miraculous medicine are also outlined. Gedokuen, then, was advertised not only as an all-purpose medicine in terms of the illnesses it could cure, but as a medicine that worked with all types of people, and even horses, cows, and other livestock. This multipurpose aspect of the medicine helped to cement ties between the temples that sold them and the consumers, who were Sōtō Zen parishioners.

Gedokuen was a herbal medicine with qualities shared with other Chinese herbs, like the specificity of its administration for different ailments. It was unique in that it was an all-purpose sacred medicine that could purportedly cure anything from the common cold to malaria. However, why was such a medicine specifically linked to the Sōtō Zen sect? The legend cited above of Dōgen and Dōshō receiving Gedokuen from the Japanese deity Inari obviously holds the key to this question. This is not because the account is historically accurate, but because its authorship coincides with records of the distribution of the pill.

Legends of Dōgen, Dōshō, and Gedokuen

The biography of Dōgen in which this account is found is the *Kenzeiki*, a text compiled by the fourteenth-generation abbot of Eiheiji, Kenzei (1415–74). Although the text was originally titled *Eihei kaisan Dōgen zenji gyōjōki*, as copies after Kenzei's death proliferated it became known simply as the *Kenzeiki* or "The Record of Kenzei."[39] There are a number of extant handwritten copies, but the story about Dōshō and the medicine Gedokuen comes from the first printed edition of the text, the *Teiho Kenzeiki* (formally the *Teiho Eihei kaisan gyōjō Kenzeiki*) edited by Menzan Zuihō in 1753, which went on to eclipse all the handwritten versions.[40] Kawamura Kōdō, in his classic study on the *Kenzeiki*, includes six versions of the text (handcopied editions—Minshū/1538, Zuichō/1589, Empō/1680, Monsu/1694, Gemmon/1738—and the printed edition, the Teiho/1753) in columns for comparison. What is striking here is that none of the handcopied versions includes the story about Dōshō and the medicine.[41] Only the 1753 version of the *Kenzeiki*, published roughly three hundred years after the original text, includes this story.

The omission of such an important incident—Dōgen's salvation from death by a miraculous medicine—by the compilers of the earlier biographies is simply not comprehensible when we think of the detailed accountings of more minor incidents.[42] But then how and why did Menzan come to include this story? The answer comes in the text itself immediately following the story where Menzan includes a lengthy explanation of the lineage of Dōshō and how he came to accompany Dōgen to China. He clearly cites his source for this information: the *Dōshōan keifu*—the family genealogy of Dōshōan—by Dōshōan Bokujun (d. 1690), the nineteenth-generation head of the family. This family genealogy is the earliest reference of Dōshō's (1172–1248) connection with Dōgen.[43] And since there is no evidence of the sale of the medicine to any Sōtō Zen temples before 1600, though we cannot completely discount the existence of Gedokuen in the medieval period, it is safe to assume that the connection between this medicine and Dōgen or the Sōtō school is an invention of the late sixteenth or early seventeenth century.[44] Bokujun was creating a genealogy for his family, like many others in this period, that legitimized not only his family's heritage, by tying them to the powerful Fujiwara, but their medicine, by relating it to sacred sources, both Dōgen and Inari. By claiming that Dōgen instructed Dōshōan's founder to "distribute this medicine of many benefits to our [Sōtō Zen] temples so that they may spread the Dharma lineage," Bokujun clearly wanted to provide a legitimate basis for selling the medicine to Sōtō Zen temples, especially Eiheiji.

Legends about the origin of the medicine were not confined to the *Dōshō'an keifu* or the *Teiho Kenzeiki*, but, as cited before, became woven into a puppet play that added many elaborate and dramatic twists. The playwright Yūki Magozaburō embellished Dōshō's life with details found nowhere else to satisfy the needs of his apparent sponsor, Dōshōan, who would most likely have advertised Gedokuen during the breaks between the acts.[45] These details include the first two acts of the drama, which recount how the young Dōgen was nearly assassinated by Kinoshita Shōkan, Dōshō's father and a servant to Dōgen's evil stepmother who wanted to eliminate him as a competitor for the position of family head. Dōshō is also tied to Dōgen in the second act in which the two enter Mt. Hiei together to pursue the Buddhist path. Training together in China, they have amazing adventures in Act 4 in which they receive teachings on Zen meditation from Bodhidharma himself (in an old man's disguise), who later saves them from a dangerous tiger by turning into a serpent.

All of the stories in this puppet play are, of course, not found in any of the earlier Dōgen biographies. Through the invention of new stories about Dōgen, the playwright made the play more appealing to a general audience. This emphasis on the legendary powers of Dōgen in order to appeal to a nonliterate audience reached its peak a hundred years later with the commissioning of numerous Dōgen picture scrolls, which Tsutsumi has argued were necessary to counter the enormously popular scrolls of Shinran and other sect founders.[46] But in the case of this play, it was not only that Dōgen was made more appealing, but also that Dōshō's role in the life of the Sōtō Zen sect's founder was upgraded.

Another key feature of this play is the medicine Gedokuen, which is given to a sick Dōshō (rather than Dōgen, as in the original) by a daughter of the dragon king after Dōgen gives her the precepts and a Zen lineage chart.[47] Not only is Gedokuen a part of their Chinese adventures, but in Act 5 the two are instructed by the emperor upon their return to Japan to help the poor and sick people of Kyoto by distributing their miraculous medicine. This section of the play ends ironically when one of the first poor, ill people they help recover with the Gedokuen (someone who is no longer able to walk) is Dōgen's evil stepmother, who had fallen destitute after her failed assassination attempt.

Although Gedokuen appears to have had its roots in the early medieval period according to these legends found in the *Dōshōan keifu* (1639),[48] the *Echizen no kuni Eiheiji kaisanki* (1689), and the *Teiho Kenzeiki* (1753), since neither the medicine story nor sales records of Gedokuen appear prior to 1600, this medicine is best thought of as a Tokugawa-period "Buddhist medicine." Because of the explosion of new medicines in the early Tokugawa period, it is not surprising that Dōshōan—which may have been producing this herb pill since the medieval period—would want to tout the uniqueness of their medicine by tying it to a sacred being (Inari or the daughter of the Dragon King) and connect it to a sales base (Sōtō Zen temples).

BROKER TO THE IMPERIAL HOUSEHOLD AND PHARMACY TO PRIESTS

The manner in which Dōshōan established its sales base—we should recall that by the early 1700s the Sōtō school included more than 17,500 temples nationwide—was not only to promote the story of the origins of the medicine, but also to use its unique position as the mediating institution between the Sōtō Zen sect and the Kyoto-based imperial household. Although Dōshōan functioned as a pharmacy, it is perhaps better known as the administrative go-between for the two headquarter temples of the Sōtō sect (Eiheiji and Sōjiji) and the imperial household in Kyoto.[49] The main reason the Sōtō Zen headquarter temples needed a connection to the imperial house was that those who became abbots of either temple required a Zen master name (zenjigo) and a purple monastic surplice (shie or murasaki no koromo), which could be awarded only by the imperial house.[50] Indeed, whether one was the day-to-day abbot of the headquarters or simply a short-term (often one-day) abbot under a system called zuisse, one could not officially move up in the Sōtō Zen hierarchy without imperial sanction. Though one could never directly petition the imperial house, the headquarter temples of other sects dealt directly with the Tensō or Kajūji houses, which were intermediaries for all requests to the imperial household. But in the case of Sōtō Zen, one further buffer existed—Dōshōan.

Japanese scholars researching Dōshōan, including Tamamuro Fumio, Hirose Ryōkō, and Kumagai Chūkō, have not yet determined why and from when Dōshōan held this special position in relation to the imperial household.[51] Although we have evidence that the head of Dōshōan, because of the family's expertise in medicine, could use the imperially sanctioned title of "Hōgen" by the late medieval period—a rank one below the highest, "Hōin," given to great doctors, craftspeople, and artists—this connection is not sufficiently significant to have allowed it to serve as the Sōtō sect's connection to the imperial house.[52] Whatever the reason for Dōshōan's elevation to this position, which can only be speculative until new documents are discovered, we have clear evidence that all abbots of Eiheiji and Sōjiji went through Dōshō'an for promotion to their ranks after 1634.[53] Dōshōan would not only handle the submission of all documents, but instruct the Zen abbots on proper etiquette when they visited the imperial palace and provide them with lodging during their stay in Kyoto. For these services, Dōshōan received payment from the abbots, a cut of the total paid to the imperial household. Though the amount increased over time, Dōshōan's fees were approximately two hundred pieces of gold for abbots and one hundred pieces of silver for *zuisse* abbots.[54] Because *zuisse* abbots never really served as abbots but simply received the title "former abbot of Eiheiji (or Sōjiji)," as Sōtō Zen expanded, the number of these monks visiting Dōshōan grew exponentially throughout the Tokugawa period. If we combine the number of *zuisse* abbots from Eiheiji (an average of 96 monks per year) with those from Sōjiji (105 monks), Dōshōan would be lodging and receiving payments from some 200 monks per year. It was to these monks and their temples that Dōshōan sold, and/or presented as a gift, the herbal medicine Gedokuen.

For instance, in the case of actual abbots of Eiheiji Temple, the head of Dōshōan might present roughly one hundred pills of Gedokuen as a "going-away gift" to the new Zen master and fifty pills to the head supervising monk.[55] As for *zuisse* abbots, a temple inventory dated 1759 from Kenkon'in Temple (Aichi Prefecture) states: "It has been the custom since the abbotship of Taibi to pass down fifty Gedokugan pills from one abbot to the next."[56] One can at least speculate, then, that while the abbots of Eiheiji or Sōjiji may have received one hundred pills for their status and the amount of money they paid to Dōshōan, lower-ranking temples may have received roughly half that quantity of medicine.[57] Putting aside the question of the exact number of pills distributed, using its unique position as the intermediary to the imperial household, Dōshōan was able to promote and sell its medicine not only to the headquarter temples, but to all midsize temples large enough that their abbots would have the prestige of going to Kyoto for promotion.

DIRECT MARKETING AND COUNTERFEIT PILLS

Selling and promoting Gedokuen while Sōtō Zen abbots were in Kyoto was one sales strategy for Dōshōan, but by the mid-1700s we have evidence that Dōshōan was selling directly to temples, even to the most low-ranking temples, abbots of which did not have to go to training monasteries, let alone were in a position to receive imperial titles. For example, a midsize temple such as Ganshōin Temple, a branch of Kichijōji Temple in Gosen City (Niigata Prefecture), recorded in its 1841 *Sōtōshū Ganshōin shoji okite* the need for abbots to prepare 250 *mon* to be paid in cash for Gedokuen pills every year.[58] Direct sales in central Japan were handled through Kasuisai Temple, a large administrative temple dealing with bakufu directives in the Kantō region. A contract dated 1746 states that the previous abbot had given permission to Dōshōan to sell the medicine to all branch temples of Kasuisai Temple, including its lowest-ranked temples. The document further informs all branch temples in the Suruga, Tōtoumi, and Mikawa regions that while Dōshōan previously needed Kasuisai Temple's permission to sell Gedokuen every seven years, henceforth their contract to sell medicine directly to temples would be valid for ten years.[59] What this contract indicates is that Dōshōan was gradually able to sell its medicine with greater autonomy to an ever expanding market, which included even the lowest-level temples.

Another way to gauge the popularity and spread of the medicine is to track the sale of imitation Gedokuen. As the medicine's popularity grew, it invited a corresponding growth in the sale of imitation brands or unlicensed sales of what were purportedly Gedokuen pills. Among Dōshōan's extant documents, more than thirty incidents (see table 6) were recorded between 1607 and 1714, though the earliest incident involved a father and son who were caught by Dōshōan selling fake Gedokuen pills in the Izumi region between 1592 and 1596.[60] Letters sent to Dōshōan accusing certain pharmacists or medicine-hawkers of illegal behavior or signed confessions promising never again to sell imitation Gedokuen are among the extant documents. These incidents involve either the unauthorized sale of Gedokuen (i.e., without Dōshōan's permission), the production and sale of imitation Gedokuen, or the sale of medicine that used names strikingly similar to Gedokuen that were deemed violations of a kind of patent law. For example, according to the 1640 *Nise gedoku hanbai hakkaku ni yori shūchin manbyōen to kaimei ni tsuki issatsu*, the Kyoto pharmacist Myōkan and six others incurred the anger of Dōshōan by selling a herbal pill, "Manbyōen," with a name similar to Dōshōan's product, and had to write a letter of apology.[61] Medical patent law violations took place especially if the medicine was popular, a good example being the sale of the well-known medicine Akadama Jinkyōgan as "Enmei Jinkyōgan" or "Jinrikigan" by unauthorized shops during the late eighteenth century.[62]

In 1663 a contract, the *Dōshōan onkerai no mono kishōmon*, was signed by 156 employees at Dōshōan who solemnly swore not to produce imitation Gedokuen or assist in unauthorized sales.[63] As was common with contracts from the mid-Kamakura period onward, employees signed their name on the back side of a special contract document called a *goō hōin* ("The Seal of the King of Buffaloes"). While there are many interpretations as to the origins of the "goō," it initially developed a reputation as a talisman protecting against epidemics and bad harvests and was issued by a number of well-known shrines and temples, each with its own design, as early as the late Heian period.[64] However, by the mid-Kamakura period, in addition to their talismanic value, *goō hōin* came to be used as sacred documents in which one swore allegiance to a feudal lord, promised not to betray one's co-conspirators in a peasant uprising, and, more generally, made contractual agreements that if broken would result in illness, death, or rebirth in hell.[65]

The Dōshōan contract is one such document, signed on the reverse of a *goō hōin* from Kumano by employees of Dōshōan who demonstrated their

Table 6
Incidents of Counterfeit Gedokuen Sales in the Early Modern Period

Year	Seller of Fake Gedokuen	Accuser(s)	Region of Sales
1607	Hōshōin, Kōjō, Chōjō (priests)	Dōshōan Jin'emon and Tōgorō	near Kyoto
1640	Sōi and his daughter	Shōzaemon and 35 others	Kyoto, Tentō no machi
1640	Sōji and his son	Shinano and 25 others	Kyoto, Furo no zushimachi
1640	Pharmacist Myōkan and 6 others	none (changed name to Manbyōen)	Kyoto, Ōkitanokōji Higashichō
1640	Seizaemon	none (self-confession)	Kyoto, Gojō Daikokuchō
1640	Dōsen of Bizenya	Dōshōan Jinbei	Shinshū Province, Kawanakajima
1640	Seibei and Ninbei	Kanesaburō	Shinshū Province, Matsushiro
1659	Sōshun	Jin'emon and 4 others	n/a
1664	Yasuke	Daitsūji	Jōshū-Gunma
1665	Yasuke	Gijenji	Jōshū-Gunma
1665	Yasuke	Ryūsen'in	Jōshū-Gunma-Koizumimura
1665	Yasuke	Keirinji	Jōshū-Gunma-Yabamura
1665	Yasuke	Ryūkōin	Yashū-Tochigi-Hanedamura
1669	Genzō	Yōan, Chōemon	Kyoto, Kuro-mondōri Danjōchō
1669	Genzō	Dōshōan Kōjun	Kyoto, Kuro-mondōri
1669	Takasaki Shirōbei	Dōshōan Kōjun	n/a
1685	Kyūbei	letter to court regarding lawsuit	Shibaimachi
1688	n/a	Dōshōan Yamauchi Seibei	Osaka
1696	Dōshō	Hashimoto Genshō	n/a
1714	Kurōbei and 1 other	none (self-confession)	n/a
n/a	n/a	Sōneiji Tennin	n/a
n/a	Murata Heiemon, Ichijihachiemon	Dōshōan Teijun	n/a
n/a	n/a	Dōshōan	Edo
n/a	n/a	Chōenji	n/a
n/a	Tokuzaemon	Niemon and Mataemon	Kyoto, Tentō no machi
n/a	Echiri and Yoemon	none (self-confession)	Izu

TABLE 6 (cont.)

Year	Seller of Fake Gedokuen	Accuser(s)	Region of Sales
n/a	n/a	Seishōji Jyotei	n/a
n/a	Nakamura Genbei	Seigenji Chigai	n/a
n/a	Genbei	Daichūji Kōzan	n/a
n/a	Yasuke	Ryūshinji	Sano Mentorimura
n/a	n/a	Seishōji Nyoshū	n/a

seriousness by adding their fingerprints imprinted using their own blood. Because these employees knew the formula for Gedokuen and had the trust of the household to sell the medicine, they also pledged never to reveal the secret formula, to uphold high business standards such as never overcharging, and to refrain from using Dōshōan's profits for their personal affairs. That such measures were made so explicit probably meant that prior to 1663, some employees did make unauthorized Gedokuen sales, shared the formula with a competitor, or spent profits on prostitutes. But the 156 employees who signed this document solemnly swore that if they ever broke these regulations, they would be severely punished by all the kami in Japan, the most common result being to fall terribly ill or to go to hell in the afterlife. A similar document from 1607 was also signed by a former wife of the Dōshōan head upon her divorce, attesting to the early interest to keep the formula a household secret.[66]

Not surprising, given Dōshōan's location, Kyoto-based pharmacists and traveling salespeople were the most frequent outside offenders. However, from as early as 1640 counterfeit Gedokuen was being sold as far away as Shinshū Province, and in 1664–65 there were five similar incidents in Jōshū and Yashū provinces.[67] The majority of these incidents seem to have been the work of one individual, Yasuke. According to the letters from temple informants, Yasuke visited temples such as Daitsūji, Gijenji, Ryūsen'in, Keirinji, and Ryūkōin posing as a pharmacist from Dōshōan. He not only charged the temples for previous deliveries of the medicine by the legitimate Dōshōan representative in the region, Ichirōbee, but sold them defective or "fake" Gedokuen and charged them upfront. Yasuke was caught and severely reprimanded in 1667 and did not face harsh penalties only because Handa Matazaemon and thirteen other Kyoto-based elders pleaded for leniency.[68]

These reports of counterfeit sales in Kyoto seem to have been made by members or informants of the Dōshōan household, while local Sōtō Zen temples were the primary informants in the Jōshū and Yashū cases. Whether it was Dōshōan employees, Sōtō temples selling the medicine, or other authorized distributors of Gedokuen, the primary interest of these parties was to stop unauthorized sales that would cut into their profit margin. As mentioned above, the pill was probably sold for a relatively high price; thus not only cheaper imitations would damage sales receipts, but the reputation of Dōshōan would also be tainted if the medicine was of inferior quality or if the household could not regulate the distribution licensing.

Dōshōan did not deal with offenders independently but used the institutional and legal authority of Eiheiji, and at times the government's Office of Temples and Shrines. Eiheiji abbots signed contracts with Dōshōan guaranteeing the household the exclusive rights for both lodging Sōtō Zen abbots in Kyoto and the sale of medicine to Sōtō Zen temples.[69] With such agreements in hand, Dōshōan not only had the ability to sell directly to temples but had Eiheiji's institutional backing should any temple be associated with unauthorized sales. Furthermore, although Dōshōan was neither a shrine nor a temple, when an incident of counterfeit medicine sales could not be resolved between the household and the offending party, the government's Office of Temples and Shrines was informed and their legal authority brought to bear. For example, in 1685 a pharmacist, Kyūbee, was taken to the Edo "supreme court" for his part in the production of fake Gedokuen.[70] By 1714 a number of incidents of unauthorized sales had also taken place in the cities of Osaka and Edo, but the total number of incidents began to dwindle, suggesting that Dōshōan's efforts to regulate the sale of Gedokuen through the issuance of licenses, informants in Kyoto and local temples, and the legal assistance of Eiheiji and the government's Office of Temples and Shrines had begun to take effect. Offenders were made to write official "letters of apology," which, like many such Tokugawa-period letters, outlined the offense and delivered sincere apologies and pledges never to commit such acts again.[71] That these offenders were caught and that their number went down was clearly related to the strengthening of the head temple–branch temple system and the powers of the government and the head temples to exercise control and implement policies that had become apparent by the early to mid-1700s.

SELLING MEDICINE, STRENGTHENING THE SECT

The period of a little over a hundred years when cheap imitation Gedokuen were sold in a growing number of provinces probably represents the most dynamic growth phase of the medicine. The market for Gedokuen seems to have stabilized by the mid-1700s, by which point Dōshōan sold directly to even the lowest-ranking temples, and competitors for medicine sales within the Sōtō sect were virtually eliminated.

With the dawn of the Meiji period and the transfer of the imperial household to the new capital of Tokyo, Dōshōan's traditional function as a mediator between the imperial house and the Sōtō Zen sect disappeared. According to the March 1880 entry in the *Eiheiji nenpyō*, however, Dōshōan Katsujun (the twenty-seventh generation head) requested permission to continue selling Gedokuen to Sōtō Zen temples as such sales were the only financial source left for Dōshōan.[72] However, the forces of modernity and a series of unfortunate mishaps spelled the doom of Gedokuen. First, Katsu-jun passed away the same year he sent in his request to Eiheiji. And although permission was granted, his two sons, Ryūjū and Ryūki, both died in a steamship accident while on their way to Kyūshū to promote the medicine. The household, near bankruptcy, sold most of their land—a portion of which was bought by Eiheiji—and somehow managed to continue produc-ing the medicine until the Second World War, when the supply of the ingre-dients came to a halt. As mentioned above, the new postwar drug-control laws banned the main ingredient of Gedokuen—the bulb of the *Lycoris ra-diata* herb (*higanbana no kyūkon*)—that effectively put a complete end to the production of what had once been a highly popular Buddhist medicine.[73]

From Dōshōan, this medicine, which had gained sufficient popularity that it invited imitators, was distributed to Sōtō Zen temples throughout Japan for the span of the Tokugawa period. The penetration of this huge market was based on the legend of the sick Dōgen's miraculous recovery, the pro-motion of Gedokuen in Kyoto when abbots lodged at Dōshōan, and direct sales to temples by the pharmacy. Above all, the skillful use of the Sōtō Zen head temple–branch temple system by both Dōshōan and the headquarter temples was a major factor in the medicine's success. By selling medicine, the sect was strengthened both financially and organizationally. Dōshōan benefited tremendously by its connection to Sōtō Zen, but by the same token, the Sōtō school also benefited from having a popular herbal pill linked to their not-so-popular founder, which helped them participate in the burgeoning Buddhist medical business of the Tokugawa period.

Togenuki Jizō: The "Splinter-Removing" Jizō

The best-known Sōtō Zen temple in present-day Tokyo is Kōganji Temple, more commonly known by its main object of worship "Togenuki Jizō" (the Splinter-Removing Jizō bodhisattva). Especially on the monthly *ennichi* (fes-tival day associated with a deity), Kōganji Temple is bustling with older peo-ple, thus earning the nickname "jīsan-bāsan no Harajuku" (the Harajuku of grandpas and grandmas, after the well-known young people's hangout).[74] An early nineteenth-century bakufu-sponsored survey of the main temples in Edo states that Kōganji Temple was founded in 1598 by Fugaku Taijo in the Ochanomizu district of Edo.[75] Although a Jizō statue is listed in the survey as a *hibutsu* (a "hidden Buddha" shown only on special occasions) alongside a statue of Śākyamuni (which was the main image of worship), the popularity of this Jizō cult did not catch the attention of outsiders until the temple moved to the Shitaya district of Edo near present-day Shinobazu Pond.[76] In its new location, this Jizō became known for performing miracu-lous healing and its popularity skyrocketed, especially after popular accounts highlighted these miracles. Accounts of noteworthy places in the city of Edo, such as the 1735 *Zoku Edo sunago onko meisekishi*, reported a new "*hayari* Jizō" (a "Jizō that's all the rage") at the Zen temple Kōganji, claiming, "Those gravely ill or those who have difficult-to-cure ailments, if they get a hold of a talisman of this Jizō statue, will definitely find relief."[77]

The name "Togenuki" (Splinter-Removing) Jizō is derived from the following story found in the 1822 *Enmei Jizōson inkō riyakuki* (A Record of the Benefits of Printing the Image of the Life-Prolonging Jizō).[78]

> For some time, the Zen monk Saijun had visited the Mōri family household [in the city of Edo]. In 1716 a female maid-servant employed by the family had casually placed a broken needle in her mouth while she was sewing and suddenly, accidentally swallowed the needle. The needle got stuck in her throat and then it worked itself down to her stomach which caused her a tremendous amount of pain. Numerous medicines and talismans were used, but to no avail. The monk, Saijun, who was visiting at that time, said, "I have a Jizō talisman that worked a miracle previously; I will give it to you." With that, the female servant drank down the talisman with some water. After a short interval, she vomited and the talisman came out. When the talisman was taken away to be cleaned, they discovered the four-*bu*-long[79] broken needle that had pierced the talisman. Everyone was amazed. Since I didn't hear of this story from just anyone, but from the monk Saijun who came to relate and vouch for this story himself, I have included it in this record of miraculous stories.
>
> Although there were many other amazing things that I witnessed with this talisman, I cannot include them all here. Indeed, I had not readily talked about this story or shown the talisman before; I do so now because the main hall at Kōganji Temple was destroyed and needs to be rebuilt. I told this story to the abbot and also donated a written version of it as well as copies of the talisman because there are plans to form a large association to help rebuild the temple quickly. To these supporters, the abbot has been giving out the miraculous talismans.

The popularity of Togenuki Jizō derived from this story in the mid-Tokugawa period, but the cult of Jizō has its roots in the medieval period. As Manabe Kōsai has suggested in his classic *Jizō bosatsu no kenkyū*,[80] by the late medieval period worship of Jizō had spread widely, based not only on texts considered to be canonical, such as the *Jizō bosatsukyō* or the *Jizō hongankyō*, but also on apocryphal texts such as the *Enmei Jizōkyō*, which expounded on the miraculous and limitless powers of Jizō to prolong life— longevity being a long-standing theme associated with certain Buddhist deities.[81] The Jizō at Kōganji Temple is one such "Enmei Jizō" (Life-Prolonging Jizō); in this case, because the bodhisattva prolonged the woman's life by removing a needle, a "splinter," from her, hence the name "Togenuki Jizō" (Splinter-Removing Jizō).

By the early modern period, Jizō had become pluriform, as evidenced in the association of this deity with a multitude of Buddhas (Amida and Mahāvairocana most commonly), bodhisattvas (Kannon or Fudō), and other non-Japanese deities (Bishamonten or the guardian of hell, Enma), as well as being credited as the "honji" (original source) of Japanese kami such as Atago Myōjin, Kasuga Daimyōjin, and Tateyama Gongen. Also by this period, Jizō had come to be associated with a variety of roles such as reviving believers from death, saving those in hell, guarding travelers, women, and children, and, of most interest to this study, healing a wide range of diseases—particularly diseases that were difficult to cure (*nanbyō*) or so-called karmic diseases (*gōbyō*).

To Drink and Print Talismans: Miracle Tales of the Healing Jizō

The alleged miraculous powers of Jizō to cure illnesses, revive the dead, protect people from hell, provide easy childbirth, and so forth were chronicled in a genre of texts known as *Jizō setsuwa*. Although a number of these compilations of miraculous tales of Jizō have been dated to the medieval period (such as the *Jizō bosatsu reigenki*),[82] most of these texts—with such titles as *Jizō bosatsu rijōki* (1688 by Myōdō Jōe), *Jizō bosatsu riyakushū* (1691 by Myōdō Jōe), *Kōshakushū* (1693 by Rentai), *Enmei Jizō bosatsukyō jikidansho* (1696 by Hitsumu), or the text cited above, the *Enmei Jizōson inkō riyakuki* (1822 by Hissai)—were compiled during the Tokugawa period.[83]

The story of the woman saved by drinking the Jizō talisman is one of twenty-one miracles that are recorded in the *Enmei Jizōson inkō riyakuki* (A Record of the Benefits in Printing the Image of the Life-Prolonging Jizō).[84] This text was compiled in 1822 by Hissai, a Zen monk from Kyoto, and was published in 1844 by Tokugyō, the abbot of the well-known Jōdo-affiliated Ekōin Temple. The text records miracles associated with this "life-prolonging" Jizō dating from 1695 to 1822.[85] Although the story of the woman swallowing the needle and being saved by the talisman occurred a hundred years previously (in 1716), the Zen monk Hissai included it at the beginning of the collection. This was because the Sōtō Zen temple Kōganji needed to raise funds after a devastating fire, and the talismans made from the same printing block were distributed to donors who were told that they, too, could prevent death and illness by drinking the Jizō talisman. Because this text, as with all miraculous tales of deities, was compiled to fit a specific purpose, these stories cannot be read as objectively reflecting the actual Jizō cult. However, even if we acknowledge Hissai's intent to inspire faith for the purpose of soliciting donations for Kōganji Temple's reconstruction, the precise inclusion of names, dates, and the locations of the miracles, which could be verified by readers as they occurred not so long ago, suggests that these stories deserve more credibility than their medieval predecessors. Unlike medieval texts such as the *Jizō bosatsu reigenki*, Tokugawa-period texts like the *Enmei Jizōson inkō riyakuki* contain stories that resonated with the period's readers more as contemporary testimonials than as legends from the medieval period.

The curative ingesting of talismans continues to this day at Kōganji Temple, though the size of the talisman is somewhat smaller than during the Tokugawa period.[86] This practice, while not common in Japan, was certainly not limited to Kōganji Temple during the Tokugawa period. Indeed, it is most likely that the practice of ingesting talismans in the popular cult of Mt. Fuji during the mid-Tokugawa period influenced the Zen monk Saijun's advice to the woman to ingest the talisman.[87] This should remind us that Sōtō Zen priests and parishioners participated in the practices of the larger landscape of Japanese religions during the Tokugawa period.

The miraculous Jizō healing text, in addition to recommending the ingestion of talismans or the sincere worship of Jizō to effect healing miracles, focuses on the practice of printing the Jizō talismans from the wooden printing block held at Kōganji Temple and later copied and held at temples of the Sōtō, Jōdo, Rinzai, and Shingon sects. More specifically, the text instructs the sick patient or a relative to hand print a total of ten thousand talismans and scatter them in a nearby river or the sea, which is why this deity is sometimes known as Ichimantai Jizō or the "Ten Thousand Images Jizō." The practice of making large numbers of Buddhist images dates back to the Heian period when aristocrats prayed for recovery from illnesses through the commissioning of statues.[88] According to the text, the reason for scattering the talismans in nearby waterways is so that fish and other sea-dwelling "dragon and water deities" who did not ordinarily have any contact with Buddhism can become intimate with the Dharma through Jizō melting into the water, even if the print has traveled to the sea from far upstream. Saving other beings, especially those who could not ordinarily come into contact with Buddhism, brought merit to the persons performing or paying for the ritual, the most central benefit highlighted in this cult being healing.

According to the 1822 text, the specifics of how to conduct this ritual cure effected through faith in the Splinter-Removing Jizō included the following:

- The printing of the ten thousand talismans of Jizō should be undertaken by the sick person him or herself. However if the illness is too grave, it is also permissible that a caretaker or a devout believer in Jizō take the sick person's place.
- The paper that should be used for printing these talismans is a sheet of regular-sized paper folded into three lengthwise and into eight along the width. This should produce twenty-four pieces of paper. The number twenty-four is related to the fact that the festival day for Jizō is held on the twenty-fourth of each month. However, this rule of having twenty-four pieces need not be strictly adhered to.[89]
- During the process of printing, idle chatter and joking are not permitted. One should simply intone the Jizō mantra with a sincere heart.
- When it is time to scatter the talismans into a waterway, either a river or the sea can be chosen, whichever is more convenient. If they are many people in the party, the talismans can be divided among them so that the Jizō mantra is recited once with every talisman put into the water. Because it may be logistically

difficult to do this with the time necessary for this ritual, it is also permissible to recite the Jizō mantra ten thousand times back at the house. One can then go out to a waterway and chant the sacred name as it seems fit.

• If the ritual is to take place at the beach, while there are those who say that one should set up a small table on a boat with offerings of incense, flowers, candles, pure water, drink, and food, or give obeisance to dragon and water deities, these types of attention-grabbing activities should be avoided because these acts detract from the true meaning and power of the ritual. One should therefore perform the ritual as discreetly as possible.

While it was preferable, according to the text, that the sick person make ten thousand talismans him or herself out of paper cut in twenty-four pieces and intone "Namu Jizō Daibosatsu" (Homage to the Great Bodhisattva Jizō) both at the time of printing and when scattering the talismans, these rules were not rigid. If the particular circumstances of the patient made it difficult, the text allows significant leeway both in changing the number of talismans printed and the identity of the person printing or reciting the Jizō mantra, under one condition—that all involved sincerely believe in the power of Jizō. This sole condition was what saved or did not save the sick person. This aspect of the Jizō healing cult distinguishes it from the herbal pills discussed above. For while Gedokuen's efficacy depended on its sacred origins, since it was part of a larger culture of treatment through herbs, seasonings, and plants, it belonged more to what Demiéville classified as "medical therapeutics proper (dietetics, pharmacy, surgery)" than to "magical therapeutics (mantras, incantations, esoteric ritual)." In the case of the Jizō healing cult, sincere faith appears to be the sole criterion for recovery. The singular importance of faith is highlighted in the following, one of the few stories in the *Enmei Jizōson inkō riyakuki* that does not involve healing as such, but the prolongation of life through revival from death.[90]

> In the city of Osaka, a rich man had heard of the miraculous powers of the great Jizō bodhisattva. He thought that if he had the ten thousand talismans made, he could obtain worldly prosperity [for his family business]. He thus ordered one of his young apprentices in the business to start making the prints though he went about his business as usual—being greedy from morning till evening and engaging in business practices completely alien to the Buddhist path. The young boy did as his master ordered, though reluctantly and without any religious devotion. Humming tunes and printing the talismans absentmindedly, bored as he was with this task, he eventually printed three thousand. Of course, humming while printing the talismans or the like is extremely disrespectful to the bodhisattva, so the boy thought that he might at least relieve his boredom by making a few prints with a more solemn attitude and recite the sacred mantra of Jizō. He ended up making five such talismans while intoning the sacred name.
>
> But all of a sudden, the boy inexplicably toppled over and died. Everyone in the household was shocked and tried to attend to him. Fortunately, soon thereafter, the boy revived to everyone's amazement and joy. They asked him what had hap-

pened and he replied: "While I was printing the Jizō talismans, I felt as though I had fallen into a deep well. I found myself in the middle of a large wild expanse and wondered where in the world I was. Before I could make head or tail of the situation, a blue demon came out of nowhere and captured me and tied me up. I was so frightened that though I tried to escape, I couldn't. It was then that I saw several dozen monks in the distance and I called out to them for help. With an eerie demeanor they just stood there grinning and looking on until maybe five or six of them came over with their staffs to hit and chase off the demon. I was so relieved and wanted to thank them, but before I could say anything, one of the monks said, 'Your master is very greedy and is always engaged in activities alien to the Buddhist path. Never thinking about the future, he only concerns himself with profiting in the present. This is a sure path for falling into the realm of the hungry ghosts.[91] Make sure to relate this to your master when you return to the *saha* world.' "[92]

The moral of this story is clearly that the talismans must be made with deep faith, honorable intentions, and a sincere heart. This story highlights the power of even a small number of talismans made in such a manner. If five talismans could rescue the boy from demons and from death, the text seems to suggest that great miracles could occur if even more talismans were printed with a sincere heart. This story of revival from death is the most extreme example in the text. Indeed, the stories recorded describe the cure of a wide range of illnesses: tuberculosis (2 stories), hereditary illness (2), typhoid fever (2), high fever (2), leprosy (2), stomach pains (2), inability to urinate (1), impotence (1), skin rash (1), and eye disease (1).[93]

As can be seen from table 7, the illnesses that were reportedly healed through Jizō's miraculous powers can be categorized into two types: difficult-to-cure diseases (*nanbyō*) and karmic diseases (*gōbyō*). In the difficult-to-cure category, each miraculous tale contains similar motifs. First, an illness—whether an ordinarily curable ailment or a normally incurable epidemic disease—becomes life-threatening. The Jizō talisman works its miracle only after treatments from doctors and from other Buddhist healing rituals have proved unsuccessful. When all conventional treatments have been exhausted, the illness is considered "difficult-to-cure." The compiler seems to want to point out the effectiveness of Jizō's healing power, particularly for "last resort" situations. This emphasis clearly distinguishes the medical category of these talismans from the herbal pills discussed above. While the herbal pills have the power to cure "any illness," they are principally used as remedies for more common ailments like stomach upsets, colds, and other non-life-threatening illnesses. With the pill, there were precise instructions on how to prepare dosage and mixtures for each specific ailment. With the Jizō talismans, there is no customization of treatment to illness, the basic "instructions" boil down to having faith in the power of both the ritual and—more importantly—in the power of Jizō.

Another type of disease cured by faith healing, as distinguished from

TABLE 7
Miracle Stories in the *Enmei Jizōson inkō riyakuki*

Year	Region	Person	Gender	Problem	Ritual
1713	Edo	wife of Tatsuke	F	Possessed by spirit	Printing
1715	Edo	servant of Mōri	F	Stomach pains	Drink talisman
1756	Edo	Kobanawa	M	Hereditary illness	Printing
1757	Izumo	Shintō priest	M	Tuberculosis	Printing
1761	Izumo	child of farmer	n/a	Hereditary illness	Printing
1766	Bungo	monk Zenso	M	Typhoid fever	Printing
1770	Bungo	wife of Sajibei	F	Typhoid fever	Printing
1770	Osaka	merchant's girl	F	Inability to urinate	Printing
1770	Osaka	unnamed man	M	High fever	Printing
1770	Ikeda	rich merchant	M	Leprosy	Printing
1771	Bungo	4-year-old girl	F	High fever	Printing
1771	Osaka	apprentice boy	M	Died	Printing
1776	Bungo	monk Shinkōji	M	Lost money	Printing
1695	Kashū	Takeuchi	M	Leprosy	Statue worship
n/a	Kyoto	workman Ganō	M	Went to hell	Statue worship
1809	Osaka	servant	M	Tuberculosis	Printing
n/a	Kyoto	16-year-old girl	F	About to commit suicide	Printing
1822	Kyoto	unnamed man	M	Impotence	Printing
n/a	Kyoto	unnamed man	M	Skin rash	Printing
1812	Kyoto	unnamed man	M	Eye disease	Printing
n/a	Kyoto	unnamed man	M	Lost calligraphy	Printing

herbal pills, is karmic diseases. These include illnesses that emerge either in an individual (a disease that is the result of an individual's bad karma) or a family (a hereditary illness that is passed down generations because of accumulated bad karma) level. The notion of karmic diseases is, of course, not limited to Japanese Buddhism, but as Terry Clifford has suggested in the case of Tibetan Buddhism, "Since the effects of the karma of previous lives may be felt in the present, some diseases are said to have a purely spiritual or karmic cause. According to Tibetan medicine, these demand, instead, spiritual or religious treatments to cure them on a level that parallels their source."[94]

To return to our 1822 Japanese text, the following story illustrates how karmic diseases could be cured with faith in Jizō.

In the spring of 1695 the Jūrindō Hall at Henshōji Temple (Kashū Province) was under construction. A great number of devoted men and women were assisting in its construction by helping carry the building materials such as soil, wood, bamboo, and stones. A man named Takenouchi lived in the village of Ashigaru, which was located behind Henshōji Temple. He was very poor and furthermore he had contracted leprosy, so it was hard for him to face his neighbors with his disfigured face. Isolated in his own hut, he nevertheless wished he could engage in devotional activities just like everyone else by carrying the building materials for the new Jūrindō Hall. Reluctantly, he remained in his humble home, not wanting to venture out to help because of his leprosy. However, he reverently intoned the name of Jizō from the confines of his own home, regretting that his karmic burden was so heavy and sincerely owning up to all his faults.

Soon thereafter, the construction of the Jūrindō Hall was complete and everyone, rich and poor, young and old, found time to stop working so that they could visit Henshōji for the Buddha-installation ceremony [that would officially mark the opening of the temple]. Hearing about the opening of the temple, Takenouchi felt an even keener wish to come closer to Jizō and, bowing deeply toward the direction of the temple, prayed to the bodhisattva. The earnestness of this man's faith was not lost on Jizō, and that night, Takenouchi saw an image of Jizō in a dream. Jizō preached the Dharma to him and explained that he was afflicted with his terrible illness because of bad karma that he had accumulated in the past. But Jizō also told the man, "Whatever your past, if you continue to be devoted to me with all your heart, the bad karma will immediately disappear and your illness will gradually be cured. Indeed, if you show unswerving faith in me, you will certainly be reborn as a human being in a noble family and live a long life free from illness. And ultimately, through faith in me, you will finally be able to cut off all bondage to the world [and achieve final liberation]." Having received these instructions from the deity, the man carried them out and soon found that his leprosy was cured. What a wondrous miracle!

In this story, Jizō intervened to help a man suffering from leprosy induced by bad karma in the past. For many Tokugawa-period Japanese, who believed in such karmic origins for a host of diseases (especially leprosy), it was inconceivable that conventional medical treatment could effect a cure. Such diseases required not so much medical attention as the removal of bad karma. In this case, the text explains this theory of karmic diseases: Jizō speaks directly to Takenouchi, and not only a medical recovery, but a "social recovery" too, are effected through the man's faith.

With the case of leprosy in particular, the sufferer was burdened not only with physical illness, but, as Takenouchi's story suggests, with many associated stigmas. Lepers were social outcasts because of the disease. Buddhist theories that the disease had karmic origins, in fact, contributed to the social discrimination faced by those afflicted with leprosy, though in the late Heian and early Kamakura periods, lepers were treated at Buddhist hospices, the most famous being that run by the monk Ninshō, who had set up a leprosaria with steam-baths at Saidaiji and Gokurakuji temples. But by the mid-Kamakura period, the mainstream Buddhist view on leprosy had changed.[95] Many sutras of Indian origin had identified leprosy as an illness born of bad karma accumulated in the past, and with the rise of *Lotus Sutra*-based cults, the idea that leprosy was the result of speaking ill of Buddhism and of the *Lotus Sutra* in particular had gained firm hold.[96] Both the second and seventh chapters of the *Lotus Sutra* contain passages equating illness, particularly leprosy, with speaking poorly of the sutra in a previous life. Having offended the Dharma, such people would return in a subhuman category. The Jizō text also seems to adopt this view, as the bodhisattva promises Takenouchi that, "if you show unswerving faith in me, you will certainly be reborn as a human being in a noble family and live a long life free from illness."

The logic behind karmic diseases, then, was that if offending the Dharma in a previous life caused the disease, having faith in Buddhism could undo the illness. As Michel Strickmann has noted of the Chinese Buddhist tradition, "Sacred scriptures were definitely not to be trifled with; if they can protect against all harm and heal all manner of afflictions, they can also infect."[97] By the mid-Tokugawa period, Nichiren temples focusing on the *Lotus Sutra* actively encouraged lepers to come to their temples to pray to rid themselves of the bad karma that caused the disease in the first place through devotion to the *Lotus Sutra*.[98] Whether it be through devotion to a sutra or to a bodhisattva like Jizō, there was a belief that both "karmic" and "difficult-to-cure" illnesses lay outside the power of ordinary medical treatments.[99]

Returning to table 7, we can also see how this Jizō faith-healing cult spread from Kōganji Temple in Edo City to regions all over Japan. The printing blocks for the Jizō talismans proliferated throughout Japan, as did the ritual of scattering the prints into waterways. Of the twenty-one stories, fifteen take place in or around one of the major urban centers of the period, namely, Edo, Osaka, Kyoto, and Kanazawa (listed on the chart as Kashū); also notable is the concentration of stories in the provinces of Izumo and Bungo. Often, the cult spread to a new region via a traveling monk or a merchant who donated a talisman or the printing block used to print the talismans to a local temple. The clustering of miracle tales in these regions can be attributed to the way in which the powers of the bodhisattva to treat ailments spread by word of mouth. What is of interest is not only how this healing cult became diffuse geographically, but that the cult of the healing Jizō is clearly not in the exclusive domain of the religious specialists. The compiler, Hissai, may or may not be reflecting a representative group with his selections of the miraculous stories, but what we can be sure of is that he wanted the reader to notice how Jizō responds to all that have faith, from lepers to rich merchants, servants to farmers, and small children to the elderly.

Faith in Jizō spread not through sectarian networks of head-branch temple structures, but through a variety of informal networks. Though the 1822 *Enmei Jizōson inkō riyakuki* was the product of a Zen monk named Hissai, it was published by a Jōdo monk named Tokugyō. Likewise, although the original woodblock for the Jizō talisman was held at the Sōtō Zen Kōganji Temple, most of the other temples identified as having copies of the printing block are other Sōtō Zen temples, as well as Jōdo, Rinzai Zen, and Shingon sect temples. In each case, the presentation of the healing Jizō would be subtly recast to conform to sectarian ideals. As a Jōdo-sect Amidist in charge of publishing a work compiled by a Zen monk, Tokugyō, for example, felt the need to justify his endeavor by stressing the identity of Jizō with Amida Buddha. In his epilogue to the Zen monk's work, he writes:

> Originally Jizō was known as the "Treasure-Bearing Tathagata [Buddha] of the South,"[100] but according to the deep, hidden teachings of the *Renge Zammai Sutra*,[101] Jizō is identified as a transformation-body of the Amida Buddha of the highest Western Pure Land who saves all sentient beings. This is why people of old have thought that the character "zō" in Jizō is the same as the "zō" in Hōzō [otherwise known as Hōzō Bosatsu or Amida Buddha]. Therefore even whilst having faith in the great bodhisattva, one should also recite the *nenbutsu* [the sacred name of Amida] to ensure rebirth in the Pure Land. This would be in accord with the bodhisattva Jizō's original intentions, as Jizō's original identity is Amida Buddha.

Each sect, then, interpreted this healing bodhisattva in a way palatable to its own sectarian frameworks.

The transsectarian nature of Jizō is also emphasized within the stories themselves. One relates the miracle of how even someone outside the Buddhist fold, a Shintō priest—the text notes that many of them are anti-Buddhist—can be healed.

> In the province of Izumo, there is a village called Higashiemura in the Tatenui district where a Shintō priest named Yashio lived. He was in charge of the shrine dedicated to Tonda myōjin. In his household, tuberculosis was a hereditary disease and family members died of it generation after generation. Yashio also died of this disease. Having no one to inherit his position, his younger brother named Shikibu became the head of the family and changed his name to Onoe. When [Onoe] reached the age of twenty, he also became afflicted with tuberculosis, and neither medical treatment nor prayers produced any hopes for recovery. Generally speaking, as a Shintō believer, he had been critical of and shown animosity toward Buddhism. But having heard of the story of [this healing Jizō], he used the wooden printing block from Kongōji Temple to make ten thousand talisman prints. He then intoned the sacred mantra [of Jizō] and scattered the prints into the sea. In time, his illness completely disappeared.

What this story points to is a larger phenomenon during the Tokugawa period in which cults of certain deities, most prominently Jizō, Kannon, Fudō, Yakushi, and Inari, did not respect the denominational or "tradition"-based temple and shrine boundaries. Each sect incorporated these popular cults—and Sōtō Zen was a leader in this regard—to draw believers to particular temples and their deities, as parish temples alone could not bring dynamism to their school.

While the example of the Jizō talisman suggests that Sōtō Zen participated in a transsectarian religious culture, the example of the herbal pill Gedokuen discussed earlier indicates the role played by medicine in strengthening sectarian identity through head- and branch-temple hierarchies. Indeed, the history of Sōtō Zen in the Tokugawa period is driven by a dual impulse to heighten sectarian ties on the one hand and to participate in a common religious culture on the other. Sōtō Zen could expand into so many regions precisely because both orientations coexisted.

We began this chapter with Demiéville's admission that the lines of demarcation that he created for the study of Buddhist approaches to illness are not entirely clear but are distinct enough to be broadly useful. I have also identified two types of movements in Sōtō Zen and healing—the sect-centered medicine and the transsectarian healing cult—though they are not completely distinct.

SENRYŪJI TEMPLE'S "DREAM MEDICINE" AND SMALLPOX TALISMANS

One good example of the overlapping of categories is the medical and healing practices conducted in the late Tokugawa period at Senryūji Temple, a Sōtō Zen temple located in Komae, present-day Tokyo.[102] This temple, perhaps best known for the popularity of its "Mawari Jizō" in the late eighteenth century, sold a medicine called Musōgan as well as the deity Benzaiten's talismans for preventing smallpox.[103] Musōgan, given its name "Dream/Vision-Medicine," probably appeared to the priest of Senryūji Temple in a dream, though there are no extant documents on the origins of this medicine. Unlike Gedokuen, the medicine was not a cure-all, as it purportedly treated only childhood and animal diseases. The instructions (fig. 6) that accompany the medicine read:

> Musōgan—Best medicine for children with weak constitutions. Take with boiled water that has cooled down. If taken this way, [the child] will recover from all sickness. If your cows or horses get sick. Mix and dissolve the medicine in water before giving it to the animal. Senryūji Temple in Izumi Village near the Tama River in Bushū Tama District.[104]

In this sense, Musōgan functioned as a pill much like Gedokuen in that precise preparation was required for specific ailments.

Although this medicine was sold from the temple, both to parishioners and to the many pilgrims who came to pay homage to their famous "Mawari Jizō," Senryūji Temple also offered talismans for the prevention of smallpox to believers in the temple's Kannon or Benzaiten statues. In a mid-nineteenth-century document on how to prevent smallpox, passed down from abbot to abbot, it is clear that the Sōtō Zen priests there believed that only faith could cure smallpox.[105]

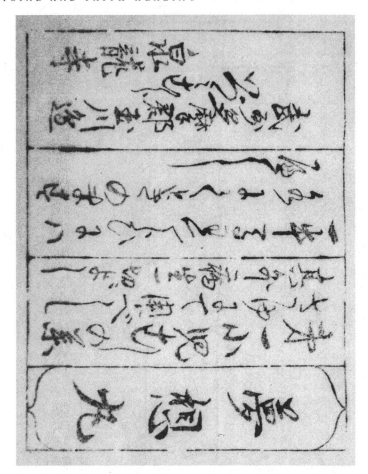

Figure 6. Senryūji's Musōgan medicine wrapper. Senryūji Temple, Komae City.

THINGS TO REMEMBER FOR PREVENTING SMALLPOX

The following Truth should be secretly transmitted to one's disciple. This document reveals how the Honji Shō Kanzeon responds to our needs and protects us. When winter comes, one should take a chicken's egg and perform prayers and incantations around it. At around six in the evening on an auspicious day, one should pray that all human smallpox be transformed and directed into the egg. Through this special method, a person afflicted with smallpox will become like an egg. That is, a prayer should be said to make the afflicted person's skin as smooth as the egg. The benefit [of such a prayer] is that the egg will take on the pox and the human body will recover. This method is called "bird-shining." For a person who is full of faith and never doubts this method is assured a life free from smallpox. But if one has the faintest doubt, for example, if one gets a fever when smallpox is affecting people close by and one thinks it might be smallpox, then indeed one may get smallpox. However even in this case, while the fever may remain, there will be no scars or disfigurement from the pox. If one is actually diagnosed with smallpox, one should take the talisman on the box (with the egg that has received prayers and incantations) outside. That talisman should be buried by the side of the shrine to Inari, our protector-deity. Those who are not afflicted with smallpox should always revere the talisman and the box with the egg, both of which should be placed on their house kami shrine shelf. Senryūji Temple in Izumi Village, of the Setagaya area in Bushū Tama district.[106]

This example of transferring smallpox into a chicken egg through prayer, keeping a talisman (see fig. 7) to ward off smallpox at one's house, and believing in the deity's power to heal is much closer to the Jizō faith-healing ideology.[107] As Hartmut Rotermund and Ann Jannetta have discussed, epidemics such as smallpox and measles, diseases that were increasingly prevalent in the eighteenth to nineteenth centuries in Edo and other cities, gave rise to many different forms of religious remedies to prevent epidemics similar to the Senryūji Temple case.[108] For example, the rising belief in the protective powers of Sagi Daimyōjin, a subshrine deity from the Grand Shrine at Izumo, to prevent smallpox by enshrining a talisman and a small stone from Izumo within one's house was a good example of this phenomenon.[109] Sōtō Zen temples in other parts of Japan, such as Tokuunji Temple in Shinshū Province, upon hearing of the smallpox epidemics in the city of Edo, also conducted special smallpox prevention ceremonies with special recitations of the *Great Perfection of Wisdom Sutra*.[110]

The Senryūji Temple smallpox prevention can therefore be thought of as one case in a much larger phenomenon of Buddhist and other deities being called on to cure ordinarily fatal diseases, a development that transcended sectarianism. In this way, Senryūji Temple's Musōgan pill is similar to Gedokuen, while the smallpox-prevention talisman resembles the key features of Jizō faith healing. What the Senryūji Temple example suggests is the fluidity of categories that existed at Sōtō Zen temples, defying later scholarly attempts to identify clean-cut categories. It was precisely this combined practice of selling divinely inspired medicine and faith-based talismans that gave dynamism to healing practices at Sōtō Zen temples.[111]

In thinking about the spread of Sōtō Zen and its incorporation into local society, the demonstration of the practical benefit of healing cannot be underestimated. When the female servant of the Mōri family ingested the Zen monk's talisman to cure what no other known therapy could heal, she accepted the Zen monk, Jizō bodhisattva, and the miraculous powers associated with them in the most direct sense possible. This type of physical incorporation of a tradition can be seen broadly in the history of religions, for example, in Sudanese Islam, where Koranic verses written on paper with ink made from soot and gum arabic are washed off with water that is then drunk by the patient.[112] In the Buddhist tradition, Strickmann has noted the

疱瘡除
和泉
辨財天

雲松山龍泉禅寺

Figure 7. Senryūji's Benzaiten smallpox talisman. Senryūji Temple, Komae City.

swallowing of the spell of Jāngulī to protect against all forms of toxic en-venomations,[113] while Brown has observed the power of water to transmit the power of Buddhism in his study of oath-taking in Sumatra and Thai-land, stating, "The notion of an oath being sworn by drinking water that has touched an object of power is well known in many areas of Southeast Asia.... It implies the ability of water to absorb and transfer the 'power' of an object, so that the oath-taker literally ingests this supernatural power."[114] In Japan, an early example of healing through the literal ingestion of the su-pernatural powers associated with Buddhism can be found in the Heian-period text, the *Genji monogatari*, which relates an episode when Genji vis-ited a holy man who prescribed the swallowing of talismans inscribed with Sanskrit *siddham* to cure a recurrent fever.[115] During the Tokugawa period, Mt. Fuji pilgrimage associations imbibed healing talismans, while at Mt.

Ōyama, believers swallowed pieces of Fudō Myōō's rope, and villagers ingested segments of the *Taima mandala* as a prophylatic against epidemics in Fukushima.[116] The absorption of Buddhism into the material body in these ways suggests the physicality of Buddhist healing practices. For Sōtō Zen temples to spread in local society, it had to participate in the work of this-worldly Buddhism, the alleviation of suffering in all its forms.

The Other Side of Zen

IN TOKUGAWA-PERIOD Sōtō Zen Buddhism, the boundaries between this world and the next—and between funerals and memorial services, translocal and local practices, sectarian and transsectarian institutions, medicine and faith healing—were important and yet malleable. Sōtō Zen operated well in this ambiguous world of multiple meanings and practices that allowed the sect to grow as a part of the larger landscape of Japanese religions without losing its distinctiveness.

This conclusion begins with a translation of a Tokugawa-period ghost story that took place at the Sōtō Zen temple, Jōsenji. Much like other legends of beings traversing this world and the world beyond, the story of the young girl Kiku takes place in the in-between world that was populated by Zen priests, Buddhist deities, ordinary villagers and townspeople, along with ghosts and demons that were central to the Sōtō Zen tradition. Famous monks, Zen meditation, philosophical concepts, and the "high culture" aspects of the tradition were not absent in this world, but our previous scholarly privileging of this side of Zen has obscured a far more complex and messy picture of the "other side of Zen."

THE YOUNG GIRL KIKU AND THE VALUABLE PLATE

During the Jōō era (1652–54), a powerful samurai family named Aoyama lived near our temple. At that time, in the Yotsuya-Ōkido District [of Edo City], there was a beautiful, willowlike girl named Kiku, the daughter of the dashing gentleman, Mukaizaki Jinnai.[1] For reasons unknown, Kiku had started working [as a maid] at the Aoyama household.[2] At the residence, there was a collection of ten plates that had long been a family heirloom, but one day, Kiku accidentally broke one of them.[3] It goes without saying that she went into a state of panic. Aoyama's wife, having been jealous of Kiku's beauty for some time, used this incident to say some terrible things about the girl to her husband. The husband did get rather upset but ultimately decided that since it was not as much of a disaster [as his wife made it out to be], Kiku's punishment would consist of having a finger cut off.[4] To atone for her deed, she was also to be locked away [in a room] for a short while.

But [after a few days], Kiku could not bear her suffering any longer. So one night, when the house guard was distracted, she escaped [from the room]. In a sad end to her life, she plunged into the well at the edge of the house compound.[5] That night, a ball of fire swept up out from the well. With a dank, warm wind blowing, Kiku's ghostly figure appeared. A melancholy voice began counting, "one, two, . . ." over and over again [up to ten]. Everyone who heard it was scared out of their wits because it was not a sound, such as from insects of the field, that anyone could identify. Fortunately [just then], a venerable monk [happened to come by]. He saved Kiku [from her ghostly existence by bestowing a Zen lineage chart upon her]. But some time later, when Zen Master Funrei (the third abbot of our temple) was engaged in evening Zen meditation, Kiku's ghostly figure reappeared. She had come to meet the master. He proclaimed the following Dharma words to her, "If you want to go back to heaven again, you must make an offering of one plate." We have recorded this incident here as it provides everyone with a suitable story to do good and avoid evil. Jōsenji Temple in the Kōjimachi District [Edo City].[6]

This condensed narrative of the origins of the worship of a special plate at Jōsenji Temple that the ghost Kiku allegedly left behind, the late-Tokugawa period *The Origins of the Girl Kiku's Plate* (*Kikunyo sara no raiyu*), contains many of the themes taken up in this study. From the late seventeenth century, Jōsenji Temple held occasional public viewings of a ceramic plate that had been offered to free Kiku's ghost.[7] Just as with the public displays of the Dōryō statue at festival times at Daiyūzan Temple, the spiritual value of this ceramic plate derived from the fact that it was concealed except on special, rare occasions. The significance of displaying Kiku's plate, however, also came from the fact that the people who flocked to Jōsenji Temple saw the plate as evidence from the other world that Zen priests were able to save those who had fallen into a miserable state in the world beyond.[8] Such salvation was framed not in terms of entering a state of nirvana, but as a powerful disruption and reversal of the karmic spiral, which Kiku had brought upon herself first by breaking a plate and then by taking her own life. This act pulled her down toward the hungry ghost and hell realms. That Kiku traveled between ghostly, heavenly, and human realms reflected the fluidity of the Buddhist cosmos, and the point of such a narrative for the temple must have been to highlight the power of Zen priests to influence matters in the world beyond.

The plate also functioned like other mementos left behind by ghosts or other suffering beings (such as ghost sleeves or fish scales) as material evidence of salvation through the bestowal of precepts or the Zen lineage chart. Similarly, tokens of appreciation from those saved, such as the Gedokuen herbal medicine from the dragon girl in the Dōgen puppet play, or spring waters from the local deities at Daiyūzan, were concrete manifestations of faith that Sōtō Zen temples could highlight to attract and maintain parishioners. The public display and sharing of such sacralized objects allowed ordinary priests and parishioners to participate in a religious world that did not require a special study of the writings of the classic Zen masters or meditative experiences, but rather required faith in the power of a small group of extraordinary Zen priests and what they represented.

"CERAMIC PLATE" AND "ORDINARY PLATE" PRIESTS

Turning to modern times, on a special occasion, we might bring out our most expensive dinner service—ceramic plates usually stored safely away. On the other hand, for regular meals, we probably use cheaper ordinary plates. If Kiku had broken an ordinary plate, the Aoyama family may have ignored the incident or at least meted out a lesser punishment.

Once Kiku had become a ghost, the plate that she brought from the other world to Jōsenji Temple came to hold special value, precisely because it was an extraordinary plate that helped her ascend to heaven. Further, among residents of Edo, this plate became known as an object that could impart various types of practical benefits, especially on the special days when the plate was displayed. High value is often assigned to the rare and extraordinary, while the ordinary and routine aspects of life, crucial to day-to-day living, are not as noticeable.

In Sōtō Zen Buddhism, there have been two types of priests. First are those endowed with extraordinary meditative powers and magical techniques who, in legends, save people, ghosts, and gods: medieval priests such as Dōgen, Ryōan, or Gennō, and Tokugawa-period priests such as Suzuki Shōsan, San'ei Honshū, or Funrei (featured in the Kiku story above). These priests are what might be termed "ceramic plate priests," extraordinary exemplars brought out of the cupboard of the Sōtō Zen tradition in times of proselytization (such as the association of Dōgen with saving ghosts or promoting medicine), at critical junctures (such as to gain patronage from local officials), or on special occasions (such as the Great Festival Day when Dōryō's power to prevent fires was heightened). I began this study arguing against a style of Zen historiography that concentrated exclusively on such extraordinary priests. And though I have deliberately decentered them, a social history of Sōtō Zen must include these figures. Their role in the construction of the tradition needs to be further studied, though future research might benefit from placing them more firmly in the broader social and institutional landscape that this research has depicted.

In contrast to these special priests were the vast majority of ordinary priests who served the bulk of the more than seventeen thousand Sōtō Zen temples in Tokugawa Japan. These priests rarely, if ever, engaged in Zen meditation or the study of Dōgen's writings, but they performed the prayers for healing or the ancestral memorial services for the ordinary parish members. These "ordinary plate priests" have been generally considered unworthy of study by Zen historians because they were so ordinary as to be negligible. In contrast, this study has tried to demonstrate that they were, in fact, a critical force in the formation of Sōtō Zen Buddhism because they are the ones who maintained the day-to-day contact with parishioners. It was they, and not the extraordinary priests, who mediated disputes such as over the fight that broke out with the drunken Dōryō association members, who dis-

tributed talismans and medicine, prayed for rain, registered parishioners for
the village headman, gave posthumous names to the ancestors of villagers,
and held Blood Pool Hell sutra ceremonies for women's groups. While Sōtō
Zen as an institution relied on the extraordinary priests to provide powerful
symbols of the special powers that Zen priests derived from Zen meditation,
the organization equally depended on ordinary village and town priests to
maintain the temples and the parish structures that formed the sect's foundation during the Tokugawa period. Indeed, it was the accumulated history
of these ordinary priests that formed each temple's Zen lineage. Over time,
even ordinary plates gain a certain value.

In this study, like Kiku, I broke some sacred plates of Zen historiography
by decentering the extraordinary Zen priests and focusing instead on the
ordinary priests who played a crucial role in the formation of the sect as a
social and cultural institution with a broad appeal. Similar to Kiku, I entered another world inhabited by ordinary priests and laypeople such as Isshin Gyōja (the charismatic pilgrim leader at Daiyūzan) or Towa (the female
parishioner sexually harassed by a parish priest). By doing so, I brought
back a new plate that might be of equal value to the older sacred plates, in
that it might better present Sōtō Zen in actual practice as a vital social institution, rather than as a static ideal.

This study of the other side of Zen highlighted the work of these ordinary
Zen priests and wove them and their parishioners into the discourse. While
hagiographical accounts of the "great monks" have tended to highlight their
superhuman abilities, by employing new types of sources such as temple diaries, letters regarding legal disputes, and fund-raising logbooks, I have tried
to present a more human picture of ordinary Sōtō Zen priests. Having to respond concretely to such social and political realities as the bakufu and head
temple regulations, local villagers' funerary customs, and the financial im-
peratives of maintaining a temple, Sōtō Zen priests can be seen as complex
individuals who struggled with everyday human issues. Only when we examine the human aspects of ordinary priests' lives can we understand the
gaps, tensions, and disconnections between such priests and legendary or
high-ranking priests.

ORDER AND MESS

Although the validity of the dichotomies between "high and low" and "elite
and popular" religion and culture have been rightly questioned in recent
years, an all-too-easy erasure of difference, based not on empirical research
but on theory, must be equally scrutinized. The extraordinary and ordinary
priests of the Sōtō Zen world coexisted in a mutually dependent manner, in
a holistic continuum that constituted the Sōtō Zen priestly order, yet which
at other times was a disjointed, contradictory, and tension-filled mess.[9] Sōtō
Zen Buddhism was able to maintain itself and grow during the Tokugawa

period in part because "order" (whether doctrinal, priestly, or political) and a more ambiguous and convoluted reality were rarely examined side by side. Priests who questioned this state of affairs, such as those in the so-called sect restoration movement, stand out precisely because they were so rare. Ordered consistency within religious traditions was simply not a priority for most priests, whether between contradictory doctrinal positions, such as that of the immediate salvation at the funeral and gradual care of the ancestors, or between cross-purposes within a sect mainly concerned with performing funerary and prayer rituals despite Dōgen's advocacy of monasticism and Zen meditation. Modern scholars attempt to make sense of and provide order to research topics, but efforts to find consistency may also prove fruitless.

For instance, although this study differentiates between the other-world salvation and management of the dead (chapters 2–3) and this-world benefits (chapters 4–5), this was primarily for the heuristic purposes of distinguishing parish and prayer temples as ideal types. Such ideal typologies, however, must ultimately give way to a much more ambiguous representation of Sōtō Zen in which this-world benefits (like medicine, healing, rain making, and protection from disasters) interacted with and were mutually dependent on funerary salvation or appeasement of ancestral and ghost spirits in the other world. As we saw with the *Blood Pool Hell Sutra*, the same text was employed at Sōtō Zen temples both to ensure salvation in the next world and to erase impurities or achieve easy childbirth in this world. Indeed, it was not simply sutras and statues at temples, but Sōtō Zen priests themselves who stood at the precipice bordering this world and the next, serving both the living and the dead, on both sides of that fluid boundary.

And yet, Sōtō Zen as an institution was, without doubt, consolidated during the first half of the Tokugawa period. Looser medieval forms of authority within the sect made way for more clearly hierarchical pyramidal structures, such as the head-branch temple and the regional administrative temple systems. For the first time, these structures organized a legally and institutionally independent Sōtō Zen order that transcended regional and lineage boundaries to encompass the whole of Japan. This government-mandated order, which was strengthened or weakened in accordance with the political strength of the bakufu and the domains, molded the very foundations of the Sōtō Zen sect. In other words, while Sōtō Zen consisted of a multiplicity of regional and lineage variations with a fluid nonsectarian dimension, it simultaneously had to operate as an institutional unit prescribed by the Tokugawa regime.

Far from transcending historical or sociopolitical considerations, the seventeen thousand temples of Sōtō Zen were deeply enmeshed in this early modern order. While prayer temples such as Daiyūzan or head training monasteries such as Eiheiji served as important nodes in the Sōtō Zen temple network, the overwhelming majority of Sōtō Zen temples were smaller parish temples. The funerary ritual life at such parish temples, based on the emergent idea of a parish household, was directly linked to the bakufu-mandated temple registration system designed to control Christians and later to monitor the entire Japanese population. Because the Sōtō Zen sect established a large number of temples in thousands of villages throughout Japan, rather than concentrating on a few large or prestigious temples in the major cities, it took advantage of every villager's mandate to become affiliated with a temple. In fact, it was not until the implementation of this system that the physical building of what we now regard as temples became widespread across Japan. Thus, though Sōtō Zen parish temples, along with similar temples of other sects, served as critical elements in enforcing the Tokugawa regime's sociopolitical order, this order in turn helped the Sōtō Zen sect construct its physical institutions.

The ritual duties and financial duties of temple parishioners meant that they were not simply being asked, but were obligated, to support their parish temple. The consequences of disobedience were harsh: defaulters were branded as heretics or taken "off register" to be shunned as social outcasts. While the Sōtō Zen sect drew adherents through promoting the extraordinary abilities of its priests to save the dead from hell or, through the power of its popular deities to protect the living from illness, fire, or other disasters, we cannot ignore these initially coercive and later customary aspects of the Tokugawa-period parish temple system.

We began this study with a question: What aspects of the Sōtō Zen school, whose temples numbered only several thousand in the early sixteenth century, enabled it to become the single largest school of Japanese Buddhism by the early eighteenth century? The sect-specific aspects of Sōtō Zen alone, such as Dōgen's writings or practices such as Zen meditation, do not answer this question. Rather, the immense growth of Sōtō Zen as an institution that transcended regional and lineage boundaries was based on a combination of two factors that came together in the early Tokugawa period: (1) funerary Zen within the new Tokugawa legal and political imperative for temple registration, and (2) this-world benefits offered by temples that drew on Zen motifs of meditative powers and on esoteric and generic Buddhist themes.

Offering the powerful combination of prayer and funerary rituals within the context of the Tokugawa bakufu's new political order certainly promoted the growth of Sōtō Zen, as well as other sects. Although Sōtō Zen managed to combine both factors in a particularly effective way to become the largest single sect, temple numbers increased for all sects during the first part of the Tokugawa period. In other words, the nonsectarian dimension of Sōtō Zen influenced its institutional growth as much as, if not more, than elements specific to the sect. To bring order to our studies of Sōtō Zen, it is tempting to reduce the sect to the teachings of its founder or to highlight the distinctive character of the tradition. But it is only when we supplement such an approach with an examination of the complex and messy participation of Sōtō Zen in the "common religion" of Tokugawa Japan that we can, for the first time, glimpse Sōtō Zen as a "lived religion."

LISTENING TO THE GHOST OF KIKU

New sources from the Tokugawa period have made easier the study of Sōtō Zen as a "lived religion." Recently discovered materials that had been lying in cardboard boxes in temples or the attics of parishioners have shed new light on the ritual life at Sōtō Zen temples. Indebted to the many local history and temple history projects that have emerged in the past twenty years, the representation of the Sōtō Zen tradition offered here was made possible by both literary texts and items from Buddhist material culture including newly discovered letters, temple logbooks, miracle tales, villager's diaries, fund-raising donor lists, talismans, and tombstones. As William Bodiford has astutely noted, "Tacit assumptions as to what is or is not 'Zen' have limited the manner in which scholars select and evaluate their data. . . . Most definitions of Japanese Zen represent an idealized image of what Zen (Ch. Ch'an) norms were supposed to have been in China."[10] The study of Tokugawa-period Sōtō Zen has suffered not only from an idealization of Chinese Chan norms, but also from definitions of an idealized Japanese Sōtō Zen of the medieval period. Bodiford made great progress in re-visioning the lived religion of medieval Sōtō Zen, and I hope this study has shed some light on its Tokugawa-period developments.

And yet, scholars necessarily limit the fashion in which they "select and evaluate their data." This study, too, could have been written differently: focusing on temples in other regions, looking at the intersection of prayer and funerary rituals instead of viewing them separately, or interspersing social history with the practices of individual exemplar priests such as Manzan and Menzan. It is hoped that future studies on Tokugawa-period Sōtō Zen adopt perspectives that are different again in selecting and analyzing the vast data that are now available from the period. The study of Tokugawa-period Buddhism is, at times, made difficult simply by the sheer number of manuscripts available; my choice in source selection and approach was guided by a search for material that has been largely overlooked. Although "the theory of Edo Buddhist degeneration" (*Edo bukkyō darakuron*), advanced by the influential historian of Japanese Buddhism, Tsuji Zennosuke, had cast the period as unworthy of study, instead of searching for the great monks and philosophical innovations during the Tokugawa period that might counter such a view, I decided to question the very premise that those elements ought to be the criteria for studying a Buddhist tradition in any period. Although focusing on eminent priests of the Tokugawa period for their doctrinal or ritual innovations would have been one way of contributing to the growing field of Tokugawa-period Buddhist studies, I opted to examine the social and ritual dimensions of prayer and parish temples, which represented the Sōtō Zen tradition for the vast majority of ordinary priests and lay followers of the sect.

While such an approach involved researching manuscripts and material culture that might be rather new and unfamiliar to some scholars of Japanese religions, Zen, or Buddhism, perhaps this study will provide some suggestions for exploring new sources in the field. Though any study of a single sect is by its nature limited due to sectarian uniqueness and nonsectarian commonality in Japanese religions, I have tried to provide a balanced approach that might be useful for others studying specific sectarian traditions (Tendai, Shingon, Nichiren, Onmyōdō, Shugendō, etc.) in the larger context of the Tokugawa religious landscape. I also hope that an understanding of the people who are Buddhists, in addition to an understanding of the ideas of Buddhism, will have a place in Buddhist studies in timeframes beyond the Tokugawa period, and in regions outside Japan. Buddhism has never existed in a sociopolitical vacuum, and its articulation within social and historical contexts brings great depth to our understanding of the tradition. While it may be difficult for a single study to incorporate a vast range of perspectives, the addition of the voices of ordinary monks, village officials, lay parishioners, traveling pilgrims, and women's associations to the words of the eminent monks surely helps us to represent Buddhism more accurately and fully.

The story of Kiku, the maid who broke a valuable plate and committed suicide only to be saved by a Zen monk, was transformed into a puppet play and comic drama during the late Tokugawa period and can be found as a motif in other temple legends.[11] Although the use of a Sōtō Zen lineage chart to save Kiku infused this story with a specifically Sōtō Zen flavor, the so-called *sarayashiki* motif (where a a woman breaks a plate, commits suicide or is murdered, and becomes a ghost) has had a transsectarian character as part of the temple legends of Daisenji Temple (Jōdo sect, Rikuchū Province) and Chōkyūji (Shingon sect, Ōmi Province). In these legends, Kiku's strange voice counted, "one, two, . . . [up to ten]" over and over again. She was obsessed with the fact that she had broken the tenth plate. As stated in the Jōsenji Temple legend above, "Everyone who heard it was scared out of their wits because it was not a sound, such as from insects of the field, that anyone could identify." Only a wandering Zen priest recognized the unfamiliar sound and saved the ghost. While we scholars may or may not have salvation in our repertoire, the ability to recognize and incorporate the less familiar into *our* studies, and to represent them in an intelligible manner, is surely a quality we ought to share with that Tokugawa-period Sōtō Zen priest.

NYONIN JŌBUTSU KETSUBONKYŌ ENGI
(THE ORIGINS OF THE BLOOD POOL HELL SUTRA FOR
WOMEN'S SALVATION)

IT IS SAID THAT AMONG the 136 hells, there is an awful one called the Ketsubon (Blood Pool) Hell that measures eighty thousand *yujun*. All women fall into this hell because of their karma. This is because women have an eight-petaled lotus flower hanging upside down between their breasts that releases blood of five colors. The red-colored blood flows out for seven days every month or eighty-four days out of the twelve months. This blood is called menstrual blood (lit. monthly water, *gessui*) that is terribly evil and impure. When this impure fluid touches the earth, it pollutes the earth deities by falling on their heads and invites the punishment of the 98,072 deities. If this blood gets into waterways, it pollutes the water deities, and if it is thrown into a mountain forest, the mountain deity is polluted. Or if clothes stained with this blood are washed in a river, and some devout person takes that river water to boil tea or cook rice and offers it to the Buddhas and kami, such an offering will not be accepted. Because women naturally pollute the deities in this way, all women after death fall into the Blood Pool Hell (*chi no ike jigoku*). Women are by nature extremely jealous and unable to reap merit because of their evil acts, which leads after death to their transformation into a poisonous snake. This snake has sixteen horns, eighty-four thousand scales, and experiences the sufferings of the "three heats" day and night. The venerable Mokuren, seeing such a figure, felt sorry for the fate of all women. He approached Śākyamuni Buddha begging for a way to save women, and the Buddha responded by giving the sermon that became the *Ketsubonkyō* (Blood Pool Hell Sutra). Therefore, if one accepts and recites or copies this sutra, one can be saved from falling into hell. This sutra, given to us by the Buddha, is the only source of women's salvation. It matters not how evil the woman is; if she accepts and recites this sutra, she is guaranteed salvation. Not only does the sutra remove the seven sufferings and three disasters of this world, but it provides an escape from the state of the eight sufferings and five hindrances (of being a woman) in the next life so that one can be reborn into the Pure Land.

I have heard that in Nakasōma District, Shimōsa Province, there is a village called Ichibu Village that used to be called Hatto Village. In this village was a temple called Hosshōji that is known for a miraculous incident. On the twenty-fourth of the fourth month, Ōei 24 (1417), a thirteen-year-old girl who was a parishioner of the temple suddenly became ill and exhibited very strange symptoms, such as becoming completely red from the waist down, emitting five-colored fire and smoke from the top of her head, and writing up and down, screaming, "I can't stand this pain." Her parents were startled and worried and immediately prayed to the Buddhas and kami. They called upon a doctor to treat her and an Onmyōdō practitioner to divine the cause of the illness, but all to no avail. It was then that the girl spoke, asking her parents to invite the abbot of Hosshōji Temple over because she urgently needed to make a request. Her parents immediately sent a servant over to the temple to relate this request and had the abbot come over to the house shortly thereafter. When he arrived, the girl went out to greet him. Prostrating herself profusely, she said, "Oh abbot, do you know who I am? Honored one, please do not doubt what I am about to say for I would like to explain why things are as they are. I am the daughter of Kamakura Hōjō Tokiyori, a nun named Hosshō, the first abbess of Hosshōji Temple. This is why my father, Tokiyori, who constructed Hosshōji Temple, named it so. Even though I was ordained as a nun, taking pride in my family background, I did not keep the three disciplines of body, speech, and mind. Not keeping the precepts or doing good, I spent each day foolishly. Unfortunately, time waits for no one, and after six years I passed away. Since the road to hell is not distinguished by whether one is rich or poor, I am currently suffering immensely in the Blood Pool Hell, having descended there upon death because of the evil I committed during my life. This evil karmic destiny caused me to be reborn as a snake with sixteen horns constantly suffering the 'three heats' and falling back into the Blood Pool Hell. Oh abbot, if you have any doubt about what I have just said, let me show you some proof." The girl then wiped her body with ten pieces of paper, and amazingly, the paper turned crimson red. She spoke to the abbot again, saying, "Look at this! What suffering, what sadness!" She then sobbed quietly for a while.

The abbot asked for a description of the Blood Pool Hell. The girl replied, "Once one has been born as a woman, whether one is the daughter of an aristocratic or *daimyō* family, no woman can escape this hell. This is because all women have the pollution of menstrual blood or the impure blood of childbirth. This blood defiles not only the earth and water deities, but all Buddhas and kami. For this, a woman falls into the hell of immeasurable suffering after death. The sufferings in this hell include, first of all, the six times a day we come out of the pool to drink blood. If we refuse to drink it because of its horridness, frightening demons come and torture us with metal rods before we get thrown back into the blood pool, screaming to no avail. In the blood pool, countless insectlike creatures with metal snouts come to pierce our skin and worm into our flesh to suck our blood, before grinding into the bone to feast on the marrow. There are no words that could describe this pain. However, at times, large five-colored lotus flowers appear from within the blood pool saving some woman or another. Seeing them, one gets envious. Those are women who fell into hell but, because of the merit accrued through their good acts in their previous life, were able to escape the torments of hell quickly. Others were able to attain release and go to heaven because their descendants performed ceremonies for the Buddhas and made offerings to the Buddhist priesthood. Oh abbot, I beg you for your great compassion and that you save me from the sufferings of this Blood Pool Hell."

The abbot asked the girl, "What kind of meritorious acts must I do to save you from the Blood Pool Hell?" She replied, "The Buddha taught the Dharma in a little over five thousand sutras, but there is a sutra entitled the *Ketsubonkyō* (which is a part of the *Hōon Sutra*). If one recites and copies this sutra one thousand times each day for seven continuous days, not only will it save me from the torments of hell, but it will transform this snake body of mine. This is not for my benefit alone; all hell-dwelling women who want to be freed from the pool's torments should wish to receive the benefits of this sutra, for it can immediately free one from the six daily blood drinks. In this world, a woman should keep the sutra on her body as a protective amulet, and when she dies she should have the sutra buried in the grave with her. A *Ketsubonshō* ceremony should be observed twice a month, after the six senses have been purified, for the benefits are great. Furthermore, if one places this sutra in the grave mound of one's deceased mother, wife, or daughter, they are guaranteed to escape the sufferings of the three evil realms and go to a Buddha land. So please go back to your temple right away to recite and copy the sutra. If you still have any doubts about what I said, go to the five-storied stone stūpa in front of the temple near the pine and willow tree where I was buried, because there will be found something miraculous." The astonished abbot said, "I will recite the *Ketsubonkyō* as you requested, but it will take me a few days to get a hold of this sutra." The ill girl then said, "Let me tell you how to obtain the sutra. The Jizō statue, which is the main image of worship at Hosshōji, was donated by my father, Hōjō Tokiyori. This Jizō has miraculous qualities so go back to the temple immediately to pray to it." The girl then collapsed and went to sleep. Her illness had disappeared.

When the abbot returned to the temple, he rang the bell to gather the monks to relate the above story. The monks went together to the five-storied stone stūpa only to find that the base of the stūpa was red. Everyone was completely amazed. On that very day, the monks performed a *Jizōkō* ceremony after which they practiced Zen meditation until eight incense sticks had burned away. Though the regular monks fell asleep after this, the abbot stayed awake, praying, "Namu Rokudō Nōge Jizō Gan'ō Bosatsu, please provide me with a copy of the *Ketsubonkyō* so that all deluded beings can be saved," after which he entered into a deep state of meditation. Later, during the hours of the cow and tiger, the abbot took a short nap. In a dream, Jizō appeared in the guise of a dignified eighty-year-old monk with a staff in his hand who said, "Your prayers have reached me, so I will present you with the *Ketsubonkyō* that has been stored in the Dragon Palace. You should go to Taganuma Marsh early tomorrow morning." The dream abruptly ceased, and very early the next day, the abbot went to Taganuma Marsh with the other monks. To their surprise, the water in the marsh suddenly started to move of its own accord. The water swept up into the sky like the waterfall at Dragon's Gate. From the depth of the water emerged a single white lotus flower that held within its petals a sutra scroll. The abbot immediately thought that this was the *Ketsubonkyō* that Jizō had promised in his dream. Prostrating himself in front of the sutra, he took it back to the temple to begin, with the other monks, the recitation and copying of one thousand sutras every day for seven continuous days. All the copied sutras were then interred in the nun's grave. Around midnight on the seventh day, the abbot, the monks, as well as the temple's parishioners all had the same dream. In the dream appeared a beautiful woman, accompanied by the sound of music, and flowers rained from a sky strewn with purple clouds. She was wearing a magnificent robe and sitting on a lotus-shaped seat surrounded by halos. She uttered the following: "Because the abbot of Hosshōji recently recited and copied the *Ketsubonkyō*, I have not only escaped the suffering of the blood pool, but my snake body has disappeared. I am now able to go to the Buddha's pure land." The next day, when everyone at the temple talked about their dream, not a single detail differed.

Because a copy of a sutra, namely, the *Ketsubonkyō*, appeared in the village, the name of the village was changed to Ichibu, "One Copy" Village. And because the nun's snake body was transformed, the "mountain name" of the temple was changed to Dairyūzan, "Great Dragon Mountain." And finally, because the sutra came out of a spring, the name of the temple was changed from Hosshōji Temple to Shōsenji, "True Spring" Temple, though the remains of the old temple still exist.

Ichibu Village, Sōma District, Shimōsa Province: The First Place in Japan Where the *Nyonin Jōbutsu Ketsubonkyō* from the Dragon Palace Appeared

This woodblock edition is dedicated as a prayer for the women of Bishū Province, in the inner compound of the castle, by the thirty-second abbot of Dairyūzan Shōsenji Temple, Seien Tairyō.

An auspicious day of the tenth month, Ansei 4 (1857), the Year of the Snake.

SHINSEN GEDOKU MANBYŌEN FUKUYŌ NO KOTO
(HOW TO PREPARE AND TAKE THE WIZARD MOUNTAIN
"POISON-DISPELLING" PILL THAT CURES ALL ILLNESSES)

FOR ANY KIND OF POISONING, take one tablet of Gedoku and dissolve it in some lukewarm water. Drink a few sips and vomit out the poison in one's body. After this, if one drinks the solution two or three times with hot water, then the rest of the poison will come out during urination. For the recovery phase, one should drink the extract taken from the ground up *hakkin* herb. In addition, if one feels ill from food poisoning, for example from eating the *fugu* fish, the above formula will work.

For all kinds of stomach ailments, take one tablet of Gedoku with hot, salty water. One can also dissolve the tablet with vinegar and rub the solution into the part of the body that hurts.

For fatigue, take one tablet of Gedoku and mix it with one *bu* of the *nanten* leaf, one *bu* of aged tea leaves, one *bu* of incense, and a pinch of salt. For stomachaches, chest pains, constipation, or other stomach-related discomfort, use the same formula as above, but also add five *bu* of the herb *kumatsuzura*.

For various types of diarrhea, take one tablet of Gedoku and mix it with two *bu* of the herb *kanawakara*, one *bu* of wood incense, one *bu* of betelnut, five *bu* of licorice, ten grains of previously harvested rice, and take it as above. But in the case of dysentery, also add one *bu* of *shibayoki* grass, one *bu* of the herb *tōki*, or if the condition continues without abating for more than a month, add one *bu* of bone marrow.

For influenza-related headaches, coughs, and phlegm, a mixture of eight *bu* of Gedoku along with one pill-size portion of ground beefsteak plant, one *bu* of dried orange peel, two *bu* of green tree bark, one slice of the white root of a scallion, and three ground ginger roots should be prepared. This same preparation should be taken by those infected during midwinter cold epidemics or those with high fevers resulting from exposure to the wind.

For malaria, one tablet of Gedoku should be taken together with a cut-up sprig from a peach tree that faces east.

For regular phlegm, one tablet of Gedoku should be taken, mixed with the sap from eight *bu* of ginger roots.

For gonorrhea, take five tablets of Gedoku and mix it in a large vat of water with a sprig of the *ikoko* tree cut thirty times, ten loquat leaves without the stems, two *bu* of corn, and three *bu* of licorice.

For bloating of the stomach, take one tablet of Gedoku and mix it with two *bu* of white *bukuryō* mushrooms, one *bu* of *bakuko* incense, one *bu* of the *shukushanin* herb, one *bu* of wood incense, two *bu* of ginseng, and two ginger roots. This formula will also work for water blisters.

For chest worms, one tablet of Gedoku should be mixed into water that has been slightly heated with steel and imbibed. In addition, a salve made from the same amount of Gedoku with mustard should be applied to the affected area.

For headaches, Gedoku in hot salty water can be taken. Also for heat strokes it can be dissolved into aged sake and taken.

For faintness, blurry vision, or mouth chapping resulting from exposure to the wind, drink some hot aged sake mixed with one tablet of Gedoku.

For stomach upset, use the same formula as above, but also add seven *bu* of honey incense.

For jaundice, take one tablet of Gedoku and mix it with one *bu* of the *yomogi* herb, one *bu* of the *shingi* herb, one *bu* of green tree bark, two *bu* of red *bukuryō* mushrooms, and take as above.

For strokes that are not serious, one should take Gedoku with some salty hot water.

For asthma, take one tablet of Gedoku and mix it with two *bu* of white bark from the *kuwa* tree, one *bu* of apricot seed, and one *bu* of a large *daikon* radish, and take it as above.

For illness like beriberi or gout, one tablet of Gedoku dissolved in salty hot water should be taken. Another method is to take the Gedoku, put it in some aged sake, and rub the mixture onto the area that hurts.

For backaches, take one tablet of Gedoku and mix it with two *bu* of *tochū* tea leaves, two *bu* of Mediterranean cress, two *bu* of regular watercress, and three ginger roots, and rub it in as above.

For constipation, take one tablet of Gedoku and mix it with one *bu* of *manin* seed, two *bu* of peach seed, and one bu of the *daiō* herb, and rub it in as above.

For tuberculosis and related ailments, take one tablet of Gedoku and mix it with one *bu* of ginseng, one *bu* of the *uyaku* herb, one *bu* of the *nanten* leaf, and take it with some high-quality aged tea.

For colic or abdominal pains, one tablet of Gedoku should be added to sap made from crushing five *bu* of the flower of eggplants and the mixture taken as above. Adding one tablet of Gedoku to two *bu* of blackened lacquer tree and drinking it down with some aged sake will also work. As a further note, for penile dysfunction, one can add some sap made from the *hakobe* grass to the above.

For spirit possession and attacks, one should take one tablet of Gedoku with some salty hot water.

For toothaches, one should grind up the Gedoku into very fine powder, mix it with some aged sake, and rub this solution into the painful surfaces. If a cavity has already appeared, one should prepare the Gedoku to fit the size of the cavity and place it into the hole.

For pain in the shoulder, neck, and back, one should mix the Gedoku with equal amount of *nikkei* incense, both in fine powder form. This mixture should be applied with some rice vinegar to the part of the body that is in pain.

For severe cases of acne and other skin disorders, one should take one tablet of Gedoku with some salty hot water. The same goes for a disease like scrofula.

For spots and smaller acne, one should grind up the Gedoku into very fine powder and mix it with some sap made from the *hakobe* grass and apply it. This works for all kinds of swelling of the skin as well.

For poisonous snake or insect bites, one should grind up the Gedoku into a very fine powder, mix it with some sap made from *hakobe* grass, and apply it directly to the bite. This works for all types of bites from farm animals as well as as dog and rat bites.

For syphilis and skin blemishes from smallpox, dissolve the Gedoku in water and apply it to the skin. It is also permissible to drink the solution.

For welts and pus, one should mix Gedoku with an equal amount of red *azuki* beans, both in fine powder, before applying. Further, for scabies, two tablets of Gedoku in powder form should be mixed with five *bu* of bamboo root oil, three *bu* of sesame seeds, and one *bu* of camphor before applying.

For skin discoloration, one should grind up one tablet of Gedoku into very fine powder and mix it with five *bu* of the *wadaiō* herb, two *bu* of sulphur, and one *bu* of white sesame seeds. These ingredients should be thoroughly mixed together before making a paste with some rice vinegar and applying the resultant solution to the skin. For better flow of *ki*, this solution will work as well.

For leprosy, one should drink one tablet of Gedoku with some hot water. It is also possible to dissolve the Gedoku into some aged sake to apply it to the skin.

For hair loss, put powder-form Gedoku into hair pomade before applying.

For sprains, bruises, fractures, and the like, get drunk on one tablet of Gedoku mixed with *morohaku* sake.

For hemorrhoids and similar pains, one or two tablets of Gedoku should be taken with some water. For faster results, take it with some aged sake.

For cuts, lightly apply finely powdered Gedoku to the wound. It is also permissible to take a tablet with water.

For burns, finely powdered Gedoku should be dissolved in sap made from the *ai* flower before applying.

If one gets a fish bone or some other object stuck in one's throat, one should take Gedoku with some salty hot water.

If one is near death from hanging, being crushed, drowning, spirit possession, freezing, or fright at coming into contact with demons, drink some hot aged sake mixed with one tablet of Gedoku.

For menstrual pains, mix one tablet of Gedoku into some freshly brewed hot water and drink it. Furthermore, for headaches, hot flashes, or faintness resulting from menstruation, one tablet of Gedoku should be mixed with one *bu* of the *senkyū* herb, one *bu* of the *saiko* herb, one *bu* of the *sanshishi* herb, and one *bu* of tree peony before taking it as above. Finally, if a woman has the symptoms of headaches and hearing loss, she should make some sap by grinding up some *sanshō* herb, then mix it into some hot miso soup before drinking it down with Gedoku.

For leucorrhea, one should take Gedoku with some salty hot water.

When menopause comes around, mix one tablet of Gedoku with two *bu* of the herb *tōki*, one *bu* of the *senkyū* herb, and one *bu* of the *benibana* flower, and take this solution as above.

For stomach cramps, mix one tablet of Gedoku with two *bu* of the herb *tōki*, two *bu* of the *senkyū* herb, and two *bu* of the *yakumō* herb, and take this solution as above.

For postpartum pains, one should drink some hot miso soup with slices of ginger root and one tablet of Gedoku.

For general health maintenance, when convalescing after a sickness, for recuperating after a walk on a hot day, for getting over a hangover, or for sea sickness, one should take Gedoku with some salty hot water. The same goes for illness resulting from drinking unfamiliar water while traveling in another province.

For any ailments affecting a hawk, one should mix Gedoku into some pear juice before giving it to the bird.

For a cow unable to urinate, one can put a Gedoku tablet directly in its anus, or crush five pills into a powder, dissolve this in water, and make the cow drink it. If neither of these two methods works, one should mix five tablets with ground miso paste and give it to the cow, which will then mysteriously recover.

For a horse having trouble breathing or moving, Gedoku can be placed directly onto the horse's tongue because it is chewable. If the cold gets to the horse and it is unable to urinate, one should mix five tablets of Gedoku with roasted miso paste and unrefined sake and wrap this mixture in something before giving it to the horse to eat. If it is too hot, it is permissible to add some cool water. If the horse's nose or throat is affected, the horse should be given three tablets of Gedoku, twenty garlic bulbs, and some unrefined sake. Or if the horse's back is painful, one should mix equal amounts of Gedoku and blackened *makoshi* grass with the sap of the *hakoba* herb before applying it to the back.

For all ailments of every type of bird and furry creature, powdered Gedoku should be administered with hot water. In the case of cats, it can be directly put on the cat's tongue.

For women and children, the amounts are the same. In any case, if one does not have any Gedoku on hand, it is fine to treat all illnesses with some salty hot water.

Ryakutō (Kyoto) Kinoshita Dōshōan, the Seal of the Monk Tokua

NOTES

CHAPTER 1   Toward a Social History of Sōtō Zen

1. Edwin O. Reischauer, "Introduction," in Martin Collcutt's *Five Mountains: The Rinzai Monastic Institution in Medieval Japan* (Cambridge: Harvard University Press, 1981), p. viii.

2. See Helen Baroni, *Ōbaku Zen: The Emergence of the Third Sect of Zen in Tokugawa Japan* (Honolulu: University of Hawai'i Press, 2000); William M. Bodiford, *Sōtō Zen in Medieval Japan* (Honolulu: University of Hawai'i Press, 1993); Collcutt, *Five Mountains*; Bernard Faure, *Visions of Power: Imagining Medieval Japanese Buddhism* (Princeton: Princeton University Press, 1996); Joseph Parker, *Zen Buddhist Landscape Arts of Early Muromachi Japan (1336–1573)* (Albany: State University of New York Press, 1999). For a review essay on the history of Japanese and Western scholarship on medieval Japanese Zen Buddhism, see Duncan Williams, "The Monastery, Popular Rituals, and the Zen Master: New Histories of Medieval Japanese Zen Buddhism," *Critical Review of Books in Religion* (1998): 255–64. William Bodiford's monograph has special bearing on this study because his work was the first in a Western language to present an overview of the medieval development of Sōtō Zen. As will become clear from the upcoming chapters, in many ways, my research is indebted to his pioneering work on medieval materials. Similar English-language work in the field of China and Korea have focused on their social contexts. See Robert Buswell, Jr., *The Zen Monastic Experience* (Princeton: Princeton University Press, 1992); Bernard Faure, *The Rhetoric of Immediacy: A Cultural Critique of Chan/Zen Buddhism* (Princeton: Princeton University Press, 1991); *Chan Insights and Oversights* (Princeton: Princeton University Press, 1993); *The Will to Orthodoxy: A Critical Genealogy of Northern Chan Buddhism* (Stanford: Stanford University Press, 1997); T. Griffith Foulk, "The 'Ch'an School' and Its Place in the Buddhist Monastic Tradition" (Ph.D. dissertation, University of Michigan, 1987); John MacRae, *The Northern School and the Formation of Early Ch'an Buddhism* (Honolulu: University of Hawai'i Press, 1986).

3. For the eighteenth-century data on temples, see the bakufu-sponsored survey of Sōtō Zen temples in 1721, which can be found in printed text form in Kagamishima Sōjun, ed., *Enkyōdo Sōtōshū jiin honmatsuchō* (Tsurumi: Daihonzan Sōjiji, 1944; rpt. Tokyo: Meicho fukyūkai, 1980). While Sōtō Zen was the largest school of Buddhism in terms of the number of temples, the Nishi and Higashi Honganji (i.e., Jōdo Shin) schools claimed the largest number of parish members during the Tokugawa period. For the most recent statistics on the number of affiliated temples for each sect, see Bunkachō, ed. *Shūkyō nenkan: Heisei jūichinenban* (Tokyo: Bunkachō bunkabu shūmuka, 2000), pp. 64–76. They are listed here in order of the number of temples affiliated with each sect: Sōtō Zen 14,687; Shingon 12,407; Jōdo Shin Honganji 10,320; Jōdo Shin Ōtani 8,694; Jōdo 6,933; Nichiren 6,891; Rinzai Zen 5,726; Tendai 4,463; and Ōbaku Zen 463.

4. I have drawn on the concept of "lived religion," though I use it in a somewhat modified way, from David Hall's study of American religious history. See David Hall, ed. *Lived Religion in America: Toward a History of Practice* (Princeton: Princeton University Press, 1997).

5. See Barbara A. Ruch, "The Other Side of Culture in Medieval Japan," in *Cambridge History of Japan*, vol. 3: *Medieval Japan*, ed. Kozo Yamamura (Cambridge: Cambridge University Press, 1990), pp. 500–543.

6. In the English-language literature alone, there are two doctoral dissertations dealing with figures central to the sect-reformation movement. See Lawrence Gross, "Manzan Dōhaku and the Transmission of the Teaching" (Ph.D. dissertation, Stanford University,

1998), and David Riggs, "The Rekindling of a Tradition: Menzan Zuihō and the Reform of Japanese Sōtō Zen in the Tokugawa Era" (Ph.D. dissertation, University of California, Los Angeles, 2002). Another important work is Menzan's biography of the "eccentric" Sōtō Zen monk, Tōsui Unkei, the *Tōsui oshō densan*, translated by Peter Haskel, *Letting Go: The Story of Zen Master Tōsui* (Honolulu: University of Hawai'i Press, 2001). There is also a translated work of another important figure in the "reform movement," Tenkei Denson: see Thomas Cleary, *Secrets of the Blue Cliff Record: Zen Comments by Hakuin and Tenkei* (Boston: Shambhala Publications, 2000). On the "reform movement" in general, see Baroni, *Ōbaku Zen*, pp. 122–64; William Bodiford, "Dharma Transmission in Sōtō Zen: Manzan Dōhaku's Reform Movement," *Monumenta Nipponica* 46/4 (1991): 423–51; and Michel Mohr, "Zen Buddhism during the Tokugawa Period: The Challenge to Go beyond Sectarian Consciousness," *Japanese Journal of Religious Studies* 21/4 (1994): 341–72, and "L'Héritage contesté de Dokuan Genkō: Tradition et conflits dans le bouddhisme Zen du XVIIe siècle," in *Repenser l'ordre, repenser l'héritage: Paysage intellectuel du Japon (XVIIe–XIXe siècles)*, ed. Frédéric Girard, Annick Horiuchi, Mieko Macé (Geneva: Librairie Droz, 2002), pp. 209–63.

7. Bernard Faure rightly acknowledges the importance of looking at the margins of Buddhist discourse but warns, "The most creative part of Buddhist discourse might be orginating in the margins. Thus, it is important to explore less conventional elements of Buddhist discourse, as long as one remains aware of their marginality, and does not try to pass them off as orthodox, or even mainstream, Buddhism." See Bernard Faure, *The Power of Denial: Buddhism, Purity, and Gender* (Princeton: Princeton University Press, 2003), p. 18.

8. James Obelkevich, ed., *Religion and the People from the Middle Ages through the Counter-Reformation: Studies in the History of Popular Religious Beliefs and Practices* (Chapel Hill: University of North Carolina Press, 1979), pp. 3–4.

9. For an important discussion of the various problems associated with the category "popular religion," in either its praxis (practices outside the established church structures) or its class (the religion of the nonprivileged) formulation, see Jacques Berlinerbau, "Max Weber's Useful Ambiguities and the Problem of Defining 'Popular Religion'," *Journal of the American Academy of Religion* 69/3 (2001): 605–26. Catherine Bell's review of the theoretical positions in the study of "popular religion" and its application to the study of Chinese religions is also very helpful. See Catherine Bell, "Religion and Chinese Culture: Toward an Assessment of 'Popular Religion'," *History of Religions* 29/1 (1989): 35–57. In the context of Zen studies, Steven Heine provides an interesting overview of the "tension model" (exemplified by Bernard Faure's works emphasizing epistemological inconsistency) and the "continuity model" (exemplified by William Bodiford's works on the seamless nature of Zen and popular religiosity). See Steven Heine, *Shifting Shape, Shaping Text: Philosophy and Folklore in the Fox Kōan* (Honolulu: University of Hawai'i Press, 1999), pp. 183–98.

10. The term "common currency" was first used by Ian Reader in his "Contemporary Thought in Sōtō Zen Buddhism: An Investigation of the Publications and Teachings of the Sect in the Light of Their Cultural and Historical Context" (Ph.D. dissertation, University of Leeds, 1983), p. 69, as a metaphor for the religious practices of the Sōtō school common to other schools of Japanese religions. More recently, he has used the term "common religion" to speak more broadly about the aspect of each tradition's practices that are not unique, but rather shared, among all religious traditions participating in Japanese religious culture. See Ian Reader and George Tanabe, *Practically Religious: Worldly Benefits and the Common Religion of Japan* (Honolulu: University of Hawai'i Press, 1998), p. 20.

11. See John Kieschnick, *The Impact of Buddhism on Chinese Material Culture* (Princeton: Princeton University Press, 2003), and Gregory Schopen, *Bones, Stones, and Buddhist Monks: Collected Papers on the Archaeology, Epigraphy, and Texts of Monastic Buddhism in India* (Honolulu: University of Hawai'i Press, 1997) and *Buddhist*

Monks and Business Matters: Some More Papers on Monastic Buddhism in India (Honolulu: University of Hawai'i Press, 2004).

12. For a useful guide to local history archives in Japan divided into two volumes, one for western Japan and the other for eastern Japan, see Chihōshi Kenkyū Kyōgikai, ed., *Rekishi shiryō hozon kikan sōran*, 2 vols. (Tokyo: Yamakawa shuppansha, rev. ed., 1990). The Council on the Study of Local History (Chihōshi Kenkyū Kyōgikai) surveyed 5,820 local history archives and institutes for information on their holdings and the availability of the collection to outside researchers. Helen Hardacre has demonstrated the importance of these local history archives to the systematic study of Tokugawa-period Japanese religions as a whole. See her "Sources for the Study of Religion and Society in the Late Edo Period," *Japanese Journal of Religious Studies* 28, 3–4 (2001): 227–60, and *Religion and Society in Nineteenth-Century Japan: A Study of the Southern Kanto Region, Using Late Edo and Early Meiji Gazetteers* (Ann Arbor: Center for Japanese Studies, University of Michigan, 2002). Three recent doctoral dissertations have also made extensive use of local archives in the study of Tokugawa religions: Barbara Ambros, "The Mountain of Great Prosperity: The Ōyama Cult in Early Modern Japan" (Ph.D. dissertation, Harvard University, 2002): Hiromi Maeda, "Imperial Authority and Local Shrines: The Yoshida House and the Creation of a Countrywide Shinto Institution in Early Modern Japan" (Ph.D. dissertation, Harvard University, 2003); and Alexander Vesey, "The Buddhist Clergy and Village Society in Early Modern Japan" (Ph.D. dissertation, Princeton University, 2002).

13. See Suzuki Taizan, *Zenshū no chihō hatten* (Tokyo: Azebō shobō, 1942; rpt. Tokyo: Yoshikawa kōbunkan, 1983), and *Sōtōshū no chiikiteki tenkai* (Kyoto: Shibunkaku shuppan, 1993).

14. See Bodiford, *Sōtō Zen in Medieval Japan*; Hanuki Masai, *Chūsei Zenrin seiritsushi no kenkyū* (Tokyo: Yoshikawa kōbunkan, 1993); Harada Masatoshi, *Nihon chūsei no Zenshū to shakai* (Tokyo: Yoshikawa kōbunkan, 1998); Hirose Ryōkō, *Zenshū chihō tenkaishi no kenkyū* (Tokyo: Yoshikawa kōbunkan, 1988). Other book-length works on particular regions include Ifune Manzen, *Kyōdo Zenshūshi: Jushu (Machino, Yanagidaudetsu o fukumu) jiin no seiritsu o chūshin ni* (Tamasu: Seisui bunko, 1972); Ōsaka Kōshō, *Akitaken Sōtōshū jiden taiyō* (Akita: Mumyōsha shuppan, 1996); *Akitaken Sōtōshū hen'nenshi* (Akita: Mumyōsha shuppan, 1999); Sasao Tetsuo, *Akitaken Sōtōshū kyōdanshi* (Akita: Daihizenji, 1971); *Kinsei Akita no tōjō zensō* (Akita: Daihizenji, 1972); Takahashi Masato, ed., *Shinshū no bukkyō jiin 3: Zenshū* (Matsumoto: Kyōdo shuppansha, 1986); and Takeuchi Michio, *Echigo Zenshūshi no kenkyū* (Tokyo: Takashi shoin, 1998).

15. Most articles focus on the Chūbu, Tōhoku, and Kantō regions, with lesser attention given to the Chūgoku, Kinki, Shikoku, and Kyūshū regions. For a survey of more than fifty articles on the spread of Zen in local society, see Duncan Williams, "Representations of Zen: A Social and Institutional History of Sōtō Zen Buddhism in Edo Japan" (Ph.D. dissertation, Harvard University, 2000), chap. 1. Although not solely on Zen, Arimoto Masao's *Kinsei Nihon no shūkyō shakaishi* (Tokyo: Yoshikawa kōbunkan, 2002) is an excellent example of this type of local and social history of Buddhism in the Tokugawa period.

16. A list of more than one hundred Sōtō Zen temple histories, which have grown in number every year since the 1970s, is included in ibid.

17. The two head temples, Eiheiji and Sōjiji, also produced temple histories, though the Eiheiji project is a much larger enterprise. In the case of Eiheiji Temple, the two-volume *Eiheijishi* (The History of Eiheiji), which was published in 1982, will be accompanied by a multivolume *Eiheiji shiryōhen* (The History of Eiheiji: Documents Edition), with reproductions of the original handwritten manuscripts and their printed text versions (the first volume, covering medieval Zen, appeared in 2002, with nine volumes slated for the next seven years). This project involved not only sorting and cataloging thousands of manuscripts held at Eiheiji, but the procurement of tens of thousands of manuscripts from more than twenty of its main branch temples. For the already published section of the his-

tory of Eiheiji Temple, see Eiheijishi Hensan Iinkai, ed., *Eiheijishi*, 2 vols. (Eiheijichō: Daihonzan Eiheiji, 1982), and *Eiheiji shiryōzensho 1* (Eiheijichō: Daihonzan Eiheiji, 2002). For the history of Sōjiji Temple, see Kuriyama Taion, *Sōjijishi* (Yokohama: Daihonzan Sōjiji, 1965). Another major ongoing project is the collection of manuscripts related to Kasuisai Temple, one of the four bakufu-appointed Sōtō Zen liaison temples with a special connection to the first Tokugawa shōgun, Ieyasu. This project began in 1989 with the collection of the first volume, including documents on the temple's history from the medieval period. The other volumes, however, focused on the Tokugawa period, including letters, diaries, and official logbooks related to Kasuisai's role as a liaison temple between the sect and the government. With the fifth and most recent volume published in 1998, the project has cataloged more than ten thousand manuscripts.

18. The Zenshū Chihōshi Chōsakai has been directed by Professor Hirose Ryōkō at Komazawa University. Zenshū Chihōshi Chōsakai, ed., *Zenshū chihōshi chōsakai nenpō* (Tokyo: Zenshū chihōshi chōsakai, 1978–98). Volume 1 (1978) surveyed 1,543 manuscripts from nine temples; volume 2 (1980), 1,511 manuscripts from ten temples; volume 3 (1982), 3,735 manuscripts from five temples; volume 4 (1988), 4,472 manuscripts from seven temples; and volume 5 (1998), 1,209 manuscripts from four temples.

19. The manuscript catalogs have also been arranged regionally and compiled (though this project is still in its infancy) into book form. See *SSCM* (vols. 1–2) and *SBCM* (vols. 3–6). Volume 1 covers the Tōkai region; vol. 2, Tōhoku and Hokkaidō; vol. 3, Kyūshū; vol. 4, Shikoku and Chūgoku, vol. 5, Kinki; and vol. 6, Kantō.

20. See Tsuji Zennosuke, *Nihon bukkyōshi 4* (Tokyo: Iwanami shoten, 1955), pp. 404–90. Other modern scholars who have discussed the issues surrounding the idea of the degeneration of Tokugawa-period Buddhism include Gerald Groemer, "A Short History of Gannin: Popular Religious Performers in Tokugawa Japan," *Japanese Journal of Religious Studies* 27/2 (2000): 41–72; Nam-Lin Hur, *Prayer and Play in Late Tokugawa Japan: Asakusa Sensōji and Edo Society* (Cambridge: Harvard University Asia Center, 2000), pp. 218–28; Shibata Minoru, "Kinsei no sezoku shugi to bukkyō," *Bukkyō shigaku* 14/1 (1968): 1–15; and Wakatsuki Shōgo, "Edo jidai no sōryo no daraku ni tsuite: Sono shorei," *KDBR* 2 (1971): 5–19. Ōkuwa Hitoshi provides a summary of the efforts of a team of scholars dedicated to overturning Tsuji's "degeneration theory" by collecting new documents that showed the vitality of Buddhism during the period and through the publication of a journal, *Kinsei bukkyō* (Early modern Buddhism). See Ōkuwa Hitoshi, *Nihon bukkyō no kinsei* (Kyoto: Hōzōkan, 2003), pp. 5–12.

21. See Peter Gregory, "The Vitality of Buddhism in the Sung," in *Buddhism in the Sung*, ed. Peter Gregory and Daniel Getz (Honolulu: University of Hawai'i Press, 1999), pp. 2–4, and John McRae, *Seeing through Zen: Encounter, Transformation, and Genealogy in Chinese Chan Buddhism* (Berkeley: University of California Press, 2003), pp. 120–23, for a discussion of the historiography behind the notion of a "golden age of the T'ang" and a "decline in the Sung."

22. Lee Butler's study of early Tokugawa government regulations makes a similar point about how authority was not unidirectional. See Lee Butler, "Tokugawa Ieyasu's Regulations for the Court: A Reappraisal," *Harvard Journal of Asiatic Studies* 54/2 (1994): 528–31 and his *Emperor and Aristocracy in Japan, 1467–1680* (Cambridge: Harvard University Asia Center, 2002), pp. 198–224.

23. For a detailed English-language study of the Tokugawa bakufu's role in establishing the institutional structure of Sōtō Zen in the seventeenth century, see Williams, "Representations of Zen," chap. 2. For pansectarian studies of the Tokugawa government's policies toward religious institutions, see Nam-lin Hur, *Death and Social Order in Tokugawa Japan: Buddhism, Anti-Christianity, and the Danka System* (Cambridge: Harvard University Asia Center, forthcoming); Peter Nosco, "Keeping the Faith: *Bakuhan* Policy Towards Religions in Seventeenth-Century Japan," in *Religion in Japan: Arrows to Heaven and Earth*, ed. Peter Kornicki and Ian McMullen (Cambridge: Cambridge University Press, 1996), pp. 136–55; and Vesey, "Buddhist Clergy," pp. 113–78.

24. For surveys of the secondary literature on Tokugawa Buddhism and an analysis of recent trends, see Hōzawa Naohide, "Kinsei," in *Nihon bukkyō no kenkyū hō*, ed. Nihon Bukkyō Kenkyūkai (Kyoto: Hōzōkan, 2000), pp. 47–61; Janine Sawada, "Tokugawa Religious History: Studies in Western Languages," *Early Modern Japan* 10/1 (2002): 39–64 Bibliography: Religion and Thought in Early Modern Japan," *Early Modern Japan* 10/1 (2002): 72–85; and Duncan Williams, "Religion in Early Modern Japan," in *Nanzan Guidebook for the Study of Japanese Religions*, ed. Paul Swanson et al. (Nanzan: Nanzan Institute for Religion and Culture, 2004).

25. For a full listing, see Williams, "Representations of Zen," chap. 1.

26. On the influence of esoteric Buddhism, Onmyōdō, Shintō, and mountain cults on the Sōtō Zen school, see Ishikawa Rikizan, "Chūsei Sōtōshū to reizan shinkō," *IBK* 33/2 (1985): 26–31, "Chūsei Zenshū to shinbutsu shūgō: Toku ni Sōtōshū no chihōteki tenkai to kirigami shiryō o chūshin ni shite," *Nihon bukkyō* 60–61 (1985): 41–56; Kimura Shungen and Takenaka Chitai, *Zenshū no darani* (Tokyo: Daitō shuppansha, 1998); Sakauchi Tatsuo, "Sōtōshū ni okeru mikkyō no juyō," *Shūgaku kenkyū* 16 (1974): 35–40; Satō Shunkō, "'Chinju Hakusan' kō (jō)," *SKK* 19 (1987): 114–24; "'Hakusan' no isō: Sōtōshū kyōdanshi kenkyū no ichi shikō," *KDBR* 19 (1988): 343–59; "Sōtōshū kyōdan ni okeru 'Hakusan shinkō' juyōshi no mondai," *Shūgaku kenkyū* 1/28 (1986): 148–51; 2/29 (1987): 157–60; 3/30 (1988): 168–71; "Kinsei sonraku shakai ni okeru Shugen to Sōtōshū jiin," *Shūgaku kenkyū* 1/34 (1992): 237–41; 2/35 (1993): 238–43; "'sesshū' no shiten kara miru Shugen jiin to Sōtōshū jiin: Kinsei kindai, Akitahan Hinai chihō ni okeru jirei hōkoku," *Kyōka kenshū* 37 (1994): 263–68; "Kinsei Shugenja no shinkō ni miru Zen to Shintō," *Shūgaku kenkyū* 38 (1996): 234–39; "Kinsei Zenshū to Taishiryū Shintō: Kugihongi Taiseikyō to Sōtōshū Tokuō Ryōkō no shūhen," *IBK* 47/1 (1998): 173–76; Tamamuro Fumio, "Sōtōshū to Shintō to no kōsho," in *Dōgen shisō no ayumi 3*, ed. Sōtōshū Shūgaku Kenkyūsho (Tokyo: Yoshikawa kōbunkan, 1993), pp. 224-47.

27. See Tamamuro Taijō, *Sōshiki bukkyō* (Tokyo: Daihōrinkaku, 1963).

28. This notion of religion as composed of the triad of institutions, doctrines, and rituals comes from Allan Grapard. He states, "It is clear to many of us engaged in research in religious studies that the questions traditionally addressed by scholars in the field have generally tended to be focused on doctrinal or philosophical issues. It would appear that scholars of religion were content to leave the problems concerning institutions to historians, the problems of ritual to anthropologists, sociologists, and psychologists, and the problems of interpreting the relations between ideas and institutions to intellectual historians, who for the most part rarely worked on the topic of religion." See his "Preface: Ritual and Power," *Journal of Ritual Studies* 4/2 (1990): xi.

29. On John McRae's critique of the "string of pearls" fallacy, which describes Zen in terms of "a sequence of individual masters like pearls on a string," see his *Seeing through Zen: Encounter, Transformation, and Genealogy in Chinese Chan Buddhism* (Berkeley: University of California Press, 2003), pp. 10–11. One Annalist, François Dosse, has summed up the orientation of the school as abandoning "significant periods in favor of the daily life of little people." See François Dosse, *New History in France: The Triumph of the Annales* (Urbana: University of Illinois Press, 1994), p. 2.

30. See Robert Sharf, *Coming to Terms with Chinese Buddhism: A Reading of the Treasure Store Treatise* (Honolulu: University of Hawai'i Press, 2001), pp. 9–10.

CHAPTER 2   Registering the Family, Memorializing the Ancestors: The Zen Temple and the Parishioner Household

1. For a detailed study of the Tokugawa bakufu's role in establishing the institutional structure of Sōtō Zen in the seventeenth century, see Williams, "Representations of Zen," chap. 2.

2. I discovered this and other letters relating to the Tetsumei affair with Professor

Tamamuro Fumio of Meiji University in 1997 at the Atsugi City Historical Archives. These letters have not been cataloged but are a part of the *Chōsenji monjo (Tetsumei jiken)* (1784–86) held at Seigen'in Temple, which is unfortunately not included in the Atsugi City Archives catalog, although it is also held at the city archives in microfilm form. Professor Tamamuro has since transcribed selected portions of the letters into printed form and published them in his *Sōshiki to danka* (Tokyo: Yoshikawa kōbunkan, 1999), pp. 209–18. Sections of Tamamuro's research have also been translated into English by Holly Sanders in his "Local Society and the Temple-Parishioner Relationship within the *Bakufu*'s Governance Structure," *Japanese Journal of Religious Studies* 28, 3–4 (2001): 260–92.

3. There are many studies on the so-called Christian century and the conversion of daimyō and those living in their domain during the sixteenth century. Two classic works are C. R. Boxer, *The Christian Century in Japan, 1549–1650* (Berkeley: University of California Press, 1951); and George Elison, *Deus Destroyed: The Image of Christianity in Early Modern Japan* (Cambridge: Council on East Asian Studies, Harvard University, 1991).

4. See Adriana Boscaro, "Toyotomi Hideyoshi and the 1587 Edicts against Christianity," *Oriens extremus* 20 (1973): 219–41, which, in addition to highlighting Hideyoshi's concern about foreign loyalty, demonstrates his concern that Christianity as a religion ran counter to the very nature of Japan as a pantheistic ("land of many gods") nation. Also see Elison, *Deus Destroyed*, pp. 109–141.

5. On the legal aspects of the ban on Christianity, see Annō Masaki, " 'Kirishitan kinrei' no kenkyū," in *Kinsei shakai to shūkyō*, ed. Fujino Tamotsu (Tokyo: Yūzankaku, 1995), pp. 321–58.

6. For an account of the increasing anti-Christian mood of the bakufu, see Joseph Sebes, "Christian Influences on the Shimabara Rebellion, 1637–1638," *Annals of the Jesuit Historical Society* 48 (1979): 140.

7. Konchiin Sūden, the Rinzai monk and bakufu advisor on religious regulations, drafted the *Bateren tsuihōrei* of 1613 before it was sent to the domains with the seal of the shōgun, Tokugawa Hidetada. A printed version of the law can be found in Ebisawa Arimichi, "Kirishitan bateren tsuihōrei," *Rekishi kyōiku* 3/9 (1955): 87–93; and in Annō Masaki, *Bateren tsuihōrei* (Tokyo: Nihon data school shuppanbu, 1989), p. 124. In his book, Annō provides a detailed analysis of the extant variants of the law. For the larger context of the law, see Ebisawa's *Kirishitan no dan'atsu to teikō* (Tokyo: Yūzankaku, 1981), pp. 22–38; Gonoi Takashi, "Keichō jūkyūnen shōgatsu no Kyoto ni okeru Kirisutokyō hakugai ni kansuru ichi kōsatsu: Shoki bakusei to Kirisutokyō," in *Kinsei shakai to shūkyō*, ed. Fujino Tamotsu (Tokyo: Yūzankaku, 1995), pp. 385–420; and Shimizu Hirokazu, "Bateren tsuihōrei no happu o megutte," In *Kinsei shakai to shūkyō*, ed. Fujino Tamotsu (Tokyo: Yūzankaku, 1995), pp. 359–84. An English translation of the law can be found in Boxer, *Christian Century*, p. 148.

8. See Léon Pagès, *Histoire de la religion chrétienne au Japon depuis 1598 jusqu'à 1651* (Paris, 1869).

9. For detailed discussion of the first survey of Christians in Kyoto during early 1614, see Toyoda Takeshi, *Nihon shūkyō seidoshi no kenkyū* (Tokyo: Kōseikaku, 1938), p. 115; for the same period in Kokura Domain in Kyūshū, see the collection at Kumamoto University (*Matsui-ke monjo*) or the study on those documents by Tamamuro Fumio, *Sōshiki to danka*, pp. 15–28. Also see Yoshimura Toyū, "Kinsei shoki Kumamotohan ni okeru Kirishitan kisei no tenkai," *Shigaku kenkyū* 149 (1980): 1–25.

10. For example, in Kokura Domain, after investigating 54 domainal retainers and their family members and servants who confessed to being formerly Christian, a survey of merchants and peasants was conducted for every district in the domain. According to Kawaguchi's study of one district in this investigation, the *Shimogegun bateren montō onaratamechō*, submitted in 1614 for the Shimoge District, 127 former Christians were reported on in detail. See Kawaguchi Kyōko, "Kirishitan korobi shōmon," *Kumamoto*

shigaku 19/20 (1961): 39–69. A study of the Christian impact on Buddhist temples in the Arima and Shimabara regions in Kyūshū is Nei Kiyoshi, "Kirishitan denrai to Arima, Shimabara chihō no jiin" *Nihon rekishi* 427 (1983): 72–78.

11. This can be found in Tamamuro Fumio, *Sōshiki to danka*, p. 21.

12. In some cases, whole villages that were formerly Christian joined the Kōzen'in Temple en masse. Kōzen'in Temple was one of the largest Sōtō Zen temples in the region because of its status as a branch temple of Senpukuji Temple, a direct branch temple of the headquarter Sōjiji Temple. See "Kokurahan jinchiku aratamechō (5)" in *Dai Nihon kinsei shiryō* for a full listing of the number of former Christians in this region. For a study of this document, see Tamamuro Fumio, *Sōshiki to danka*, pp. 25–27.

13. A good English-language introduction to Suzuki Shōsan's thought and activities is Royall Tyler's *Selected Writings of Suzuki Shōsan* (Ithaca: China-Japan Program, Cornell University, 1977), which includes translations of Shōsan's moral tracts (*Mōanjō* and *Banmin tokuyō*), a melodramatic tale (*Ninin bikuni*), and recorded sayings and stories of Shōsan compiled by his disciple, Echū (*Roankyō* and *Kaijō monogatari*). Also see Arthur Braverman, *Warrior of Zen: The Diamond-Hard Wisdom Mind of Suzuki Shōsan* (Tokyo: Kōdansha International, 1994); Elison, *Deus Destroyed*, pp. 224–31; Herman Ooms, *Tokugawa Ideology: Early Constructs, 1570–1680* (Princeton: Princeton University Press, 1985), pp. 123–43, and "'Primeval Chaos' and 'Mental Void' in Early Tokugawa Ideology: Fujiwara Seika, Suzuki Shōsan, and Yamazaki Ansai," *Japanese Journal of Religious Studies* 13/4 (1986): 245–60; and Royall Tyler, "The Tokugawa Peace and Popular Religion: Suzuki Shōsan, Kakugyō Tōbutsu, and Jikigyō Miroku," in *Confucianism and Tokugawa Culture*, ed. Peter Nosco (Princeton: Princeton University Press, 1984), pp. 92–119.

14. There is a large body of literature on Suzuki Shōsan's establishment of Buddhist temples in the Amakusa region during the early Tokugawa period. See Aomori Tōru, "Suzuki Shōsan ni okeru kinsei bukkyō shisō no keisei katei," *Bukkyō shigaku kenkyū* 18/1 (1976): 1–33; Kurachi Katsunao, "Suzuki Shōsan no shisō: Bakuhansei seiritsuki no shihai shisō ni tsuite no hitotsu no kokoromi," *Nihonshi kenkyū* 155 (1975): 24–49; Okumoto Takehiro, "Kinsei zenki no jiin fukkō undō: Suzuki Shōsan o chūshin to shite," *Ryūkoku shidan* 87 (1986): 35–56; rpt. in *Nihon joseishi ronshū 5: Josei to shūkyō*, ed. Sōgō joseishi kenkyūkai (Tokyo: Yoshikawa kōbunkan, 1998), pp. 106–26; and Ōkuwa Hitoshi, "Kinsei shoki no bukkyō fukkō undō: Suzuki Shōsan to sono shūhen," in *Nihon ni okeru kokka to shūkyō*, ed. Shimode Sekiyo Hakase Kanreki Kinenkai (Tokyo: Daizō shuppan, 1978), pp. 219–46, and "Bakuhansei bukkyō no keisei: Suzuki Shōsan to sono shūhen," *Ronshū Nihonjin no seikatsu to shinkō*, ed. Ōtani Daigaku Kokushi Gakkai (Kyoto: Dōhōsha, 1979), pp. 765–800.

15. For a catalog of the original manuscript and early editions of this text's printing, see Ebisawa Arimichi, *Christianity in Japan: A Bibliography of Japanese and Chinese Sources (Part 1, 1543–1858)* (Tokyo: International Christian University, 1960), p. 45. An English translation of the text can be found in Elison, *Deus Destroyed*, pp. 377–89. Also see Fujiyoshi Jikai, "Suzuki Shōsan to kirisutokyō," *Zen bunka kenkyūsho kiyō* 11 (1979): 127–47; rpt. in *Suzuki Shōsan no Zen* (Kyoto: Zen bunka kenkyūsho, 1984), pp. 181–202; and Katayama Shūken, "Suzuki Shōsan no chosaku oyobi jūishū ni okeru ichi kōsatsu to Shimabarashi toshokanzō 'Ha Kirishitan' no shōkai," *SKKK* 5 (1973): 128–29. For other Zen monks' anti-Christian activities in support of the bakufu's policies, see Fréderic Girard, "Discours bouddhiques face au christianisme," In *Repenser l'ordre, repenser l'héritage: Paysage intellectuel du Japon (XVIIe–XIXe siècles)*, ed. Fréderic Girard, Annick Horiuchi, and Mieko Macé (Geneva: Librairie Droz, 2002), pp. 167–207, which focuses on Sessō and Bankei in addition to Suzuki Shōsan; also see Murai Sanae, "Bakuhansei seiritsuki ni okeru haiya katsudō: Zensō o chūshin ni," in *Kinsei shakai to shūkyō*, ed. Fujino Tamotsu (Tokyo: Yūzankaku, 1995), pp. 457–87; Ōkuwa Hitoshi, ed. *Sessō Sōsai: Zen to kokka to kirishitan* (Kyoto: Dōhōsha shuppan, 1984), and "Kinsei shoki bukkyō shisōshi ni okeru shinshōron: Sessō Sōsai 'Zenkyō Tōron' o megutte," in

Ronshū Nihon bukkyōshi: Edo jidai, ed. Tamamuro Fumio (Tokyo: Yūzankaku shuppan, 1986), pp. 157–78.

16. Both Ebisawa and Tamamuro have emphasized the significance of the Shimabara Rebellion as a turning point that was followed by the unflagging efforts of government officials to check on and control potential religiously based subversive elements; see Ebisawa, *Kirishitan no dan'atsu to teikō*, pp. 190–212; and Tamamuro Fumio, "Bakuhan taisei to bukkyō: Kirishitan danatsu to danka seido no tenkai," in *Ronshū Nihon bukkyōshi: Edo jidai*, ed. Tamamuro Fumio (Tokyo: Yūzankaku shuppan, 1986), pp. 1–42. Joseph Sebes has reviewed the debate on whether the Shimabara Rebellion ought to be understood as a Christian uprising joined by peasants or a peasant rebellion in which Christianity played a part. Sebes, "Christian Influences," 136–48.

17. For more on the relationship between Suzuki Shōsan and his younger brother, Suzuki Shigenari, as well as other bakufu officials, see Murakami Tadashi, "Higo no kuni Amakusa ni okeru tenryō no seiritsu katei: Daikan Suzuki Shigenari, Shigetoshi o chūshin ni," *Komazawa joshi tanki daigaku kenkyū kiyō* 3 (1969): 25–40; and Okumoto, "Kinsei zenki no jiin fukkō undo."

18. See Murai, "Bakuhansei seiritsuki ni okeru haiya katsudō," p. 461.

19. The sum of the reward money for bringing in suspected Christians ranged widely. For a discussion of this practice, see Tamamuro Fumio, *Nihon bukkyōshi: Kinsei* (Tokyo: Yoshikawa kōbunkan, 1987), p. 72. We might also recall here that all Jesuit missionaries were supposed to have been expelled under the 1613 *Bateren tsuihōrei*, but obviously some still remained in Japan twenty-five years later. Nam-lin Hur's *Death and Social Order in Tokugawa Japan*, chap. 1, discusses the evolution of these fees for informants. Indeed, the history of hidden Christians (*kakure Kirishitan*) who managed to maintain their faith despite the rigorous attempts to weed them out is a fascinating one. For the ways in which Christians hid their faith, such as worshipping a Kannon statue as Mary (Maria Kannon) or a Jizō statue with a cross discreetly engraved on it, see Matsuda Shigeo, *Kirishitan tōrō no shinkō* (Tokyo: Kōbunsha, 1988). See Williams, "Religion in Early Modern Japan," for a listing of the Western-language literature on the hidden Christians.

20. Officially, the bakufu's directive to conduct *fumi-e* was sent out in 1629, but the practice probably originated before the official directive. For a summary of the different theories of the origins of the *fumi-e* (in both its paper and metallic versions), see Takemura Satoru, *Kirishitan ibutsu no kenkyū* (Tokyo: Kaibunsha shuppan, 1964), pp. 259–61.

21. For more on the Nagasaki Bugyō and the persecution of Christians, see Lane Earns, "The Nagasaki Bugyo and the Development of Bureaucratic Rule in Seventeenth-Century Japan," *Asian Culture* 22/2 (1994): 66–67.

22. In addition to Kyūshū, the practice of *fumi-e* was undertaken at the Kirishitan Yashiki (the "house for Christians") in Edo. See Takemura, Satoru, *Kirishitan ibutsu no kenkyū*, p. 261.

23. On the 1659 Christian survey (*Kirishitan aratame*), see Tamamuro Fumio, *Nihon bukkyōshi*, pp. 75–77. On the *goningumi* and their role in these surveys, see Hubert Cieslik, "Die Goningumi im Dienste der Christenüberwachung," *Monumenta Nipponica* 7 (1951): 112–20; Hozumi Nobushige, *Goningumi seido* (Tokyo: Yūhikaku shobō, 1903); and Rudolf Schüffner, *Die Fünferschaft als Grundlage der Staats- und Gemeindeverwaltung und des sozialen Friedens in Japan zur Zeit der Taikwa-Reform und in der Tokugawa-Periode* (Leipzig: Harrassowitz, 1938). On the development of the *goningumi* system at the local level, see Aoyama Kōji, "Kanagawakenka no goningumichō, 1–2," *Kanagawa kenshi kenkyū* 7 (1969): 40–60; 8 (1970): 39–58.

24. This time lag of roughly thirty-five years between the first surveys and the general surveys of all provinces has been studied by Kanzaki Akitoshi, "Ryōshu to nōmin: Kenchichō to ninbetsuchō," in *Kinsei kyōdoshi kenkyūhō: Kyōdoshi kenkyū kōza 4*, ed. Furushima Toshio et al. (Tokyo: Akakura shoten, 1970), p. 149.

25. See Hirose Ryōkō, *Zenshū chihō tenkaishi no kenkyū*, p. 187.

26. The survey taken by the Sōtō Zen headquarters can be broken down as follows: temples built in the Nara/Heian period (5.3 percent), Kamakura/Muromachi/Azuchi Momoyama periods (30.4 percent), Tokugawa period (41.2 percent), and post-Meiji period (23.1 percent). See Sōtōshū Shūmuchō, *Sōtōshū shūsei sōgō chōsa hōkokusho* (Tokyo: Sōtōshū shūmuchō, 1995), p. 142. The earlier dates, because they are legendary in main cases, must be taken cautiously. Approximately 85 percent of temples of the Jōdo and Jōdo Shin schools were also built during the same period. See Takeda Chōshū, *Minzoku bukkyō to sosen shinkō* (Tokyo: Tokyo daigaku shuppankai, 1971), pp. 69–87.

27. For a comprehensive overview of the connection between the anti-Christian campaign and the temple-registration system, see Nam-lin Hur, *Death and Social Order in Tokugawa Japan*; and Tamamuro Fumio, "Kirishitan kinsei to terauke seido," in *Le vase de béryl: Études sur le Japon et la Chine en hommage à Bernard Frank*, ed. Jacqueline Pigeot and Hartmut Rotermund (Arles, France: Éditions Philippe Picquier, 1997), pp. 581–606.

28. Indeed, as if to foresee the bakufu order, Hosokawa Tadatoshi, the daimyō of Kumamoto Domain, ordered a version of the temple-registration system several months prior to the bakufu order because of the overwhelming number of Christians in his domain. Using a system of village administration particular to Kumamoto, the *tenaga* system, in which village heads reported to their representatives who in turn were accountable to domain officials, all family representatives first had to receive a temple certificate declaring that they were not Christian before handing it to the village head (and from there, up the bureaucratic links to the domain officials). Villages were supposed to hold meetings twice a month in these years to weed out and gather information on suspicious characters. For more on the *tenaga* and temple-registration systems in Kumamoto Domain, see Tamamuro Fumio, *Sōshiki to danka*, pp. 38–48. Since Kyoto was also a hotbed of Christian activity, we can also find extant 1635 temple-registration certificates from the Rinzai Zen temple, Nanzenji. See Fujii Manabu and Sakurai Keiyū, eds. *Nanzenji monjo, gekan* (Kyoto: Nanzenji shūmu honsho, 1988), pp. 20–21.

29. This document, *Kono tabi Kirishitanshū on'aratame ni tsuki danna bōzu shōmon sashiage*, is part of a private collection, Mitsuhashi Monjo (Hatori Village, Fujisawa City). It can be found in printed text form in Tamamuro Fumio, *Nihon bukkyōshi*, p. 62, and translated in Williams, "Representations of Zen," chap. 6.

30. Because of this type of data gathering on individuals throughout Japan, many social historians have examined *shūmon aratamechō* and documents in that genre for information on family structure, life expectancy, and population expansion. For example, the work of Kitagawa links this type of Tokugawa-period social history to the French Annales approach; see Kitagawa Toyouji, "Dewa no kuni Murayamagun Yoshikawamura shūshi ninbetsuchō ni yoru kazokushi no kenkyū: Anāru gakuha narabi ni Kenburiji sukūru no shosetsu o joron to shite," *Tōyō daigaku shakaigaku kiyō* 21 (1984): 217–42.

31. For the ideological aspects of the banning of various religious organizations during the Tokugawa period, see Kikuchi Takeshi, "Kinsei bukkyō tōsei no ichi kenkyū: Ihōgi hatto no jittai to sono haikei," *Nihon rekishi* 365 (1978): 66–88. In English, see Nosco, "Keeping the Faith," esp. 152–53; and Ooms, *Tokugawa Ideology*, pp. 186–93.

32. On the Nichirenshū Fuju Fuse sect, see Aiba Shin, *Fuju fuseha junkyō no rekishi* (Tokyo: Daizō shuppan, 1975); and Miyazaki Eishū, *Fuju fuseha no genryū to tenkai* (Kyoto: Heirakuji shoten, 1969). In English, see Aizawa Yoichi, "Almsgiving and Alms Refusal in the Fuju-Fuse Sect of Nichiren Buddhism with a Consideration of These Practices in Early Indian Buddhism" (Ph.D. dissertation, University of Pennsylvania, 1984); and Kasahara Kazuo, ed., *A History of Japanese Religions* (Tokyo: Kōsei Publishing Co., 2001), pp. 387–408.

33. The temple-registration system in Satsuma Domain was unique not only because of the ban on the Ikkō (Jōdo Shin) school, but because virtually everyone was commanded to wear wooden identification tags stating their sect affiliation. For more on this regional

system, see Robert Sakai, et al., trans., *The Status System and Social Organization of Satsuma: A Translation of the "Shūmon Tefuda Aratame Jōmoku"* (Honolulu: University of Hawai'i Press, 1975), in which the "Regulations for the Investigation of Religious Sects and Identification Tags" (the earliest version is dated 1635, though the version used here is dated 1852) is translated in full. The regulations in Satsuma Domain differed from those adopted by other domains. For example, "In compliance with the *Bakufu* proscription of Christianity, religious sect identification tags were issued long ago for the entire population of the lord's domain. Accordingly, the following pertain to regulations concerning Christianity and the Ikkō sect in connection with the present directive for tag inspections. Special care shall be taken in investigating Christian sects. Persons about whom there is any doubt should be arrested immediately and reported. Moreover, the Ikkō sect, which is prohibited within the lord's domain, also shall be carefully investigated. Of course, persons who are affiliated with this sect shall be reported" (p. 45). For more on the ban on the Ikkō sect, see Hoshino Gentei, "Satsumahan no Shinshū kinsei to Honganji no dōkō," *Shinshū kenkyū* 17 (1972): 16–25; "Satsumahan no shoki Shinshū kinsei seisaku," in *Bukkyō no rekishi to bunka*, ed. Bukkyō Shigakkai (Kyoto: Dōhōsha shuppan, 1980), pp. 757–84; and "Satsumahan no kenchiku shihai to Shinshū kinseisaku," *Shinshū kenkyū* 28 (1984): 1–16.

34. This document, *Sashi age mōsu danna ukejogata no koto*, is part of a private collection, Mitsuhashi Monjo (Hatori Village, Fujisawa City). It can be found in printed text form in Tamamuro Fumio, *Nihon bukkyōshi*, pp. 168–69.

35. On the differences between *shūmon aratamechō* and *kasū ninbetsu aratamechō*, see Kanzaki, *Ryōshu to nōmin*, pp. 136–62. These registers have been sources for a number of population studies pertaining to the social history of the Tokugawa period, especially the study of mortality rates and epidemics. For English-language research, see Laurel Cornell and Akira Hayami, "The *Shumon aratame-chō*: Japan's Population Registers," *Journal of Family History* 11 (1986): 311–28; Ann Jannetta, *Epidemics and Mortality in Early Modern Japan* (Princeton: Princeton University Press, 1987), and "Famine Mortality in Nineteenth-Century Japan: The Evidence from a Temple Register," *Population Studies* 46 (1992): 427–43; and Kinoshita Futoshi, "Mortality Crises in the Tokugawa Period: A View from the *Shūmon Aratame-Chō* in Northeastern Japan," *Nichibunken Japan Review* (1998): 53–72.

36. Sakai, *Status System*, p. 6. For a similar argument, especially as applied to the particularly strict set of control mechanisms in the Satsuma Domain, see Momozono Keishin, "Sappan ni okeru shūmon tefuda aratame no jisshi kaisū ni tsuite," *Kadai shigaku* 2 (1954): 27–33.

37. Village-level registers were organized in a number of different systems, including the temple-to-village headman-to-magistrate-to-domainal office example cited above. But another very important organization unit was the *goningumi* system, which involved five households (*goningumi*) checking on and taking mutual responsibility for verifying each household's adherence to the law. Indeed, by the beginning of the eighteenth century, the *goningumi* had begun to take over some of the functions of the temple's certification process. The 1684 *Goningumi sadamegaki* law proscribed by the bakufu put the responsibility on the five-household units to check on all members (including servants and renters) for Christians or Fuju Fuse members. Three years later, the bakufu issued another law applicable only to bakufu-held domains, the 1687 *Domin shiokijō*, which further determined that *goningumi* would be responsible for carrying out the inspections once a month. For more on these two laws, see Tamamuro Fumio, *Nihon bukkyōshi*, pp. 176–78.

38. The standardization of *shūmon aratamechō* prefaces was based on a style recommended by the bakufu "elder statesman" Ryōshu. This style first appeared in 1665, in the oldest *shūmon aratamechō* from the Kantō region, the *Sōshū Nishigun Nishisuji Chitsushima Kirishitan aratamechō* from Odawara Domain. For discussion of this document and Ryōshu's role in standardizing these registries, see ibid., pp. 94–100.

39. The religious affiliation in this village has been analyzed in detail by Tamamuro Fumio, "Danka seido no tenkai katei: Sagami no kuni Ashigarakamigun Chitsushima-mura shūmon ninbetsuchō no bunseki," in *Kinsei shakai to shūkyō*, ed. Fujino Tamotsu (Tokyo: Yūzankaku, 1995), pp. 171–88.

40. The 1665 *Sagami no kuni Ashigara Kamigun Chitsushimamura shūmon ninbetsu aratamechō* is kept at Meiji University's Keiji Hakubutsukan Museum. The section on Bun'eemon has been published in Tamamuro Fumio, *Nihon bukkyōshi*, pp. 98–100. For another English translation of this kind of register, see Wigmore's translation of a 1683 document regarding parishioners of a Zen temple, Jōkōji, in John Henry Wigmore, ed., *Law and Justice in Tokugawa Japan: Materials for the History of Japanese Law and Justice under the Tokugawa Shogunate, 1603–1867* (Tokyo: Kokusai bunka shinkōkai, 1969), pp. 36–38.

41. The *kata-danka* or *han-danka* phenomenon, in which a member of a household may have a sect affiliation different from that of the head of the family, was relatively un-usual. Generally, the only admissible grounds for changing sect affiliation were if, at the time of marriage, a daughter marrying out or a son adopted into a new family adopted the sect affiliation of that family (and thus adopted a new sect, if the new family was of a different sect). There were also regions where men and women customarily belonged to different parish temples (but here, it was often within the same sect: men at the head tem-ple, women at the branch temple). However, in some exceptional cases—particularly with Jōdo Shin and Nichiren sect believers—a person's religious faith could be cited as a rea-son for sect change. This phenomenon has been discussed by Morimoto Kazuhiko, "Fukudanka kara ikka ichiji e: Dewa no kuni Murayamagun Yamaiemura no jirei," in *Mizoku girei no sekai*, ed. Mori Takao (Osaka: Seibundō shuppan, 2002), pp. 250–69; Noguchi Takenori, "Fukudankasei to fūfubetsu, oyakobetsu bosei: Nihon no shinzoku kenkyū no ichi shikaku," in *Sōso bosei kenkyū shūsei 4*, ed. Mogami Takayoshi (Tokyo: Meichō shuppan, 1979), pp. 375–403, and "Han dankasei," in *Kōza Nihon no minzoku shūkyō 5: Minzoku shūkyō to shakai*, ed. Gorai Shigeru et al. (Tokyo: Kōbundō, 1980), pp. 124–37; Ōkuwa Hitoshi, *Jidan no shisō* (Tokyo: Kyōikusha, 1979), pp. 184–89, and "Jidan seido no seiritsu katei," in *Kinsei shakai to shūkyō*, ed. Fujino Tamotsu (Tokyo: Yūzankaku, 1995), pp. 195–205; Fukuda Ajio, "Kinsei jidan seido no seiritsu to fuku-danka," *Shakai denshō kenkyū 5* (1976): 32–49, and "Kinsei jidan seido to fukudanka," in *Bukkyō minzokugaku taikei 7: Tera to chiiki shakai*, ed. Togawa Anshō (Tokyo: Me-ichō shuppan, 1992), pp. 49–66. The phenomenon of *nijū dankasei* (double parish mem-bership), where parishioners might belong to two temples in a village because of local custom, has been explored by Sakurai Tokutarō, "Fukudankasei seiritsu no kiban: Dan-nadera to sokusaidera," *Shūkyō kenkyū 70/4* (1997): 290–91. Sakurai's research focuses on the Wakasa region in Fukui Prefecture in which monks from both a Shingon temple (Tenmanji) and a Jōdo Shinshū temple (Ryōnenji) jointly performed funerals because of the unique division of labor between the Shingon temple, which performed prayer rituals only, and the Jōdo Shinshū temple, which took over funeral and temple-registration functions for parishioners of both temples. Although the bakufu had banned this practice, a good example of how hard it was to implement in regions that customarily had more than one affiliation can be seen in a series of mutual agreements signed by nineteen tem-ples (of the Sōtō Zen, Shingon, and Jōdo Shin) in the Gosen region of Niigata. See an 1846 code of conduct, the *Han danka ni tsuki jikata no torikime*, signed by temples, which referred to older agreements that finally developed into a set of rules about how to treat double membership. For a printed text version of this agreement, see Gosen Shishi Hensan Iinkai, ed., *Gosen shishi: Shiryō 3, kinsei 2* (Gosen, Niigata: Gosenshi, 1997), pp. 611–13.

42. See Watanabe Masao, *Miura hantō no nōmin seikatsu* (Kanagawa Pref.: Rōkkō shōkai, 1979), pp. 277–78.

43. In addition to further persecution of Christians and their descendents, the cam-paign against the Nichiren Fuju Fuse sect continued, especially in strongholds such as

Okayama Domain. The ban of the Fuju Fuse was first ordered in 1669 and was periodically reissued until the last official directive in 1691. The continual discovery of *kakure daimyō* believers (members of the Fuju Fuse who secretly chanted the *daimoku*, the title of the Lotus Sutra) in Okayama Domain caused concern for both the domain and the bakufu. The campaign included measures to close down temples with such believers and rebuild new Nichiren temples after the sect members recanted and testified that they no longer held illegal mandalas or mortuary tablets of Fuju Fuse priests, which could become objects of devotion. For more on the Okayama campaign, see Tamamuro Fumio, *Nihon bukkyōshi*, pp. 242–50.

44. For a comprehensive survey of the system for identifying Christian descendents (those who fell into this category by marriage, adoption, sibling relations, etc.), see Tamamuro Fumio, *Sōshiki to danka*, pp. 173–77.

45. For the procedures surrounding the salt preservation of the Christian dead, see Gonoi Takashi, *Tokugawa shoki Kirishitanshi kenkyū* (Tokyo: Yoshikawa kōbunkan, 1983), pp. 117–54; and Mita Genshō, *Kirishitan denshō* (Tokyo: Hōbunkan shuppan, 1975), p. 177.

46. However, as Mita has noted, hidden Christians (*kakure Kirishitan*) had their own methods by which to "purify" the dead who received Buddhist funerals, and they performed secret Christian funerary ceremonies. Mountain graves of Christians or their relatives had crosses engraved into the bottom section of the tombstone where no one would see it; examples have been found in the Nagasaki region. See Mita *Kirishitan denshō*, pp. 176–77.

47. The section of the law on how to treat descendents of Christians at death can be found in Tamamuro Fumio, *Nihon bukkyōshi*, p. 236. He includes an estimate of the number of such people (p. 242).

48. For a general overview of the relationship between temples and parishioners, see Kōmoto Mitsugi, "Jiin to danka no sōshiki," in *Kōza Nihon no minzoku shūkyō 5: Minzoku shūkyō to shakai*, ed. Gorai Shigeru et al. (Tokyo: Kōbundō, 1980), pp. 100–23. For a case study of the Jōdo Shin tradition, see Morioka Kiyomi, *Shinshū kyōdan ni okeru 'ie' seido* (Tokyo: Sōbunsha, 1981). For English-language studies, see Kenneth Marcure, "The *Danka* System," *Monumenta Nipponica* 40/1 (1985): 39–67; and Vesey, "The Buddhist Clergy," pp. 347–71.

49. See the Tokugawa-period usage in, for example, a study of wealthy patrons of the Sōtō Zen temple, Chōkokuji, "Chōkokuji o sasaeta hitobito (dai dan'otsu)," in *Azabu Chōkokujishi*, ed. Chōkokujishi Hensan Iinkai (Tokyo: Eiheiji Tokyo betsuin Chōkokuji, 1977), pp. 111–21.

50. Much secondary literature exists concerning the development of the *ie* (household) in Japanese society. A few representative studies include Aruga Kizaemon, "Nihon ni okeru senzo no kannen: Ie no keifu to ie no honmatsu no keifu to," in *Nihon no shakaigaku 19: Shūkyō*, ed. Miyake Hitoshi et al. (Tokyo: Tokyo daigaku shuppankai, 1986), pp. 86–97; Itō Kanji, "Sosen sūhai to ie," in *Sorei shinkō*, ed. Akata Mitsuo (Tokyo: Yūzankaku, 1991), pp. 371–86; Morioka, *Shinshū kyōdan ni okeru 'ie' seido*. For English-language accounts, see Mary Nagata and Chiyo Yonemura, "Continuity, Solidarity, Family and Enterprise: What Is an IE?" in *House and Stem Family in Eurasian Perspective*, ed. Antoinette Fauve-Chamoux and Emiko Ochiai (France: Proceedings of the Twelfth International Economic History Congress, 1998), pp. 193–214; Mary Nagata, "Why Did You Change Your Name? Name Changing Patterns and the Life Course in Early Modern Japan," *The History of the Family: An International Quarterly* 4/3 (1999): 315–38; Ōbayashi Tarō, "*Uji* Society and *Ie* Society from Prehistory to Medieval Times," *Journal of Japanese Studies* 11/1 (1985): 3–27; Wakita Haruko, "Women and the Creation of the *Ie* in Japan: An Overview from the Medieval Period to the Present," *U.S.-Japan Women's Journal English Supplement* 4 (1995): 83–105, and "The Formation of the *Ie* and Medieval Myth: The *Shintōshū*, Nō Theatre, and Picture Scrolls of Temple

Origins," in *Gender and Japanese History,* vol. 1, ed. Wakita Haruko, Anne Bouchy, and Ueno Chizuko (Osaka: Osaka University Press, 1999), pp. 53–85.

51. However, Barbara Ambros makes a useful distinction between the use of the terms *danna/danka* in the context of temple registration at parish temples (*tera-uke danna/danka*) and in the context of household affiliates held by pilgrim guides (*oshi*) of pilgrimage sites and sacred mountains, such as at Mt. Ōyama; see Barbara Ambros, "Localized Religious Specialists in Early Modern Japan: The Development of the Ōyama *Oshi* System," *Japanese Journal of Religious Studies* 28/3–4 (2001): 341–44. One can also see the use of the term "danka" in terms of Shugen temples as "prayer temple danka" (*kitō danka*). See Tanaka Yōhei, "Kinsei ni okeru shugen jiin no kaidan to kitō jidan kankei," *Fūzoku shigaku* 16 (2001): 18–31. Ōkuwa Hitoshi also makes a useful distinction among *montō, danna,* and *danka* in "Jidan seido no seiritsu katei," pp. 192–95.

52. A comprehensive overview of parish temples can be found in Ōkuwa, "Jidan seido no seiritsu katei," pp. 189–228. Ōkuwa has divided scholarship on the subject into three types: (1) studies that emphasize the role of the temples in enforcing the bakufu's policies for the control of its populace; (2) studies that emphasize the economic aspects of parish temples; and (3) those that emphasize the social unit of the "household" and its connection to the temple. For an English-language study of the Tokugawa-period temple-parishioner system, see Marcure, "The *Danka* System."

53. This document (also known as the *Tōshōgū Jūgokajō*), translated here in a slightly abridged form, can be found in Tamamuro Fumio, *Nihon bukkyōshi,* pp. 183–86, and in his *Sōshiki to,* pp. 183–88. While this document has the air of a government directive outlining parishioner responsibilities to the parish temple, as Tamamuro Fumio has demonstrated, it was not written by bakufu officials and cannot be dated back to the fifth month of 1613. What makes this document resemble an order from the bakufu is the reference in its preamble to the ban on the teachings of the so-called four heretical religions: the Bateren (Christian fathers), Kirishitan (Christians in general), Fuju Fuse (the Nichiren "No-receiving, no-giving" school), and Hidenshū (another reference to the Fuju Fuse sect). But these four groups were not officially banned until after the date written on the document: the Bateren in the twelfth month, 1613, the Kirishitan in 1638, the Fuju Fuse in 1669, and the Hidenshū in 1691. Moreover, Tamamuro argues, how could parishioner obligations be written up in this way in 1613, when the temple-registration system was not even operative until 1635? Since there is no record in the government's internal archives of the bakufu ever issuing this document, Tamamuro has concluded that this document was most likely written not by a bakufu official, but by a Buddhist priest probably after 1691 (when the Hidenshū was banned). For Tamamuro's arguments, see his *Nihon bukkyōshi,* pp. 180–86. On similar "fake" directives such as the Stipulations for All Temples (*Sho jiin jōmoku*) dated 1691, see Tamamuro Fumio, "Sōtōshū to danka seido," in *Shūkyō shūdan no ashita e no kadai: Sōtōshū shūsei jittai chōsa hōkokusho,* ed. Odawara Rinin (Tokyo: Sōtōshū shūmuchō, 1982), pp. 307–8.

54. For the growth of temple size after 1700, see Tamamuro Fumio, "Sōtōshū to danka seido," pp. 310–11.

55. I have relied here on Tamamuro's research. For several case studies of households taken off the register, see Tamamuro Fumio, *Sōshiki to danka,* pp. 200–202.

56. This story, "Otōto no yūrei ani ni on o nasu koto tsuketari aniyome ni tsukeru koto," is number 14.3 in *Inga monogatari, jōkan,* in *Koten bunko 185,* ed. Yoshida Kōichi (Tokyo: Koten bunko, 1962). For an interpretation of the *Inga monogatari* as a didactic, but secularized, form of the telling of "strange and mysterious tales," see Noriko Reider, "The Emergence of *Kaidan-shū*: The Collection of Tales of the Strange and Mysterious in the Edo Period," *Asian Folklore Studies* 60/1 (2001): 79–100.

57. George Smith, *Ten Weeks in Japan* (London: Longman, Green, Longman, and Roberts, 1861), p. 31.

58. For an overview of the medieval Sōtō Zen interpretation of precepts, see Nakao

Ryōshin, "Zenmon no sōgi to kaimyō jūyo," *Nihon bukkyō gakkai nenpō* 63 (1998): 136–45; and Bodiford, *Sōtō Zen in Medieval Japan*, pp. 163–84.

59. For a more detailed discussion of the multiple usage of the term *kaimyō* and its historical development, see Sasaki Kōkan, "Kaimyō no shūkyō: Shakaiteki imi ni tsuite," in *Kaimyō no imi to kinō*, ed. Sōtōshū Gendai Kyōgaku Center (Tokyo: Sōtōshū gendai kyōgaku center, 1995), p. 15.

60. Hirose's study focused on the earliest records of mass precept ordinations held at a Sōtō Zen temple (Kenkon'in in Aichi Prefecture): the *Kechimyakushū* (which covers 724 individuals from 1477 to 1488) and the *Shōshichō* (which covers 77 individuals in 1490–91). A somewhat later record, the *Tōji zenjū sūdai no kaichō* of Tokushōji Temple (Shiga Prefecture), which provided Hirose with a point of contrast, recorded 418 individuals from 1535 to 1568. Since these records kept track of not only the individual's new "precept name," but also their social background, Hirose determined that a wide range of people (from the daimyō on down to female servants) participated in these ceremonies. Such mass ordinations had precedents in the Rinzai school under Eisai during the fourteenth century, who established a pattern of holding such events on auspicious occasions such as the Buddha's birthday or a *parinirvana* (*nehan-e*) ceremony, and in the Sōtō school under Keizan and Gasan in the fourteenth century. See Hirose Ryōkō, "Chūsei Zen'in no unei to keizai katsudō: Owari no kuni Chitagun Kenkon'in shozō 'ichimaigami utsushi' no bunseki o chūshin to shite," *Komazawa shigaku* 24 (1977): 72–91, and "Chūsei Zensō to jukai-e: Aichiken Chitagun Kenkon'inzō 'Kechimyakushū' 'shōshichō' no bunseki o chūshin to shite," in *Minzoku shigaku no hōhō* (Tokyo: Yūzankaku, 1977), pp. 305–59, rpt. in his *Zenshū chihō tenkaishi no kenkyū* (Tokyo: Yoshikawa kōbunkan, 1988), pp. 422–81.

61. See Hirose Ryōkō, "Nihon Sōtōshū no chū, kinsei ni okeru jukai to kaimyō," in *Kaimyō no imi to kinō*, ed. Sōtōshū Gendai Kyōgaku Center (Tokyo: Sōtōshū gendai kyōgaku center, 1995), p. 62.

62. This can be found in the letter "Padre Cosmo de Torres shokan," in *Iezusukaishi Nihon tsūshin, jō*, ed. Yanagiya Teruo (Tokyo: Yūshōdō shoten, 1968), p. 23.

63. See Jacques Le Goff, *Your Money or Your Life: Economy and Religion in the Middle Ages* (New York: Zone Books, 1988), p. 44. For the theme of paying for salvation, also see Francesco L. Galassi, "Buying a Passport to Heaven: Usury, Restitution, and the Merchants of Medieval Genoa," *Religion* 4 (1992): 313–26.

64. For the economics of paying for the erasure of karma in the afterlife in Chinese Buddhism, see Hou Ching-lang, *Monnaies d'offrande et la notion de trésorerie dans la religion chinoise* (Paris: Institut des Hautes Études Chinoises, Collège de France, 1975). While the practice of offering religious paper money to the gods, ghosts, and ancestors was not found in Japan, the practice of putting a small "money bag" or coins (*rokudō-sen*, lit. money for the six realms) in the coffin could be found in some regions of Japan. For an extensive review of Hou Ching-lang's work on the financial dealings between this world and the next, see Anna Seidel, "Buying One's Way to Heaven: The Celestial Treasury in Chinese Religions," *History of Religions* 17/3–4 (1978): 419–31.

65. For more discussion of the gap between priestly and lay understanding of posthumous names, see Sasaki, "Kaimyō no shūkyō," p. 16.

66. Although a Sōtō Zen sectwide standard on the assignment of posthumous names did not exist, Sōtō Zen priests followed certain conventions. Manuals on how to assign such titles and names likely began in the sixteenth century, especially among Rinzai and Sōtō Zen circles. The earliest Sōtō Zen manual that provided guidelines for creating posthumous names was the *Shōhō shingi*, which only dealt with the creation of such names before death (*gyakushū*), a popular practice during the Muromachi period; see Shiina Kōyū, "Nihon Sōtōshū ni okeru kaimyō (chūsei)," in *Kaimyō no imi to kinō*, ed. Sōtōshū Gendai Kyōgaku Center (Tokyo: Sōtōshū gendai kyōgaku center, 1995), p. 54. On the Rinzai side, the *Shoekō shingi*, edited by Tenrin Fuin in 1565 (though not published until 1657), included a section on how to create posthumous names for memorial

tablets. This manual was also used in the Sōtō school; see Matsumoto Kōichi, "Kaimyō shinkō no rekishi to mondaiten," in *Kaimyō no imi to kinō*, ed. Sōtōshū Gendai Kyōgaku Center (Tokyo: Sōtōshū gendai kyōgaku center, 1995), p. 9.

67. This most common way of assigning posthumous names in the Zen school is taken from Egaku Kyokusui, ed., *Zenshū no ingō, dōgō, kaimyō jiten* (Tokyo: Kokusho kankōkai, 1989), pp. 11–13.

68. The use of the character "in" for posthumous names began during the Muromachi period. The tendency to create high-ranking posthumous names with a long string of Chinese characters for those of high social standing was most clearly exemplified at the beginning of the Tokugawa period with the assignment of the name "Tōshō Daigongen Antokuinden Tokurensha Sūyo Dōwa Daikoji" for the first Tokugawa shōgun, Ieyasu.

69. See Tamamuro Fumio, *Sōshiki to danka*, p. 194.

70. Hirose has studied both temple bulletins giving price lists for posthumous names at Jutokuji Temple (Sagami Province) from 1661 and notices sent out in 1796 from Jikōji Temple (Mikawa Province) to inform parishioners of the going rate for the various ranks. See Hirose, "Nihon Sōtōshū no chū," p. 79, and also his "Mura no jiin to murabito no kaimyō," in *Shōen to mura o aruku*, ed. Fujiki Hisashi and Arano Yasunori (Tokyo: Azekura shobō, 1997), pp. 409–11. Tamamuro has also conducted research on posthumous name rates in Kantō region temples in the early 1800s. The Sōtō Zen average fee seems to have been around three to five *ryō* for the "Ingō"-level prefix, while the "Koji/Daishi" suffix sold for roughly one *ryō*, the "Shinji/Shinnyo" for two *kanmon*, and the "Zenjōmon/Zenjōni," or the basic two-character precept name, for one *kanmon*. These rates, Tamamuro claims, are relatively high compared to rates he found at Ji sect temples. Although it is hard to determine the market rate for these posthumous names throughout the Tokugawa period, the general trend seems to have been a decrease in prices for higher ranks, putting them within the reach of greater numbers of parishioners. See Tamamuro Fumio, *Sōshiki to danka*, p. 196.

71. This can be found in the *Kyōkokunai shingi*, in SZ *Shingi*: 555–74.

72. For an English-language introduction to the genre of documents known as *kirigami* (secret transmission or secret initiation manuals), originally slips of paper, see Ishikawa, "The Transmission of *Kirigami* (Secret Initiation Documents): A Sōtō Practice in Medieval Japan," in *The Koan: Text and Context in Zen Buddhism*, ed. Steve Heine and Dale Wright, trans. Seishū Kawahashi (Oxford: Oxford University Press, 2000), pp. 233–43. For a survey of this kind of "culture of secret transmission," see Susan Klein, *Allegories of Desire: Esoteric Literary Commentaries of Medieval Japan* (Cambridge: Harvard University Asia Center, 2002), pp. 145–50. On Menzan's critique of such *kirigami*, see Matsumoto, "Kaimyō shinkō no rekishi to mondaiten," p. 10. These critiques took place in the context of a dialogue among key doctrinal specialists of the tradition, like Menzan and Manzan, who, in the so-called sect restoration movement, reflected on the correct interpretation of precepts in the Zen tradition. On this topic, see Shiina Kōyū, "Edoki Zenkairon no tenkai," in *Kaimyō no imi to kinō* Sōtōshū, ed. Gendai Kyōgaku Center (Tokyo: Sōtōshū gendai kyōgaku center, 1995), pp. 82–87.

73. Hirose Ryōkō, in his study of 4,176 posthumous names inscribed in the temple registry at a Sōtō Zen temple in Ibaraki, showed that during the first half of the Tokugawa period almost all the posthumous names consisted of the lowest-ranking two-character "Zenjōmon" (male) or "Zenjōni" (female) suffixes. However, from the mid-Tokugawa period, the same suffixes with four characters began to appear. Finally, by the end of the Tokugawa period, the four-character "Shinji" (male) and "Shinnyo" (female) suffixes became standard. The same pattern existed at Jutokuji Temple (Sagami Province), with the low-ranking two-character "Zenjōmon/Zenjōni" virtually disappearing by 1760. This suggests that even peasants and those low on the social hierarchy could assure themselves of a better name in the afterlife if they made suitable monetary contributions. Indeed, in his analysis of who received higher-ranking posthumous names, Hirose discovered a correlation between property ownership and/or the size of temple donations (especially when

temple buildings needed repair) with higher-ranking names. In line with the generally accepted practice in Japan when using data from temple registries, Hirose opted to keep the name of the Ibaraki temple anonymous. His study of 1,500 posthumous names at a Shingi Shingon sect temple revealed that this basic pattern of higher ranks and more elaborate naming toward the mid- to late-Tokugawa period was not limited to the Sōtō sect. See Hirose, "Nihon Sōtōshū no chū," pp. 66, 80–81. Also see Hirose's "Kakochō' kara mita kinsei no Sueyoshimura," In *Hachijōjima Sueyoshichiku bunkazai chōsa hōkoku*, ed. Kyōikuchō (Tokyo: Kyōikuchō, 1981), pp. 121–39, and "Mura no jiin to murabito no kaimyō," pp. 402–3, 411–20.

74. Though the earliest *kakochō* can be traced to the medieval period, the standardization of these registries began in the 1650s, and their nationwide use began in the Genroku-Kyōhō era (1688–1716). Of course, since these registers were not ordered by bakufu law, it is hard to determine the precise date at which their use became widespread. For more on the development of the *kakochō* in the late medieval and early Tokugawa period, see Kyōka Kenshūjo, ed., *Shūmon sōsai no tokushitsu o saguru* (Kyoto: Dōhōsha shuppan, 1985), p. 314, as well as Tamamuro Fumio, *Sōshiki to danka*, pp. 188–90. These registries of the deceased, which "accounted" for the dead, came in three types: (1) the Annual (*Nenji shokei*) Style: These registries recorded the funeral date of parishioners by year, month, and day. Each successive abbot filled in new deaths during their tenure in chronological order. (2) the Calendrical (*Himekuri* or *Kuridashi*) Style: These registries were divided by each day of the month so that when a death occurred, it would be recorded under the correct month and day. This type of register would be kept in the main hall of the temple available for the priest checking up on whose memorial services needed to be held on any given day. The format of the register was that at the beginning of each day's entry, a short list of the highest-ranking parishioners or abbots of the temple would be recorded, before a general list of regular parishioners, in chronological order. (3) the Household-by-Household (*Iebetsu*) Style: These registries were written for each household, adding the name of the most recently deceased to the family genealogy of the dead. This type of registry might be held at the family residence (in the family Buddhist altar along with the memorial tablets), or at the memorial tablet hall of the parish temple, where this family list would be placed together with the household's permanent tablet. It was useful in planning ancestral memorial services, especially if combined services for more than one ancestor were to be held. Although all three types of *kakochō* developed during the Tokugawa period, the "day-of-the-month" type was used most frequently by priests and is generally what people today refer to as *kakochō*. This typology can be found in Tamamuro Fumio, *Soshiki to danka*, p. 190.

75. Hirose, "Nihon Sōtōshū no chū," p. 66.

76. Although a particular person's death anniversary would occur only once a year, with this style of *kakochō* it was possible to perform a memorial service on every day that matched the original date (i.e., twelve services per year). This style of memorial service where family members paid a lump sum for monthly services grew in popularity during the Tokugawa period. For example, in the case of a certain Suzuki Hirobee, his family donated one *tan* six *se* (equivalent to 1,584 square meters) of land to Jutokuji Temple in 1749 as a "monthly memorial service fee." See Hirose, "Mura no jiin to murabito no kaimyō," pp. 399–406.

77. For a good English-language overview of the issue of discrimination in Sōtō Zen registers of the dead and posthumous names, see William Bodiford, "Zen and the Art of Religious Prejudice: Efforts to Reform a Tradition of Social Discrimination," *Japanese Journal of Religious Studies* 23/1–2 (1996): 1–28.

78. For a general overview of the literature on the status categories of *hinin*, *kawata* (lit. "leather workers) and *eta* (lit. "plentiful dirt" or "full of defilement"), see Amino Yoshihiko, "Asobi onna to hinin, kawaramono," in *Sei to mibun*, ed. Miyata Noboru (Tokyo: Shunjūsha, 1989), pp. 93–128; Gerald Groemer, "The Creation of the Edo Outcaste Order," *Journal of Japanese Studies* 27, 2 (2001): 263–94; Hatanaka Toshiyuki,

"*Kawata*" *to heijin: Kinsei mibun shakairon* (Kyoto: Kamogawa shuppan, 1992); Nagahara Keiji, "Medieval Origins of the Eta-Hinin," *Journal of Japanese Studies* 5/2 (1979):
385–403; and Herman Ooms, *Tokugawa Village Practice: Class, Status, Power, Law*
(Berkeley: University of California Press, 1996), chap. 5. For the link between *eta-hinin*
and the Buddhist ideology of discrimination, see Ian Laidlaw, "The Origins and Future of
the Burakumin" (M.A. thesis, University of Otago, 2001), pp. 17–27. For discussion of
these status categories in the context of the modern liberation of such peoples, see Ian
Neary, *Political Protest and Social Control in Prewar Japan: The Origins of Buraku Liberation* (Manchester: Manchester University Press, 1989).

79. See Kobayashi Daiji, *Sabetsu kaimyō no rekishi* (Tokyo: Yūzankaku shuppan,
1987), pp. 173–75. For a discussion of religious itinerants who often came close to being
classified as "hinin" by the bakufu, see Groemer, "A Short History of *Gannin.*"

80. Reprinted in Sōtōshū Jinken Yōgo Suishin Honbu, ed., "*Ashiki gōron*" *kokufuku
no tame ni* (Tokyo: Sōtōshu shūmuchō, 1987), p. 4. For a discussion in English, see Bodiford, *Zen and the Art of Religious Prejudice*, p. 15.

81. There is now a large body of research on how this view of karma shaped social discrimination. In the case of the Sōtō sect, in particular, see Ishikawa Rikizan, " 'shōbōgenzō' no gōron to 'Denkōroku,' 'shushōgi' no gōron," *Shūgaku kenkyū* 33 (1991):
105–12; Kudō Eishō, "Sabetsu no ronri kōzō: Sōtōshū sabetsu kirigami ni okeru gō,
rinne, busshō shisō ni tsuite," *Shūgaku kenkyū* 30 (1988): 131–36; Sōtōshū Jinken Yōgo
Suishin Honbu, ed. "*Ashiki gōron,*" and "*Gō*" *ni tsuite: Dōgen zenji no ningenkan to buraku kaihō* (Tokyo: Sōtōshū shūmuchō, 1993); Sōtōshū shūmuchō, " 'Gō' ron ni tsuite:
Dōgen Zenji no jinkenkan to buraku kaihō," *Genshoku kenkyū* 12 (1991): 6–82. For
more general studies, see Nishida Shin'in, "Sabetsu mondai kara nani ga towareteiru no
ka: Zen'aku ingaron ni mondaisei ni tsuite no joron," *Shinshū Ōtaniha kyōgaku
kenkyūsho kyōka kenkyū* 99 (1989): 100–158; and Zen Nihon Bukkyōkai, ed., *Sabetsu
mondai to gōron ni tsuite* (Tokyo: Zen Nihon bukkyōkai, 1987).

82. The issue of Japanese Buddhism and social discrimination against outcasts has received considerable attention in the last two decades. Secondary literature on this subject
includes Andachi Itsuo, *Bukkyō to buraku mondai kankei shiryō shūsei*, 2 vols. (Kobe:
Hyōgo buraku kaihō kenkyūsho, 1995–97); Iwaya Kyōju, "Buraku jiinsei ni tsuite no
ichi kōsatsu: Harima no kuni Shinshū kyōdan o chūshin ni," *Dōwa kyōiku ronkyū* 10
(1988): 128–51; Monma Sachio, "Shūmon ni okeru sabetsu jishō," *Shūgaku kenkyū* 28
(1986): 97–106; Nishiki Kōichi, "Kinsei Kantō ni okeru 'chōri' jidan kankei," *Chihōshi
kenkyū* 219 (1989): 26–40, and "Kinsei Kantō no 'chōri' to dannadera: Sabetsu no
rekishiteki ichizuke o mezashite," *Buraku mondai kenkyū* 98 (1989): 43–63; Saitō Manabu, " 'Buraku sabetsu to Jōdo shinshū kenkyū kōsō nōto," *Dōwa kyōiku ronkyū* 10
(1988): 152–66; Yamamoto Naotomo, "Kinsei buraku jiin no seiritsu ni tsuite," *Kyoto
burakushi kenkyūsho kiyō* 1/1 (1981): 80–126; 2/2 (1982): 34–62.

83. The detailed ritual prescriptions on how to perform such discriminatory funerals
were described in *kirigami*, such as the *Hinin narabi tenkyōbyō kirigami* (1611, Shinsōji
Temple, Shinano Province). This can be found in *Shinano shiryō, hoi ge* (Nagano: Shinano shiryō kankōkai, 1971), p. 189. Also see Ishikawa Rikizan, *Zenshū sōden shiryō no
kenkyū ge*, vol. 2 (Kyoto: Hōzōkan, 2001), pp. 1023–33.

84. See Ishikawa Rikizan, "Sabetsu kirigami to sabetsu jishō ni tsuite," *Shūgaku
kenkyū* 27 (1985): 140.

85. For more on these talismans, see Hirose, "Nihon Sōtōshū no chū," p. 67.

86. The *Hinin indō no kirigami*, which served as the manual for these rituals, increased
in number throughout the Tokugawa period. The 1630 *kirigami* is from Saimyōji Temple
(Aichi Prefecture); see Ishikawa Rikizan, "Chūsei Sōtōshū kirigami no bunrui shiron 4,"
KDBR 15 (1984): 153.

87. Various incidents sparked concern about discriminatory posthumous names and
rituals within the Sōtō Zen sect, especially the so-called Machida incident of 1979 when
the head of the Sōtō school, Machida Muneo, convinced delegates at the World Confer-

ence on Religion and Peace (held in United States that year) to delete any mention of Japanese outcasts from the conference report. See Sōtōshū Shūmuchō, "Sōtōshū ni taisuru buraku kaihō dōmei no kakunin kyūdankai keika hōkoku," *Sōtō shūhō* 551 (1981): 354–60, and "Buraku kaihō dōmei no mōshiire ni taisuru Sōtōshū no kaitōsho," *Sōtō shūhō* 573 (1983): 1–52. In English, see Bodiford, *Zen and the Art of Religious Prejudice*, pp. 1–4.

88. On the use of the term "sendara" in social discrimination, see Hayashi Hisayoshi, *Bukkyō ni miru sabetsu no kongen: Sendara, etori hōshi no gongen* (Tokyo: Akashi shoten, 1997); Kudō Eishō, "Sendara sabetsu no ideologii kōzō," *Shūgaku kenkyū* 40 (1998): 267–72; Taira Masayuki, "Tabous et alimentation carnées dans l'histoire du Japon," in *Identités, marges, méditations: Regards croisés sur la société japonaise*, ed. Jean-Pierre Berthron, Anne Bouchy, and Pierre Souyri (Paris: École Française d'Extrême-Orient, 2001), p. 173; and Yuji Sogen, "Shūtenchū no 'sendara' ni taisuru gendaigo yaku ya chūki no mondai ni tsuite," *Shūgaku kenkyū* 37 (1995): 292–97.

89. For the most comprehensive analysis of ways to write the discriminatory posthumous names, see Kobayashi Daiji, *Sabetsu kaimyō no rekishi* (Tokyo: Yūzankaku shuppan, 1987), pp. 273–312. For a more detailed, English-language discussion, see Bodiford, *Zen and theArt of Religious Prejudice*, p. 15. On discriminatory posthumous names in general, see Matsune Taka, "Jōhōsarenakatta sabetsu hōmyō," *Buraku kaihō* 347 (1992): 28–36; Shiroyama Daiken, "Hōshōji kakochō sabetsu kisai e no tori kumi," *Buraku kaihō kenkyū* 1 (1994): 21–27; Nichirenshū Jinken Mondai Taisaku Kaigi, ed., *Sabetsu kaimyō to wa* (Tokyo: Nichirenshū shūmuin, 1992); and Sōtōshū Shūmuchō, *"Sabetsu kaimyō" no kaisei ni tsuite* (Tokyo: Sōtōshū Shūmuchō, 1994).

90. Kobayashi Daiji, *Sabetsu kaimyō no rekishi*, pp. 273–79.

91. Members of the outcast community were classified as "garden sweepers" rather than "parishioners" in Chōfukuji Temple's temple registry. See Kizu Yuzuru, "Sabetsu kaimyō ni zange," *Buraku kaihō* 398 (1995): 85–86.

92. Tomonaga Kenzō, "Gendai no buraku mondai," in *Buraku kahōshi: Netsu to hikari*, ed. Buraku Mondai Kenkyūsho (Osaka: Buraku mondai kenkyūsho, 1989), p. 221. This number conflicts with the official number reported by the Sōtō Headquarters (for example, only 235 registries were reported in a survey taken in 1994). The widespread nonreporting and underreporting of Sōtō Zen temples makes the headquarter's survey unreliable. At the same time, the numbers were perhaps inflated by the Buraku Liberation Movement. I nevertheless use them here because even if figures were inflated, it is not specific to a particular Buddhist school and thus allows for comparative analysis.

93. Challenges to bakufu authority at a local village level are a major theme of Herman Ooms's important work on village life and law, *Tokugawa Village Practice*, and Alexander Vesey's study of parishioners, local society, and temple relations, "The Buddhist Clergy."

94. A 1688 bakufu missive, the *Jiin bōsha ni nyonin kakaeokubekarazu no koto*, prohibited women from living on temple grounds, even if they were the sister or mother of the temple priest. It further prohibited any sexual relations for priests, the consequence being execution by beheading. For this missive, see *EJTS*: 178. Richard Jaffe has chronicled various bakufu laws regarding clerical fornication and adultery in the eighteenth century, including such punishments as banishment to a remote island, public humiliation, and execution. See his *Neither Monk nor Layman: Clerical Marriage in Modern Japanese Buddhism* (Princeton: Princeton University Press, 2001), pp. 20–25. The best survey of recorded cases of clerical indiscretion during the Tokugawa period is Ishida Mizumaro's *Nyobon: Hijiri no sei* (Tokyo: Chikuma shobō, 1995), pp. 153–215.

95. The original text can be found in the *Chōsenji Monjo* held at Seigen'in Temple. This letter can be found in printed form, see Tamamuro Fumio, *Sōshiki to danka*, pp. 213–14.

96. On the social and legal history of adultery during the Tokugawa period, see Mega Atsuko, *Hanka no naka no onnatachi: Okayamahan no kiroku kara* (Tokyo: Heibonsha,

1995); and Ujiie Mikito, *Fugimitsū: Kinjirareta ai no Edo* (Tokyo: Kōdansha, 1997). Bernard Faure has also written on the "clerical vices" of Buddhist priests during the Tokugawa period and details several cases where monks who had engaged in sexual relations were executed by crucifixion in his *The Red Thread: Buddhist Approaches to Sexuality* (Princeton: Princeton University Press, 1998), pp. 149–50, 186–89.

97. A section of this letter can be found in Tamamuro, *Sōshiki to danka*, pp. 217–18.

98. See Williams, "Representations of Zen," chap. 2.

99. On the increasing powers of the wealthy lay temple "officers" (known alternatively as *danka sōdai, dangashira, danna sōdai,* or *danchū sōdai*) to represent the temple's parishioners, see Takemura Makio, "Sōdai seido no hensen ni tsuite," *Shūkyōhō kenkyū* 2 (1981): 79–105.

100. The Jōjō can be found in Tamamuro Fumio, *Nihon bukkyōshi*, pp. 89–91. An English summary can be found in Kasahara, *History of Japanese Religions*, pp. 336–37.

101. Cited in Tamamuro Fumio, *Nihon bukkyōshi*, p. 188.

102. The excessive burdens that Buddhist temples placed on parishioners were problematized in the Okayama Domain by domainal authorities who criticized the lack of sect choice for parishioners and the financial burdens involved for temple membership. Following the domain's campaign to restructure Buddhist temples, begun in 1666, 57.8 percent of all Buddhist temples were destroyed, and a short-lived effort to switch to a Shintō shrine registration system also reflected criticism of the Buddhist temples. For the Okayama Domain's anti-Buddhist campaign, see ibid., pp. 131–66; Tamamuro Fumio, "Okayamahan no jisha seiri seisaku ni tsuite," *Meiji daigaku jinbun kagaku kenkyūsho kiyō* 40 (1996): 364–82, and *Sōshiki to danka*, pp. 100–28. For the Shintō registration campaign in Okayama, see Maeda Hiromi, "Ikeda Mitsumasa's Shrine Reform during the Kanbun Period (1661–1672)," paper presented at Nov. 1999 American Academy of Religion meeting, Boston). For attempts to introduce Shintō funerals during the early modern period, see Endō Jun, "'The Shinto Funeral Movement' in Early Modern and Modern Japan," *Nihon bunka kenkyūsho kiyō* 82 (1998): 1–31.

103. Approximately 200 ounces of rice.

104. The 1714 bakufu missive, *Jisha keidai no shibai narabi ni yūjo goginmi no koto,* which prohibited theatrical performances and prostitutes on temple grounds, was obviously not strictly kept. For this missive, see *EJTS*: 182. In a well-known incident from 1796, bakufu police officers rounded up seventy Buddhist priests in the red-light district of Yoshiwara in an early morning raid. For more on this incident, see Hur, *Prayer and Play in Late Tokugawa Japan*, p. 73.

105. The 1825 *Chōsenji hōjō aitedori murakata danka no uchi yonjūrokunin fukie no ikken* by Zenbee and Kyūemon can be found in the *Seigen'in monjo* (Atsugishishi hensan shitsu, microfilm no. 72).

106. Here I am relying heavily on the discussion of this case by Tamamuro Fumio, *Sōshiki to danka*, pp. 203–7. The letters that went back and forth are collected in Shin Kumamotoshishi Hensan Iinkai, ed., *Shin Kumamotoshishi: Shiryōhen 3, kinsei 1* (Kumamoto: Kumamotoshi, 1996), pp. 861–70.

107. Shin Kumamotoshishi Hensan Iinkai, ed., *Shin Kumamotoshishi.*

CHAPTER 3   Funerary Zen: Managing the Dead in the World Beyond

1. Smith, *Ten Weeks in Japan*, p. 145.

2. For more on this cleansing practice, see Tamamuro Taijō, *Sōshiki bukkyō*, p. 83.

3. This can be found in the *Keizan shingi* (SZ 2, 449) and has been translated by Nara Yasuaki, "May the Deceased Get Enlightenment! An Aspect of the Enculturation of Buddhism in Japan," *Buddhist-Christian Studies* 15 (1995): 38–39. Satō has noted the influence of Jōdo and Ritsu practices of *Taiya nenju* on this Sōtō Zen version. See Satō Shōshi, "Shūmon sōsai girei no hensen 1," *Kyōka kenshū* 33 (1990): 55.

4. Suzuki Hikaru outlines the shift from locally based "community funerals" to the postwar "commercial ceremonies" in her *The Price of Death: The Funeral Industry in Contemporary Japan* (Stanford: Stanford University Press, 2000), see esp. chap. 2.

5. See Tamamuro Taijō, *Sōshiki bukkyō*, p. 83.

6. The interrelation between sectarian Buddhist and non- and pre-Buddhist funerary practices is complex and has received substantial research from Japanese Buddhist scholars, anthropologists, and historians. Halldór Stefánsson has classified three major approaches to the study of funerals: (1) studies that emphasize the Buddhist aspect of funerals, that is, focusing on how Buddhism took over an aspect of Japanese religious life that had previously been considered taboo (e.g., Haga Noboru); (2) studies that emphasize the non-Buddhist aspects of funerals, that is, highlighting the indigenous roots of funerary and ancestral rites (e.g., Yanagita Kunio and Takeda Chōshū); and (3) studies that emphasize the structural or systemic aspects of funerals (e.g., Herman Ooms) to which Stefánsson adds his approach that focuses on the collective forms of concern for the dead (such as village-level practices). See Halldór Stefánsson, "On Structural Duality in Japanese Conceptions of Death: Collective Forms of Death Rituals in Morimachi," in *Ceremony and Ritual in Japan: Religious Practices in an Industrialized Society*, ed. Jan van Bremen and D. P. Martinez (London: Routledge, 1995), pp. 83–107. To these four approaches, I would add another: studies that emphasize the role Confucian ideas played in forming funerary practices (e.g., Kaji Nobuyuki). For Haga Noboru's work, see *Sōgi no rekishi* (Tokyo: Yūzankaku, 1970). For Takeda Chōshū, see *Sosen sūhai* (Kyoto: Heirakuji shoten, 1957) and *Minzoku bukkyō to sosen shinkō*. For Yanagita Kunio, see "Senzo no hanashi," in *Teibon Yanagita Kunio 10* (Tokyo: Chikuma shobō, 1969), pp. 1–152; *Sōsō shūzoku goi* (Tokyo: Kokusho kankōkai, 1975); "Sōei no enkaku shiryō," *Teibon Yanagita Kunio 15* (Tokyo: Chikuma shobō, 1969), pp. 521–52. For Herman Ooms, see "A Structural Analysis of Japanese Ancestral Rites and Beliefs," in *Ancestors*, ed. William Newell (The Hague: Mouton, 1976), pp. 61–90. For Kaji Nobuyuki, see *Chinmoku no shūkyō: Jukyō* (Tokyo: Chikuma shobō, 1994).

7. This section on Zen funerals as found in monastic regulations is largely based on the research of Hareyama Shun'ei, Itō Yoshihisa, Kirino Kōgaku, Matsuura Shūkō, Narikawa Mineo, Satō Shōshi, Takeuchi Kōdō, and Tsunoda Tairyū. See Hareyama Shun'ei, "Jukai nyūi ni tsuite," *Shūgaku kenkyū kiyō* 14 (2001): 127–46; Itō Yoshihisa, "Sōtōshū kyōdan ni okeru sōsaishi: Keizan zenji no shūhen made," *Shūgaku kenkyū kiyō* 14 (2001): 219–32; Kirino Kōgaku, "Shūmon no sōsō to shinkō: Dōgen zenji ni okeru sōsōkan o megutte," *Shūgaku kenkyū kiyō* 14 (2001): 177–91; Matsuura Shūkō, *Zenke no sōhō to tsuizen kuyō no kenkyū* (Tokyo: Sankibō busshorin, 1969), and *Sonshuku sōhō no kenkyū* (Tokyo: Sankibō busshorin, 1985); Narikawa Mineo, "Zenshū no sōsai girei," *Aichi gakuin daigaku Zen kenkyūsho kiyō* 24 (1995): 121–66; Satō Shōshi, "Shūmon sōsai girei no hensen, 1–2"; Takeuchi Kōdō, "Keizan zenji monka no sōgikan," *Shūgaku kenkyū* 45 (2003): 133–38; and Tsunoda Tairyū, "Sōtōshū ni okeru sōsai no shūgiteki igizuke," *Shūgaku kenkyū kiyō* 14 (2001): 119–25. Satō compares the monastic funeral in eleven Chinese and Japanese monastic regulations. For the lay funeral, he omits the Chinese monastic codes, since they do not address the topic of lay funerals, but he adds two Japanese Rinzai texts as well as later Sōtō manuals in his analysis. William Bodiford has also written an overview of medieval Zen funerary practices in his "Zen in the Art of Funerals." *History of Religions* 32/2 (1992): 146–64. He discusses the developments in Chinese Chan monastic funerals (shifts in invocations to Amitābha to the use of esoteric *daranis* like the *Daihi jinshu* and the *Ryōgonshu*, for example) and their relationship with medieval Japanese rites in his *Sōtō Zen in Medieval Japan*, pp. 188–89. For an alternate view on Chan funerals, see Alan Cole, "Upside Down/Right Side Up: A Revisionist History of Buddhist Funerals in China," *History of Religions* 35/4 (1996): 307–38. There is also a translation of one of the Chinese Chan monastic codes, the *Chanyuan qinggui* (twelfth century); the section on monastic funerals can be found in Yifa, "The Rules of Purity for the Chan Monastery: An Annotated Translation and Study

of the Chanyuan qinggui" (Ph.D. dissertation, Yale University, 1996), pp. 330–40, and also her *Origins of Buddhist Monastic Codes in China* (Honolulu: University of Hawai'i Press, 2002).

8. With Dōgen's death, his disciple Ejō simply recited the *Shari raimon* without performing a Chan/Zen funeral. See Bodiford's *Sōtō Zen in Medieval*, p. 192.

9. For an overview of the history of the various extant copies and printed editions of the *Keizan shingi*, ascribed to the fourth-generation monk Keizan Jōkin in 1324, but not widely circulated until 1681, see Ichimura Shōhei, trans. and ed., *Zen Master Keizan's Monastic Regulations* (Tsurumi: Daihonzan Sōjiji, 1994), pp. 365–92. The 1681 edition, edited by Manzan Dōhaku and Gesshū Sōko, is commonly called the *Enpō* edition of the *Keizan Oshō shingi* (though earlier handwritten editions used the title *Noto Tōkokusan Yōkōzenji gyōji jijo*).

10. The Chinese Chan monastic codes reflected the coexistence of Chan and Pure Land practices, but Keizan decided to replace, for instance, the recitation to Amida Buddha (*Amida butsu jūnen*) with the recitation of the Names of the Ten Buddhas (*jūbutsumyō*). However, as Satō has noted, the Pure Land elements returned in later Sōtō Zen monastic regulations as the idea of the soul going to a Pure Land after death became part of the common culture of later medieval and Tokugawa period Japanese funerary culture. See Satō Shōshi, *Shūmon sōsai girei no hensen 1*, 59. Furthermore, by the time of the funerals of the well-known Sōtō monks, Meiho in 1350 and Tsūgen in 1391, the recitations included a more elaborate set of esoteric Buddhist *dhāranī* and the *Kōmyō shingon*.

11. On the incorporation of Onmyōdō ideas about directional taboos or coffin placement into Zen funerary practices, see Ozaki Masayoshi, "Sōtōshū sōsai girei to Onmyōdō," (1) *IBK* 45/1 (1996): 202–5; (2) *SKK* 28 (1997): 219–38. Regarding the dispute between Sōtō Zen and Honzan-ha Shugen, see Kanno Yōsuke, "Kinsei no sōryo, shugen to mura shakai," *Komazawa daigaku shigaku ronshū* 32 (2002): 65–78.

12. Scholars have widely cited Tamamuro Taijō's account of the growth of funerary practices in the later medieval period based on his study of funeral sermons. See Tamamuro Taijō, *Sōshiki bukkyō*, pp. 128–30. However, William Bodiford has correctly critiqued Tamamuro's misleading methodology of counting page numbers in the "Zen master's sayings" (*goroku*) to suggest the growing significance of funerary Buddhism and the relative insignificance of Zen meditation. For example, pages counted as "funerary" because they are funeral sermons also make reference to Zen monastic practices, according to Bodiford; see his *Sōtō Zen in Medieval Japan*, pp. 197–99. While Bodiford's critique of Tamamuro's methodology is accurate, Tamamuro's conclusions are nevertheless well founded. Funerary practices for Sōtō Zen priests become increasingly dominant in the late medieval and early modern period, while Zen meditation was virtually nonexistent. However, this evidence should not be culled from sources such as *goroku*, but from sources such as temple logbooks and from documents related to temple economics, although admittedly this is harder to do for the medieval period on which Bodiford and Tamamuro concentrate.

13. See Satō's study of two Sōtō Zen lay funerary rituals from the Meiji period, Satō Shōshi, *Shūmon sōsai girei no hensen 2*, 39–53. Indeed, a clear distinction between the three types of funerals that are currently performed (i.e., high priest, ordinary priest, and layperson) was made for the first time in the *Shōwa kaitei Sōtōshū gyōji kihan* (1950) by the Sōtō Zen headquarters.

14. Bodiford, *Sōtō Zen in Medieval Japan*, p. 195.

15. See William Bodiford, "Zen in the Art of Funerals: Ritual Salvation in Japanese Buddhism," *History of Religions* 32/2 (1992): 146–64.

16. For the *Motsugo sasō jukai shiki*, see Ishikawa (8) *KDBR* 17 (1986): 186, (9) *KDBK* 45 (1987): 173, or *Zenshū sōden shiryō no kenkyū*, pp. 995–1006.

17. The English translation is Bodiford's; see his *Sōtō Zen in Medieval Japan*, pp. 195–96. For the *Motsugo jukai sahō* and the similar *Mōja jukai kirigami* as well as the discussion of these two texts, see Ishikawa (2) KDBR 14 (1983) 128–29, (4) *KDBR* 15

(1984): 158–59, (7) *KDBK* 44 (1986): 266, and "Chūsei Sōtōshū ni okeru jukai girei ni tsuite: Shuju no jukai girei shinansho no hassei to sono shakaiteki kinō," *Bukkyō shigaku kenkyū* 32, 3 (1989): 65–66.

18. This English translation can be found in Faure's *Visions of Power*, p. 64. This *kirigami*, the *Busso shōden bosatsukai no kechimyaku saigoku mujō no daiji*, can be found in Ishikawa, (14) *KDBR* 20 (1989): 129.

19. On the roots of the *kechimyaku* in Japanese Buddhism, see Nakao, "Zenmon no sōsai to kaimyō juyo," pp.145–47.

20. See Faure, *Visions of Power*, p. 64.

21. For the notion of the power of writing Buddhist texts in blood, see Patricia Fister, "Creating Devotional Art with Body Fragments: The Buddhist Nun Bunchi and Her Father, Emperor Gomizuno-o," *Japanese Journal of Religious Studies* 27/3–4 (2000): 232–35; and John Kieschnick, "Blood Writing in Chinese Buddhism," *Journal of the International Association of Buddhist Studies* 23/2 (2000): 177–94.

22. Belief in the talismanic power of the Zen lineage chart to fight off evil spirits, robbers, and diseases also seems to have begun at about the same time. See Hirose, "Nihon Sōtōshū no chū," p. 63.

23. This can be found under the section titled *Dōgen zenji Eiheiji konpon dō kechimyaku ike no koto* in the *Getsuan suiseiki*, held at Kyoto University Library. A similar text also appeared under the title *Kechimyakudo rei* in the 1673 *Eihei kaisan Dōgen Oshō kōroku*, as well as the 1808 *Kaisan Genzen Daishi kōjō denbunki*, the 1811 *Eihei Dōgen zenji kōjō zue*, the 1817 edition of the *Teiho Kenzeiki zue,* 1819 *Eihei Dōgen zenji kōjō no zu*, and the (Bunka/Bunsei era) *Kōsō daishi on'eden*. For more on Dōgen saving a ghost in these texts, see Tsutsumi Kunihiko, "Ano yo no shōkohin: Kinsei setsuwa no naka no katasode yūreitan," *Setsuwa denshōgaku* 7 (1999): 138–41.

24. The early nineteenth century witnessed a boom in legends of ghosts and ghost stories narrated in popular literature and performance. Midori Deguchi suggests that the Bunka-Bunsei period was the peak of this boom; see her "One Hundred Demons and One Hundred Supernatural Tales," in *Japanese Ghosts and Demons: Art of the Supernatural*, ed. Stephen Addiss (New York: George Braziller, 1985), pp. 15–24.

25. This story, the "Tsumi naku shite korosaru mono onrei to naru koto," is number 10.1 in *Inga monogatari, jōkan*. Scholars generally agree that the *hiragana* syllabary version came out in either 1658 or 1659, while the *katakana* syllabary version appeared in 1661. For secondary literature on the *Inga monogatari*, see Fujiyoshi Jikai, *Suzuki Shōsan no Zen* (Kyoto: Zen bunka kenkyūsho, 1984), pp. 229–56; Tsutsumi Kunihiko, *Kinsei Bukkyō setsuwa no kenkyū: Shōdō to bungei* (Tokyo: Kanrin shobō, 1996), pp. 299–339, and *Kinsei setsuwa to zensō* (Osaka: Izumi shoin, 1999), pp. 207–10.

26. Tsutsumi Kunihiko, *Kinsei setsuwa to zensō*, pp. 172-73. The need for religious specialists to respond to ghosts, though, seems more universal, as Le Goff suggests in the case of Christianity: "Purgatory is also a place where ghosts are sorted out. From it issue ghosts for whom God permits or orders a brief return to earth to prove the existence of Purgatory and to beg their dear ones to hasten their deliverance by their suffrage, as did the usurer of Liège. They must be heeded." See Le Goff, *Your Money or Your Life*, pp. 79–80.

27. Tsutsumi surveys such ghost sleeves (*katasode yūrei*) among temples of different sects in his "Ano yo no shōkohin," 138–41.

28. On the Enjōji Temple legend, see legend no. 3471 in Oikawa Jun, ed. *Hanamaki no densetsu* (Tokyo: Kokusho kankōkai, 1983).

29. For the story of the salvation by the Tokushōji Temple abbot of a jealous wife who turned into a ghost, see the "Yūrei saido eden ryaku engi" in Tokushōji Gojikai, ed., *Tokushōji engi to jihō* (Niigata: Tokushōji, 1994), pp. 18–20.

30. This list can be found as a part of the *Banshōzan Kikyūhō Tokuunji yuraisho* in *ZSZ, Jishi*: 119–23. For a discussion of this text, see Tsutsumi, *Kinsei setsuwa to zensō*, pp. 181–83.

31. See Tsutsumi, "Ano yo no shōkohin," pp. 133–34.

32. Sasaki Kōkan, "'*Hotoke* Belief' and the Anthropology of Religion," trans. Norman Havens, *Nihon bunka kenkyūsho kiyō* 81 (1998): 41.

33. Tamamuro Taijō, among others, has identified three types of pre-Buddhist notions of spirits (*tama* or *rei*): (1) *Ikimitama* (a spirit while still alive), (2) *Aramitama* (a "rough" spirit who has just passed away and still in an indeterminable state), and (3) *Mitama* (a good, calm spirit that has settled into a dwelling such as the top of a mountain). The *Aramitama*-type of spirit required appeasement rituals. See Tamamuro Taijō, *Sōshiki bukkyō*, pp. 79–80. For a fine overview of early Japanese views of death in English, see Gary Ebersole, *Ritual Poetry and the Politics of Death in Early Japan* (Princeton: Princeton University Press, 1989).

34. One of best-known associations of Tokugawa-period Sōtō Zen temples (Ten'ōji, Sōgan'in, and Zenjūji) with the belief in the deceased's passage to and through mountain ranges is the so-called *mori no yama kuyō* in the Shōnai region of Yamagata Prefecture. For more on the rites to the dead held both at the temples and the mountain ranges of the region, see Suzuki Iwayumi, "'shisha kuyō' no ichi kōsatsu: 'Mori kuyō' o megutte," *Shūkyō kenkyū* 64/3 (1981): 289–91, and "'Mori kuyō' no jiin gyōjika," *Shūkyō kenkyū* 69/4 (1996): 258–59; Watanabe Shōei, "Mori kuyō to Zenshū jiin ni tsuite no ichishiten," *Shūkyō kenkyū* 68/4 (1985): 210–11, and "'Mori kuyō' ni okeru Zenshū jiin no ichi," *SKKK* 17 (1986): 134–48.

35. See, for instance, Murayama Shūichi, *Tenjin goryō shinkō* (Tokyo: Hanawa shobō, 1996). Powerful people, such as Sugawara no Michizane, who had been wrongfully denied their rightful positions in society, and others holding grudges toward the living were believed to be particularly prone to attack or to possess the living. These spirits also included those who had suffered untimely deaths through murder, natural disasters, or childbirth. In English, see Robert S. Borgen, *Sugawara no Michizane and the Early Heian Court* (Cambridge: Council on East Asian Studies, Harvard University, 1986).

36. One method of "containing" unruly spirits can be seen in the practice of guiding and shutting them inside special boards at the altar of the hungry ghosts; see Kawakami Mitsuyo, "Two Views of Spirits as Seen in the Bon Observances of the Shima Region," *Japanese Journal of Religious Studies* 15/2–3 (1988): 127.

37. Sasaki Kōkan, "*Hotoke* Belief," p. 46. Daimon also suggests the variability of the term *hotoke* to mean *buddha* (as a religious term) and *tama* (soul/spirit as a magical term); see Daimon Kōzen, "Anshin no tame no shūkyō gyōji no ichi kōsatsu: Sōsai o chūshin to shite," *Kyōka kenshū* 39 (1996): 129.

38. The folklorist Yanagita Kunio put forward the well-known and intriguing, though highly implausible, thesis that the term *hotoke* was a degeneration of the term *hotoki* (a household tablet into which the ancestors descended). Aruga Kizaemon has argued, instead, that the term was popularly used among the early medieval aristocracy to refer to the Buddha but does not explain how this is related to the use of the term *hotoke* to refer to a dead person. See Aruga Kizaemon, "Hotoke to iu kotoba ni tsuite: Nihon bukkyōshi ichi sokumen," in *Sōsō bosei kenkyū shūsei 3*, ed. Takeda Chōshū (Tokyo: Meicho shuppan, 1979), pp. 93–113.

39. On the development of the six realms (*rokudō*) concept in Japan, see Erika Peschard-Erlih, *Les mondes infernaux et les peintures des six voies dans le Japon bouddhique* (Paris: Institut national des langues et civilisations orientales Paris 3, 1991); Barbara Ruch, "Coping with Death: Paradigms of Heaven and Hell and the Six Realms in Early Literature and Painting," *Flowing Traces: Buddhism and the Literary and Visual Arts of Japan*, ed. James Sanford, Masatoshi Nagatomi, and William LaFleur (Princeton: Princeton University Press, 1992), pp. 93–130; William LaFleur, *The Karma of Words: Buddhism and the Literary Arts in Medieval Japan* (Berkeley: University of California Press, 1983), pp. 26–59.

40. See Stephen Teiser's detailed explanation of this sutra (T. 2003), which he translates as *The Sutra on the Prophesy of King Yama to the Four Orders Concerning the*

Seven [Rituals] to Be Practiced Prepatory to Rebirth in the Pure Land, in The Ghost Festival in Medieval China (Princeton: Princeton University Press, 1988), pp. 182–84. For a historical overview of the development of the worship of the Ten Kings in China, see Stephen Teiser, *The Scripture on the Ten Kings and the Making of Purgatory in Medieval Chinese Buddhism* (Honolulu: University of Hawai'i Press, 1994).

41. The cycle of rites and the Ten Kings and the Corresponding Buddha (or Bodhisattva): (1) 7th day after death: King Shinkō and Fudō; (2) 14th day: King Shokō and Shaka; (3) 21st day: King Shūtai and Monju; (4) 28th day: King Gokan and Fugen; (5) 35th day: King Enma and Jizō; (6) 42nd day: King Henjō and Miroku; (7) 49th day: King Taisen and Yakushi; (8) 100th day: King Byōdō and Kannon; (9) 1st year: King Tochō and Seishi; (10) 3rd year: King Godōrinten and Amida. Early Ten Kings (*jūō*) rites in Japan were based on the Japanese apocryphal sutra, the *Jizō jūōkyō* (*Jizō bosatsu hosshin innen jūōkyō*), unlike in China where they were based on the *Shiwang shengqijing* (Jpn. *Jūō shōshichikyō*). For a summary of the differences in Chinese and Japanese Ten Kings beliefs, see Watanabe Shōgo, *Tsuizen kuyō no hotokesama: Jūsanbutsu shinkō* (Tokyo: Keisuisha, 1989), pp. 162–63.

42. These practices continue even today at twenty-seven temples (15 Jōdo, 6 Sōtō Zen, 2 Ji, 2 Rinzai Zen, 1 Shingon, and 1 Jōdo Shin). See Enomoto Chika, "Yamagataken Murayama chihō no jigoku-e to etoki," *Etoki kenkyū* 4 (1986): 16–32. A further study on the same region was conducted by Watanabe Shōgo; see his *Chūseishi no minshū shōdō bungei* (Tokyo: Iwata shoin, 1995), pp. 253–56.

43. The Thirteen Buddha Rites (Time of Ritual and Corresponding Buddha or Bodhisattva): (1) 7th day after death: Fudō; (2) 14th day: Shaka; (3) 21st day: Monju; (4) 28th day: Fugen; (5) 35th day: Jizō; (6) 42nd day: Miroku; (7) 49th day: Yakushi; (8) 100th day: Kannon; (9) 1st year: Seishi; (10) 3rd year: Amida; (11) 7th year: Ashuku; (12) 13th year: Dainichi; (13) 33rd year: Kokuzō. The thirty-three-year period was interpreted in the Tōzan Shugen tradition, from which Sōtō Zen received much of their Thirteen Buddha Rites, as if it were a pregnancy cycle in which a person was reborn only to repeat the cycle of life and death over and over until final *nirvana* (which is beyond life and death). In the Tōzan Shugen tradition in the late medieval and early Tokugawa period, the wake was considered the inception of the pregnancy, with each memorial rite representing different stages of nurturing in the "womb": (1) 1st week memorial service—Fudō—1st month of pregnancy; (2) 2nd week—Shaka—2nd month; (3) 3rd week—Monju—3rd month; (4) 4th week—Fugen—4th month; (5) 5th week—Jizō—5th month; (6) 6th week—Miroku—6th month; (7) 7th week—Yakushi—7th month; (8) 100 days—Kannon—8th month; (9) 1st year—Seishi—9th month; (10) 3rd year—Amida—10th month; (11) 7th year—Ashuku—birth into present life; (12) 13th year—Dainichi—old person; (13) 33rd year—Kokuzō—end of birth and death. Tokugawa-period texts, such as the *Tsuizen kuyō no susume*, used by *yamabushi* affiliated with Tōzan Shugen and Kumano *bikuni* nuns in their preaching (*etoki*), reveal that the dead males, in this system, were thought to go into the womb of their wife (who stayed with the deceased through the night of the wake). Once the deceased was buried, he entered the womb of the earth and grew as an embryo (along the pattern of the memorial anniversaries) until he became a Buddha beyond birth and death. A similar Sōtō Zen *kirigami*, *Jutai shushō kirigami* or the *Tainai sagashi no kirigami*, describes this connection between posthumous enlightenment and the cycle of pregnancy; see Ishikawa Rikizan, (8) *KDBR* 17 (1986): 201–3. For a detailed study of pregnancy metaphors in rebirth within the Shingon school, see James Sanford, "Wind, Waters, Stupas, Mandalas: Fetal Buddhahood in Shingon," *Japanese Journal of Religious Studies* 24, 1–2 (1997): 1–38.

44. For the Thirteen Buddha *kirigami*, which explained the meaning of each Buddha at each rite, see Ishikawa Rikizan, (7) *KDBK* 44 (1986): 263–65, and (10) *KDBR* 18 (1987): 181–91, or *Zenshū sōden shiryō no kenkyū jō*, pp. 411–13. For a broader study of the spread of the cult of the Thirteen Buddhas, see Nakamura Gashun, "Jūsanbutsu

shinkō no denpa ni tsuite: Kyoto Seiganji Jūsanbutsudō o chūshin to shite," *Mikage shi-gaku* 12 (1987): 45–65.

45. Rev. Shinohara Eiichi, the current abbot of Chōjuin Temple, kindly gave me permission to use this untitled document.

46. The significance of the number forty-nine has a number of interpretations. For example, in medieval popular literature, the forty-ninth day corresponded to the forty-ninth day "nails" that the guardian king of hell, King Enma, was supposed to drive into the person to keep them in hell. This led to local customs such as making soft rice cakes on that day so that the nails would go into the cakes rather than the flesh. See Tamamuro Taijō, *Sōshiki bukkyō*, p. 157.

47. Smith has noted that in certain regions of Japan, this lifting of the dead person's pollution, while forty-nine days for men, was shorter (thirty-five days) for women. See Robert J. Smith, *Ancestor Worship in Contemporary Japan* (Stanford: Stanford University Press, 1974), p. 92. Tamamuro has also noted that the significance of the number forty-nine was based on the Buddhist seven-day unit system, and that prior to the introduction of Buddhism, the mourning period lasted fifty days. See Tamamuro Taijō, *Sōshiki bukkyō*, p. 147.

48. See Wada Kenju, "Bukkyō sōsō jibutsu no hatten hikaku kō," *KDBK* 39 (1981): 30–31.

49. There are several theories about the significance of the number thirty-three; the most popular one refers to Kannon having thirty-three transformation bodies. Another theory points to the fact that Śākyamuni was thirty-three years of age when he gave a sermon to Maya at Tōriten (one of the thirty-three heavens). For more discussion of such theories, see Wada Kenju, "Bukkyō shūzoku ni arawareta kazu no kōsatsu: Kuyō shūzoku o chūshin to shite," *KDBK* 28 (1970): 31–45; and Watanabe Shōgo, *Tsuizen kuyō no hoto kesama*, pp. 186–90.

50. The layout of the Thirteen Buddhas differs by sect. As Watanabe has pointed out, although nonsectarian scrolls depict all thirteen as being of equal size, the esoteric schools usually placed Dainichi at the center, shown slightly larger. The Pure Land schools did the same with Amida, as did the Zen schools with Śākyamuni. See Watanabe Shōgo, *Tsuizen kuyō no hotokesama*, p. 251.

51. For esoteric and Shugendō interpretations of the Earth Womb conception model of rebirth, see Miyake Hitoshi, "Tsuizen kuyō no etoki: Tōzanha Shugen no chiiki te-ichaku," *Keiō gijuku daigakuin shakaikagaku kenkyūka kiyō* 36 (1997): 65–68, and *Shugendō: Essays on the Structure of Japanese Folk Religion* (Ann Arbor: Center for Japanese Studies, University of Michigan, 2001), p. 245.

52. Stephen F. Teiser, *Ghost Festival*, p. 13.

53. R. Smith, *Ancestor Worship*, p. 3. Smith also points out that this transformation occurs at the fifty-year mark in a few regions of Japan, which he attributes to Shintō influences (p. 76). Of course, in contemporary Japan, memorial rites to mark the fiftieth or hundredth year after death are not uncommon. Harold Bolitho also remarks on the complex feelings of the descendants of the dead during the Tokugawa period in his *Bereavement and Consolation: Testimonies from Tokugawa Japan* (New Haven: Yale University Press, 2003).

54. Ibid., p. 69.

55. See Le Goff, *Your Money or Your Life*, p. 75.

56. The *Ketsubonkyō*—or, more formally, the *Bussetsu daizō shōkyō ketsubonkyō*—can be found in MZZK 1–87.4, 299. As in the *Urabonkyō*, the Buddha's disciple Mokuren (in most variants), after having seen the immense suffering of women in the Blood Pool Hell, asked the Buddha for help, which resulted in the *Ketsubonkyō*. Women are condemned to this hell because they "every month leak menses or in childbirth release blood which seeps down and pollutes the earth gods. And, more, they take their filthy garments to the river to wash, thereby polluting the river water. Later, an unsuspecting

good man or woman draws some water from the river, boils it for tea, and then offers it to the holy ones, causing them to be impure." To this problem, the sutra provides a solution: "you only need to carefully be a filial son or daughter, respect the Three Jewels, and, for the sake of your mom, hold Blood Bowl Meetings to which you invite monks to recite this sutra for a full day, and have confessions. Then there will be a *prajñā* boat to carry the mothers across the River Nai He, and they will see five-colored lotuses appear in the blood pool, and the sinner will come out happy and contrite and they will be able to take rebirth in a Buddha Land." This translation is Alan Cole's; the entire text can be found in Alan Cole, *Mothers and Sons in Chinese Buddhism* (Stanford: Stanford University Press, 1998), pp. 199–206. A somewhat different English translation of the sutra (partial) can be found in Takemi Momoko, "'Menstruation Sutra' Belief in Japan," *Japanese Journal of Religious Studies* 10/2–3 (1983): 230, 232.

A number of extant Chinese, Korean, and Japanese variants are analyzed by Takemi (p. 231). The *Ketsubonkyō*'s origins in China (and its Taoist versions as well) are explored by Michel Soymié, "Ketsubonkyō no shiryōteki kenkyū," In *Dōkyō kenkyū 1*, ed. Michel Soymié and Iriya Yoshitaka (Tokyo: Shōshinsha, 1965), pp. 109–66. Extant *Ketsubonkyō* texts in Japan have been cataloged and categorized most broadly into the Gankōji type, Genshōji type (which cites childbirth blood as the reason for women falling into the Blood Pool Hell), and the Wage type (which includes both the sutra and commentary and cites both childbirth and menstruation as reasons). For these classifications, see Matsuoka Hideaki, "Waga kuni ni okeru Ketsubonkyō shinkō ni tsuite no ikkōsatsu," In *Nihon joseishi ronshū 5: Josei to shūkyō*, ed. Sōgō joseishi kenkyūkai (Tokyo: Yoshikawa kōbunkan, 1998), pp. 259–64.

57. Soymié disputes the early history of the *Ketsubonkyō* in Japan, arguing that it was introduced to Japan in between 1250 and 1350, while Takemi and Kōdate lean toward a late Muromachi dating. See Soymié, "Ketsubonkyō no shiryōteki kenkyū," pp. 137–38; Takemi Momoko, "Nihon ni okeru Ketsubonkyō shinkō ni tsuite," *Nihon bukkyō* 41 (1981): 44; and Kōdate Naomi, "Chi no ike jigoku no esō o meguru oboegaki: Kyūsaisha to shite no Nyoirin Kannon no mondai o chūshin ni," *Etoki kenkyū* 6 (1988): 53; rpt. in *Jigoku no sekai*, ed. Sakamoto Kaname (Tokyo: Keisuisha, 1990), p. 668. In any case, there is a general consensus that the sutra's popularity did not spread until the early Tokugawa period. For English-language scholarship on the *Ketsubonkyō*, see Cole, *Mothers and Sons*, pp. 197–214; Faure, *The Power of Denial*, pp. 67–81; Hank Glassman, "The Religious Construction of Motherhood in Medieval Japan" (Ph.D. dissertation, Stanford University, 2001), chap. 4; and "At the Crossroads of Birth and Death: The Blood-Pool Hell and Postmortem Fetal Extraction," in *Death Rituals and the Afterlife in Japanese Buddhism*, ed. Mariko Walter and Jacqueline Stone (Honolulu: University of Hawai'i Press, 2004); Manabe Shunshō, "Hell of the Bloody Pond and the Rebirth of Women in the Paradise." *Indogaku bukkyōgaku kenkyū* 43/1 (1994): 34–38; and Takemi, "'Menstruation Sutra' Belief in Japan."

58. The earliest version of the founding legend from 1736 has been attributed to Senjō Jitsugan (1722–1802) by the team assembled at the Sōtō Zen Headquarters; see Sōtōshū Shūhō Chōsa Iinkai, "Shūhō chōsa iinkai chōsa mokuroku oyobi kaidai: Shōsenji," *Sōtō shūhō* 628 (1992): 410. However, as Nakano Yūshin has argued, Jitsugan's authorship would be highly unlikely as he would have been just fifteen years old. Since Jitsugan also wrote in his well-known *Yūkoku yoin* that he received it from a monk named Ryōkan (who is said to have gotten the text from Shōsenji Temple) during the time he was abbot of Chōkokuji Temple (Nagano Prefecture, served 1779–92), his authorship is improbable. This text was therefore probably written by a fairly unknown Shōsenji monk prior to Jitsugan's time, but his name became associated with the text when the other text attributed to him, *Yūkoku yoin*, was well received. For this line of argument, see Nakano Yūshin, "Sōtōshū ni okeru Ketsubonkyō shinkō 2," *Sōtōshū shūgaku kenkyūsho kiyō* 7 (1994): 129–30.

59. Though the *Ketsubonkyō* activities at Shōsenji Temple centered around the bod-

hisattva Jizō, most pictorial depictions of the Blood Pool Hell center on the salvific powers of Nyoirin Kannon. The association of Kannon with this particular hell not only is founded on mandalas, but examples exist of gravestones of women with Nyoirin Kannon engraved on the stone. For a detailed study of Nyoirin Kannon and the *Ketsubonkyō*, see Kōdate Naomi with Makino Kazuo, "Ketsubonkyō no juyō to tenkai," in *Onna to otoko no jiku 3*, ed. Okano Haruko (Tokyo: Nihon joseishi saikō 6, bekkan 1, Fujiwara shoten), esp. pp. 86–94. Another rare example that ties Jizō to the Blood Pool can be found with the Jizō at Chatōden in Minoge Village, Kanagawa Prefecture; for this example, see Tokieda Tsutomu, "Sekibutsu to Ketsubonkyō shinkō: Ōyama sanroku Minoge no Jizōson o megutte," *Nihon no sekibutsu* 32 (1984): 27–33.

60. The notion that menstrual blood appeared in the form of a Blood Pool Hell is also related to a broader Buddhist theory on the transference of bodily substances elsewhere, such as to the world of the hungry ghosts, who consume spit and semen. As William LaFleur has noted, " 'Where,' they [the people] might ask, 'do you suppose the shit in the latrine eventually goes? Or the cadaver that lies exposed out in the public cemetery? Or the semen or menstrual blood that falls from the body to the ground?' " See William LaFleur, "Hungry Ghosts and Hungry People: Somacity and Rationality in Medieval Japan," in *Fragments for a History of the Human Body, Part One*, ed. Michael Feher (New York: Urzone, 1989), p. 289.

61. Various scholars have studied the history of Kumano *bikuni* (nuns), who were also deeply involved in spreading the notion of the Blood Pool Hell through the use of pictorial diagrams such as the *Kanjin Jukkai Mandara*. For example, see Faure, *The Power of Denial*, pp. 250–54; Hagiwara Tatsuo, "Kumano bikuni no seitai," in *Nihon minzoku fūdoron* Chiba Tokuji, ed. (Tokyo: Kōbundō, 1980), pp. 269–82; *Miko to bukkyōshi* (Tokyo: Yoshikawa kōbunkan, 1983), pp. 24–63, 163–69; "Kumano bikuni to etoki," in *Nihon no koten bungaku 3: Issatsu no kōza, Etoki* (Tokyo: Yūseidō, 1985), pp. 57–67; Hayashi Masahiko, "Kumano bikuni no etoki," in *Zōho Nihon no etoki: Shiryō to kenkyū* (Tokyo: Miyai shoten, 1984), pp. 126–46; "Etoki suru Kumano bikuni," in *Imēji rīdingu sōso: Kaiga no hakken* (Tokyo: Heibonsha, 1990), pp. 143–52; D. Max Moerman, "Localizing Paradise: Kumano Pilgrimage in Medieval Japan" (Ph.D. dissertation, Stanford University, 1999), pp. 183–99 and *Localizing Paradise: Kumano Pilgrimage and the Religious Landscape of Premodern Japan* (Cambridge: Harvard University Asia Center, 2004); and Barbara Ruch, "Woman to Woman: *Kumano bikuni* Proslytizers in Medieval and Early Modern Japan," in *Japanese Women and Buddhism*, ed. Barbara Ruch (Ann Arbor: Center for Japanese Studies, University of Michigan, 2002), pp. 567–75. Hagiwara makes a rather far-fetched argument in an attempt to link the Kumano *bikuni* and Shōsenji Temple (linking the Kumano *bikuni* supporter, Hōttō Kokushi of Myōshinji Temple, to Hōjō Tokiyori. This link was made by Tokiyori's daughter, the nun Hōsshō-ni, the founder of Shōsenji Temple, featured in the *Ketsubonkyō* legend above). See Hagiwara, Miko to bukkyōshi, p. 20, and "Kumano bikuni no shimei," in *Kumano sanzan shinkō jiten*, ed. Katō Takahisa (Tokyo: Ebisu kōshō shuppan kabushiki gaisha, 1998), pp. 304–9. Hank Glassman makes an important point that the performances of stories about the Blood Pool Hell by Kumano *bikuni* became a major vehicle for teaching women about not only the doctrine, but the topography of the hell. See Glassman, "At the Crossroads of Birth and Death."

62. Jōdo school monks in the early Tokugawa period connected their special funerary ceremonies for women who died during childbirth to ceremonies to be used for all women through the ideology propounded in the *Ketsubonkyō*. For a study of Jōdo school propagation manuals such as the 1698 *Jōka shōekō hōkan*, which connected funerary ritual with faith in the *Ketsubonkyō*, see Kōdate Naomi, "Shiryō shōkai 'Ketsubonkyō wage': Kinseiki Jōdoshū ni okeru Ketsubonkyō shinkō," *Bukkyō minzoku kenkyū* 6 (1989): 59–91; and Matsuoka, "Waga kuni ni okeru," esp. p. 269.

63. Mt. Tateyama was another major site for *Ketsubonkyō* ritual activities in the early Tokugawa period because of its well-known Blood Pool Hell at the sacred mountain into

which copies of the sutra were placed. For a detailed study of Tateyama and the *Ketsu-bonkyō*, see Kōdate Naomi, "Ketsubonkyō shinkō reijō to shite no Tateyama," *Sangaku shugen* 20 (1997): 75–84. The influence of Tendai-affiliated Shugen practitioners on the spread of the ideas in the *Ketsubonkyō*, including their presence at Mt. Tateyama (a Tendai-affiliated site), is detailed in Tokieda Tsutomu, "Chūsei Tōgoku ni okeru Ketsu-bonkyō shinkō no yōsō: Kusatsu Shiranesan o chūshin to shite," *Shinano* 36, 8 (1984): 28–45. Here, Tokieda includes useful charts and maps of the regional spread of the faith in *Ketsubonkyō*. For research on Mt. Tateyama in English, see Susanne Formanek, "Pil-grimage in the Edo Period: Forerunner of Medieval Domestic Pilgrimage? The Example of the Pilgrimage to Mt. Tateyama," in *The Culture of Japan as Seen through Its Leisure*, ed. Sepp Linhart and Sabine Frühstück (Albany: State University of New York Press, 1993), pp. 165–94; and Anna Seidel, "Descante aux enfers et rédemption des femmes dans le Bouddhisme populaire Japonaise: le pèlerinage du Mont Tateyama," *Cahiers d'Extrême-Asie* 9 (1996–97): 1–14. The "red-colored waters" of Mt. Tateyama, which were related to the hot springs at the sacred mountain, reminded people of the Blood Pool Hell. Another site where hot springs and hells were linked was Osorezan, a sacred moun-tain in Aomori Prefecture with a Sōtō Zen temple (Entsūji) as its official center. Though not as well known as Tateyama for its *Ketsubonkyō* activities, the same practice of plac-ing the sutra into the "hell" at Osorezan to rescue women from hell continued until very recently. See Miyazaki Fumiko and Duncan Williams, "The Intersection of the Local and Translocal at a Sacred Site: The Case of Osorezan in Tokugawa Japan," *Japanese Journal of Religious Studies* 28/3–4 (2001): 424–25. In China, the monthly period of Yang Taizhen, an imperial consort to the Tang emperor Zuan Zong, was said to appear as "red maculations" at the warm springs of Chang-an. See Edward Schafer, "The Development of Bathing Customs in Ancient and Medieval China and the History of the Floriate Clear Palace," *Journal of the American Oriental Society* 76 (1956): 81.

64. Shōsenji Temple had not always been a Sōtō Zen temple. Founded in 1263 as a nunnery for Hōsshō-ni, the daughter of Hōjō Tokiyori, it was named Hosshōji and nom-inally affiliated with the Rinzai sect until the *Ketsubonkyō* incident, when it was renamed. The temple was turned into a Sōtō Zen temple in the fifteenth century by Shunpō Shūō (d. 1506), who had been the abbot of Shinnyoji Temple (also in Shimousa Province) prior to his changing the sectarian affiliation of the temple. As the *engi* chronicles, the name of the village was also changed at the time of the Hōsshō-ni incident from Hatto Village to Ichibu (One Section) Village because a section (the *Ketsubonkyō*) of the larger sutra (the *Hōonkyō*) appeared in the village. The village is currently a part of Abiko City, Chiba Prefecture. On the history of Shōsenji and Tokuō Ryōkō, see Shiina Hiroo, "Tokuō Ryōkō to Shimousa Shōsenji," *Abikoshishi kenkyū* 4 (1979): 548–62; and Satō Shunkō, "Tokuō Ryōkō no Shintō shisō," *Shūgaku kenkyū* 41 (1999): 211–16.

65. Among the extant *Ketsubonkyō engi*—or founding legends that explain the ap-pearance of the sutra in Japan—all of them except one were produced at Shōsenji Temple and contain the same basic story of Hōsshō-ni and her telling the priest how to find the sutra at Taganuma Marsh. The version I translated from 1857, the *Nyonin jōbutsu Ket-subonkyō engi*, differs from the other Shōsenji Temple versions in only one respect: it dates the Hōsshō-ni incident twenty years later, to 1417, while earlier versions date it to 1397. The earliest versions date from the eighteenth century: the 1736 *Ketsubonkyō engi* and 1792 *Ketsubonkyō Jizōson engi* (both at Shōsenji Temple). However, it was the nine-teenth-century woodblock-print book versions (*kanpon*) such as the 1837 *Bussetsu daizō Ketsubonkyō bon (en)gi*, the 1837 *Ryūgū shitsugen nyonin jōbutsu Ketsubonkyō engi*, the 1841 *Nyonin jōbutsu Ketsubonkyō engi kan*, and the 1857 *Nyonin jōbutsu Ketsu-bonkyō engi* (all held at Shōsenji), that enabled the increased circulation of this founding legend that tied the *Ketsubonkyō* to this Sōtō Zen temple. For a partial cataloging of these *engi*, see Nakano Yūshin, "Sōtoshū ni okeru Ketsubonkyō shinkō," pp. 127–28. The one *Ketsubonkyō engi* with a different explanation of the origins of the sutra in Japan is the

1713 *Ketsubonkyō Nihon ruden kaiban no yurai* "'*Daizōshōkyō Ketsubonkyō wage*'," which holds that either Jishinbō Sonsui (the founder of Mt. Seichō) or Kakugen (Nikkōzan Jakkōji) brought the sutra back after a visit to the Palace of King Enma. For more on these variants, see Takemi, "Menstruation Sutra," pp. 237–38. The Shōsenji Temple legend also spread to other Sōtō Zen temples throughout Japan, as evidenced in extant Tokugawa-period texts that cite the legend at the following temples: Anyōji (Hyōgo Prefecture, *SBCM* 5: 443); Chōanji (Chiba Prefecture, *SBCM* 6: 774); Eitenji (Hyōgo Prefecture, *SBCM* 5: 397); Jōkeiji (Fukui Prefecture, *SBCM* 5: 176); Keirinji (Kyoto, *SBCM* 5: 99); Shōgenji (Shimane Prefecture, *SBCM* 4: 296); Tōkōin (Osaka, *SBCM* 5: 176); Tōkōji (Shimane Prefecture, *SBCM* 4: 307); Tōrinji (Fukuoka Prefecture, *SBCM* 3: 23); Zuisenji (Miyagi Prefecture, *SSCM* 2: 121). Although the current Sōtōshū Headquarters has tried to downplay the *Ketsubonkyō*, I put together the above list from the medieval and early modern manuscript surveys of Sōtō Zen temples conducted under the headquarters' auspices.

66. The information on the sign can be found in Tagami Taishū, *Bukkyō to sei sabetsu* (Tokyo: Tokyo shoseki, 1992), p. 203. Kōyōji Temple in Wakasa Province claimed to be another Sōtō Zen center for women's salvation. During the mid-Tokugawa period, the temple started circulating a legend that a "dragon jewel" left by a dragon girl saved by a former abbot of the temple symbolized women's ability to be saved at the temple. For the Kōyōji Temple case, see Tsutsumi, "Ano yo no shōkohin," p. 133.

67. This lecture, entitled *Ketsubonkyō yūshutsu inyu suishu*, is part of a collection of Dharma lectures given by Unrei Taizen at *jukai-e* (precept ceremonies). The collection, the *Kaie rakusōdan*, can be found in printed form in *SZ Zenkai*, pp. 704–20.

68. See Susan B. Klein, "Women as Serpent: The Demonic Feminine in the Noh Play *Dōjōji*," in *Religious Reflections on the Human Body*, ed. Jane Marie Law (Bloomington: Indiana University Press, 1995), pp. 105–6. Klein offers interesting psychoanalytical interpretations of the relationship among women, temple bells, sexuality, and salvation. For an analysis of how this legend was spread through illustrated scroll performances, see Hayashi Masahiko, "Bukkyō setsuwaga to etoki: 'Dōjōji engi emaki' no tenkai," *Komazawa daigaku bukkyō bungaku kenkyū* 6 (2003): 35–59. For a translation of the *engi emaki* version of the story, see Virginia Skord Waters, "Sex, Lies, and the Illustrated Scroll: The *Dōjōji Engi Emaki*," *Monumenta Nipponica* 57/1 (1997): 59–84.

69. The notion that women, by their very nature, faced obstacles to Buddhist salvation is an enduring theme. On the so-called five obstacles, see Faure, *The Power of Denial*, pp. 62–64; and Nagata Mizu, "Transitions in Attitudes toward Women in the Buddhist Canon: The Three Obligations, the Five Obstructions, and the Eight Rules of Reverence," in *Japanese Women and Buddhism*, ed. Barbara Ruch (Ann Arbor: Center for Japanese Studies, University of Michigan, 2002), pp. 279–96.

70. The text of this *kirigami* can be found in full in Sugimoto Shunryū, *Tōjō shitsunai kirigami sanwa kenkyū narabi hiroku* (Tokyo: Sōtōshū shūmuchō, 1956; rev. ed. 1982), pp. 16–17. It is also reprinted in Sōtōshū Jinken Yōgo Suishin Honbu, ed. "*Ashiki gōron*" *kokufuku no tame ni* (Tokyo: Sōtōshū shūmuchō, 1987), p. 134. The earliest version of this *kirigami* is attributed to Yūten in 1810, though it is unclear from whom he received this teaching, which makes it a rather late *kirigami*; see Sugimoto, p. 20. Takemi Momoko, a leading scholar of the *Ketsubonkyō*, has noted three Niigata-area Sōtō Zen temples that until recently distributed the sutra to women so as to "cancel" the impurity of womanhood, enabling them to worship the Buddha in a "pure" state. Takemi, "Menstruation Sutra," p. 243.

71. For more on the cult of Ususama, especially in the Sino-Tibetan tradition, see Michel Strickmann, *Chinese Magical Medicine* (Stanford: Stanford University Press, 2002), pp. 156–61.

72. Yoshida has noted this dynamic in Mahayana scriptures in general. He suggests that women's salvation is predicated on the notion that "women are belittled then enno-

bled." See Yoshida Kasuhiko, "The Enlightenment of the Dragon King's Daughter in *The Lotus Sutra*," in *Japanese Women and Buddhism*, ed. Barbara Ruch (Ann Arbor: Center for Japanese Studies, University of Michigan, 2002), p. 303.

73. Although it was still relatively rare for women to hand-write Chinese-character sutras in the eighteenth century, extant copies by Sōtō Zen members at Shōsenji Temple attest to this practice. A 1783 sutra copy, for example, written by the mother of Matsudaira Sagami no kami, included a prayer she wrote expressing her hope to achieve rebirth into the Western Pure Land. See Takemi, "Menstruation Sutra," p. 243.

74. *Segaki* rituals were rites dedicated to the *gaki* (hungry ghosts) and *muenbotoke*, to feed the hungry ghosts and to console those unable to receive proper ancestral services (such as those who did not have any descendants—i.e., those who were childless or whose children died young—or had only unfilial descendents). Originally, *segaki* ceremonies were held after large-scale natural disasters (fires, flood, earthquakes) because so many spirits become hungry ghosts or *muenbotoke* on such occasions. Such hungry ghosts and other spirits were thought to bother the living, especially during the *Obon* summer festival season, when ancestors and other spirits were thought to return to this world for a period of time. To appease and ease the sufferings of such spirits, though the *segaki* rite was independent of *Obon* rites, during the Tokugawa period, *segaki* rituals were often held at the same time, with households preparing a special altar for their ancestors and a different one for the other spirits. For more on the practice of *segaki*, see LaFleur, "Hungry Ghosts and Hungry People"; Ozaki Masayoshi, "Segaki-e ni kansuru ichi kōsatsu," *IBK* 43/1 (1994): 131–34, and *SKK* 26 (1995): 91–104; and Richard Payne, "Shingon Services for the Dead," in *Religions of Japan in Practice*, ed. George J. Tanabe, Jr. (Princeton: Princeton University Press, 1999), pp. 159–65. For studies on types of *muenbotoke* and ritual manuals, see Asano Hisae, "'Muen' no na o motsu shomotsu tachi: Kinsei sōshiki tebikisho shōkai," *Bukkyō minzoku kenkyū* 7 (1991): 1–21; Mogami Takayoshi, "Muenbotoke ni tsuite," in *Sōsō bosei kenkyū shūsei 3*, ed. Takeda Chōshū (Tokyo: Meicho shuppan, 1979), pp. 386–93.

75. See Takemi, "Menstruation Sutra," p. 241.

76. See Kōdate and Makino, "Keysubonkyō no juyō to tenkai," p. 111. The late Tokugawa period *Kishin meibo* (Donations Logbook) is also discussed in Chibaken Kyōikuchō Shōgai Gakushūbu Bunkaka, ed. *Chibaken no shitei bunkazai 8* (Chiba: Chibaken kyōiku iinkai, 1998), p. 13.

77. This legend is included in a *kirigami* from Yōkōji Temple, the *Kawara konpon no kirigami*, which Ishikawa dated to roughly 1628. For a printed text version of the *kirigami*, see Ishikawa Rikizan, *KDBR* 15 (1984): 165. An English translation of the *Ketsubonkyō* section of the *kirigami* can be found in Bodiford, *Sōtō Zen in Medieval Japan*, p. 207.

78. Hank Glassman has written on the theme of death in childbirth among Buddhist schools in general, as well as on a Sōtō Zen temple in Shizuoka called Ubume Kannon ("Birthing Woman" Kannon); see "At the Crossroads of Birth and Death." For more on "ubume" and "kosodate yūrei," see Iwasaka Michiko and Barre Toelken, *Ghosts and the Japanese: Cultural Experience in Japanese Death Legends* (Logan: Utah State University Press, 1994), pp. 63–66.

79. For a study of funerals under "special circumstances," see Namihira Emiko, "Ijō shisha no sōhō to shūzoku," in *Bukkyō minzokugaku taikei 4: Sosen saishi to sōbo*, ed. Fujii Masao (Tokyo: Meicho shuppan, 1988), pp. 141–60.

80. The following list, first compiled by Tsutsumi Kunihiko, has been rearranged somewhat to make it more compact. (1) "Ko haha betsubuku no kirigami"/"Haha ko betsubuku no kirigami" (Kōrinji Temple—Sagami Province/1633 and 1636; Saimyōji Temple—Mikawa Province/1637; Myōōji Temple—Mino Province/1659; Yōkōji Temple—Kaga Province/1687); (2) "Taijin sanbun daiji" (Kōanji Temple—Edo Fuchū /1694); (3) "Kaitai mōja otosu no kirigami"/"Kaitai mōja otosu no sanwa" (Shōryūji Temple—Musashi Province/1724; Shojōji Temple—Echigo Province/1771; Shōjurin Temple—

1776); (4) "Taiji no kirigami" (Shōryūji Temple—Musashi Province/mid-Tokugawa period); (5) "Ko betsubuku kirigami" (Yōkōji Temple—Kaga Province/mid-Tokugawa period); (6) "Ubume mōjo indō shiyaku" (Fukuzōji Temple—Mikawa Province/1845); (7) "Taijo ketsuen daiji" (Myōgonji Temple—Ōmi Province/late Tokugawa period). See Tsutsumi, *Kinsei setsuwa to zensō*, p. 141. For an overview of these *kirigami*, see Ishikawa Rikizan, "Kirigami denshō to kinsei Sōtōshū: 'Betsubuku,' 'motsugo sasō' kankei kirigami no kinseiteki henyō o megutte," in *Minzoku shūkyō no kōzō to keifu*, pp. 298–322; *Zenshū sōden shiryō no kenkyū jō*, pp. 482–500; and *Zenshū sōden shiryō no kenkyū ge*, pp. 995–1006.

81. See Katsurai Kazuo, "Kama no gara ni kansuru kinpi: Taiji bunri no koshū nōto," *Tosa minzoku* 30 (1976): 1–3; rpt. in *Sōsō bosei kenkyū shūsei Vol. 1: Sōhō* (Tokyo: Meicho shuppan, 1979), pp. 291–95; Minakata Kumakusu, "Haramifu no shigai yori taiji o hikihanasu koto," *Kyōdo kenkyū* 5/4 (1931): 245–246; Namihira, "Ijō shisha no sōhō to shūzoku," pp. 149–53; Sōtōshū Dendōbu Eidōka, ed., *Jinken kara mita baikaryū eisanka* (Tokyo: Sōtōshū shūmuchō, 1992), pp. 46–47; Yamaguchi Yaichirō, "Shitai bunri maisō jiken: Ninpu sōsō girei," *Minkan denshō* 17/5 (1953): 50–52.

82. These secret transmission manuals also recommended quietly chanting the names of the Ten Buddhas by reciting them into the left ear of the dead woman and drawing Sanskrit diagrams of the Five Buddhas on the face of the woman to ensure salvation. Finally, the coffin would be closed and hit with "a branch of an eastern-facing peach tree." For a *kirigami* that explains where to draw the Sanskrit letters, the *Betsubuku menjō bongyō*, see Ishikawa Rikizan, (9) *KDBK* 45 (1987): 178–89, or *Zenshū sōden shiryō no kenkyū*, vol. 1, pp. 485–90. Another example of such a *kirigami* would be the *Tabi taiji mōja*. The motif of the peach tree being used to ward off demons or evil spirits was common in Chinese magical practices. One can find this motif in the Japanese chronicle, the *Kojiki*, in which the creator deity, Izanagi, threw peaches at the denizens of the land of *yomi* (darkness) who were following him. See Donald Philippi, trans. *Kojiki: Translated with an Introduction and Notes* (Tokyo: The Institute for Japanese Culture and Classics, Kokugakuin University, 1959), p. 65. It was also thought that ghosts came in and out of the other world through an entrance found underneath the northeast branches of a large peach tree. See Wang Xiuwen, "Momo no densetsushi," *Nihon kenkyū* 20 (2000): 125–72.

83. Tsutsumi has explored the motif of a child being born in a coffin or a grave (several well-known Sōtō Zen monks, such as Tsūgen Jakurei, were born in a grave after their mother died in childbirth. See his "Kosodate yūreitan no genzō: Sōtōshū sōsō girei o tegakari to shite," *Kyoto Seika daigaku kiyō* 4 (1993): 244–56; rpt. in *Setsuwa: Sukui to shite no shi*, ed. Setsuwa Denshō Gakkai (Tokyo: Kanrin shobō, 1994), pp. 117–42, and *Kinsei setsuwa to zensō* (Osaka: Izumi shoin, 1999), pp. 133–52. On Tsūgen Jakurei's case, see Tsutsumi, *Kinsei setsuwa to zensō*, pp. 135–40.

84. The practice can also be found in esoteric and Shugen traditions. Quoted in Tsutsumi, *Kinsei setsuwa to zensō*, p. 146. Also see Iizuka Daiten, "Chūsei Sōtōshū ni okeru kirigami no sōden ni tsuite," *Shūgaku kenkyū* 41 (1999): 177, for Menzan's critique of these *kirigami*.

85. For discussion of the recognition, or the lack thereof, of fetuses and young children as human during the Tokugawa period, see Helen Hardacre, *Marketing the Menacing Fetus in Japan* (Berkeley: University of California Press, 1997), p. 25.

86. On the question of separate children's graves (*kobaka*), whether at the regular gravesite, under the house, or in a special children's gravesite, see Tanaka Hisao, "Kobaka: Sono sōsei ni shimaru ichi ni shite," *Minzoku* 29 (1965): 14–24; rpt. in *Sōsō bosei kenkyū shūsei 1*, ed. Doi Takuji and Satō Yoneshi (Tokyo: Meicho shuppan, 1979), pp. 314–30. The age at which children might receive funerals is a complex issue, differing by region. On dead children in the world beyond, see Watari Kōichi, "Osanaki mōjatachi no sekai: 'sai no kawara' no zuzō o megutte," in *"Sei to shi" no zuzōgaku*, ed. Meiji Daigaku Jinbun Kagaku Kenkyūsho (Tokyo: Kazama shobō, 1999), pp. 197–243.

87. See Sawayama Mikako, "Sendaihan ryōnai akago yōiku shihō to kanren shiryō: Higashiyama chihō o chūshin ni," in *Kinsei Nihon mabiki kankō shiryō shūsei*, ed. Ōta Motoko (Tokyo: Tōsui shobō, 1997), pp. 33–127. This article includes materials from Shōonji Temple, held at Shiraishi Hitoshi Ke Monjo, under the headings "Sendai Shōonji akago o gai shi kyōka o su gojunkō nasare sōrō yoshi no koto," "Shōonji ni te shichigatsu jūhachi nichi goshutatsu gojunkō nasare sōrō yoshi no koto," and "Taishinin akago yōiku kanjin no hiki, aiwatasare yoshi no koto"; see pp. 111–19. Arimoto has written on the taboo against infanticide in the Jōdo Shinshū tradition; see Arimoto Masao, *Shūkyō shakaishi no kōzō: Shinshū monto no shinkō to seikatsu* (Tokyo: Yoshikawa kōbunkan, 1997), pp. 74–102. On the general question of the prevalence of infanticide in Tokugawa Japan, see Laurel Cornell, "Infanticide in Early Modern Japan? Demography, Culture, and Population Growth," *Journal of Asian Studies* 55/1 (1996): 22–50.

88. The sermons are the 1791 *Akago yōiku kanjin no hiki* by Daiken (Rinnōji Temple, held at Katō Shin'ichi Ke Monjo) and the 1811 *Ikuji kyōka no bun shōryaku* by Daikō (Kōkenji Temple, held at Katō Shin'ichi ke Monjo). Both can be found in Sawayama, "Sendaihan," pp. 119–22.

89. A good example is a painting dated 1813 from Jōsenji Temple (Shirakawa, Fukushima Prefecture) donated by the shogunal advisor, Matsudaira Sadanobu, to the temple's chief abbot for the purpose of warning the local populace of the eventual outcome of committing infanticide. See a reproduction of the painting in Itabashi Kuritsu Bijutsukan, ed., *Ano yo no jōkei* (Tokyo: Itabashi kuritsu bijutsukan, 2001), pp. 24–25.

90. For a study of women's childbirth associations in this region, see Ōshima Tatehiko, "Koyasu jinja to koyasukō: Chibashi Hanamigawaku Hatachō," *Seikō minzoku* 169 (1999): 24–29. Of course, the temple also sponsored safe-childbirth rites. There the sutra was placed in the pregnant woman's waistband, and after birth the seven Sanskrit characters representing Jizō were cut out of the sutra. Each Sanskrit character was drunk on seven consecutive nights (which commemorates the seven nights the abbot copied the sutra in the original legend). The family took back the remaining uncut section of the sutra to the temple so that a new sutra could be obtained for the period until the mother fully recovered.

91. For more on the Matsudōkō, see Iishiro Kazuko, "Matsudo daigongen to Matsudōkō: Shinai ni okeru nyoninkō no hensen katei o tōshite," *Abikoshishi kenkyū* 9 (1985): 173–99.

92. These hymns can be found in Nakano Jūsai, "Shūmon fukyōjō ni okeru sabetsu jishō 1: Sei sabetsu 'Ketsubonkyō' ni tsuite," *Kyōka kenshū* 30 (1987): 288–89; or in Tagami, *Bukkyō to sei sabetsu*, pp. 205–6. As Iishiro Kazuko and Seki Tadao argued, the fire at Shōsenji Temple during the Meiwa era (1764–71) provided a catalyst for the temple to engage these women's groups in new fundraising that focused on *Ketsubonkyō* activities. See Iishiro, "Matsudo daigongen to Matsudōko," p. 193; and Seki Tadao, "Shōsenji no bunkazai, shikō," *Abikoshishi kenkyū* 10 (1986): 96.

93. In the 1990s a number of Komazawa University scholars started to highlight this discrepancy, both doctrinally and in terms of their ritual practice (since many of them were Zen priests serving parish temples). This theme is one aspect of a project on Sōtō Zen funerals that was inaugurated as the first joint research project under the auspices of the newly established Sōtōshū Center for Buddhist Studies (*Sōtōshū sōgō kenkyū sentā*), which began in April 1999. But the important point here is that the need to account for the discrepancy, either for doctrinal consistency or as an explanation to parishioners, is a modern, not a Tokugawa-period, problem.

94. Mariko Walter's "Structure of the Japanese Buddhist Funeral," in *Death Rituals and the Afterlife in Japanese Buddhism*, ed. Mariko Walter and Jacqueline Stone (Honolulu: University of Hawai'i Press, 2004), details the problems inherent in this dual structure of Japanese funerary practices.

CHAPTER 4 The Cult of Dōryō Daigongen: Daiyūzan and Sōtō Zen Prayer Temples

1. Alexander Vesey similarly cautions against reducing Tokugawa Buddhists to funeral liturgists or registrars for the government. Vesey's work focuses on temples, including Sōtō Zen ones, as sites for the mediation of social disputes and contestations. Much like the resolution of the fight that began this chapter, Vesey examines the role of temples in handling village contention, including assaults, marriage disputes, and accidental fires. His work represents an important new direction in the social history of local Buddhism during the Tokugawa period. See Alexander Vesey, "Entering the Temple: Priests, Peasants, and Village Contention in Tokugawa Japan," *Japanese Journal of Religious Studies* 28/3–4 (2001): 293–328, and "The Buddhist Clergy."

2. This document, "Naisai torikawashi shōmon no koto," is held at Daiyūzan Saijōji (as yet uncataloged). A printed version of the manuscript and photos of the original can be found in Watanabe Shōei, "Edo kara Meiji made no kaichō," in *DTG*, pp. 110–12.

3. Literally "*sake* of the gods."

4. The text continues, "mediated by Kaizōji Temple in Hayakawa Village, Sōfukuji Temple in Sannōhara Village, Tennōin Temple in Tsukahara Village, as well as the Tsukahara Village headman Heinosuke and his deputies Uhei and Hanemon."

5. The text was sent to Takematsu Village Daishōji Temple, its village headman (Kurōemon), and deputies (Kakuemon, Rinnai, Yazaemon, Riemon) by Kano Village residents, including the village representative, Tōemon; the village deputies, Yōzaemon, Ubee, and Ichiemon; and members of the *goningumi* heads [of the five injured]: Gonzaemon group (Magoemon), Chūemon group (Yaheiji), Inosuke group (Riemon), Hikōemon group (Kakuemon), Hikojirō group (Shigeuemon); *goningumi* heads [of the five injured]: Gonzaemon group (Enzaemon), Chūemon group (Yōzō), Inosuke group (Yaheiji), Hikōemon group (Yōzō), and Hikojirō group (Genshichi); and the fathers of Chūemon (Hannai), Inosuke (Seiemon), and Hikojirō (Den'emon). This is followed by the seals of the mediators, Tsukahara Village deputies (Chūemon and Uhei) and headman (Heinosuke); Sannōhara Village Sōfukuji Temple; Tsukahara Village Tennōin Temple; Hayakawa Village Kaizōji Temple.

6. This 1819 *kaichō* was recorded by outside observers like Saitō Gesshin, a powerful landowner in the Kanda district of Edo and chronicler of the *Bukō nenpyō*. In his diary, in which he recorded almost all the *kaichō* in the city of Edo during his lifetime, he notes that the Dōryō gongen statue from Sekimoto was on display at Chōkokuji Temple. For a printed version, see Saitō Gesshin, *Bukō nenpyō*, ed. Kaneko Mitsuharu (Tokyo: Heibonsha, 1968), p. 62.

7. Temple mediation in this type of dispute was quite common. In 1738 a priest from the Sōtō Zen temple Kōsenji mediated with village officials regarding a group of young men from two different villages involved in a melee. Twenty years later, in 1758, some young men became rowdy during the annual Bon festival and hurt a certain Ninsuke from Koguma Village. Since the village headman was a parishioner of the Sōtō Zen temple Shōzenji, the incident was resolved through the temple's mediation. For documents related to these two incidents, see Gosen Shishi Hensan Iinkai, ed., *Gosen Shishi*, pp. 607–11. A similar incident in 1646, in which two drunk men killed a number of villagers in Iinoya Village (Shizuoka Prefecture) during a festival associated with the annual summer festival dance, required the mediation of a Rinzai temple (Ryōtanji) for the two assailants to escape the death penalty. The men's lives were spared on the condition that they become monks at the temple. For the diary of a village official that relates this incident, see Nakai Yagozaemon, *Nakai nikki* (1684), in *Shizuoka kenshi shiryōhen 12: Kinsei 4*, ed. Shizuokaken (Tokyo: Gyōsei, 1995), pp. 685–86. Takeuchi Makoto has also argued for "the festival" as an "autonomous zone of action" in which fights are viewed differently by government officials. He takes up the resolution of fights at the Sanja Festival of Sensōji Temple during the eighteenth century in his "Festivals and Fights: The

Law and the People of Edo," in *Edo and Paris: Urban Life and the State in the Early Modern Era*, ed. James McClain, John Merriman, and Ugawa Kaoru (Ithaca: Cornell University Press, 1994), pp. 384–406. The writing of social history through disputes and local village legal practices is the hallmark of the works of Ooms, *Tokugawa Village Practice*; and Vesey, "The Buddhist Clergy." Both refer frequently to the role of Buddhist temples of all sects in meditating disputes.

8. According to the 1727 *Nihon tōjō rentōroku*, Ryōan was from Sagami Province (though the 1693 *Nichiiki tōjō shosoden* claims he was born in Hitachi Province)—born in Kasuya Village (in present-day Isehara City)—and returned to his home province after training with both Gasan and Tsūgen at Sōjiji and Yōtakuji, respectively. Before he founded Daiyūzan, Ryōan served as abbot at a number of well-known Sōtō Zen temples, including Sōneiji, Yōtakuji, and Ryūsenji. These two texts are the best-known Tokugawa-period biographies of Sōtō Zen monks. The *Nihon tōjō rentōroku*, which includes the biographies of 743 Sōtō monks after Dōgen, was compiled by Reinan Shūjo as a twelve-volume work, published in 1742. The *Nichiiki tōjō shosoden*, which includes biographies of Sōtō monks after Dōgen, was compiled by Tangen Jichō in two volumes in 1693. A later addition to this text by Tokuō Ryōkō (1709; 4 vols.) and by Zōzan (1717; 4 vols.) added the biographies of eighty and ninety monks, respectively. Both texts can be found in printed form in the *Dai Nihon Bukkyō zensho* 70: 213–37; and the *SZ shiden jō*, 287–346. An important study on the *Nihon tōjō rentōroku* is Iwanaga Shōsei et al., "'Nihon tōjō rentōroku' no kenkyū (1)," *KDZN* 15 (2003): 145–204. For the most comprehensive study of Ryōan, see Matsuda Bunyū, *Daiyūzan to gokaisansama: Ryōan Emyō zenji no ashiato o tazunete* (Minami Ashigara: *Daiyūzan* Saijōji, 1984.) For more on Ryōan, see Andō Yoshinori, *Chūsei Zenshū bunken no kenkyū* (Tokyo: Kokusho kankōkai, 2000), pp. 270–78; and Kumamoto Einin, "Ryōan Emyō no Saijōji kaisō ni kansuru ichi kōsatsu," *Shūkyō kenkyū* 61, 9 (1988): 199–200, and "Ryōan Emyō to sono monka ni tsuite," *Shūkyō kenkyū* 63, 4 (1990): 196–97.

9. Scholars debate the exact date of the opening of the temple. Some have suggested for an earlier dating of 1394, but Matsuda Bunyū has convincingly argued that the zodiac sign assigned to the founding date refers to 1395 instead. See *Daiyūzan to gokaisansama*, pp. 61–62.

10. For a discussion of the theories about original sponsor of Daiyūzan (whether it be the Ōmori or the Ōta family), see Matsuda's argument, ibid., pp. 76–82. The Tokugawa-period history of five generations of the Odawara Hōjō family by Kōsei no Itsushishi, the *Hōjō godai jikki* (also known as the *Odawara Hōjōki* or *Odawaraki*, held at the National Diet Library), mentions the history of their patronage and the original patronage of the Ōmori in the entry for the eighth month of 1560. For a detailed study, see *Odawara Hōjōki*, ed. Kishi Masanao (Tokyo: Kyōikusha, 1980). Also see Nakano Keijirō, "Ōmorishi no sūbutsu seisaku to sono bukkyō bunka," *Shidan Ashigara* 2 (1964): 36–44, which discusses the role of Ansō Sōryō, the tenth-generation abbot of Daiyūzan and an Ōmori family descendant, in the completion of the Daiyūzan temple buildings.

11. For the term *godai kitō jiin*, see Misawa Chishō, "Daiyūzan Saijōji to itoku jintsū Dōryō daisatta," *Shidan Ashigara* 29 (1991): 8–10.

12. On the cult of Toyokawa Inari and Myōgonji, see Steven Heine, "Sōtō Zen and the Inari Cult: Symbiotic and Exorcistic Trends in Buddhist-Folk Religious Amalgamations," *Pacific World* 10 (1994): 80–87.

13. No nationwide Tokugawa-period data on the primary images of worship exist, but since these statues have not undergone drastic changes, the survey conducted by the Sōtōshū Shūmuchō every ten years (since 1965) provides national data that are instructive: Śākyamuni as the object of worship in the main hall, 47.5%; Kannon, 22.6%; Yakushi, 7.1%; Jizō, 6.7%; Amida, 6.6%; and others. As for the worship of deities in the other halls of the temple, where in many senses the real worship of deities occurred on temple grounds, the worship of Jizō and Kannon can be found at 62.2% and 57.6% of all temples, respectively. These data can be found in Sōtōshū Shūmuchō, *Sōtōshū shūsei*

sōgō chōsa hōkokusho, pp. 111–13. I have, however, conducted a regional survey of Tokugawa-period temple main images of worship. For the roughly 400 Sōtō Zen temples in Sagami Province, the figures for the main hall images are: Śākyamuni, 151 temples; Kannon, 86 temples; Yakushi, 41 temples; Jizō, 39 temples; Amida, 24 temples; Kokuzō, 12 temples; Fudō, 3 temples; other deities, 2 temples.

14. For an overview of prayer temples in the Tokugawa period, see Tamamuro Fumio, "Sōsai kara kitō e: Kinsei bukkyō ni okeru taiwa naiyō no henka," in *Fukyōsha to minshū to no taiwa*, ed. Nihon Shūkyōshi Kenkyūkai (Kyoto: Hōzōkan, 1968), pp. 128–35.

15. For a good overview of rain-making prayers in the Sōtō school, see Satō Shunkō, "Kinsei Sōtō Zensō no seiu girei." Satō shows how Tokugawa-period Sōtō priests used prayers derived from Buddhist canonical texts, secret transmission documents, and local dragon deity traditions as sources for their rituals. For one such secret transmission document, see Ishikawa, "Chūsei Sōtōshū kirigami no bunrui shiron 21," *KDBK* 51 (1993): 122–24. For English-language literature on rain-making rituals, the best overview of early textual sources and practices is Brian Ruppert's "Buddhist Rain-making in Early Japan: The Dragon King and the Ritual Careers of Esoteric Monks," *History of Religions* 42, 2 (2002): 143–74. Also see Marinus Willem De Visser's study of dragon worship and rain-making in his *The Dragon in China and Japan* (Amsterdam: Verhandelingen der Koniklijke Akademie van Weteschappen, 1913), pp. 113–21, 178; and Sherry Fowler's study of dragons and rain-making in her "In Search of the Dragon: Mt. Murō's Sacred Topography," *Japanese Journal of Religious Studies* 24/1–2 (1997): 145–62.

16. For example, by the late Tokugawa period, Zenpōji Temple in the Shōnai region (present-day Yamagata Prefecture)—one of the best-known Sōtō Zen prayer temples— had tens of thousands of believers from coastal fishing villages along the eastern Japan Sea coast. The phrase "Nishi no Konpira, Higashi no Zenpōji" (In the West, Konpira and in the East, Zenpōji) was developed in the Meiji period to denote the two sites (Konpira Shrine in Shikoku, i.e., western Japan, and Zenpōji in the east), which specialized in rituals for fishermen and seafarers. Zenpōji's talismans, believed to both protect fishermen from the rough seas and bring in large catches of fish, had prints of two dragon deities (Ryūō and Ryūjo). These dragon deities had been part of the temple's history (it was originally a Tendai temple named Ryūgeji) before the temple was converted into a Sōtō Zen temple by Tainen Jōchin (although some temple histories attribute the conversion of the temple to Gasan Jōkin), who enshrined the dragon deities in a Dragon King Hall (Ryūōden) in 1446. The cult of the dragon deities (*ryūjin shinkō*) developed into a much more powerful aspect of this Sōtō temple's ritual life than the main image of worship (Yakushi), especially in the late Tokugawa and early Meiji periods, when fishing routes along the Tōhoku sea coasts expanded dramatically. The special prayers of such temples functioned to solve problems once they occurred (to protect the person in a dangerous situation such as in a storm out at sea) as well as to invite good fortune (bringing in large catches of fish). This dual function of this-world benefits is discussed in terms of *yakudoke* (protection from external dangers) and *kaiun* (bringing good fortune) in a study of *genze riyaku* in contemporary Japanese religions. See Reader and Tanabe, *Practically Religious*, pp. 45–46. Another important late-Tokugawa-period Sōtō Zen center known for its "protection-at-sea Jizō" was Osorezan Bodaiji on the Shimokita Peninsula. For the cult of this Jizō, see Miyazaki and Williams, "The Intersection of the Local and Translocal at a Sacred Site," pp. 427–30, and "Chiiki kara mita Osorezan," *Rekishi Hyōron* (September 2002): 59-73; and Miyazaki Fumiko, "Reijō Osorezan no tanjō," *Kan: Rekishi, kankyō, bunmei* 8 (2002): 366–71.

17. This distinction between *kitō* performed at regular parish temples and those at prayer temples (*kitō jiin*) that are almost exclusively run for the purpose of offering prayers for "this-world benefits" has also been made by Abe Shinken in "Kitō ni yori kyōka keitai no ichi kōsatsu: Daiyūzan Saijōji o rei to shite," *Komazawa daigaku bukkyōgakkaishi* 11 (1969): 29–41.

18. One *chō* is equivalent to 109 meters.

19. The *Hakone nikki* by Shimazu Hamaomi (1814) is held at the Kanazawa Bunko.

20. Dōryō seems to have been pronounced Dōryū in rare cases such as in the Tokugawa-period *Tōkaidō meisho no banzukehyō* (The Ranking of Famous Sites along the Tōkaidō). For more on this text and the pronunciation of Dōryō as Dōryū, see Misawa Chishō, "Daiyūzan Saijōji to itoku jintsū," p. 9.

21. For documents related to Dōryō's training at Miidera, see the excerpts from the *Kumano sanzan genki* reproduced in *Daiyūzanshi*, ed. Daiyūzan Saijōji (Minami Ashigara: Saijōji, 1961), p. 17. On the connection between Sagamibō and tengu, see Ōwa Iwao, *Tengu to tennō* (Tokyo: Hakusuisha, 1997), pp. 175–79.

22. See Matsuda Bunyū, *Daiyūzan to gokaisansama*, p. 172.

23. A variant to this story from manuscripts from Miidera states that Dōryō had already turned himself into a tengu in 1393 when he left Miidera and flew to Sagami Province. For this document, see the *Onjōji gakutōdai Hokurin'in nikki* in printed-text form in *Daiyūzanshi*, p. 17.

24. As a tengu, Dōryō was thought of as a kami, but in the pre-Meiji period, the distinction between kami and Buddhist deities was not at all clear. However, the appellation "gongen" used for Dōryō and his enshrinement in the Dōryōgū or Dōryō Shrine indicates his status as a kami. After the *haibutsu kishaku* movement to separate Buddhism and Shintō in the Meiji period, like many complex institutions, Daiyūzan had to designate Dōryō as either a Shintō kami or a Buddhist deity. Though many Sōtō Zen institutions (the best-known being the case of Akibadera, which was turned into Akiba Shrine) took the route of designating their "mixed" deities as Shintō deities, Daiyūzan renamed Dōryō Gongen first as Dōryō Bosatsu and then as Dōryō Daisatta (short for bodhisattva) to retain his Buddhist identity.

25. Kumamoto has also noted how the rebuilding of the Dōryō statue (in the figure of a *shō tengu*) and the assignment of a special posthumous name to Dōryō, Myōkaku Dōryō Oshō, by an anonymous monk from Ryūneiji Temple in 1850 helped consolidate the image of Dōryō as tengu. See Kumamoto Einin, "Dōryōson to Daiyūzan Saijōji ni kansuru rekishiteki ichi kōsatsu," *Shūkyō kenkyū* 62/4 (1989): 307.

26. Also by the medieval period, two different iconographic images of the tengu emerged: (1) the *dai tengu* with a red face and protruding nose and (2) the *shō tengu* with a bird's beak instead of the long nose, sometimes called *karasu tengu* (crow tengu). For a good summary of the development of the figure of the tengu, see Andō Yoshinori, "Tengu kō: Tenguzō no keiseishi," *SKK* 20 (1988): 55–70; and Ōwa, *Tengu to tennō*. In English, see Patricia Fister, "*Tengu*, the Mountain Goblin," in *Japanese Ghosts and Demons: Art of the Supernatural*, ed. Stephen Addiss (New York: George Braziller, 1985), pp. 103–28; Marinus Willem De Visser, "The Tengu," *Transactions of the Asiatic Society of Japan* 36/2 (1908): 25–99; and Haruko Wakabayashi, "Tengu: Images of the Buddhist Concepts of Evil in Medieval Japan" (Ph.D. dissertation, Princeton University, 1995), and "The Dharma for Sovereigns and Warriors: Onjō-ji's Claim for Legitimacy in *Tengu zōshi*," *Japanese Journal of Religious Studies* 29/1–2 (2002): 35–66.

27. The Sanskrit etymology can be found in Monier Monier-Williams, *Sanskrit-English Dictionary* (New Delhi: Munshivam Manoharlal, 1999), p. 218.

28. A Shintō priest and Kokugaku scholar from Fuchū Rokushonomiya, Saruwatari Moriaki, wrote in his 1832 diary, the *Namaoyomi no nikki*: "At Saijōji, a Sōtō Zen temple, there was a selfish, evil monk full of pernicious wisdom called Dōryō who studied under Ryōan (who was a monk five generations after Dōgen). He eventually went to the spirit world (*makai*) and became a tengu. The spirit of this tengu is worshipped at the shrine, according to the *Tōyūkō nōshō*. There is a similar story about a monk, Hōshōbō, of Mt. Myōgi of Kōzuke Province, but these stories are pretty suspicious." This text can be found in print form in *MAS* 6: 551–52.

29. The unique aspect of Dōryō was that while most associations of tengu and *yamabushi* are very vague, the original identity of this tengu is clear. However, there seems to have been a shift in the Dōryō iconography from a *shō tengu* (bird-beaked style) as rep-

resented by the early statue in the Dōryō Shrine (donated by Betsuzan Shōun in 1676), to the later Tokugawa image depicting Dōryō as a long-nosed tengu (as seen in woodblock prints). This can be partially explained by the report that during the late seventeenth century, the wings from the "bird" tengu dropped off. For more on the Dōryō tengu statuary, see Chigiri Kōsai, *Zushū tengu retsuden: Nishi Nihon hen* (Tokyo: Miki shobō, 1977), p. 471. This is also a good two-volume overview of tengu in Japan (a volume each on western and eastern Japan). A Tokugawa-period *banzuke* (a ranking chart that used terminology from sumo) reprinted in this volume—the *Nihon Dai Tengu Banzuke*—lists the Dōryō tengu as a fourth-level *maegashira* of eastern Japan (p. 494).

30. For more on the cult of Akiba, see Nakano Tōzen and Shun'ei Yoshida, eds., *Akiba shinkō* (Tokyo: Yūzankaku, 1998); Takei Shōgu, "Akihasan no shinkō," In *Fuji, Ontake to chūbu reizan*, ed. Suzuki Shōei (Tokyo: Meicho shuppan, 1978), pp. 202–18; Watanabe Shōei, "Zenshū jiin to Akiba shinkō to shomin: Akibadera no himatsuri o chūshin ni," *Shūkyō kenkyū* 60, 4 (1987): 333–35, "Akiba shinkō to Akiba sanjakubō no nana-jūgozen ni tsuite," *Shūkyō kenkyū* 63/4 (1990): 254–56, "Akiba shinkō ni okeru shinkō taishō no ichirei ni tsuite," *Shūkyō kenkyū* 69/4 (1996): 306–7, "Akiba shinkō to daisankō no genjō ni tsuite," *Shūkyō kenkyū* 71/4 (1998): 399–401, "Minzoku shūkyō kara mita Akiba shinkō no ichi," *Shūkyō kenkyū* 72/4 (1999): 323–24, "Minzoku bukkyō to shite no Akiba shinkō to zenshū jiin ni tsuite," *Shukyō kenkyū* 74/4 (2001): 353–54; Yoshida Shun'ei, "Sōtōshū ni okeru Akiba shinkō," *Shūgaku kenkyū* (1992–95) (1) 34: 242–47; (2) 35: 244–50; (3) 36: 211–16; (4) 37: 239–44, "Minkan shinkō no kyōkagakuteki ichi kōsatsu: Akibakō no chōsa jirei kara," *Kyōka kenshū* 39 (1996): 194–200. For more on Kashōzan's tengu, see Numata Shishi Hensan Iinkai, "Kashōzan no minzoku shinkō," in *Numatashi shi: minzokuhen*, ed. Numata Shishi Hensan Iinkai (Numata: Numata shishi hensan iinkai, 1998), pp. 973–1012; and Watanabe Shōei, "Zenshū jiin to tengu shinkō to ichi rei: Kashōzan to Numata matsuri no baai," *Shūkyō kenkyū* 69/4 (1986): 305–6. For a comparison between Daiyūzan's and Kashōzan's tengu legends, see Yamaoka Ryūkō, "Jiin engi ni mirareru tengu denshō no motif to sono imi," *Komazawa daigaku shūkyōgaku ronshū* 13 (1987): 69–74. The Kashōzan case is remarkably similar to Daiyūzan's, and given its historical connection (the founder—Tenson—was also the seventh-generation abbot of Daiyūzan), it would not be surprising that the legend of a founder's disciple turning into a tengu became a motif for the Ryōan lineage. Furthermore, the Sanshakubō Shrine at Daiyūzan, which features the deity Iizuna Gongen of Akibadera, is clearly the combination of two deities, Fudō and a tengu. See Robert Duquenne, "Sanshakubō Gongen, an Aspect of Fudō Myō-ō," *Transactions of the International Conference of Orientalists in Japan* 17 (1972): 119–20.

31. The earliest reference I can find to the Dōryō festival is the *Saijōji utsushi tozanyū kyūmeiji* (*Gokurakuji monjo*, uncataloged) of 1724. The earliest reference to the ceremony being called Gokūshiki is from the 1867 document, the *Saijō rinjū kiroku* (*Daiyūzan monjo*, uncataloged). The best Tokugawa-period description of this festival can be found in an 1818 entry in the Daiyūzan abbot's logbook, the *Saijō rinjū dainikkan*, which I have translated in "Representations of Zen," chap. 3. Butsujō copied this 1818 entry during his tenure as abbot of Daiyūzan in 1867. His text includes the various rules and regulations at Daiyūzan, a daily log of rituals held, duties of members of the temples as well as the local villagers, and incidents that the abbot thought it proper to record. A total of twelve extant Daiyūzan logbooks (with alternate titles such as *rinjūroku, rinjū kiroku,* or *rinjū nikki*) exist, but this manuscript is currently held as part of the Ryūtaiji Monjo (Aichi Gakuin University Library). A printed version is included in the ZSZ 2: 141–75, but because of numerous errors in its transcription, a new edition will be released by the members of the Bukkyō Minzokugaku Kenkyūkai at Komazawa University. See Duncan Williams et al., ed., "Saijō rinjū dainikkan ni tsuite, " *Minzoku bukkyō kenkyūkai kiyō* 2 (2004).

32. While the major elements of the Tokugawa-period ceremony—now called Gokūshiki—have been retained, some elements have changed. For example, the cere-

mony now starts earlier (at 8:30 p.m.) to accommodate pilgrims who do not stay the night. This reflects the fact that the ceremony has become more pilgrim- and *yamabushi*-oriented in the postwar period (as opposed to being primarily a monastic ceremony to gain magical powers that happened also to include lay believers, as was the case during the Tokugawa period). Today, the members of the Byakuekai—the main *yamabushi* organization made up of lay Dōryō believers—blow the conch horns, distribute the pieces of sacred rope (which is said to "rope in" money), and sprinkle sacred water over kō members. Instead of Zen meditation by the monks, the ceremony ends at 10 p.m. with a Dharma talk by the abbot in the main hall. The sake drinking, though, has remained a constant.

33. A pilgrim belonging to a Mt. Fuji pilgrimage association recorded his visit to Daiyūzan on the 28th, expressing his astonishment at the festiveness of the *kaichō* at the Dōryō Shrine. See the *Fuji Ōyama dōchū zakki* (1838).

34. Another variant of this talisman is "Okanoin." In another version of this story, found in the 1841 *Shinpen Sagami no kuni fudokikō*, Mishima Myōjin, rather than Iizawa and Yagura Myōjin, led Ryōan to the site.

35. *Tōzan kaibyaku narabini kunin rōjin no kien* by Kōkoku Eishun (1648) is held at Daiyūzan. A printed version can be found in *MAS* 8: 282–84.

36. This can be found, for example, in the *Saijōji engi wasan*, *MAS* 8: 290–93.

37. For more on the "Diamond Water," see Shidan Ashigara, "Kongōsui," *Shidan Ashigara* 32 (1994): 92–93.

38. The regulation, the *Yūhō kongō hōin okite*, is among the still uncataloged *Daishōji monjo*, but a printed version of the text can be found in *DTG*, pp. 122–23. A full translation of the text is in Williams, "Representations of Zen," chap. 3.

39. In fact, another notice issued in 1822 repeats the same points about the number of talismans allowed per pilgrim, which suggests that meeting pilgrims' demands was an ongoing problem. For the 1822 notice, see *Daiyūzanshi*, p. 15.

40. See the entry under the twelfth of the sixth month. Mori Mozaemon's diary of 1827 chronicling his travel to Mt. Fuji, the *Kōshin nikkichō*, is privately owned by Nishigai Kenji, who kindly shared this document with me.

41. The 1848 *Shinrozan dōchūki* by Akutsu Shōemon notes his travels on the way to Ise Shrine.

42. Jippensha Ikku, *Dōryō gongen Hakone gongen nanayu meguri* (1822), is held at the Kanagawaken kyōdo shiryōkan. A printed version was privately circulated by the Kanagawaken kyōdo shiryōkan and also appears in *Daiyū*, vol. 41 (1988): 2.

43. *Shinpen Sagami no kuni fudokikō*, vol. 1. (rev. ed., Tokyo: Yūzankaku, 1998), p. 258.

44. Although we do not know the anonymous author of this story from 1821, it is found under the title "Senyokō no otoshibanashi" in a collection of Tokugawa-period short stories compiled by Miyao Shigeo, ed., *Kobanashi nido no memie* 8 (Tokyo: Kobanashi hanpukai, 1933).

45. These talismans remain because, unlike most talismans (which were kept in family altars and shrines for one year before being replaced), they were stored among the roof beams of the Numata household in Hiratsuka City. These talismans from Daiyūzan were numbered 4 out of a total of 322 (the vast majority being talismans from Mt. Ōyama) kept by the family to prevent lightning from striking the roof and causing a fire. For more on the discovery of these talismans, see Hiratsukashi Hakubutsukan Shishi Hensangakari, ed., *Hiratsukashishi 12: Betsuhen minzoku* (Hiratsuka: Hiratsuka, 1993), pp. 774–76.

46. For example, Kōshin kō, Inari kō, or Jizō kō.

47. For example, Nenbutsu kō or Daimoku kō.

48. For example, Ise kō, Zenkōji kō, Fuji kō, or Ōyama kō. A general survey of this type of pilgrimage association is Sakurai Tokutarō's *Kō shūdan no kenkyū* (Tokyo: Sakurai Tokutarō chosakushū 1, Yoshikawa kōbunkan, 1988). A brief, English-language

overview of kō can be found in Lucy Itō, "Kō: Japanese Confraternities," *Monumenta Nipponica* 8 (1952): 411–15.

49. This is among the documents of the *Daiyūzan monjo*, which I have accessed, but which has not yet been made public. It is, however, listed in a catalog of Daiyūzan's holdings in Zenshū Chihōshi Chōsakai, ed., *Zenshū chihōshi chōsakai nenpō*, pp. 1–36. The donation of tree saplings by individuals, kō organizations, and rotating abbots, as well as the subsequent protection of the forest surrounding Daiyūzan, was an important way of showing support for the temple. Although at the time of Ryōan an already sizable natural forest surrounded the temple, it grew into an extensive manmade forest (more than half a million donated trees are still standing) because of the practice of offering tree saplings to the temple. In addition to the Shin Yoshiwara kō example, if we examine the number of tree saplings (mainly cedar, followed by pine) offered just by pilgrimage organizations during the Tokugawa period, we can see the significance attached to this practice: 1806—8,000 cedar; 1806—8,000 pine; 1818—2,500 cedar; 1818—5,200 pine; 1820—10,000 cedar; 1834—52,000 cedar; 1857—10,000 cedar; 1860—10,000 cedar; 1861—50,000 cedar; 1863—10,000 cedar; 1864—10,000 cedar; 1865—10,000 cedar; 1866—3,000 pine; 1866—10,000 cedar; 1867—10,000 cedar. I compiled this list from a general listing of tree donations in Daiyūzan Saijōji, ed. *Daiyūzanshi*, pp. 125–38.

50. For the full list of 434 stone markers, see *MAS* 8: 434–93. For a partial list, just of stone markers from the Tokugawa period, see Nishigai Kenji, *Minshū shūkyō no inori to sugata: Maneki* (Tokyo: Gyōsei, 1997), pp. 46–53.

51. In a later period, the Odawara Seishin kō left a very visible "mark" at Daiyūzan with their donations of stone markers designating each *chō* (sixty steps) up the twenty-eight-*chō* mountain. Their 1864 donation came with the following explanation etched into the stone of the twenty-eighth-*chō* marker: "To get to the mountain gate, go through a thick forest, which takes about 1,680 steps from the base of the mountain. It takes about sixty steps to walk one *chō* and this is the twenty-eighth-*chō* marker. The Odawara Seishin pilgrimage confraternity donated these polished stone markers out of gratitude [to Dōryō], one at each *chō*. Each stone marker has a place to put burning oil to light up this path. On festival occasions, they are lit up for all who visit." A printed version of this inscription can be found in *Daiyūzanshi*, p. 106.

52. In 1657 the pleasure quarters of Yoshiwara moved from Nihonbashi to the Asakusa District of Edo as Shin Yoshiwara. At its peak in 1858, 3,875 women were reported to be working in the district. On these numbers and the history of Yoshiwara, see Ishii Ryōsuke, "Yoshiwara," in *Nyonin sabetsu to kinsei senmin*, ed. Ishii Ryōsuke and Arai Kōjirō (Tokyo: Akashi shoten, 1995), pp. 9–178; Cecilia Sagawa Seigle, *Yoshiwara: The Glittering World of the Japanese Courtesan* (Honolulu: University of Hawai'i Press, 1993); and Yasutaka Teruoka, "The Pleasure Quarters and Tokugawa Culture," in *18th Century Japan: Culture and Society*, ed. C. Andrew Gerstle (London: Allen and Unwin, 1989), pp. 3–32. See Seigle, p. 174, for more on Daikokuya Shōroku.

53. This stone marker was rebuilt in 1880 under the initiative of a caretaker of the Shin Yoshiwara kō, Suzuki Kamakichi. Also named as contributors to the rebuilding of the marker are the kō leader and owner of the brothel Nakabeerō, and a kō leader representative (*kōmoto sōdai*) Tamaru Kitarō. Thirty other people are unnamed but listed as contributors.

54. This estimate of the number of pilgrims is taken from Nishigai Kenji's *Minshū shūkyō no inori to sugata*, p. 44. Official figures of the number of kō (the practice of registering with the temple) did not start until the Taishō period (in 1920, 151 kō), with a slight decline in the early Shōwa period (1930, 123 kō). Today, there are approximately 370–80 kō officially registered at Daiyūzan, with an average of 50 members per group, although the largest kō have memberships of 800–1,000. Most postwar kō have become more uniform in their names—usually Dōryōkō or Daiyūkō and incorporating their geographic location as part of their name. The number of informal pilgrimage groups (*sampaikai* or *kyōkai*), women's groups, and groups from distant regions (such as Hiroshima,

Osaka, Kyoto, Nagoya, and Fukuoka) has increased, though more than 50 percent are concentrated in the Tokyo-Kanagawa region. On the Taishō data, see Daiyūzan, ed., "Gokaichō kōchū sanpai hiwari," *Daiyū jihō* 1/2 (1920): 16–17. On the Shōwa 5 (1930) data, see Watanabe Shōei, "Zenshū jiin no kaichō ni tsuite: Daiyūzan Saijōji no baai," *SKKK* 18 (1986): 123–24. On the regional distribution, see Shūkyō to Gendai Henshūbu, "Daiyūzan o sasaeru Dōryōson no kō," *Shūkyō to gendai* 4/5 (1982): 58.

55. Nishigai Kenji has noted two patterns among Fuji pilgrims: Mt. Fuji-Dōryō or Mt. Fuji-Mt. Ōyama-Dōryō. See *Mihshu shūkyō no inori to sugata*, p. 46.

56. For a good survey of travel and travel restrictions in the Tokugawa period, see Constantine Vaporis, *Breaking Barriers: Travel and the State in Early Modern Japan* (Cambridge: Council on East Asian Studies, Harvard University Press, 1994), esp. pp. 137–59, for a discussion of the differences between travel permits (*sekisho tegata*) and passports (*ōrai tegata*). Marcia Yonemoto also provides an overview of Tokugawa-period travel and travel writing in *Mapping Early Modern Japan: Space, Place, and Culture in the Tokugawa Period (1603–1868)* (Berkeley: University of California Press, 2003).

57. Two major roads led to Daiyūzan (sometimes called Saijōjimichi) during the Tokugawa period, both coming off from the Kōshūmichi (which itself is a split-off of the main Tōkaidō highway): (1) A direct route from the Sekimoto station town, and (2) a winding road known locally as the Odawaramichi, which went by Sumiyakijo, Nakanuma, Kano, and Iizawa villages. For more on the transportation routes to Daiyūzan, see *MAS* 6: 515.

58. On the first occasion, the term Fuji kō was not specifically used, but it is clearly used subsequently to ban the popular groups. See Tamamuro Fumio, *Nihon bukkyōshi*, pp. 335–36.

59. There was, however, a dispute in 1774 as to whether Fuji pilgrims could stay at one of the temple lodgings up at Daiyūzan or instead needed to secure a place at an inn down at the station town of Sekimoto. This dispute—which was decided by local magistrates in favor of Sekimoto—suggests that the economic basis of a station town like Sekimoto was pilgrims. They could not afford to have a vital source of income siphoned off by the temple. For more on this dispute, see *An'ei nenchū kakuan e rōzeki ni tsuki Sekimoto yori wabi issatsu* in *MAS* 8: 420–21. On a similar type of dispute at Mt. Ōyama between villager inns and *oshi* lodgings, see Ambros, "Localized Religious Specialists," 344–45. Sekimoto and other surrounding villages received privileges (such as exclusive rights to house pilgrims or permits to use sections of Daiyūzan's forest for fuel and fertilizer) in exchange for yearly donations of rice, help during the three major festivals and when the rotating abbots came to Daiyūzan, and contributions for temple rebuilding. On the village's role during large ceremonies, see *Rinban kōtai sansairei nado ni okeru Sekimotomura yakuninshū no toriatsukai ni tsuki gijōsho* by Saijōji (1850), Sekimoto Jichikai Collection, which has been printed in *MAS* 8: 421–22. On farmers' contributions in times of temple rebuilding, see *MAS* 8: 75.

60. See the entry under the twelfth of the sixth month of Mori Mozaemon's diary of 1831, chronicling his travel to Mt. Fuji and Mt. Ōyama, the *Fuji tozan nikki oboechō*.

61. On bakufu restrictions on pilgrimages in general, see Vaporis, *Breaking Barriers*, pp. 198–216.

62. This point has also been observed by Hara Jun'ichirō in his "Ōyama, Fuji, Enoshima," *Chihōshi kenkyū* 274 (1998): 25.

63. This stone marker is dated as being reconstructed in 1884. It is likely that the original was from around the Bunsei period (1818–30) because the same kō built a still extant (located about 100 meters from the road marker) stone monument to "Fuji Sengen daigongen" in 1830. For more on the Yagurazawa Road, see Yamamoto Mitsumasa, "Sōshū Yagurazawa ōkan ni tsuite," *Kanagawa kenshi kenkyū* 19 (1973): 46–56.

64. Of the sixty-four stone markers and guideposts—along seven routes that pass by Daiyūzan (Kōzu to Tsukahara; Odawara to Kōshū; Saijōji Road; Yagurazawa Road; Mt. Ōyama to Kaisei; Yamakitachō to Mt. Fuji; Gotemba to Mt. Fuji)—studied by the Ashigara shidankai (Historical Society of Ashigara City), twenty-nine markers showed

the way to Daiyūzan, while twenty-two also gave directions to Mt. Fuji and thirteen to Mt. Ōyama. The significance of Dōryō can be seen in these stone markers as well in the use of the term "Saijōji" during the early Tokugawa period, while "Dōryō" became the norm by the late Tokugawa and early Meiji periods. See Ashigara Shidan Chōsa Kenkyūbu, "Shinkō no michi: Dōhyō chōsa," *Shidan Ashigara* 1 (1997) 35: 10–27; 2 (1998) 36: 10–38.

65. See Ōno Ichirō, "Seichi no settoka to shinkō no sōgō kanren," *Chihōshi kenkyū* 274 (1998): 33–37.

66. This point has also been made by Hara, "Ōyama, Fuji, Enoshima," p. 26.

67. For this prayer, see *Hakusan daigongen, Dōryō daigongen jotōsai norito* (1777), Tenaka Tadashi private collection. A printed text version can be found in Isehara shishi henshū iinkai, ed., *Isehara shishi shiryōhen: Zoku Ōyama* (Isehara: Isehara, 1994), pp. 179–80.

68. This can be found in *Isehara shishi shiryōhen*, p. 323. Both Tanaka Sen'ichi and Hirano Eiji have analyzed this document: Tanaka Sen'ichi, "Sōshū Ōyamakō no oshi to danka," in *Ōyama shinkō*, ed. Tamamuro Fumio (Tokyo: Yūzankaku, 1992), pp. 63–90; and Hirano Eiji, "Fujikō, Ōyamakō no junpai to yūzan," *Chihōshi kenkyū* 274 (1998): 29–32.

69. On the notion of the development of a "culture of movement" in form of travel guides, maps, travel literature, and woodblock prints depicting interesting destinations, see Vaporis, *Breaking Barriers*, p. 14.

70. Ryōan was supposedly at Jikudoan Temple (currently Jikudoji) when an eagle flew off with his robe in the direction of Ashigara and dropped it on a pine tree there. This legend was first recorded in the 1508 *Gokurakuji monjo* (though, as discussed above, this dating is suspiciously early) and later cited in full in the 1693 *Nichiiki tōjō shosoden jō*. The location where the eagle supposedly dropped the robe still exists and is known as the "Kesagake no matsu." The earliest mention of such a site can be found in the 1672 village survey—the *Ashigara Kamigun Iizawamura meisaichō*—which means that this legend must have existed prior to that. Barbara Ambros has pointed out the similarity of this legend to a legend at Mt. Ōyama where its founder, the monk Rōben, was led to Kasuga for training by an eagle, and to the famous Shinano Zenkōji story of a woman led to the temple by a cow (*ushi ni hikarete Zenkōji mairi*). In this case, however, since it is an eagle, perhaps the phrasing would be *washi ni hikarete Daiyūzan*.

71. Other legends featured an eagle taking Ryōan's robe given to him by Tsūgen Jakurei and depositing the robe at Daiyūzan. For a full survey of legends associated with Daiyūzan, see table 5.

72. This legend is from the *Kōgen Daitsū zenji sengoshū* (vol. 2) by Daitsū Takushū (1644–1715). A printed version of the Ōyama story can be found in *SZ Goroku* 4: 31–32.

73. For more on Zen priests and hot springs, see Duncan Williams, "Arai to iyashi no bunka: Bukkyō to onsen," in *Nihon de mitsuketa takaramono*, ed. Imanishi Shōko (Tokyo: Kōdansha, 1999), pp. 64–65, and "Nihon bukkyō ni okeru seisui: Shingonshū no keisusutadī," in *The Proceedings of the Fourth Symposium on Global Perspectives in Japanese Studies: Encountering Japanese Studies Abroad* (Tokyo: Ochanomizu University, 2003), pp. 219–25; Miyazaki and Williams, "The Intersection of the Local and Translocal at a Sacred Site," 413–21; Hirose Ryōkō, "Sōtōshū no tenkai to chiiki shakai 5–6," *Chōryū* 563 (1997): 25–31; 564: 25–28; and Yokoi Noriaki, "'sesshōseki' densetsu kō: Shūkyō jinruigaku no hōhō to shiza kara," *KDBR* 30 (1999): 291–309, "Gennō oshō no densetsu to onsen," *Zen no kaze* 21 (2000): 68–71, "Zendera no densetsu to onsen no bunka," *Sōtōshū kenkyūin kenkyū kiyō* 30 (2000): 145–56.

For the broader theme of "shinjin kedo" (or the incorporation of kami into the Zen fold and their support and protection given in return), see Andō Yoshinori, *Chūsei Zenshū bunken no kenkyū*, pp. 47–58; Enomoto Chika, "Morinji to bunbuku kagama," *Ōtsuma joshi daigaku kiyō* 26 (1994): 135–57; Hanuki Masai, "Tōmon zensō to shinjin kedo no setsuwa," *Komazawa shigaku* 10 (1962): 44–51; rpt. in *Chūsei Zenrin seiritsushi no kenkyū* (Tokyo: Yoshikawa kōbunkan, 1993), pp. 335–40; Hirose Ryōkō, "Sōtō Zen sō ni okeru shinjin kedo, akurei chin'atsu," *IBK* 31/2 (1983): 233–36; rpt. in *Zenshū chihō tenkaishi no kenkyū* (Tokyo: Yoshikawa kōbunkan, 1988), pp. 415–21, and *Zen to sono rekishi*, ed. Ishikawa Rikizan and Hirose Ryōkō (Tokyo: Perikansha, 1999), pp. 275–84; Tsutsumi Kunihiko, "Tōmon Zensō to shinrei saido setsuwa: Wakasa Kōyōji no engi o chūshin," *Denshō bungaku kenkyū* 41 (1993): 25–45, and "Zensō no hōriki: Sōtōshū kanyo no higuruma setsuwa to kinsei kidan bungei," *Setsuwa bungaku kenkyū* 28 (1993): 53–73; Yoshida Dōkō, "Den Jakushitsu Kenkō 'Fukuan Jukai no Enyu' kō: 'shinjin kedo' to 'jukai jōbutsu' ni tsuite," *IBK* 47/1 (1998): 167–72. For an English-language treatment of this theme, see William Bodiford, "The Enlightenment of Kami and Ghosts: Spirit Ordinations in Sōtō Zen," *Cahiers d'Extrême-Asie* 7 (1993–94): 267–82.

74. *Tōzan kaibyaku narabini kunin rōjin no kien* by Kōkoku Eishun (1648) is held at Daiyūzan. A printed version can be found in *MAS* 8: 282–84.

75. For more on Yagura(zawa) Myōjin and its shrine, see *MAS* 8: 246–51.

76. As can be seen from table 5, a similar legend cycle involving nine deities disguised as old men coming to Ryōan to learn Zen meditation appears in a number of texts. Ryōan dreams that the nine local and translocal deities and personages—Hakusan Myōri Daigongen, Ise Tenshō Daijin, Kamakura Hachiman Daibosatsu, Hasedera Kannon Bosatsu, Kumano Nachisan Fudō Myōō, Yagurazawa Daimyōjin, Tendōzan Nyojō Zenji, Wachō Dōgen Zenji, and Iizawa Myōjin—became protector kami for Daiyūzan.

77. For more on this aspect of the Sanmen Daikokuden Hall, see Misawa Chishō, "Daiyūzan Saijōji no bunkazai," *Shūkyō to gendai* 4/5 (1982): 45.

78. Due to this type of relationship between the temple and the two tutelary deities, new abbots were obliged to visit the Iizawa and Yagurazawa shrines to receive talismans before starting their appointments as Daiyūzan abbots. See Zenshū Chihōshi Chōsakai, ed., *Zenshū chihōshi chōsakai nenpō* 3, p. 12.

79. On the development of the road to Hakone and the travel diaries of hot springs visitors, see Hakone Chōritsu Kyōdo Shiryōkan, ed., *"Tōji no michi" kankei shiryō chōsa hōkokusho* (Hakone: Hakone chōritsu kyōdo shiryōkan, 1997).

80. Jippensha Ikku, *Dōryō gongen Hakone gongen nanayu meguri* (1822), is held at the Kanagawaken kyōdo shiryōkan. A printed version was privately circulated by the Kanagawaken kyōdo shiryōkan and also appears in *Daiyū*, vol. 41 (1988): 2. In addition, Ikku's 1833 *Hakonezan nana onsen Enoshima Kamakura meguri*—which describes his visit to Hakone hot springs before Daiyūzan—includes the following sketch of Daiyūzan: "The Dōryō Gongen of Saijōji is well known for miraculous benefits, but especially for the prevention of fire and burglary which has drawn many believers from near and far to come and receive these benefits. Especially in the Eastern Capital [i.e., Edo], many kō associations have sprung up and pilgrims never seem to stop going. The temple has thus expanded and is a pleasant place to see." This is reproduced in Tsuruoka Tokio, ed., *Jippensha Ikku "Hakone, Enoshima, Kamakura dōchūki"* (Tokyo: Senshūsha, 1982), pp. 26–29.

81. *Tamakushige futatsu ideyu michi no ki* by Hara Masaoki (1839) is archived at the National Diet Library. A printed version can be found in Itasaka Yōko ed., *Edo onsen kikō* (Tokyo: Heibonsha, 1987), pp. 127–228.

82. The connection with Hakone continued in the post-Meiji period, when the Hōon'in subtemple at Daiyūzan was dismantled and transferred to the hot spring resort. Under the new name, Daiyūzan Hakone Betsuin, temple construction began at a hot springs site in 1923, though it was not completed until 1933. For more on the Hakone Betsuin, see *Daiyūzanshi*, pp. 20–21.

83. For Fuji (the sixth month from the beginning to the twenty-third) and Ōyama (the twenty-seventh of the sixth month to the seventeenth of the seventh month). For more on the climbing season for Mt. Fuji and Mt. Ōyama, see Hara, "Ōyama, Fuji, Enoshima," p. 26.

84. For a fuller listing of occupational kō of the period, see Shūkyō to Gendai Hen-shūbu, "Daiyūzan o sasaeru Dōryōson no kō," p. 61.

85. William Kelly discusses the dangers of firefighting in his "Incendiary Actions: Fires and Firefighting in the Shogun's Capital and the People's City," in *Edo and Paris: Urban Life and the State in the Early Modern Era*, ed. James McClain, John Merriman, and Ugawa Kaoru (Ithaca: Cornell University Press, 1994), pp. 310–31.

86. For more on the development of *daisankō* in Japan, see Setagayaku Kyōdo Shiryōkan, ed., *Shaji sankei to daisankō* (Tokyo: Setagayaku kyōdo shiryōkan, 1992).

87. I am not the first to have noticed the relatively passive attitude of *daisankō* as opposed to the activities of kō led by charismatic leaders. See Yamaoka Ryūkō, "Daiyūzan Saijōji no kō no ichi kōsatsu," *Shūkyō kenkyū* 65/3 (1982): 184–85.

88. For more on kō members' perspectives on the function of *sendatsu*, see ibid., p. 184. While the *sendatsu* in the Tokugawa and Meiji period, partly because of their limited number, tended not to form associations with other *sendatsu*, by the early Shōwa period associations such as the Shugenkai and the Byakuekai had strengthened their mutual ties.

89. I have drawn heavily from the research on the Isshin kō conducted by Abe Shinken, "Dōryōson to shomin shinkō," *Shūkyō to gendai* 4/5 (1982): 38–39; and Shūkyō to Gendai Henshūbu, "Daiyūzan," p. 59.

90. See Nakagawa Sugane, "Inari Worship in Early Modern Osaka," in *Osaka: The Merchant's Capital of Early Modern Japan*, ed. James McClain and Osamu Wakita (Ithaca: Cornell University Press, 1999), pp. 180–212.

91. See the *Onjōji gakutōdai Hokurin'in nikki*, printed in *Daiyūzanshi*, p. 17, for more on Dōryō and the Eleven-Faced Kannon. This Kannon was installed in the current Oku-no-in structure in 1930. See Misawa Chishō, "Daiyūzan saijōji," p. 45.

92. These buildings for specific kō were abandoned by the Shōwa period, and multi-kō buildings became the norm. See Abe Shinken, "Dōryōson," p. 38.

93. However, during the Shōwa period, the nearly extinct Isshin kō was revived under Akinaga Masao—the third-generation *kōmoto*—who trained at Mt. Ontake and got his practitioner's license there. Believing that Dōryō had spared his life while a soldier during World War II, he initiated a postwar revival of the Isshin kō. Today, the group consists of roughly two hundred members, divided into units (*han*) such as the Nihonbashi-han or Fukagawa-han, who go to Daiyūzan in late May for a special prayer service. Afterward, they routinely go to Atami Hot Springs for *shōjin otoshi* ("to drop their state of abstinence," in other words, to get drunk and play around). The short-lived nature of many of these kō led by charismatic leaders makes them a difficult research subject even though they clearly represented the larger kō of the late Tokugawa and early Meiji periods. Abe estimates there were around fifty charismatic *sendatsu*-led kō before World War II, most of which have disappeared. See ibid., pp. 38–39. However, one should also note a number of charismatically led kō that turned into officially recognized temples under the Religious Corporations Law in the postwar period. They include Jigenji (formerly Jigen'an) in Yokosuka (Kanagawa); Dōryōji in Edogawa-ku (Tokyo), started by Kameido Shin-jinkō (this temple has twenty Dōryō kō even today); Dōryōsan Kōtokuji in Kosae (Shizuoka), built in a house before being turned into a formal temple by a kō leader who was also a Mt. Ontake *sendatsu* in 1953; Daiyūin in Nagakute (Aichi), whose kō leader was possessed by Dōryō and who performed fortune telling and healing; Shinryūji in Se-tagayaku (Tokyo); Genjūji in Asahimachi (Okayama); Kōgenji in Kyoto; Tōkōin and Hokkeji in Osaka. Watanabe Shōei takes up the history of Kōtokuin and Daiyūin in his "Zenshū to minshū ni tsuite: Daiyūzan Saijōji no baai," *SKKK* 13 (1981): 166–84.

94. A good overview of the concept of "hidden or secret Buddhas" (*hibutsu*) is Fabio Rambelli's "Secret Buddhas: The Limits of Buddhist Representation," *Monumenta Nipponica* 57/3 (2002): 271–307. For more on Tokugawa-period *kaichō*, see Hiruma Hisashi, "Edo no kaichō, Edo kaichō nenpyō," in *Edo chōnin no kenkyū 2*, ed. Nishiyama Matsunosuke (Tokyo: Yoshikawa kōbunkan, 1973), pp. 273–548, and *Edo*

no kaichō (Tokyo: Yoshikawa kōbunkan, 1980); Kitamura Gyōon, *Kinsei kaichō no kenkyū* (Tokyo: Meicho shuppan, 1989); Watanabe Shōei, "Edo kara Meiji made no kaichō," pp. 110–12; and Yuasa Takashi, "Edo ni okeru kinseiteki kaichō no tenkai," *Shikan* 99 (1988): 87–98, and "Edo no kaichōfuda," *Kokuritsu rekishi minzoku hakubutsukan kenkyū hōkoku* 67 (1996): 197–224. For an account of a kaichō at a Sōtō Zen temple in contemporary Japan, see William Bodiford, "Sōtō Zen in a Japanese Town: Field Notes on a Once-Every-Thirty-Three-Years Kannon Festival," *Japanese Journal of Religious Studies* 21/1 (1994): 3–36.

95. There are two major sources for information on kaichō held in the city of Edo: (1) *Bukō nenpyō*, a diary kept by Saitō Gesshin, the powerful town official from Edo Kanda who was also the compiler of the *Edo meisho zue*, and (2) the bakufu's record of kaichō that were given government approval, the *Kaichō sashi yurushichō*.

96. Ekōin was founded by the Zōjōji Temple (Jōdo school) abbot Kioku for the repose of the victims of the great Meireki (1655–57) fire in Edo, which killed more than 108,000 people. It grew to be one of the most popular, nonsectarian Buddhist temples in the city, in part because it was the resting grounds of *muenbotoke* (deceased souls without relatives) and the place for memorial services following disasters like the fire mentioned above as well as the 1783 Mt. Asama volcano eruption and the 1855 earthquake and fire. Priests from all schools of Buddhism would come and recite sutras for these souls without regard to sectarian affiliation. In much the same way, kaichō held at Ekōin also spanned all schools. Besides Ekōin, other popular "host temples" for Edo degaichō were Eitaiji, Jōshinji, Gotokuji, and Yushima Tenjin Shrine.

97. The process of obtaining bakufu permission to hold a degaichō included, first, a meeting of bakufu officials to assess the merits of the temple proposal, especially in regard to whether the event was necessary for fund-raising efforts. When this hurdle was cleared, permission was granted to hold a kaichō lasting up to sixty days after first receiving clearance from the "host temple" in Edo. For more on this process, see Watanabe Shōei, "Edo," p. 86.

98. This *degaichō* was held from the fifteenth of the third month until the fifth of the fifth month according to the entry in the *Bukō nenpyō* 1, p. 214.

99. Watanabe discusses the Tenmei kaichō in detail. See ibid., pp. 98–103.

100. Watanabe has argued for the financial success of the Tenmei kaichō from another angle, namely, the cancellation of outstanding loans from Daiyūzan subtemples to the head temple. See ibid., pp. 96–97.

101. Reference to this fire is made in the temple history, *Daiyūzanshi*, p. 251.

102. In the end, Ryōan's anniversary passed in 1810, and it was only in the following year that they received permission to recast the main bell. Three years later, the main hall was finally rebuilt.

103. The *Bukō nenpyō* 2, p. 62, includes this kaichō but fails to mention the exact dates. Chōkokuji Temple was a midlevel Sōtō Zen temple (which later became the *betsuin* for Eiheiji Temple in Tokyo).

104. This is the actual period in which the temple was officially established, taking over an abandoned temple, Ryūun'in. The temple history claims an earlier establishment of the temple when a small roadside Kannon shrine was converted into a temple in 1598, but this is rather unreliable. For a history of Chōkokuji Temple, see Chōkokujishi Hensan Iinkai, ed., *Azabu Chōkokujishi*.

105. For a printed version of this letter, see Watanabe Shōei, "Edo," pp. 105–8.

106. A letter remaining at Daiyūzan recorded thirty *kan* being raised by several Fuji kō members along the route to Edo. For a printed version of this letter, see ibid., pp. 116–17.

107. The exact wording on the bulletin boards can be seen in *MAS* 8: 377–78. Chōkokuji Temple was allowed to post a large sign just outside the temple gates, while smaller ones with roughly the same information (of where, when, and what was being displayed) were posted throughout Edo. For a broader study on these bulletin boards for kaichō, see Yuasa, "Edo no kaichōfuda."

108. The *Bukō nenpyō* 2, pp. 238–39, mentions the dates of this kaichō: from the twentieth of the third month for sixty days. Although sixty days were scheduled, because the display was so successful the statue returned to Daiyūzan after thirty-nine days.

109. As with the 1819 degaichō, advertising was handled by the kō both through word-of-mouth and by placards posted at prime locations. The larger placards were placed before the Ekōin Temple gate, the mid-size ones at four sites (Nishi Ryō-goku Hirokōji, Asakusa Kaminarimon, Shitaya Sanmeabashi, Tamachi Fuda no tsuji), and smaller ones at ten sites (including Senjōhashi, Hongō Oiwake, and Yotsuya Ōkido).

110. They included Jinzaemon of the vegetable store Aonoya, Kyūjirō of the sweets store Izumiya, Yasubee of the dried fish and seaweed store Mikawaya, and Chōbee of the tailor Shitateya.

111. The original letter from the four merchants is reproduced in Watanabe Shōei, "Edo," p. 133.

112. The meeting records, which still exist, note how everyone stayed overnight at the house. Although the kō ultimately responsible for this meeting was the Yoyogi kō, *sendatsu* (such as Isshin, the charismatic leader described above) and kō leaders (the *Daiyūzan Dōryō daisattason Tokyo onkaichō shokiroku* lists twenty-six kō representatives while the *Gokaichō konseijō* lists twenty-eight) from around Edo promised to cooperate at this meeting. The list included kō such as the Yoyogi, Eizokumoto, Kanda Eizoku, Isshin, Misugi, Jinriki, Yoshiwara, Shitoku, Gozen, Suginae Uetsuke, Gokūjo, Han'eimoto, Eikyū, Anshō, Shintoku, Tōei, Gorin, Kaiun, Shinjin, Shinsei, Eitai Gozen, Ryōgoku Wagō, and Eifuku. This list can be found in Shōei, ibid., pp. 137–38, while the estimate and the receipt of payment can be found on pp. 139–40.

113. For more on the Meiji *haibutsu kishaku* campaign in English, see Barbara Ambros, *"The Mountain of Great Prosperity,"* pp. 311–61; Martin Collcutt, "Buddhism: The Threat of Eradication," in *Japan in Transition: From Tokugawa to Meiji*, ed. Marius Jansen and Gilbert Rozman (Princeton: Princeton University Press, 1986), pp. 143–67; Allan Grapard, "Japan's Cultural Revolution: The Separation of Shinto and Buddhist Divinities in Meiji (*shimbutsu bunri*) and a Case Study: Tōnomine," *History of Religions* 23/3 (1984): 240–65; James Ketelaar, *Of Heretics and Martyrs in Meiji Japan: Buddhism and Its Persecution* (Princeton: Princeton University Press, 1990); and Tamamuro Fumio, "On the Suppression of Buddhism," in *New Directions in the Study of Meiji Japan*, ed. Helen Hardacre and Adam Kern (Leiden: E. J. Brill, 1997), pp. 499–505.

114. The advertisements for the Meiji Dōryō degaichō referred to the deity as "Dōryō Daisatta" or "Dōryō Bosatsu" (bodhisattva). There was probably a period of confusion about what to rename the deity, though by the later Meiji period the temple seems to have settled on "Dōryō Daisatta."

115. The print master, originally named Chinpei, became a disciple of the well-known Hiroshige and married his teacher's daughter before being commissioned to do these prints of the Dōryō kaichō. For more on the prints, see Iwasaki Sōjun, "'Dōryōgū Tokyo kaichō sankeizu' ni tsuite," *Shidan Ashigara* 12 (1974): 10–12.

116. This letter is printed in Honda Hideo, "Meijiki no Sekimotojuku to Saijōji (3)," *Daiyū* 27 (1983): 22.

117. This is known from the 1720 document, *Bodai no tame mainen kinsu sanryō hōnō no ken shōnin*, which is the earliest reference to Daiyūgan. This document is held privately by Nakamura Toseko but cataloged as "Nakamura Tosekoshi shozō shiryō 1" in Minami Ashigara Shishi Hensanshitsu, ed., *Minami Ashigarashi shiryō shozai mokuroku 1* (Minami Ashigara: Minami Ashigara shishi hensanshitsu, 1987), p. 38.

118. Even today, the Nakamura family owns the Daiyūgan Yakkyoku (Pharmacy) in Tsukahara Village. Though prominently displaying a sign proclaiming the origins of the pharmacy from the Kyōho era (1716–35), the pharmacy is today a regular Chinese herbal medicine store, no longer selling Daiyūgan. The main reason for this was the prohibition against the trade in endangered species as outlined in the Convention on International

Trade in Endangered Species of Wild Fauna and Flora (Washington Convention), because Daiyūgan apparently had orangutan liver as one of its ingredients.

119. A printed version of this letter, headed *Osorenagara kakitsuke motte mōshiage tatematsuru onkoto*, can be found in Honda, "Meijiki," p. 22.

120. On the medicine Uirō, see Tokoro Rikiyo's "Uirō uri kō," in *Sengokuki shokunin no keifu: Sugiyama Hiroshi hakase tsuitō ronshū*, ed. Tokoro Rikiyo and Nagahara Keiji (Tokyo: Kadokawa shoten, 1989), pp. 323–37; and Suzuki Akira, *Denshōyaku no jiten: Gama no abura kara yakuyōshū made* (Tokyo: Tokyodō shuppan, 1999), pp. 9–14.

121. I have relied here on the research by Honda Hideo regarding Daiyūgan's ingredients and manufacture. See Honda, "Meijiki," pp. 23–24.

122. On the history of the temple buildings, see Shiga Myōgen, "Daiyūzan Saijōji no kaisō engi ni tsuite," *SKK* 20 (1988): 23–28. He argues, based on maps found in the 1672 *Ashigarakamigun Iizawamura meisaichō*, that Daiyūzan was still primarily a training monastery. However, by examining the temple layout shown in the 1841 *Shinpen Sagami no kuni fudokikō*, for example, a clear shift can be seen in which the Dōryō Shrine and its prayer functions on the west side of the compound become central. Shiga's thesis, based on temple architecture, approximates my findings on the history of kō cultic activity at Daiyūzan.

123. For an analysis of the Meiji shifts, see Yamaoka Ryūkō, "Bukkyō jiin ni okeru shūkyōteki fukugō no ichi keitai: Daiyūzan Saijōji no jirei," *SKKK* 11 (1979): 160.

CHAPTER 5   Medicine and Faith Healing in the Sōtō Zen Tradition

1. The original is *ryū*, the measuring unit for medical tablets or pills.

2. A weight equal to approximately six grams.

3. This herb is more commonly known as *nozeri*.

4. See Smith, *Ten Weeks in Japan*, pp. 92–93. By the 1860s, even in many rural areas, those who could afford the doctor's fee often opted for the doctor over the priest. This report, however, captures an economic reality that the vast majority of nineteenth-century Japanese could only afford to rely on Buddhist priests and other nondoctors.

5. On the history of medicine and healing in early Buddhism and the Theravada tradition, see Hattori Toshirō, *Shaka no igaku* (Nagoya: Reimei shobō, 1982); Wetera Mahinda, "Medical Practice of Buddhist Monks: A Historical Analysis of Attitudes and Problems," in *Recent Researches in Buddhist Studies: Essays in Honour of Professor Y. Karunadasa*, ed. Kuala Lumpur Dhammajoti et al. (Colombo: Y. Karunadasa Felicitation Committee, 1997), pp. 454–65; Jinadasa Liyanaratne, "Sinhalese Medical Manuscripts in Paris," in *Medical Literature from India, Sri Lanka and Tibet*, ed. G. Jan Meulenbeld (Leiden: E. J. Brill, 1991), pp. 73–90; "Sri Lankan Medical Manuscripts in the Bodleian Library, Oxford," *Journal of the European Ayurvedic Society* 2 (1992): 36–40; "Buddhism and Traditional Medicine in Sri Lanka," *The Pacific World* 11 (1995): 124–42; Oda Susumu "Bukkyō to igaku," *Mitsugi to shugyō*, ed. Yuasa Yasuo (Tokyo: Shunjūsha, 1989), pp. 276–319; Sukumar Sengupta, "Medical Data in the Milindapañha," in *Dr. B. M. Narua Birth Centenary Commemoration Volume* (Calcutta: Bengal Buddhist Association, 1989), pp. 111–17; Arvind Sharma, "The Relation between Disease and Karma in the Milindapañha," in *Amala Prajña: Aspects of Buddhist Studies, Professor P. V. Bapat Felicitation*, ed. N. H. Samtani (Delhi: Sri Satgun Publications, 1989), pp. 139–49; and Kenneth Zysk, *Asceticism and Healing in Ancient India: Medicine in the Buddhist Monastery* (New York: Oxford University Press, 1991), and "New Approaches to the Study of Early Buddhist Medicine: Use of Technical Brāhmanic Sources in Sanskrit for the Interpretation of Pali Medical Texts," *The Pacific World* 11 (1995): 143–54. Most of these works on early Buddhism focus on the scriptural prohibition on the practice of medicine by monks and the actual practice of healing and writing of medical treatises by monks. There is also a recent English translation of one of the major scriptures related to

the healing Buddha, Bhaisajyaguru (Jpn. Yakushi); see Hsing Yun, *Sutra of the Medicine Buddha with an Introduction, Comments and Prayers* (Hacienda Heights, CA: Buddha's Light Publishing, 2002). For Tibetan and Tantric traditions of medicine, see Terry Clifford, *Tibetan Buddhist Medicine and Psychiatry: The Diamond Healing* (York Beach, ME: Samuel Weiser, 1984); Elisabeth Finckh, *Foundations of Tibetan Medicine*, vol. 1 (London: Watkins, 1978); Gerti Samel, *Tibetan Medicine: A Practical and Inspirational Guide to Diagnosis, Treating and Healing the Buddhist Way* (London: Little, Brown, 2001); William Stablein, "A Descriptive Analysis of the Content of Nepalese Buddhist *Pūjās* as a Medical-Cultural System with References to Tibetan Parallels," in *Himalayan Anthropology*, ed. James Fisher (The Hague: Mouton, 1978), pp. 529–37; Vesna Wallace, "Buddhist Tantric Medicine in the *Kālacakratantra*," *The Pacific World* 11 (1985): 155–74; and Leonard Zwilling, "On Bhaisajyaguru and His Cult," in *Studies in the History of Buddhism*, Narain A. K. ed. (Delhi: B. R. Publishing Co., 1980), pp. 413–21.

6. Paul Demiéville, "Byō," in *Hōbōgirin, Fasc. 3* (Paris: Librairie d'amérique et d'Orient, 1937) p. 225. Also see the English translation by Mark Tatz, *Buddhism and Healing: Demiéville's Article "Byō" from Hōbōgirin* (Lanham, MD: University Press of America, 1985).

7. On East Asian Buddhism and medicine, see Raoul Birnbaum, *The Healing Buddha* (Boston: Shambhala Publications, 1979), and "Seeking Longevity in Chinese Buddhism: Long Life Deities and Their Symbolism," *Journal of Chinese Religions* 13–14 (1985–86): 143–76; Jean Filliozat, "La médecine indienne et l'expansion bouddhique en Extrême-Orient," *Journal Asiatique* 224 (1934): 301–11; John Kieschnick, *The Eminent Monk: Buddhist Ideals in Medieval Chinese Hagiography* (Honolulu: University of Hawai'i Press, 1997), pp. 83–96; and Strickmann, *Chinese Magical Medicine*. Another excellent study on a popular Taoist cult's control of disease and epidemics is Paul Katz's *Demon Hordes and Burning Boats: The Cult of Marshal Wen in Late Imperial Chekiang* (Albany: State University of New York Press, 1995).

8. See, for example, Hattori Toshirō, *Edo jidai igakushi no kenkyū* (Tokyo: Yoshikawa kōbunkan, 1978); Fujikawa Yū, *Fujikawa Yū cho sakushū* 3 (Kyoto: Shibunkaku shuppan, 1980), pp. 62–63; or Yoshioka Shin, *Kinsei Nihon yakugyōshi kenkyū* (Tokyo: Yakuji nippōsha, 1998), pp. 100–103. A recent exception is Yamada Keiji and Kuriyama Shigehisa's edited volume, *Rekishi no naka no yamai to igaku* (Kyoto: Shibunkaku shuppan, 1997). This work includes a study of the development of herbal medicines within the esoteric Buddhist schools. See Nihonyanagi Kenji, "Nihon mikkyō igaku to yakubutsugaku," in *Rekishi no naka no yamai to igaku*, ed. Yamada Keiji and Shigehisa Kuriyama (Kyoto: Shibunkaku shuppan, 1997), pp. 545–66. For other Western-language studies of medicine in the Tokugawa period, see Harm Beukers et al., eds., *Red-Hair Medicine: Dutch-Japanese Medical Relations* (Amsterdam: Rodopi, 1991); Mieko Macé, "Evolution de la médecine japonaise face au modèle chinois: Des origines jusqu'au milieu du XVIIIe siècle, L'autonomie par la synthèse," *Cipango: Cahiers d'études japonaises* 1 (1992): 111–60; "L'anatomie occidentale et l'expérience clinique dans la médecine japonaise du XVIe au XVIIIe siècle," in *Nombres, astres, plantes et viscères*, ed. I. Ang and P. Will (Paris: Mémoires de l'institut des Hautes Etudes Chinoises 35, Collège de France, 1994), pp. 135–75; "Otsuki Gentaku (1757–1827) et la médecine chinoise," in *Mélanges offerts à René Sieffert à l'occasion de son soixante-dixième anniversaire* (Paris: Institut national des langues et civilisations orientales/Centre d'études japonaises, 1994), pp. 397–418; "La médecine de Hoashi Banri (1778–1852): Recherche d'une médecine universelle par un naturaliste encyclopédiste de la première moitié du XIXe siècle," in *Le vase de béryl: Études sur le Japon et la Chine en hommage à Bernard Frank*, ed. Jacqueline Pigeot and Hartmut Rotermund (Arles: Éditions Philippe Picquier, 1997), pp. 405–15; "Le chinois classique comme moyen d'accès à la modernité: La réception des concepts médicaux occidentaux dans le Japon des XVIIIe et XIXe siècles," *Daruma* 4 (1998): 79–103; "La pensée médicale de l'époque d'Edo et la modernité," in *Tradition et modernité: Quelques aspects du Japon d'Edo et de Meiji*, ed. S. Murakami-Giroux and

C. Séguy (Strasbourg: Université Marc Bloch-Strasbourg, 1998), pp. 83–109; "Japanese Medicine and Modernity in the First Half of the 19th Century: A Case in Point, Hoashi Banri," in *Current Perspectives in the History of Science in East Asia*, ed. Kim Yung Sik and Francesca Bray (Seoul: Seoul National University Press, 1999), pp. 504–16; "Takano Chōei (1804–1850): Un savant pris au piège de son temps," in *Repenser l'ordre, repenser l'héritage: Paysage intellectuel du Japon (XVIIe–XIXe siècles)*, ed. Frédéric Girard, Annick Horiuchi, and Mieko Macé (Geneva: Librairie Droz, 2002), pp. 449–95; Wolfgang Michel, "On the Reception of Western Medicine in Seventeenth Century Japan," in *Higashi to nishi no iryō bunka*, ed. Yoshida Tadashi and Yasuaki Fukuse (Kyoto: Shibunkaku shuppan, 2001), pp. 3–17; Ellen Nakamura, "Takano Choei and his Country Friends: A Receptive History of Rangaku" (Ph.D. dissertation, Australian National University, 2000); Wai-ming Ng, *The I Ching in Tokugawa Thought and Culture* (Honolulu: University of Hawai'i Press/Association for Asian Studies, 2000), pp. 150–67; Norman Ozaki, "Conceptual Changes in Japanese Medicine during the Tokugawa Period" (Ph.D. dissertation, University of California, San Francisco, 1979); and Yoshioka, *Kinsei Nihon yakugyōshi kenkyū*.

9. Two works by Tatsukawa Shōji highlight the role of deities in faith healing of the period. See his *Kinsei byōsōshi: Edo jidai no byōki to iryō* (Tokyo: Heibonsha, 1979), and *Byōki o iyasu chiisa na kamigami* (Tokyo: Heibonsha, 1993).

10. See Duncan Williams, "Temples, Pharmacies, Traveling Salesmen, and Pilgrims: Buddhist Production and Distribution of Medicine in Edo Japan," *Supplement to the Japanese Religions Bulletin*, New Series 23 (February 1998): 20–29.

11. The original has "Shakatta" Dragon King, but this is probably "Shagara," the main Dragon King among the eight types listed in the *Lotus Sutra*.

12. The sufferings of the "three heats" (*sannetsu*) are experienced in the beastly realm by dragons and snakes according to the *Ōjōyōshū*. They are (1) the heat from extremely hot winds and sands that burn one's skin, flesh, and marrow; (2) the loss of shelter and clothes caused by terrible winds; and (3) the loss of one's child because a "golden bird" devours the child.

13. The king of the lowest of the Six Heavens.

14. This text, *Echizen no kuni Eihei kaisanki*, is held by the Historiographical Institute, Tokyo University (Katei Bunko no. E22 776725). A printed version of the text appears in Yokoyama Shigeru, ed., *Sekkyō shohonshū 1* (Tokyo: Kadokawa shoten, 1968), pp. 248–70. The translated portion of the text can be found on pp. 262–66.

15. For a general overview of *jōruri* as a genre, see C. J. Dunn, *The Early Japanese Puppet Drama* (London: Luzan and Co., 1966).

16. The Mahāyāna Buddhist motif of the "salvation of the dragon king's daughter" can be found in the *Lotus Sutra*. For more on this theme, see Faure, *The Power of Denial*, pp. 91–99; Yoshida Kasuhiko, "The Enlightenment of the Dragon King's Daughter;" and Yoshida Yoshiyuki, "Ryūnyo no jōbutsu," in *Shiriizu, Josei to bukkyō 2: Sukui to oshie*, ed. Ōsumi Kazuo and Nishiguchi Junko (Tokyo: Heibonsha, 1989), pp. 45–91.

17. See Marcelle Lalou, "Le culte des Nāgas et la thérapeutique," *Journal Asiatique* 226 (1938): 1–19; and De Visser, *The Dragon in China and Japan*, p. 113. Tanaka Takako has also noted an early Tokugawa-period local history of Kyoto, the *Yōshū fushi*, which relates the legend of a Muromachi-period physician who received an easy childbirth medicine from a young girl he had treated, whose real identity was a dragon living a nearby pond. See her *Sei naru onna: Saigū, Megami, Chūjōhime* (Kyoto: Jinbun shoin, 1996), pp. 22–23.

18. The *Teiho kenzeiki* was compiled by Menzan Zuihō in 1753 as an annotated edition of Dōgen's biography by Kenzei, the fourteenth abbot of Eiheiji Temple. The reliability of this text is debatable and discussed below.

19. The *Dōshōan keifu* by Bokujun (1595–1670), the nineteenth-generation head of Dōshōan, is the official family genealogy. There are several variants, though the source text found among the *Dōshōan monjo* at Eiheiji Temple is available only in manuscript

form. Menzan quotes from the text but incorrectly identifies it as the *Dōshōan keifu ki*. One major variant is the *Dōshōan gansoden* (The Legend of the Founder of Dōshōan); a printed version can be found in the *DNBZ* 115: 559–60. Another variant of a different monk, also named Dōshō, as recorded in the 1150 *Fusō ryakki*, involves the monk having gone to China in 651 and returning to Japan with a small kettle for preparing medicines (which he had received from the well-known Chinese monk, Xuan Zong, who had picked it up during his travels to India). In De Visser's account of the legend, it was said that "all diseases could be cured by means of the medicines cooked in [the kettle]. One of Dōshō's companions, who fell ill before they left China, was cured at once thanks to the marvelous utensil. On their way to Japan, in the midst of the ocean, the ship suddenly stopped and did not move for seven days, while wind and waves were raging around it in a terrible way. Then a diviner said, 'There is something on board which is wanted by the Sea-god. I think it is the kettle.' First the abbot refused to give up his treasure, and said that there was no reason why the Dragon-king should ask for it." Ultimately, though, Dōshō threw the kettle into the sea and storm abated, which allowed the two monks to arrive safely back in Japan. This legend could have been one of several root sources for the Tokugawa-period rendition of Dōshō and Dōgen, who obviously lived several centuries after these events were supposed to have taken place. See De Visser, *The Dragon in China and Japan*, p. 187. For more on this Dōshō, see Hannelore Eisenhofer-Halim, *Dōshō (629–700): Leben und Werken eines japanischen Buddhisten vor dem Hintergrund der chinesisch-japanischen Beziehungen im 7. Jh* (Frankfurt am Maim: Peter Lang, 1995). This theme of Buddhist powers to calm the sea and wind gods may be an old motif. Sengupta notes a similar incident of a violent storm being calmed by the contemplations of the Indian monk Bodhisena during his sea journey to Japan in 736. See Sudha Sengupta, "Early Buddhism in Japan and the First Indian Priest," in *Amala Prajña: Aspects of Buddhist Studies, Professor P. V. Bapat Felicitation*, ed. N. H. Samtani (Delhi: Sri Satgun Publications, 1989), pp. 423–30.

20. This picture is from the *Teiho kenzeiki zue*, a version of the *Kenzeiki* with illustrations that was re-edited in 1802 but not available until 1817. It can be found in *SZ, Shiden 2*. Tsutsumi argues that the illustrations enabled a much wider audience to become familiar with Dōgen's biography. On the history of the *Teiho kenzeiki zue*, see Tsutsumi Kunihiko, "Dōgen eden no seiritsu," in *Shūso kōsōeden (etoki) shū*, ed. Watanabe Shōgo and Masahiko Hayashi (Tokyo: Miyai shoten, 1996), pp. 281–340.

21. This incident was one of a number of legends that tied Inari to the Sōtō Zen sect as a protective deity. See Ishikawa Rikizan, "Chūsei Sōtōshū kirigami no bunrui shiron 6," *KDBR* 16 (1985): 147.

22. Although the *Teiho Kenzeiki* uses the name Gedokugan, in this chapter I refer to the medicine as Gedokuen, as this is the name most commonly used in the primary sources of Dōshōan itself. The term *shinsen* can be interpreted in several ways. The most obvious is to connect it to the Taoist term *shinsen* (Wizard Mountain) and immortality, as a medicine that can cure all ailments logically leads to immortality. Taoist alchemical use of herbs and mushrooms, for instance, also suggests translating *shinsen* here as "immortality providing." However, the other way to interpret the term—as something "bestowed from a kami—also makes sense here, as the medicine (or at least its formula) was given to Kinoshita Dōshō by a deity, Inari, or a dragon-girl in a variant version. On Taoist wizard imagery in Japan, see Janet Carpenter, "*Sennin*: The Immortals of Taoism," in *Japanese Ghosts and Demons: Art of the Supernatural*, ed. Stephen Addiss (New York: George Braziller, 1985), pp. 57–80. For other medicines described with the same prefix, see the stomach medicine Shinsen Jirigan and the restorative Shinsen Mankintan, in Aoki Infu and Kojima Mikako, eds., *Kusuri kanban* (Kawajimachō: Naitō kinen kusuri hakubutsukan, 1986), pp. 30, 39.

23. There is, of course, the longstanding Taoist interest in the "pill of longevity" or the elixir of immortality. See J. C. Cooper, *Chinese Alchemy: The Taoist Quest for Immortality* (New York: Sterling Publishing Co., 1990), pp. 46–52.

24. Another term with this type of play on Buddhist doctrine and healing within the Sōtō school is the name of the healing Jizō bodhisattva, Togenuki Jizō, of Kōganji Temple in Edo. The term "Togenuki" literally means "splinter removing" and refers to the story of a woman suffering with severe stomach pains after swallowing a needle or "splinter" who was miraculously cured by drinking a Jizō talisman that "removed" the needle. This Sōtō temple skillfully used the term *Toge*, which was supposed to sound like *Toga* or transgressions, to explain that the bodhisattva was, in fact, plucking the evil karma out of all sentient beings.

25. As with most Tokugawa-period medicines, the formula for its production was zealously guarded, but Kinoshita Jūzō, a thirtieth-generation descendant of the Dōshōan family, revealed in a 1981 article that the main ingredient of Gedokuen was the *Lycoris radiata* herb (*higanbana no kyūkon*). In traditional Chinese medicine, this herb or flower was used mainly for treating phlegm and inducing vomiting, but it had often been shunned because of its classification as a poison. It was in fact outlawed by the new Japanese drug-control laws implemented after the Second World War. Gedokuen might have been a very concrete expression of the Zen maxim of poisons dissolving poisons. See Kinoshita Jūzō, "Dōshōan ni tsuite," *Sanshō* 457 (1981): 66.

26. For a broad examination of the role of dreams in Buddhist revelations and miracle stories, see Kawatō Masashi, *Nihon no yume shinkō* (Machida: Tamagawa daigaku shuppanbu, 2002), pp. 228–357.

27. Ryōō was also known as Dōkaku and was a Sōtō Zen monk before becoming an Ōbaku Zen monk according to the *Nihon bukkyō jinmei jitten*, ed. Washio Junkei (Tokyo: Tokyo bijitsu, 1903), pp. 861–62. His pharmacy, Kangakuya, flourished in the Kanbun era, and from the profits accrued from selling Kintaien, Ryōō built a sutra storage hall on an island within Shinobazu Pond and funded a number of social welfare projects. For more on Ryōō and his pharmacy, see Morimoto Sangai, "Ryōō," *Zen bunka* 18 (1960): 47–50; and Yoshioka Shin, *Edo no kigusuriya* (Tokyo: Seiabō, 1994), pp. 230–32.

28. See Suzuki Akira, *Edo no myōyaku* (Tokyo: Iwasaki bijutsusha, 1991), p. viii.

29. The first pharmacy in the city of Edo was built in 1590 in the Motomachi District. It stocked medicines for eye diseases, which were rampant in Edo. According to the 1687 *Edo rokushi*, the city of Edo had thirty-seven *kigusuriya*, but the *Edo sōrokushi*, printed in 1751, lists 124 pharmacies, a number that peaked at 206 shops in 1800. See Yoshioka, *Edo no myōyaku*, pp. 123, 143; also see his *Kinsei Nihon yakugyōshi kenkyū*, pp. 117–213.

30. Yoshioka, *Kinsei Nihon*, pp. 29–32.

31. For more on the development of the sale of medicines by the Toyama no gyōshōnin under the protection of the Maeda family, see Endō Kazuko, *Toyama no kusuri uri* (Tokyo: Simul shuppansha, 1993). On the religious roots of the Toyama no gyōshōnin, see Nei Kiyoshi, "Toyama baiyaku to shugenja ni tsuite," *IBK* 28/2 (1980): 116–17. For more on *shugenja* and medicine, see Imamura Michio, *Nihon no minkan iryō* (Tokyo: Kōbundō, 1983), pp. 16–22. For a study of the distribution of medicine in the Kantō area by Mt. Ōyama *oshi*, see Ambros, "The Mountain of Great Prosperity," pp. 188–91.

32. Though *daranisuke* was originally associated with Mt. Kōya, other regions, such as Mt. Yoshino and Mt. Ōmine, developed their own *daranisuke*. See Suzuki Akira, *Edo no myōyaku*, p. 59; and Danitani Behei, *Ōmine koborebanashi* (Osaka: Tōhō shuppan, 1997), pp. 118–27.

33. For a more detailed study on the development of new venues for the production and distribution of Buddhist-inspired medicines, see Williams, "Temples," pp. 20–29.

34. The original is *ryū*, the counter for medical tablets or pills.

35. Gedoku is the term generally used in this text for Gedokuen.

36. A weight measure equal to approximately six grams.

37. The text includes the reading "babensō" for this herb.

38. I discovered this manuscript among the Tokugawa-period documents held at

Ryūsanji, a Sōtō Zen temple in Sagami Province. Though the document is not dated, given its place among the other documents at Ryūsanji, it is probably from the mideighteenth century. The manuscript is available on microfilm at the Isehara City Archives in Kanagawa Prefecture, cataloged in the *Iseharashishi shiryō shozai mokuroku 4* (Isehara: Iseharashi, 1990), p. 67, as "Ryūsanji shiryō no. 127."

39. This explanation of the origins of the title *Kenzeiki* is found in Kawamura Kīdō, *Shohan taikō Eihei kaisan Dōgen zenji gyōjō Kenzeiki* (Tokyo: Taishukan shoten, 1975), p. 199.

40. Ibid., p. 202.

41. This story is also not found in other biographies of Dōgen, including the most logical text, the *Hōkyōki*, the record of his travels in China. The list of those accompanying Dōgen given in the *Hōkyōki* reads, "The abbot of Kennin-ji, Myōzen, Dōgen, Kakunen, Kōshō and others came down the Western Sea Road to sail across the ocean. Passing custom after custom, spending night after night, they passed inspection without difficulty." This translation is from James Kodera, *Dōgen's Formative Years in China: An Historical Study and Annotated Translation of the "Hōkyō-ki"* (London: Routledge & Kegan Paul, 1980), p. 34. The monk Kakunen has been at times identified (without any credible evidence) as Dōshō. James Kodera correctly, I think, identifies Kakunen rather as a Kenninji Temple disciple of Myōzen (p. 150, n. 129).

42. Indeed, one important biography, the *Eihei kaisan genzenji gyōjō denmonki* (commonly known as the "Denmonki"), omits the figure of Dōshō altogether. Though it features a story similar to that of the puppet play version, the major differences, in addition to the omission of Dōshō, are (1) the incident at sea happens on the way to China rather than on the way back, (2) Dōgen doesn't get sick, but everyone else on the boat does, (3) two deities appear in the form of an old man (the deity of the Iwashimizu Hachiman Shrine) and a young girl (the female deity of the Fushimi Inari Shrine) who reveal the formula to Dōgen after they heal everyone by serving the medicine in some rice gruel. For an extended discussion of this text and the larger question of Dōgen and his relationship to local protective deities, see Hasebe Hachirō, "Sōden ni miru 'densetsu' no igi: 'Eihei kaisan genzenji gyōjō denmonki' o megutte," in *Dōgen zenji kenkyū ronshū: Dōgen zenji nanahyaku gojukai daionkinen shuppan* (Eiheijichō: Daihonzan Eiheiji daionki kyoku, 2002), pp. 538–64.

43. While his most commonly used Dharma name is Dōshō, his given name was Fujiwara Ryūei, and because he had received imperial land in the Kinoshita area of Kyoto (roughly one kilometer northwest from the Imperial Household), he also was often referred to as Kinoshita Dōshō. Although the Dōshō of these texts appears to be a monk, it is highly unlikely that he was a fully ordained monk but instead, like many doctors of his day, was an ordained lay Buddhist who shaved his hair. On pre-Tokugawa-period references to Dōshō in diaries and other sources, see Kumagai Chūkō, "Kinoshita Dōshō ni tsuite: 'Korefusa Kōki' tōjō no jigenin Dōshō kara," *Shūgaku kenkyū* 39 (1997): 139–44; and Nakaseko Shōdō, *Dōgen zenjiden kenkyū zoku* (Tokyo: Kokusho kankōkai, 1997), pp. 127–32.

44. The earliest extant document suggests that Gedokuen was being made in 1578. See Awano Toshiyuki, "Dōshōan monjo (3): 'Kinoshita Sōko, Gotō Genjō rensho keijo'," *Sanshō* 690 (2001): 92–93.

45. The identity of the actual sponsor is not clear. While Nakano Tōzan has argued that Eiheiji might have been the sponsor of this puppet play, it is highly unlikely to have received Eiheiji's imprimatur, let alone sponsorship, given that these stories are so far off the orthodox versions of his life. The evidence that Nakano provides is that both the thirty-second- and thirty-third-generation Eiheiji abbots (Tairyō and Tetsuō) are originally from Edo and could possibly have met the playwright, Yūki Magozaburō, who was a resident of the city. I think that since Dōshō is given almost as much play time as Dōgen, it is far more likely that Dōshōan itself or certainly a person looking to promote Dōshō and/or Gedokuen was involved. For the playwright to have procured so much informa-

tion on Dōshō—who, we must remember, did not "exist" in any record until Bokujun's *Dōshōan keifu* thirty years earlier—we must come to the conclusion that someone intending to boost the image of Dōshō was the sponsor. Nakano's arguments can be found in Nakano Tōzen, "Sekkyōbushi 'Echizen no kuni Eiheiji kaisanki' o tōshite mita Dōgen zenji shinkō," *Kyōka kenshū* 43 (1999): 49–50. For a different example of the use of performance to sell medicine, Hur's comments on medicine sales at Sensōji Temple grounds on special days are instructive: "Comic dramas performed by child prodigies as a prelude to the selling of 'cure-all' lotions attracted crowds." See Hur, *Prayer and Play in Late Tokugawa Japan*, p. 65. Kagamishima Hiroyuki has also suggested that the Hatano family, a traditional patron of Eiheiji, could have been the sponsor of the play. Since the Hatano family was also involved in the buying and selling of Gedokuen in Echizen Province (as noted by Suzuki Taizan), that this family could have been the sponsor is another strong possibility. For Kagamishima's argument, see his "Sekkyōbushi ni okeru Dōgen zenji denki no kyakushoku: Eiheiji kaisanki ni tsuite," *Dōgen* 4/3 (1937): 11. Suzuki Taizan has deduced Hatano's involvement with Gedokuen because of extant medicine boxes with "Dōshōan Echizen Hatano Yakuho" written on them, which were sold until the Taishō period; see his *Sōtōshū no chiikiteki tenkai*, p. 9.

46. For Tsutsumi's argument, see Tsutsumi Kunihiko, "Dōgen eden no seiritsu"; and "'Dōgen eden' to etoki," *Kokubungaku kaishaku to kanshō* 64/12 (1999): 151–63. Pictorial scrolls (*eden*) of Dōgen were produced relatively late compared with those of the founders of other schools of Kamakura Buddhism. See Watanabe Shōgo, *Chūseishi no minshū shōdo bungei*, p. 225. For a discussion of kabuki plays featuring Dōgen, see Kumamoto Einin, "Dōgen to Tokiyori o meguru nidai no kabuki," *KDBR* 33 (2002): 211–20.

47. The text has the deity as "Princess Toyotama" (Toyotama hime), the daughter of the dragon king (*ryūō no musume*). Nakano Tōzen has noted in addition that two later biographies of Dōgen—the *Eihei kaisan Dōgen zenji gyōjō denbunki* of 1805 and the *Eihei Dōgen zenji gyōjō zue* of 1808—include stories of Dōgen being cured in China. In the first text, Dōgen is cured by the main deity of Iwashimizu (Hachiman), and in the latter text, through Gedokuen, transmitted by Inari. See Nakano Tōzen, "Sekkyōbushi," p. 48. See also his earlier work on this text, "Kōsōden ni okeru shomin geinō no eikyō: Sekkyōbon 'Echizen no kuni Eiheiji kaisanki' ni tsuite," *Shūgaku kenkyū* 11 (1969): 61–66.

48. This dating should be taken as approximate since the *Dōshōan keifu* by Bokujun includes no date. However, as noted above, a close variant of the text, the *Dōshōan gansoden*, also by Bokujun, is dated 1639. The *Dōshō'an yuishoki* by Bokujun, a later text held by Sōkōji Temple, is dated 1662 and can be found in *ZSZ Shiden/Jishi* 30: 109 and *SK Gekan*: 323–24.

49. See Tamamuro Fumio, "'Dōshōan Monjo' ni tsuite," *Sanshō* (1995) 622: 19–25; 623: 20–28; 624: 26–39, and also chapter 2 of his *Edo jidai no Sōtōshū no tenkai* (Tokyo: Sōtōshū shūmuchō, 1999). See also Eiheijishi Hensan Iinkai, ed., "Edoki no zuisse," in *Eiheijishi jō*, chap. 5.3. This was written by Hirose Ryōkō using the same collection of documents as Tamamuro. Although Tamamuro has written about Dōshōan as if it were a temple—see his chapter 2, p. 65—neither Eiheiji Temple nor the bakufu considered it a temple. If it were, it would have appeared in the so-called Enkyō Register, from which it is absent. Also see Hirose Ryōkō's "Chū-kinsei ni okeru Kinoshita Dōshōan to Sōtōshū kyōdan," in *Dōgen zenji kenkyū ronshū: Dōgen zenji nanahyaku gojukai daionkinen shuppan* (Eiheijichō: Daihonzan Eiheiji daionki kyoku, 2002), esp. pp. 567–98. For more in English on Dōshōan and its administrative functions, see Williams, "Representations of Zen," chap. 2.

50. This practice of the imperial house awarding "purple" (or imperial-color) robes precedes the Tokugawa period and was imported to Japan from China.

51. One possibility advanced was the connection made through the Shimazu family,

whose links to the imperial family are well known. As Dōshōan served as a refuge for Shimazu family members during the warring states period, the domain had awarded 300 *koku* of land to Dōshōan. Kinoshita Jūzō has also shown an early connection between Dōshōan and Fukushōji Temple in Kagoshima (a large Sōtō Zen temple that served as the parish temple for the Shimazu family). See Kinoshita Jūzō, "Dōshōan to Kagoshima Shimazuke ni tsuite," *Sanshō* 535 (1988): 88–93.

52. The titles "Hōin" and "Hōgen" are also the highest ranks used among the Buddhist priesthood, but in this case, the Dōshōan heads are not being recognized as Buddhist priests, but in their capacity as doctors or medical experts.

53. Although we have a 1628 document from Sōjiji chronicling a dispute at Dōshōan about its legitimate heir and from whom Sōtō temples should buy their Gedokuen, we do not have any evidence of use of Dōshōan as the go-between with the imperial household until 1634. In other words, the sale of medicine probably preceded its function as the intermediary. For the two documents, see Eiheijishi Hensan Iinkai, ed., *Eiheijishi jō*, pp. 597–98. Since Ieyasu's legal directives for Sōtō Zen issued in 1615 do not mention the legal need to go through Dōshōan for imperially sanctioned Zen names and purple robes, it is likely that this practice started sometime in the 1620s or '30s, with legal recognition of Dōshōan's role coming only with Dōshōan Bokujun's 1661 directive, the *Nihon Sōtōshū Eihei kaisan daizenjiha shusse no shidai*. Bokujun's directive can be found in ed. ibid., pp. 599–600.

54. Tamamuro has worked out the calculations for actual abbots. See "'Dōshōan Monjo' ni tsuite," 624: 31. He has also estimated the total cost of obtaining a Zen master name and a purple robe for actual abbots of Eiheiji and Sōjiji to to be a little over two thousand *ryō* (in present-day terms, approximately two hundred million yen or two million dollars). See his conclusions in *Edo jidai no Sōtōshū no tenkai*, p. 137. The calculations for the *zuisse* abbots, who receive the title "former abbot of Eiheiji/Sōjiji" but do not actually serve in that capacity, has been worked out by Hirose. See Eiheijishi Hensan Iinkai, ed., *Eiheijishi jō*, pp. 599–600.

55. See Tamamuro Fumio, "'Dōshōan Monjo' ni tsuite," 624: 38, or his *Edo jidai no Sōtōshū no tenkai*, pp. 136–37.

56. This document in not yet in print, but the original can be found in microfilm no. 241 of the "Kenkon'in monjo" at the Higashi-Ura city archives.

57. Hirose Ryōkō has also noted two cases in Jōshū Province where fifty pills were delivered to Daitsūji Temple and one hundred pills to Gigenji Temple. See Hirose Ryōkō, "Chū-kinsei," pp. 612–13.

58. Ganshōin Temple's *Sōtōshū Ganshōin shoji okite* of 1841 is a compilation of rules and events that each abbot ought to be aware of during the annual ritual calendar. It has been included in Gosen Shishi Hensan Iinkai, ed., *Gosen shishi*, pp. 613–34. See p. 625 for information on Gedokuen.

59. Professor Sakai Tatsurō kindly gave me permission to use this document, which is a part of the "Kasuisai monjo." Recently, a printed version of this manuscript has been included in Kasuisai Shiryōshū Hensan Iinkai, ed., *Kasuisai shiryōshū*, vol. 5 (Kyoto: Shibunkaku shuppan, 1998), p. 52.

60. On the first fake Gedokuen incident, see Awano Toshiyuki, "Dōshōan monjo (11): 'sōchin, Matashirō rensho shojō'," *Sanshō* 698 (2001): 46–47. Also see his "Dōshōan monjo (15): 'Jin'emon, Tōgorō rensho shōjō'," *Sanshō* 702: 74–75. A partial survey of these incidents can be found in Hirose Ryōkō, "Chū-Kinsei," pp. 598–614.

61. The 1640 *Nise gedoku hanbai hakkaku ni yori shūchin manbyōen to kaimei ni tsuki issatsu* by Myōkan and six others can be found in the Dōshōan Monjo, microfilm no. 2164005009. Also see Hirose Ryōkō, "Chū-Kinsei," p. 604.

62. On medicinal patent laws, see Usami Hideki, "Kinsei Yakuho no 'shōhyō, Shōgoken' hogo," *Shiga daigaku keizaigakubu fuzoku shiryōkan* 30 (1997): 83–107, which focuses on incidents of unauthorized sales of Jinkyōgan in Hikone Province as well as Yosh-

ioka Shin, *Kinsei nihon yakugyōshi kenkyū*, pp. 174–76. Also, on the history of bakufu policies on the production and monitoring of herbal medicines, see Ōishi Manabu, *Kyōhō kaikaku no chiiki seisaku* (Tokyo: Yoshikawa kōbunkan, 1996), pp. 460–506.

63. This document, written by Murakami Hisauemon and others, can be found in the *Dōshōan monjo*, Microfilm 2166312017.

64. Mt. Kumano—the three-legged crow; Tōdaiji and Tōji temples—a snake or dragon; Hachiman Shrine—a dove; Mt. Hiko—an eagle; Hasedera—a cow.

65. The history of *Goō hōin* is best summed up in Machida Shiritsu Hakubutsukan, ed., *Goō hōin: Inori to chikai no jufu* (Machida: Machida shiritsu hakubutsukan, 1991). On the use of these documents as contracts and the different types issued by the various shrines and temples, see Chijiwa Haru, "Goō hōin to kishōmon," in ibid., pp. 7–14. On Kumano's *Goō hōin*, in particular, see Shimazu Norifumi, "Kumano shinkō to Nachidaki hōin," in ibid., pp. 120–24, and "Kumano goō hōin: Inori no gofu," in *Kumano sanzan shinkō jiten*, ed. Katō Takahisa (Tokyo: Ebisu kōshō shuppan kabushiki gaisha, 1998), pp. 260–75. In English, see Ooms, *Tokugawa Village Practice*, pp. 230–33, for several village disputes that involved the use of a Kumano *Goō hōin*.

66. The divorce papers can be found in Awano Toshiyuki, "Dōshōan monjo (24)," *Sanshō* 711 (2002): 74–75.

67. Awano Toshiyuki has looked at fake sales in Shinshū Province; see his "Dōshōan monjo (17): 'Bizen no kuni Dōsen Shijō issatsu'," *Sanshō* 704: 68–69.

68. See Hirose Ryōkō, "Chū-Kinsei," p. 613.

69. Among the extant contracts in the *Dōshōan monjo* are those by Sonkai in 1671, Tetsuō in 1680, Yūzen in 1736, Engetsu in 1741, Ōgen in 1751, Esshū in 1755, Tankai in 1758, Mizan in 1764, Tōgen in 1768, Taimyō in 1781, Daikō in 1786, Gentō in 1796, Senpō in 1809, Ikai in 1814, Mankai in 1819, Daien in 1822, and Kanzen in 1845.

70. See the 1685 *Sashi age mōsu issatsu no koto* by Kyūbee, in *Dōshōan monjo*, microfilm no. 2168511014.

71. On Tokugawa-period letters of apology, see Miyahara Ichirō, "Kinsei wabishōmon no kōzō to seishitsu: Chichibu Ōnomura no jirei kara," *Kokugakuin daigaku daigakuin kiyō* 29 (1997): 305–21.

72. See Kumagai Chūkō, *Eiheiji nenpyō* (Tokyo: Rekishi toshosha, 1978), p. 250.

73. Most of the information on the post-Meiji decline of Gedokuen is taken from Kinoshita Jūzō, "Dōshōan ni tsuite," *Sanshō* 457 (September 1981): 64–67.

74. The Kōganji Jizō *en'nichi* is the fourth, fourteenth, and twenty-fourth of each month.

75. The Tokugawa bakufu decided to sponsor a local historical and geographical survey in 1810 that resulted in the *Shinpen Musashi no kuni fudokikō* (The New Regional and Historical Survey of Musashi Province). However, since the city of Edo was so large, a separate *Gofunai fudoki* (Regional and Historical Survey of Metropolitan Edo), which ran to 145 volumes, was commissioned in 1826. The notes left from that project included a separate section on shrines and temples. The entry on Kōganji Temple can be found in *Gofunai jisha bikō*: Vol. 5, *Ōbaku, Sōtō* (Tokyo: Meicho shuppan, 1987), pp. 214–17.

76. In 1891 Kōganji Temple shifted locations again, from Shitaya to the Sugamo district of Tokyo, due to the reorganization of Tokyo by city planners. Today, in fact, the temple is commonly called "Tokyo Sugamo Togenuki Jizō." Tanaka has noted that when the temple first relocated to its new Sugamo location, no one came until the abbot hit upon the idea of putting up signs with "Togenuki Jizō this way" on the newly erected city telephone poles. See Tanaka Masaaki, "'ichimantai inzō Jizō kan'ōki' no koto domo," in *Minkan no Jizō shinkō*, ed. Ōshima Tatehiko (Tokyo: Keisuisha, 1992), p. 112.

77. The *Edo sunago onko meisekishi*, the best-known contemporaneous local history and survey of Edo, was compiled by Kikuoka Senryō in six volumes. Quotes from this work and its followup edition in five volumes are included in ibid., p. 111. In some versions, the entry is *reigen aru Jizō* (a Jizō with "miraculous powers") instead of *hayari Jizō* (a "Jizō that's all the rage"). For more on the popularity of Kōganji Temple in the Toku-

gawa period, see Suzuki Kazuo, *Edo, mōhitotsu no fūkei: Ōedo jisha hanjōki* (Tokyo: Yomiuri shinbunsha, 1998), pp. 178–84.

78. On the various regional "Togenuki Jizō," see ibid., pp. 184–85.

79. The needle was therefore 1.2 cm.

80. Manabe Kōsai, *Jizō bosatsu no kenkyū* (Kyoto: Sanmitsudō shoten, 1960).

81. Three "Jizō sutras" are commonly dealt with as a set: (1) *Jizō bosatsu hongankyō* (T. 13, 777–90) or the "Sutra on the Original Vow of the Bodhisattva Jizō," said to have been translated from the Sanskrit into Chinese by Siksānanda (652–710) but probably of Central Asian or Chinese origin, outlines Jizō's past lives and the benefits of his cult (an English translation can be found in Heng Ching, trans., *Sutra of the Past Vows of Earth Store Bodhisattva* (New York: Buddhist Text Translation Society/Institute for Advanced Studies of World Religions, 1974); (2) *Jizō jūringyō* (T. 13, 721) or the "Jizō Ten Rings Sutra," supposedly translated by Xuan Zang, which describes how Jizō will serve to save all beings in this world until the appearance of Miroku (Maitreya), a study of which can be found in Françoise Wang-Toutain, *Le bodhisattva Kṣitigarbha en Chine du Ve au XIIIe siècle* (Paris: Presses de l'École Française d'Extrême Orient, 1997), pp. 16–71; and (3) *Sensatsu zen'akugyōkyō* (T. 17, 901). In addition, there are quite a number of Japanese apocryphal sutra, such as the *Enmei Jizōkyō* or the *Bussetsu Jizō bosatsu hosshin in'en jūokyō*, which eventually gained at least as much popularity as the so-called canonical versions.

Raoul Birnbaum has noted the prevalence of the life-prolonging motif in Chinese religions, particularly in the worship of Amida (longevity gained through rebirth into paradise), Yakushi (through healing powers), Kannon (through rescue from dangerous situations and with the elixir of longevity), and Fugen (healing through the recitation of the deity's mantra). See Birnbaum, "Seeking Longevity in Chinese Buddhism."

82. The *Jizō bosatsu reigenki* was compiled by Jitsuei of Miidera in the mid-Heian period, although the fourteen-volume version (with 152 stories) edited by Ryōkan was published in 1684. For a fully annotated version of the text, see Ōshima Tatehiko, et al., eds., *Jūyonkanbon Jizō bosatsu reigenki* (Tokyo: Miyai shobō, 2002–03) 2 vols. For a partial English translation, see Yoshiko Kurata Dykstra, "Jizō, the Most Merciful: Tales from *Jizō Bosatsu Reigenki*," *Monumenta Nipponica* 33/2 (Summer 1978): 178–200.

83. On Myōdō Jō'e and his Jizō miracle tale compilations, see Nishida Kōzō, "Myōdō Jō'e: Shi no wakare," *Edo jidai bungakushi* 8 (1991): 11–45; and Watari Kō'ichi, "Jō'e to kinsei Jizō setsuwashū: 'Enmei Jizō bosatsukyō jikidanshō' no haikei," *Setsuwa bungaku kenkyū* 22 (1988): 1–9; "'Jizō bosatsu riyakushū' no sekai: Jōkyō, Genroku jidai no minkan Jizō shinkō," *Bukkyō minzoku kenkyū* 6 (1989): 39–58; "'Jizō bosatsu rijōki' ni tsuite," *Meiji daigaku kyōyō ronshū* 242 (1991): 39–59. Myōdō Jō'e also propagated an apocryphal sutra, the *Jizō bosatsu mujukyō*, which was said to have been told in a dream to a nun in 1684. For more on this sutra, see Watari Kōichi, "'Jizō bosatsu mujukyō' ni tsuite," *Meiji daigaku kyōyō ronshū* 257 (1993): 235–62. Myōdō Jō'e was also influential in the Jōdo monk Hitsumu's compilation of the 1696 *Enmei jizō bosatsukyō jikidansho*. Hitsumu incorporated three Jizō stories of Myōdō Jō'e's *Jizō bosatsu rijōki* and three stories of his *Jizō bosatsu riyakushū*. On the Shingon-Ritsu monk, Rentai, and his *Kōshakushū*, see Tsukada Akinobu, "Rentai no Kōshakushū: Kinsei shōdō setsuwa no ichikōbō," *Bungaku ronsō* 52 (1977): 76–93. For a brief introduction to these early modern *Jizō setsuwa*, see Manabe Kōsai, *Jizō bosatsu no kenkyū*, pp. 157–70. Watari Kōichi has also provided an important account of the development of *Jizō setsuwa* literature from the medieval versions to the early modern ones that developed out of temples hoping to ascribe miraculous origins to their Jizō (*Jizō engishū*). See Watari Kōichi, "Kinsei Jizō setsuwashū to Jizō engi: Jūyonkanbon 'Jizō bosatsu reigenki' no baai," *Musashino bungaku* 33 (1986): 14–18.

84. This text is currently housed among the special collection "Kōshaku Mōrike monjo" at the Meiji University Library in Tokyo. The manuscript has been transcribed and analyzed by Tamamuro Fumio in his "'Enmei jizō inkō riyakuki' ni tsuite," *Meiji*

188

NOTES TO CHAPTER 5

daigaku kyōiku ronshū 243 (1992): 141–63; "Nihon ni okeru minzoku shinkō: Togenuki Jizō shinkō," in *Rekishi no naka no minshū bunka,* ed. Meiji Daigaku Jinbun Kagaku Kenkyūsho (Tokyo: Kazama shobō, 1999), pp. 5–64; "Edo jidai no jibyō shūkyō: 'Togenuki Jizō' o chūshin to shite," *Kumamoto igakkaishi* 72/2–3 (1999): 190–99; and "Togenuki Jizō to byōki," in *Kurashi no naka no sukui,* ed. Nihon Fūzokushi Gakkai (Tokyo: Tsukubanekai, 2000), pp. 72–108. Although Tamamuro has "Enmei Jizō" in his title, the original text title starts "Enmei Jizōson." For a full translation of this text into English, see Duncan Williams, "The Healing Jizō Bodhisattva in Tokugawa Japan: The 1822 *Enmei Jizōson inkō riyakuki,*" *Monumenta Nipponica* (2004): forthcoming.

85. A major section of the text is the *Ichimantai inzō Jizōson kan'ōki,* a description of which can be found in Tanaka Masaaki, "'ichimantai inzō Jizōson kan'ōki' (gen Sugamo Jizō) ni tsuite," *Bukkyō minzoku kenkyū* 5 (1980): 41–48.

86. The size of the talisman recorded in "A Summary of the Origins of the Printing of the Ten Thousand Jizō Talismans" section of the *Enmei Jizōson inkō riyakuki* is 1 *sun,* 3 *bu* (or 3.9 cm). Today these talismans, which are still faithfully swallowed with water, measure a full centimeter less. This discrepancy in size can be attributed in part to the loss of the original text and wooden printing block in a fire at Kōganji Temple during the Meiji period.

87. On the cult of Mt. Fuji and the ingesting of talismans to effect cures, see Inobe Shigeo, *Fuji no shinkō* (Tokyo: Kokin shoin; rpt. Tokyo: Heibonsha, 1983), pp. 319–20. Here, sheets of thirty-two or eighty-four prints were cut up into individuals talismans.

88. For Heian-period commissioning of Buddhist statues at times of illness and epidemics, see Mimi Yiengpruksawan, "The Visual Ideology of Buddhist Sculpture in the Late Heian Period as Configured by Epidemic and Disease," in *Bukkyō bijutsu kenkyū ni okeru zuzō to yōshiki* (Tokyo: 14th International Taniguchi Symposium, Kokusai kōryū bijutsushi kenkyūkai, 1996), pp. 69–80. Tanaka Masaaki has pointed out, however, that the upper limit for Jizō talisman printing or statue making seems to be one thousand during the medieval period. See Tanaka Masaaki, "'ichimantai Jizō kanōki' no koto domo," p. 110. Twenty-one "Sentai Jizō" are listed in Okumura Hirozumi, ed., *Shinpen Nihon Jizō jiten* (Tokyo: Murata shoten, 1989), pp. 458–59, with the vast majority of them located in present-day Tokyo, Saitama, Chiba, and Kanagawa prefectures. The Sōtō Zen headquarters temple of Eiheiji also incorporated a "Sentai Jizōson" during the early eighteenth century. See Hirose Ryōkō, "Sentai jizōson zō," *Sanshō* (May 1979): 14–15.

89. The twenty-fourth is cited in the *Jizō bosatsu jissainichi* (T. 85, 1300) as an auspicious day to visualize Jizō to avoid hell for one thousand *kalpas.* It is also found in the seventh fascicle of the *Konjaku monogatari* as the *en'nichi* (day closely related to the particular bodhisattva) of Jizō.

90. Five miracles not involving healing are recorded. Three involve saving a person from death, suicide, or the hell realms, and two involve Jizō helping people find something they have misplaced.

91. One of the six realms in Buddhist cosmology that is beneath the human and animal realms.

92. The *saha* world here refers to the "dusty" world from which the boy came.

93. This motif of returning from the dead is explored in Robert Campany's "Return-from-Death Narratives in Early Medieval China," *Journal of Chinese Religion* 18 (1990): 91–125.

94. Clifford, *Tibetan Buddhist Medicine and Psychiatry,* p. 8. Arvind Sharma, in "Relation between Disease and Karma," pp. 147–49, has also argued that early Buddhist texts also insist that bad karma can cause diseases, while good karma can lead to the remission of diseases, though not all diseases can be attributed to karma.

95. For an account of Ninshō's building of facilities at various temples in both the Kyoto-Nara and Kamakura regions, see Akizuki Suiko's *Gokurakuji Ninshō* (Tokyo:

Gyōbunsha, 1998), especially pp. 80–85, and Terabayashi Shun's *Kyūsai no hito: Kosetsu, Ninshō* (Tokyo: Tōyō keizai shinpōsha, 1998). According to Akizuki, the first facility that Ninshō set up at Saidaiji, for example, was a *yuya* (steam-bath house) where he invited lepers living at one of the seven outcast houses in the Yamato region to come and receive daily baths. Ninshō apparently believed the minority view espoused by his Kōfukuji Temple Yogācāra master Hōin that leprosy, as with all phenomena, was born from the mind and not from external karmic circumstances. Ninshō taught lepers to turn their minds toward faith in Monju bodhisattva and in the power of hygiene through daily cleansing at the bathhouse (which he separated for those with leprosy and without). This suggests that he understood the communicable character of leprosy and that the symptoms could be aggravated by unhygienic conditions.

96. These include the *Daijōbosatsu shōbōkyō* (T. 11. 834b), the *Daihōtōdaishūkyō* (T. 13. 147a), the *Shō Kanzeon bosatsu shōjō dokugai darani jukyō* (T. 20. 37b), and the *Daihannya haramitakyō* (T. 33. 63 c). For an analysis of the view of leprosy in Buddhist canonical and extra-canonical literature, see Nakamura Kaoru, "Bukkyō to rai (hansen byō) (3)," *Dōhō bukkyō* 28 (1993): 73–140. A different view of Buddhism and leprosy can be found in Ivette Vargas-O'Brian, "The Life of dGe slong ma dPalmo: The Experience of a Leper, the Founder of a Fasting Ritual, a Transmitter of Buddhist Teachings on Suffering and Renunciation in Tibetan Religious History," *Journal of the International Association of Buddhist Studies* 24/2 (2002): 157–86. In addition to Nakamura's work, the literature on leprosy and Buddhist discrimination include Kudō Eishō, "Raibyōsha sabetsu ni ideologii kōzō: Sabetsu ideologii hihan e no kōsō," *Shūgaku kenkyū* 39 (1997): 300–305; Nakano Jūsai, " 'ashiki gōron' no kokufuku: Hansenbyō ni okeru kakuri to danzetsu," *Shūgaku kenkyū* 40 (1998): 267–72; Sōtōshū Jinken Yōgo Suishin Honbu, ed., "Hansenshibyō ga 'gō' ni yoru mono to suru 'kirigami' no jirei," in "*Ashiki gōron" kokufuku no tame ni*, pp. 26–28. For Sōtō Zen *kirigami* that explain the procedure for performing funerals for people afflicted with leprosy, see Ishikawa Rikizan, "Chūsei Sōtōshū kirigami no bunrui shiron 4," *KDBR* 15 (1984): 164–68, or *Zenshū sōden shiryō no kenkyū ge*, pp. 1034–36. A separate discriminatory funeral was also held for those who had died from tuberculosis, another disease feared because of its contagious nature; see the manual *Denshibyō danzetsu no higen*, in Ishikawa Rikizan, (11) *KDBK* 46 (1988): 141.

97. Strickmann, *Chinese Magical Medicine*, p. 98.

98. I have drawn heavily on Yamamoto Shun'ichi's history of leprosy in Japan for the discussion of the Nichiren and *Lotus Sutra*–based perspectives on the disease. He argues that the ambivalent Buddhist view of leprosy in the medieval period provided an opening for Christian missionaries to build leprosaria to win converts in Sakai and Ōita provinces; see Jurgis Elisonas, "The Jesuits, the Devil, and Pollution in Japan," *Bulletin of Portuguese Japanese Studies* 1 (2000): 22; and Yamamoto Shun'ichi, *Nihon raishi* (Tokyo: Tokyo daigaku shuppankai, 1993), pp. 7–12.

99. On rites used by Sōtō Zen monks to "treat" fox possession, see Ishikawa Rikizan, "Chūsei Sōtōshū kirigami no bunrui shiron 21," *KDBK* 51 (1993): 113.

100. In the *Jizō bosatsu reigenki* as well as in the *Konjaku monogatari*, Jizō is said to come from the south to lead people at the time of death to the Pure Land of Miroku.

101. The *Renge Zanmai Sutra*'s main teaching is that Kannon had entrusted all sentient beings in the six realms to Jizō. The cult of the "Roku Jizō" (six Jizōs) developed from the notion that Jizō had six names, one for each realm of existence.

102. There has been no research on Senryūji Temple's medicine or smallpox prevention talismans. The documents and talismans discussed below were kindly provided by the current abbot of Senryūji, Sugawara Shōei, who is also a professor of Japanese history at the Historiographical Institute, Tokyo University.

103. On Senryūji's "Mawari Jizō" and pilgrimage associations, see Nakajima Keiko, "Senryūji no mawari Jizō," in *Minkan no Jizō shinkō*, ed. Ōshima Tatehiko (Tokyo:

Keisuisha, 1992), pp. 121–78; and Matsuzaki Kenzō, "Mawari Jizō no shokeitai: Higashi Nihon no mawari Jizō o chūshin ni," *Nihon bukkyō* 48 (1979): 19–37.

104. This document is among the *Senryūji monjo*, cataloged as no. 66 in Zenshū Chihōshi Chōsakai, ed. *Zenshū chihōshi chōsakai nenpō*, p. 100.

105. This dating is approximate since there is no date on the document. The date can also be inferred from its place in the *Senryūji monjo* collection. The earliest it could be is approximately the 1820s, and the latest is the early Meiji period.

106. This document is among the *Senryūji monjo*, cataloged as no. 54 in ibid., p. 99.

107. For an earlier example of Sōtō Zen smallpox prevention based on faith in Jizō, see the Tenneiji Temple *Hōsō no mamori*, in Ishikawa Rikizan, "Chūsei Sōtōshū kirigami no bunrui shiron 21," *KDBK* 51 (1993): 114. For a study on the worship of Yuo Daimyōjin, a smallpox-prevention deity associated with the Matsudaira family, at Kaizōji Temple, see Ōshima Tatehiko, "Yuo Daimyōjin," in *Edo shomin no tera: Kaizōjishi*, ed. Samura Ryūei and Kugai Shōkō (Tokyo: Kaizōji, 1994), pp. 89–99.

108. Ann Bowman Jannetta has shown the epidemic levels of both smallpox and measles in her *Epidemics and Mortality in Early Modern Japan*. For an analysis of people's religious understandings of smallpox and measles, see Hartmut Rotermund, *Hōsōgami ou la petite vérole aisément: Matériaux pour l'étude des épidémies dans le Japon des XVIIIe, XIXe siècles* (Paris: Maisonneuve & Larose, 1991); "Demonic Affliction or Contagious Disease? Changing Perceptions of Smallpox in the Late Edo Period," *Japanese Journal of Religious Studies* 28/3–4 (2001): 373–98; and "Krankheitsbilder in Krankheits-Bildern: Zu den sozial-historischen Bezügen der Darstellungen der Masern (*Hashika-e*)," in *Buch und Bild als gesellschaftliche Kommunikationsmittel in Japan einst und jetzt*, ed. Susanne Formanek and Sepp Linhart (Druck: Literas, 1995), pp. 107–38. Rotermund's book has more recently been translated into Japanese; see *Hōsōgami: Edo jidai no yamai o meguru minkan shinkō no kenkyū* (Tokyo: Iwanami shoten, 1995).

109. For more on Sagi Daimyōjin, see Hartmut Rotermund, *Hōsōgami*, pp. 35–37.

110. For the smallpox prevention ceremony at Tokuunji Temple in 1858, see Tanigawa Zenryū, ed., *Sōtōshū Fukudasan Tokuunji* (Matsumoto: Tokuunji, 1993), p. 217.

111. Higuchi has noted the emergence of medicine and faith-healing as a dual system by the late medieval period; see Higuchi Seitarō, "Chūsei ni okeru kitō to iryō," *Nihon ishigaku zasshi* 21/3 (1975): 224–36.

112. See Abdullahi Osman El-Tom, "Drinking the Koran: The Meaning of the Koranic Verses in Berti Erasure," *Africa* 55/4 (1985): 414–31.

113. In the Tantric tradition, the protective powers of Jāngulī ("Jungle-Women"), as found in the *Book of the Incantations and Dhāraṇī of the Jāngulī Woman* (T. 1265), appears in the form of a spell. Michel Strickmann has noted in the case of snakebites, "Jāngulī's spell is to be recited over water, which is then swallowed by the sufferer. Such water is to be held in the mouth while the sufferer recites the spell silently seven times; then all the root causes of the envenomation will be removed, and he will come to no harm." See Strickmann, *Chinese Magical Medicine*, p. 152.

114. Robert Brown, "The Miraculous Buddha Image: Portrait, God, or Object?" in *Images, Miracles, and Authority in Asian Religious Traditions*, ed. Richard Davis (Boulder: Westview Press, 1998), p. 47.

115. See Royall Tyler, trans., *The Tale of Genji* (New York: Viking, 2001), p. 83.

116. On the cult of Mt. Fuji and the ingesting of talismans to effect cures, see Inobe, *Fuji no shinkō*, pp. 319–20. Here, sheets of thirty-two or eighty-four prints were cut into individual talismans. For the ingestion ritual at Mt. Ōyama, see Barbara Ambros, "Mountain of Great Prosperity," p. 209. Elizabeth ten Grotenhuis has also noted the practice of eating pieces of a *Taima mandala* among villagers in Fukushima during the 1870s as a prophylatic against an epidemic; see her *Japanese Mandalas: Representations of Sacred Geography* (Honolulu: University of Hawai'i Press, 1999), p. 13.

CONCLUSION   The Other Side of Zen

1. Mukaizaki Jinnai was known as a skilled swordsman.

2. The head of the Aoyama household at this time was Aoyama Shūzen, an officer in charge of apprehending arsonists and thieves for the Banchō District, which is why this legend is sometime referred to as the "Banchō sarayashiki." Other versions of this legend state that Aoyama Shūzen caught Mukaizaki Jinnai in the act of stealing, which led to his execution. The sixteen-year-old surviving daughter, Kiku, was thus taken into the Aoyama household as an adopted daughter and maid servant. See Taii Yukiko, "Okiku," in *Nihon fushigi kaku-u denshō jinbutsu dokuhon*, ed. Miyazaki Miyu (Tokyo: Shinjin-butsu ōraisha, 1994), p. 210.

There are as many as forty-eight versions of this legend in various provinces throughout Japan, clustered in Kagoshima, Miyazaki, Shimane, Hyōgo, Niigata, and Miyagi prefectures and Tokyo City. The most comprehensive survey of the Kiku legends and their proliferation throughout the provinces is Itō Atsushi, *Nihon no sarayashiki densetsu* (Fukuoka: Kaichōsha, 2002). Most scholars have linked the "Banchō sarayashiki" story to an earlier legend, the "Banshū sarayashiki," which was first performed in Osaka and Kyoto as a *kyōgen* play in 1720. An English-language translation (or, rather, adaptation) of several versions of this story can be found in James De Benneville, *The Yotsuya Kwaidan or O'iwa Inari* (Philadelphia: Lippincott, 1917), pp. 218–35, who draws from Momogawa Jōen's *Banchō sarayashiki* as well as Byōhaku Kakuchi's and Hōgyūsha Tōko's texts of the same title.

3. One version of the story explains that the plate was an heirloom given to the family by Tokugawa Ieyasu for Aoyama Shūzen's work as an officer. See De Benneville, *Yotsuya Kwaiden*, p. 221. Itō has analyzed extant "Kiku plates" and concluded that, by legend, the "precious plates" originated from China (ten cases), Korea (three), and Europe (two). See Itō, *Nihon no sarayashiki densetsu*, p. 53. He has also noted purported graves of Kiku throughout Japan. In addition, she is enshrined as a kami at the Kiku Daimyōjin Shrine in Usui Town (Fukuoka Prefecture).

4. Aoyama decided upon this punishment by reasoning that, as she had broken one plate out of ten, one of her ten fingers should be cut off.

5. Other variants of the legend explain that Kiku's anger about her treatment and her father's execution at the hands of Aoyama Shūzen came to a head at this point. With Aoyama's wife pregnant, Kiku's last thought as she plunged into the well was to curse the baby that was to come into the world. When the baby was born, it was missing one finger.

6. This story can be found as part of the *Jōsenji ryaku engi* (exact date unknown), which is included in Nakano Takeshi, *Ryaku engi shūsei 1* (Tokyo: Renseisha, 1995), pp. 160–61. Since Jōsenji Temple was closed down in 1908 and had earlier in the Tokugawa period lost its documents due to fires, extant versions of the original text can be found only in the "Enji sōsho" collection at the Tokyo Toritsu Chūō Library. I am basing much of the historical background of the Kiku story on Itō, *Nihon no sarayashiki densetsu*, pp. 34–36, 69–71; Taii, "Okiku," pp. 210–11; and Tsutsumi, *Kinsei setsuwa to zensō*, pp. 174–80. For a brief account in English, see Brenda Jordan, "*Yūrei*: Tales of Female Ghosts," in *Japanese Ghosts and Demons: Art of the Supernatural*, ed. Stephen Addiss (New York: George Braziller, 1985), pp. 27–28. Jordan also provides an account of the emergence of female ghost legends in the Tokugawa period, including the Kiku (Okiku) legend and the most renowned, the Ōiwa Yotsuya Kaidan.

7. A variant copy of this story was discovered among the temple treasures during a *kaichō* of the plate by a certain Yamazaki Yoshinari in 1819. See Tsutsumi, *Kinsei setsuwa to zensō*, p. 174.

8. Another version of the story has not a Zen monk, but an Amidist priest, Ryōyō Shōnin, save Kiku's ghost through a three-week chanting of the *nenbutsu*, which was capped with the priest shouting "ju" (Ten) for the tenth plate. See De Benneville, *Yotsuya Kwaidan*, pp. 254–56.

9. This idea of reality as a mess upon which order is imposed is a Bakhtinian concept, which Karen Smyers skillfully uses in her discussion of the variety of forms in which the worship of Inari exists in contemporary Japan. See her *Fox and the Jewel: Shared and Private Meanings in Contemporary Japanese Inari Worship* (Honolulu: University of Hawai'i Press, 1998).

10. Bodiford, *Sōtō Zen in Medieval Japan*, p. 2.

11. Again, see Tsutsumi, *Kinsei setsuwa to zensō*, p. 175, for more on this motif.

Akiba Daigongen　秋葉大権現

akuryō chin'atsu　悪霊鎮圧

amagoi　雨乞い

Amakusa daikan　天草代官

bakufu　幕府

bakuhansei　幕藩制

bakumatsu shinshukyo　幕末新宗教

Bateren tsuihōrei　伴天連追放法令

Benzaiten　弁財天

betsubuku　別腹

betsuin　別院

bodaiji　菩提寺

bosatsukai　菩薩戒

Bukō nenpyō　武江年表

bunrei　分霊

Buraku kaiho dōmei　部落解放同盟

Bussetsu enmei jizō bosatsukyō　佛説延命地蔵菩薩経

butsudan　仏壇

chinju　鎮守

chi no ike jigoku　血の池地獄

chō hazure　帳外れ

Chōkokuji　長谷寺

Daihiju　大悲呪

daihonzan　大本山

Daijiin　大慈院

Daijoji　大乗寺

daikan　代官

daimyō　大名

Daimyōjin　大明神

daisankō　代参講

Daiyūgan　大雄丸

Daiyūzan Saijōji　大雄山最乗寺

danka　檀家

danka sōdai　檀家総代

danna　檀那

dannadera　檀那寺

dan'otsu　檀越

danshintō　檀信徒

darani　陀羅尼

degaichō　出開帳

Dōgen　道元

dokuyaku　毒薬

Doryō Daigongen　道了大権現

Doryōsai　道了祭

Dōshō　道正

Dōshōan　道正庵

Dōshōan keifu　道正庵系譜

eden　絵伝

Edo bukkyō darakuron　江戸仏教堕落論

Eiheiji　永平寺

Eihei kaisan Dōgen zenji gyōjō Kenzeiki　永平開山道元禅師行状建撕記

Eihei shingi　永平清規

ekibyo　疫病

Ekōin　回向院

engi　縁起

Enma　閻魔

Enmei Jizōkyō　延命地蔵経

Enmei jizōson inkō riyaku ki　延命地蔵尊印行利益記

ennichi　縁日

eta hinin　穢多非人

etoki　絵解き

Fudō Myōō　不動明王

Fuju fuse　不受不施

fumi-e　踏絵

gaki　餓鬼

Gasan Joseki　峨山紹碩

Gedokuen　解毒円

Gennō Shinshō　源翁心昭

genze riyaku　現世利益

gidayu jōruri　義太夫浄瑠璃

gōbyō　業病

gofu　護符

Gofunai jishabikō　御府内寺社備考

goma　護摩

gongen　権現

Gongensui　権現水

goningumi　五人組

goō hōin　牛王宝印

goroku　語録

goryō　御霊

gozan　五山

gyōja　行者

haibutsu kishaku　廃仏毀釈

Ha Kirishitan　破切支丹

Hakone gongen　箱根権現

Hakusan　白山

handanka　半檀家

Hannya shingyo　般若心経

hannyatō　般若湯

hatto　法度

hayarigami　流行神

hibutsu　秘仏

hinin　非人

hinin koseki　非人戸籍

honji　本寺

honmatsu seido　本末制度

honzan seido　本山制度

honzon　本尊

Hōon'in　報恩院

Hōshōji　法性寺

Hōshōni　法性尼

hōsō　疱

hotoke　仏

Ichimantai Jizō　一万体地蔵

igaicho　居開帳

ihai　位牌

Inari　稲荷

Inga monogatari　因果物語

jashūmon　邪宗門

Jigenji　示現寺

jikkai　十戒

Jinken Yōgo Suishin Honbu　人権擁護
　推進本部

Jippensha Ikku　十返舎一九

Jisha bugyō　寺社奉行

jisha densō　寺社伝奏

Jizō bosatsu　地蔵菩薩

Jizō bosatsu reigenki　地蔵菩薩霊験記

Jizō bosatsu riyakushū　地蔵菩薩利益集

jōruri　浄瑠璃

Jōsenji　常仙寺

ju　呪

Jūichimen Kannon　十一面観音

jūji　住持

jukai　授戒

Jūō　十王

Jūsanbutsu　十三仏

kaichō　開帳

kaimyō　戒名

kaisan　開山

kaji kitō　加持祈祷

kakochō　過去帳

kami　神

kamidana　神棚

Kan'ei shoshū matsujicho　寛永諸宗末
　寺帳

Kangan Giin　寒巌義伊

kan'in　監院

kanmon　貫文

Kannon bosatsu　観音菩薩

Kansansetsu　関三刹

Kansu　監寺

Kasuisai　可睡斎

Kasu ninbetsu aratamechō　家数人別
　改帳

kata mairi　片参り

katasode yūrei　片袖幽霊

kawa segaki　川施餓鬼

kechien　結縁

kechimyaku　血脈

kegare　穢

Keizan Jōkin　瑩山紹瑾

Keizan shingi　瑩山清規

Kenkon'in　乾坤院

Kenninji　建仁寺

Kenzeiki　建撕記

kesa　袈裟

keshin　化身

Ketsubonkyō　血盆経

Ketsubonkyō engi　血盆経縁起

kigan　祈願

kigusuriya　き薬屋

Kiku　菊

Kikunyo sara no raiyu　菊女皿の来由

Kinoshita Dōshō　木下道正

Kintaien　錦袋円

kirigami　切紙

Kirishitan　切支丹

Kirishitan aratame　切支丹改め

Kirishitan ruizoku koseki　切支丹類族
　戸籍
kishōmon　起請文
kitō jiin　祈祷寺院
kō　講
Kōbō Daishi　弘法大師
kōchū　講中
Kōganji　高岩寺
kōkatsuchō　交割帳
komonjo　古文書
Kōmyō shingon　光明真言
Kongōsui　金剛水
korobi Kirishitan　転び切支丹
Kōya hijiri　高野聖
Kōyasan　高野山
Kūkai　空海
Kumano bikuni　熊野比丘尼
Matsudō daimyōjin　待道大明神
Matsudōkō　待道講
manbyōyaku　万病薬
Manzan Dohaku　卍山道白
Matsudaira Sadanobu　松平定信
matsuji　末寺
Mawari Jizō　廻り地蔵
Meihō Sotetsu　明峰素哲
Menzan Zuihō　面山瑞方
Miidera　三井寺
mikkyōka　密教化
mikoshi　神輿
misemono　見世物
mon　文
mondō　問答
monme　匁
monzeki　門跡
monzen　門前
Mōri　毛利
motsugo sasō　没後作僧
muenbotoke　無縁仏
Musōgan　夢想丸
Nagasaki bugyō　長崎奉行
nanbyō　難病
Namu Amida butsu　南無阿弥陀仏
Namu Jizo daibosatsu　南無地蔵大菩薩
nanushi　名主
Nichiiki tōjō shosoden　日域洞上諸祖伝

niseyaku　偽薬
Nyoirin Kannon　如意輪観音
Nyojō　如浄
nyoninkō　女人講
Okanain　お金いん
Okunoin　奥院
oni　鬼
Onmyōdō　陰陽道
onryo　怨霊
osenbetsu　御餞別
oshi　御師
Osorezan　恐山
Ōyama　大山
Ōyama Myōō　大山明王
raise kuyō　来世供養
rakan　羅漢
reigenki　霊験記
rinban　輪番
rinji　綸旨
rinjū seido　輪住制度
reijō　霊場
rinka　林下
Rinzaishu　臨済宗
rokudo　六道
ryō　両
Ryōan Emyō　了庵慧明
ryōhonzansei　両本山制
ryūjin　龍神
ryūō no musume　龍王の娘
Ryūonji　龍穏寺
Ryūtaiji　龍泰寺
sabetsu kaimyō　差別戒名
Saijoji　最乗寺
Saitō Gesshin　斎藤月岑
sandai kito jiin　三大祈祷寺院
sankin kotai　参勤交代
Sanmen Daikokuden　三面大黒殿
sanmon　山門
sarayashiki　皿屋敷
segaki-e　施餓鬼会
Seigen'in　清源院
Sekigahara　関ヶ原
sekisho　関所
Sekison daigongen　石尊大権現
Senjō Jitsugen　千丈実巌

Senryūji　泉竜寺

senzo　先祖

seppō　説法

sewanin　世話人

shaku　尺

shie chokkyo jiken　紫衣勅許事件

shihō　嗣法

shijūku nichi　四十九日

Shimabara　島原

shinbutsu bunri　神仏分離

shingi　清規

Shingon　真言

shinjin kedo　神人化度

Shinpen Sagami no kuni fūdokikō　新編
　相模国風土記稿

Shinsen gedoku manbyōen　神仙解毒万
　病円

Shinsen Gedoku Manbyōen Fukuyō no
　Koto　神仙解毒万病円服用の事

Shin Yoshiwara　新吉原

Shōbōgenzō　正法眼蔵

shonanoka　初七日

Shōsenji　正泉寺

Shoshū matsuji okite　諸宗末寺掟

Shugendō　修験道

shukke　出家

Shumon aratamechō　宗門改帳

Shumon ninbetsuchō　宗門人別帳

Shumon ninbetsu aratamechō　宗門人
　別改帳

shushi　宗旨

Shushi aratamechō　宗旨改帳

sōdō　僧堂

Sōjiji　総持寺

Sōneiji　総寧寺

sōshiki bukkyo　葬式仏教

Sōtōshū　曹洞宗

Sōtōshū komonjo　曹洞宗古文書

Sōtōshū shūmuchō　曹洞宗宗務庁

Sōtōshū zensho　曹洞宗全集

Sumiyoshi myōjin　住吉明神

sun　寸

Suzuki Shōsan　鈴木正三

Taineiji　泰寧寺

tairyō kigan　大漁祈願

Taiya nenju　逮夜念誦

Takeda Shingen　武田信玄

Tateyama　立山

Teiho Kenzeiki　訂補建撕記

tengu　天狗

Tenkei Denson　天桂伝尊

tenryō　天領

Tentakuji　天沢寺

tenzo　典座

Tenzo kyōkun　典座教訓

terakoya　寺子屋

tera-uke　寺請

Tetsumei　哲明

toba　塔婆

Togenuki Jizō　とげぬき地蔵

tōji　湯治

Tokugawa Ieyasu　徳川家康

Tokugyō　得行

Tokuō Ryōkō　徳翁良高

tōrō　灯籠

Towa　とわ

Toyama no gyoshonin　富山の行商人

Toyokawa Inari　豊川稲荷

Tsūgen Jakurei　通幻寂霊

tsuizen kuyō　追善供養

Tsukahara　塚原

Tsuji Zennosuke　辻善之介

Ususama　烏枢沙摩

ujidera　氏寺

ukiyo-e　浮世絵

unsui　雲水

Urabonkyō　盂蘭盆経

Yagurazawa　矢倉沢

Yakushi　薬師

yamabushi　山伏

Yōkōji　永光寺

Yoshiwara　吉原

yūjo　遊女

yujun　由旬

Yūki Magozaburō　結城孫三郎

zaike　在家

zazen　坐禅

Zennen shingi　禅苑清規

Zenpoji　善宝寺

zuisse　瑞世

BIBLIOGRAPHY

Primary Texts (Handwritten Manuscripts Unavailable in Printed Form)

Bodai no tame mainen kinsu sanryō hōnō no ken shōnin. By Izumiya Sakuemon (1720). Nakamura Toseko private collection, Minami Ashigara Shishi Hensan Shitsu, uncataloged.

Chōsenji hōjō aitedori murakata danka no uchi yonjūrokunin fukie no ikken. By Zenbee et al. (1819). Seigen'in Temple Archives, Atsugishishi Hensan Shitsu Seigen'in Monjo, microfilm no. 72.

Chōsenji Monjo (Tetsumei jiken). By Tetsumei Towa et al. (1784–86). Seigen'in Temple Archives, uncataloged.

Dōshōan keifu. By Dōshōan Bokujun (ca. 1690). Eiheiji Sanshōkai Collection, uncataloged.

Dōshōan onkerai no mono kishōmon. By Murakami Hisauemon et al. (1663). Dōshōan Monjo, microfilm no. 2166312017.

Hōsō yoke onkokoroe gaki. By Senryūji (n.d.). Senryūji Temple Collection, microfilm no. 54.

Jisha bugyō hanketsu. By Makino Etchū no Kami et al. (1741). Tentakuji Monjo, microfilm no. 22.

Kōkatsubo. By Anonymous (1793). Daiyūzan Monjo, Komazawa University Library, uncataloged.

Kōkatsuchō. By Anonymous (1759). Higashi-Ura City Archives Kenkon'in Temple Collection, microfilm no. 241.

Kōkatsu shinchō no bu. By Anonymous (1874–80). Daiyūzan Monjo, Komazawa University Library, uncataloged.

Kōshin nikkichō. By Mori Mozaemon (1827). Nishigai Kenji private collection, uncataloged.

Musōgan hangi. By Senryūji (n.d.). Senryūji Temple Collection, microfilm no. 66.

Nise gedoku hanbai hakkaku ni yori shūchin manbyōen to kaimei ni tsuki issatsu. By Myōkan et al. (1640). Dōshōan Monjo, microfilm no. 2164005009.

Rokujusei chokushi Daikō Myōkaku Zenji ondōchū kudasaremono kiroku. By Daikō Myōkaku (1848). Dōshōan Monjo, microfilm no. 2184806099.

Rokusho sōroku ikken todome. By Ryūon'in Temple (1653). Tentakuji Temple Monjo, microfilm no. 6.

Saijōji nenban onrei shinangaki. By Anonymous (1827). Daiyūzan Monjo, Komazawa University Library, uncataloged.

Saijōji utsushi tozanyū kyūmeiji. By Gokurakuji (1724). Gokurakuji Temple Collection, uncataloged.

Saijō rinjū kiroku By Daiyūzan (1867). Daiyūzan Temple Collection, uncataloged.

Sashi age mōsu issatsu no koto. By Kyūbee (1685). Dōshōan Monjo, microfilm no. 2168511014.

Shinsen Gedoku Manbyōen Fukuyō no Koto. By Dōshōan Tokua (mid-Edo period). Isehara City Archives Ryūsanji Temple Collection, microfilm no. 127.

Primary Texts

Aburakōji Akai Takasada kyōki sōkan sōtō shidai. By Aburakōji (ca. 1673–80). *Sōjijishi*: 242 or *Eiheijishi jō*: 596.

An'ei nenchū kakuan e rōzeki ni tsuki Sekimoto yori wabi issatsu. By Sekimoto Village headman et al. (1774). Daiyūzan Monjo. *MAS* 8: 420–21.

Banshōzan Kikyūhō Tokuunji yuraisho. By Kakuin (1446). *ZSZ, Jishi:* 119–23.

Bukō nenpyō. By Saitō Gesshin (1806; ed. 1850). Edited by Kaneko Mitsuharu. Tokyo: Heibonsha, 1968, 2 vols.

Daijiin zenjichō. By Chidō Kōshō and Tesshin Goshū (1659). *MAS* 8 (betsuhen).

Daiyūzan Saijōji gokaisan engi. By Endō Tamemasa (1737). Endō Masuo private collection. *MAS* 8: 285–87.

Dōryō gongen Hakone gongen nanayumeguri. By Jippensha Ikku (1822). Kanagawaken Kyōdo Shiryōkan. *Daiyū,* vol. 41 (1988): 2.

Dōshōan gansoden. By Dōshōan Bokujun (1639). Eiheiji Sanshōkai Collection. *DNBZ* 115: 559–60.

Dōshōan yuishoki. By Fujiwara Tokuyū/Bokujun (1662). Sōkōji Temple. *ZSZ Shiden/ Jishi* 30: 109; *SK Gekan:* 323–24.

Echizen no kuni Eiheiji kaisanki. By Yūki Magazaburō (1689). Tokyo University Katei Bunko, microfilm no. E22 776725. Edited by Yokoyama Shigeru. *Sekkyō shohonshū 1.* Tokyo: Kadokawa shoten, 1968, pp. 248–70.

Eiheiji shohatto. By Anonymous (1615). *SK jō:* 20.

Enmei jizōson inkō riyakuki. By Hissai (1822). Meiji University Library Kōshaku Mōrike Monjo. Edited by Tamamuro Fumio. *Meiji daigaku kyōiku ronshū* 243 (1992): 141–63.

Fuji Ōyama dōchū zakki. By an anonymous Fuchū villager (1838). Kanagawa Kenritsu Kyōdo Shiryōkan. *Daiyū,* vol. 38 (1987): 2.

Gosaireichū shoshūnō hikaechō. By Murayamabō (1831). Murayamabō Temple Collection. *Isehara shishi shiryōhen zoku Ōyama.* Isehara: Isehara, 1994, p. 323.

Hakone yokutōki. By Anonymous (1818). Kanagawaken Kōbunshokan, *Kyōdo Kanagawa* 34: 37–45.

Hakonezan nana onsen Enoshima Kamakura meguri. By Jippensha Ikku (1833). National Diet Library. Edited by Tsuruoka Tokio. *Jippensha Ikku "Hakone, Enoshima, Kamakura dōchūki."* Tokyo: Shimpan ezōshi series 61, Senshūsha, 1982.

Hakusan daigongen, Dōryō daigongen jotōsai norito. By Anonymous (1777). Tenaka Tadashi private collection. Edited by Isehara shishi henshū iinkai. *Isehara shishi shiryōhen: Zoku Ōyama.* Isehara: Isehara, 1994, pp. 179–80.

Han danka ni tsuki jikata no torikime. By Ganjōji Temple and 18 other temples (1846). Kōsenji Temple Collection. Edited by Gosen Shishi Hensan Iinkai. *Gosen shishi: Shiryō 3, kinsei 2.* Gosen, Niigata: Gosenshi, 1997, pp. 611–13.

Hinin narabi tenkyōbyō kirigami. By Shinsōji Temple (1611). Shinsōji Temple Collection. *Shinano shiryō, hoi ge.* Nagano: Shinano shiryō kankōkai, 1971, p. 189.

Hōjō godai jikki. 10 vols. By Kōsei no Itsushishi (1615–24). National Diet Library. Edited by Kishi Masanao. *Odawara Hōjōki.* Tokyo: Kyōikusha, 1980.

Honkō Kokushi nikki. By Konchiin Sūden (1615–33). Matsugaoka Bunko. *DNBZ* 79–82.

Hōon'in zenjūchō. By Chidō Kōshō and Tesshin Goshū (1659). *MAS* 8 (betsuhen).

Inga monogatari. By Suzuki Shōsan (1658). *Koten bunko* 185. Edited by Yoshida Kōichi. Tokyo: Koten bunko, 1962.

Jiteihō. By Jutokuji Temple (1661). Jutokuji Temple Collection. Edited by Sōtōshū Gendai Kyōgaku Center. *Kaimyō no imi to kinō.* Tokyo: Sōtōshū gendai kyōgaku center, 1995, p. 79.

Kasuisai yurai ryakki. By Anonymous (1702). *SK jō:* 424.

Keizai mondō hiroku. By Shōji Kōji (1833). *Nihon shisō tōsō shiryō* 6. Edited by Washio Junkei. Tokyo: Tōhō shoin.

Ketsubonkyō yūshutsu inyu suishu (Kaie rakusōdan). By Unrei Taizen (1804). Komazawa University Library. *SZ Zenkai:* 704–20.

Kikunyo sara no raiyu. By Jōsenji Temple (late Tokugawa period). Tokyo Toritsu Chūō

Library Engi Sōsho Collection. Edited by Nakano Takeshi. *Ryaku engi shūsei 1.* Tokyo: Renseisha, 1994, pp. 160–61.

Kōgen Daitsū zenji sengoshū. By Daitsū Takushū (1721). *SZ goroku* 4: 23–128.

Kono tabi Kirishitanshū on'aratame ni tsuki danna bōzu shōmon sashiage. By Sōken'in (1635). Hatori Village, Fujisawa City Mitsuhashi Monjo. Edited by Tamamuro Fumio. *Nihon bukkyōshi: Kinsei.* Tokyo: Yoshikawa kōbunkan, 1987, p. 62.

Naisai torikawashi shōmon no koto. By Kano Village representatives (1819). Daiyūzan Monjo. *DTG:* 110–11.

Nakai nikki. By Nakai Yagozaemon (1684). Edited by Shizuokaken. *Shizuoka kenshi shiryōhen 12: Kinsei 4.* Tokyo: Gyōsei, 1995, pp. 649–771.

Nichiiki tōjō shosoden. 2 vols. By Tangen Jichō (1693). Komazawa University Library. *DNBZ* (Vol. 70): 287–346 and *SZ shiden* 1: 191–522.

Nihon tōjō rentōroku. 12 vols. By Reinan Shūjo (1727). Komazawa University Library. *DNBZ* (Vol. 70): 213–37 and *SZ shiden* 1: 33–87.

Nyonin jōbutsu Ketsubonkyō engi. By Seien Tairyō (1857). Shōsenji Temple Collection. Edited by Hagiwara Tatsuo. "Ansei yonenban Ketsubonkyō engi (Abikoshi Shōsenji shozō)." *Shiryō to denshō* 1 (1980): 20–22.

Padre Cosmo de Torres shokan. By Cosmo de Torres (1551). *Iezusukaishi Nihon tsūshin, jō.* Edited by Yanagiya Teruo. Tokyo: Yūshōdō shoten, 1968, pp. 19–25.

Rinban kōtai sansairei nado ni okeru Sekimotomura yakuninshū no toriatsukai ni tsuki gijōsho. By Saijōji (1850). Sekimoto Jichikai Collection. *MAS* 8: 421–22.

Ryūtaiji rinjū nikkan. By Butsujō (1723–34). Aichi Gakuin University Library Ryūtaiji Temple Collection. *ZSZ* 2: 141–75.

Sagami no kuni Kōzagun Hatorimura Hachirōemon tō shūshiuke tegata. By Senyo (1665). Hatori Village, Fujisawa City Mitsuhashi Monjo. Edited by Tamamuro Fumio. *Nihon bukkyōshi: Kinsei.* Tokyo: Yoshikawa kōbunkan, 1987, pp. 92–93.

Saijōji engi wasan. By Anonymous (late Tokugawa period). Nakamura Toyoko private collection. *MAS* 8: 290–93.

Saijō zenji rintōchō. By Chidō Kōshō and Tesshin Goshū (1659). *MAS* 8 (betsuhen).

Saitō Gesshin nikki. By Saitō Gesshin (1830–36). Edited by Tōdai Shiryō Hensanjo. Tokyo: Iwanami shoten, 1997.

Sashi age mōsu danna ukejogata no koto. By Hachirōemon (1669). Hatori Village, Fujisawa City Mitsuhashi Monjo. Edited by Tamamuro Fumio. *Nihon bukkyōshi: Kinsei.* Tokyo: Yoshikawa kōbunkan, 1987, pp. 168–69.

Shinpen Sagami no kuni fudokikō. By Anonymous (1841). Edited by Ashida Korehito. 6 vols. Tokyo: Meichō shuppan, 1975; rev. ed., Tamamuro Fumio, Tokyo: Yūzankaku, 1998.

Shoshū kaikyū. By Anonymous (1801). *Zokuzoku Gunsho ruiju* 12. Tokyo: Kokusho hankōkai, 1907, pp. 356–401.

Sōjiji shohatto. By Anonymous (1615). *SK jō:* 83.

Sōtōshū Ganshōin shoji okite. By Ganshōin (1841). Gosen City Archives. Edited by Goṣen Shishi Hensan Iinkai. *Gosen shishi: Shiryō 3, kinsei 2.* Gosen, Niigata: Gosenshi, 1997, pp. 613–34.

Sōtōshū shukke seiritsu saisho yori Eiheiji no tenshō no shidai. By Anonymous (1802). *Zokuzoku gunsho ruiju* 12. Tokyo: Kokusho hankōkai, 1907.

Sōtōshū sōto shusse kaikyū kakiage. By Kansansetsu (1801). *Zokuzoku gunsho ruiju* 12. Tokyo: Kokusho hankōkai, 1907.

Tamakushige futatsu ideyu michi no ki. By Hara Masaoki (1839). National Diet Library. Edited by Itasaka Yōko. *Edo onsen kikō.* Tokyo: Heibonsha, 1987, pp. 127–228.

Tōzan kaibyaku narabini kunin rōjin no kien. By Kōkoku Eishun (1648). Daiyūzan Temple Collection. *MAS* 8: 282–84.

Yūhō kongō hōin okite. By Sōneiji and Ryūonji (1764). Daishōji Temple Collection. *DTG:* 122–23.

SECONDARY LITERATURE

Abe Shinken. 1969. "Kitō ni yori kyōka keitai no ichi kōsatsu: Daiyūzan Saijōji o rei to shite." *Komazawa daigaku bukkyōgakkaishi* 11: 29–41.
———. 1982. "Dōryōson to shomin shinkō." *Shūkyō to gendai* 4/5: 37–41.
———. 1997. "Kaisan Ryōan Emyō zenji o shinonde." *Shidan Ashigara* 35: 57–71.
Adachi Yūkō. 1982–85. " 'Shinpen Sagami no kuni fudokikō' ni miru Sōtōshū jiin: Sono seiritsu to bunpu o chūshin to shite." *Hadanoshishi kenkyū* (1) 2: 46–100; (2) 5: 72–89.
Aiba Shin. 1975. *Fuju fuseha junkyō no rekishi.* Tokyo: Daizō shuppan.
Aizawa Yoichi. 1984. "Almsgiving and Alms Refusal in the Fuju-Fuse Sect of Nichiren Buddhism with a Consideration of these Practices in Early Indian Buddhism." Ph.D. dissertation, University of Pennsylvania.
Akizuki Suiko. 1998. *Gokurakuji Ninshō.* Tokyo: Gyōbunsha.
Ambros, Barbara. 2001. "Localized Religious Specialists in Early Modern Japan: The Development of the Ōyama *Oshi* System." *Japanese Journal of Religious Studies* 28/3–4: 329–72.
———. 2002. "The Mountain of Great Prosperity: The Ōyama Cult in Early Modern Japan." Ph.D. dissertation, Harvard University.
Amino Yoshihiko. 1989. "Asobi onna to hinin, kawaramono." In *Sei to mibun.* Edited by Miyata Noboru. Tokyo: Shunjūsha, 93–128.
Andachi Itsuo. 1995–97. *Bukkyō to buraku mondai kankei shiryō shūsei.* 2 vols. Kobe: Hyōgo buraku kaihō kenkyūsho.
Andō Seiichi. 1976. *Fuju Fuseha nōmin no teikō.* Osaka: Seibundō.
Andō Yoshinori. 1988. "Tengu kō: Tenguzō no keiseishi." *SKK* 20: 55–70.
———. 1998. "Daiyūzan to Dōryōsama (1)." *Daiyū* 72: 22–26.
———. 2000. *Chūsei Zenshū bunken no kenkyū.* Tokyo: Kokusho kankōkai.
Annō Masaki. 1989. *Bateren tsuihōrei.* Tokyo: Nihon data school shuppanbu.
———. 1995. " 'Kirishitan kinrei' no kenkyū." In *Kinsei shakai to shūkyō.* Edited by Fujino Tamotsu. Tokyo: Yūzankaku, 321–58.
Aoki Infu and Kojima Mikako, eds. 1986. *Kusuri kanban.* Kawajimachō: Naitō kinen kusuri hakubutsukan.
Aomori Tōru. 1976. "Suzuki Shōsan ni okeru kinsei bukkyō shisō no keisei katei." *Bukkyō shigaku kenkyū* 18/1: 1–33.
Aoyama Kōji. 1969–70. "Kanagawakenka no goningumichō" *Kanagawa kenshi kenkyū* (1) 7: 40–60; (2) 8: 39–58.
———. 1979. "Edo jidai no Sōshū no tera: Sono sūryōteki sokumen, Kōzagun no baai." *Fujisawashishi kenkyū* 12: 75–82.
———. 1979–84. "Edo jidai Sōshū no jiin." *Kanagawa kenshi kenkyū* (1) 38 (1979): 1–52; (2) 40 (1979): 36–63; (3) 41 (1980): 38–59; (4) 45 (1981): 58–63; (5) 47 (1982): 56–63; (6) 49 (1983): 78–87; (7) 51 (1984): 64–73.
———. 1987–94. "Sagami no kuni Miuragun no mura meisaichō." *Miura kobunka* (2–1) 42: 61–114; (2–2) 43: 47–100; (2–3) 46: 103–52; (2–4) 47: 63–87; (2–5) 48: 51–68; (2–6) 49: 82–114; (2–7) 55: 97–124.
Arimoto Masao. 1997. *Shūkyō shakaishi no kōzō: Shinshū monto no shinkō to seikatsu.* Tokyo: Yoshikawa kōbunkan.
———. 2002. *Kinsei Nihon no shūkyō shakaishi.* Tokyo: Yoshikawa kōbunkan.
Aruga Kizaemon. [1974]. 1979. "Hotoke to iu kotoba ni tsuite: Nihon bukkyōshi ichi sokumen." In *Sōsō bosei kenkyū shūsei 3.* Edited by Takeda Chōshū. Tokyo: Meichō shuppan, 93–113.
———. 1986. "Nihon ni okeru senzo no kannen: Ie no keifu to ie no honmatsu no keifu to." In *Nihon no shakaigaku 19: Shūkyō.* Edited by Miyake Hitoshi, Mitsugu Kōmoto, and Shigeru Nishiyama. Tokyo: Tokyo daigaku shuppankai, 86–97.

Asano Hisae. 1991. "'Muen' no na o motsu shomotsu tachi: Kinsei sōshiki tebikisho shōkai." *Bukkyō minzoku kenkyū* 7: 1–21.

Ashigara Shidan Chōsa Kenkyūbu. 1997–98. "Shinkō no michi: Dōhyō chōsa." *Shidan Ashigara* (1) 35: 10–27; (2) 36: 10–38.

Atsugishi Hishobu Shishi Hensanshitsu, ed. 1986. *Atsugishishi: Kinsei shiryōhen 1, shaji.* Atsugi: Atsugishi.

Awano Toshiyuki. 2001. "Dōshōan monjo (1): 'ittei yuzurijō' (1)." *Sanshō* 688: 84–85.

———. 2001. "Dōshōan monjo (3): 'Kinoshita Sōko, Gotō Genjō rensho keijo'." *Sanshō* 690: 92–93.

———. 2001. "Dōshōan monjo (11): 'Sōchin, Matashirō rensho shojō'." *Sanshō* 698: 46–47.

———. 2002. "Dōshōan monjo (15): 'Jin'emon, Tōgorō rensho shōjō'." *Sanshō* 702: 74–75.

———. 2002. "Dōshōan monjo (17): 'Bizen no kuni Dōsen Shijō issatsu'." *Sanshō* 704: 68–69.

———. 2002. "Dōshōan monjo (24)." *Sanshō* 711: 74–75.

Baba Hiroomi. 1990. "Saijōjiryō no daikan to jiryō hyakushō ni tsuite." *Ashigara* 2: 1–22.

Barnes, Nancy J. 1989. "Lady Rokujō's Ghost: Spirit Possession, Buddhism, and Healing in Japanese Literature." *Literature and Medicine* 8: 106–21.

Baroni, Helen J. 1994. "The Emergence of Ōbaku as the Third School of Zen in Japan." *Supplement to the Japanese Religions Bulletin* New Series 18: 1–5.

———. 1994. "Bottled Anger: Episodes in Ōbaku Conflict in the Tokugawa Period." *Japanese Journal of Religious Studies* 21/2–3: 191–210.

———. 2000. *Ōbaku Zen: The Emergence of the Third Sect of Zen in Tokugawa Japan.* Honolulu: University of Hawai'i Press.

Bell, Catherine. 1989. "Religion and Chinese Culture: Toward an Assessment of 'Popular Religion'." *History of Religions* 29/1: 35–57.

Berlinerbau, Jacques. 2001. "Max Weber's Useful Ambiguities and the Problem of Defining 'Popular Religion'." *Journal of the American Academy of Religion* 69/3: 605–26.

Beukers, Harm, et al., eds. 1991. *Red-Hair Medicine: Dutch-Japanese Medical Relations.* Amsterdam: Rodopi.

Birnbaum, Raoul. 1979. *The Healing Buddha.* Boston: Shambhala Publications.

———. 1985–86. "Seeking Longevity in Chinese Buddhism: Long Life Deities and Their Symbolism." *Journal of Chinese Religions* 13–14: 143–76.

Blacker, Carmen. 1978. "The Snake Woman in Japanese Myth and Legend." In *Animals in Folklore.* Edited by J. R. Porter and W.M.S. Russell. Cambridge: D. S. Brewer for the Folklore Society, 113–25.

Bodiford, William M. 1991. "Dharma Transmission in Sōtō Zen: Manzan Dōhaku's Reform Movement." *Monumenta Nipponica* 46/4: 423–51.

———. 1992. "Zen in the Art of Funerals: Ritual Salvation in Japanese Buddhism." *History of Religions* 32/2: 146–64.

———. 1993. *Sōtō Zen in Medieval Japan.* Honolulu: University of Hawai'i Press.

———. 1993–94. "The Enlightenment of Kami and Ghosts: Spirit Ordinations in Sōtō Zen." *Cahiers d'Extrême-Asie* 7: 267–82.

———. 1994. "Sōtō Zen in a Japanese Town: Field Notes on a Once-Every-Thirty-Three-Years Kannon Festival." *Japanese Journal of Religious Studies* 21/1: 3–36.

———. 1996. "Zen and the Art of Religious Prejudice: Efforts to Reform a Tradition of Social Discrimination." *Japanese Journal of Religious Studies* 23/1–2: 1–28.

Bolitho, Harold. 2003. *Bereavement and Consolation: Testimonies from Tokugawa Japan.* New Haven: Yale University Press.

Borgen, Robert S. 1986. *Sugawara no Michizane and the Early Heian Court.* Cambridge: Council on East Asian Studies, Harvard University.

Boscaro, Adriana. 1973. "Toyotomi Hideyoshi and the 1587 Edicts against Christianity." *Oriens extremus* 20: 219–41.

Bouchy, Anne-Marie. 1983. *Tokuhon, ascète du nenbutsu: Dans le cadre d'une étude sur les religieux errants de l'époque d'Edo.* Paris: E.P.H.E., Cahiers d'études et de documents sur les religions du Japon 5.

Boxer, C. R. 1951. *The Christian Century in Japan, 1549–1650.* Berkeley: University of California Press.

Braverman, Arthur. 1994. *Warrior of Zen: The Diamond-Hard Wisdom Mind of Suzuki Shōsan.* Tokyo: Kōdansha International.

Brown, Robert L. 1998. "The Miraculous Buddha Image: Portrait, God, or Object?" In *Images, Miracles, and Authority in Asian Religious Traditions.* Edited by Richard Davis. Boulder; Westview Press, 37–54.

Bunkachō, ed. 2000. *Shūkyō nenkan: Heisei jūichinenban.* Tokyo: Bunkachō bunkabu shūmuka.

Buswell, Robert E., Jr. 1992. *The Zen Monastic Experience.* Princeton: Princeton University Press.

Butler, Lee A. 1994. "Tokugawa Ieyasu's Regulations for the Court: A Reappraisal." *Harvard Journal of Asiatic Studies* 54/2: 509–51.

———. 2002. *Emperor and Aristocracy in Japan, 1467–1680.* Cambridge: Harvard University Asia Center.

Campany, Robert. 1990. "Return-from-Death Narratives in Early Medieval China." *Journal of Chinese Religion* 18: 91–125.

Carpenter, Janet. 1985. "*Sennin*: The Immortals of Taoism." In *Japanese Ghosts and Demons: Art of the Supernatural.* Edited by Stephen Addiss. New York: George Braziller, 57–80.

Chiba Jōryū. 1977. *Kinsei Shinshū no ichigakushō: Shinzenin sōboku no shōgai.* Kyoto: Dōhōsha.

Chiba Jōryū, Fujii Manabu, and Tamamuro Fumio, eds. 1985. *Rekishi kōron 2: Kinsei no bukkyō.* Tokyo: Yūzankaku.

Chibaken Kyōikuchō Shōgai Gakushūbu Bunkaka, ed. 1998. *Chibaken no shitei bunkazai 8.* Chiba: Chibaken kyōiku iinkai.

Chigiri Kōsai. 1977. *Zushū tengu retsuden: Nishi Nihon hen.* Tokyo: Miki shobō.

Chihōshi Kenkyū Kyōgikai, ed. 1990. *Rekishi shiryō hozon kikan sōran.* 2 vols. Tokyo: Yamakawa shuppansha.

Chijiwa Haru. 1991. "Goō hōin to kishōmon." In *Goō hōin: Inori to chikai no jufu.* Edited by Machida Shiritsu Hakubutsukan. Machida: Machida shiritsu hakubutsukan, 7–14.

Ching, Heng, trans. 1974. *Sutra of the Past Vows of Earth Store Bodhisattva.* New York: Buddhist Text Translation Society/Institute for Advanced Studies of World Religions.

Chōkokujishi Hensan Iinkai, ed. 1977. *Azabu Chōkokujishi.* Tokyo: Eiheiji Tokyo betsuin Chōkokuji.

Cieslik, Hubert. 1951. "Die Goningumi im Dienste der Christenüberwachung." *Monumenta Nipponica* 7: 102–55.

Cleary, Thomas. 2000. *Secrets of the Blue Cliff Record: Zen Comments by Hakuin and Tenkei.* Boston: Shambhala Publications.

Clifford, Terry. 1984. *Tibetan Buddhist Medicine and Psychiatry: The Diamond Healing.* York Beach, ME: Samuel Weiser.

Cole, Alan. 1996. "Upside Down/Right Side Up: A Revisionist History of Buddhist Funerals in China." *History of Religions* 35/4: 307–38.

———. 1998. *Mothers and Sons in Chinese Buddhism.* Stanford: Stanford University Press.

Collcutt, Martin. 1981. *Five Mountains: The Rinzai Monastic Institution in Medieval Japan*. Cambridge: Harvard University Press.

———. 1986. "Buddhism: The Threat of Eradication." In *Japan in Transition: From Tokugawa to Meiji*. Edited by Marius B. Jansen and Gilbert Rozman. Princeton: Princeton University Press, 143–67.

Cooper, J. C. 1990. *Chinese Alchemy: The Taoist Quest for Immortality*. New York: Sterling Publishing Co.

Cornell, Laurel. 1996. "Infanticide in Early Modern Japan? Demography, Culture, and Population Growth." *Journal of Asian Studies* 55/1: 22–50.

Cornell, Laurel L., and Akira Hayami. 1986. "The *Shumon aratame-chō*: Japan's Population Registers." *Journal of Family History* 11: 311–28.

Daimon Kōzen. 1996. "Anshin no tame no shūkyō gyōji no ichi kōsatsu: Sōsai o chūshin to shite." *Kyōka kenshū* 39: 127–33.

Daiyūzan Saijōji, ed. 1920. "Gokaichō kōchū sanpai hiwari" *Daiyū jihō* 1/2: 16–17.

———. 1961. *Daiyūzanshi*. Minami Ashigara: Saijōji.

Danitani Behei. 1997. *Ōmine koborebanashi*. Osaka: Tōhō shuppan.

De Benneville, James Seguin. 1917. *The Yotsuya Kwaidan or O'iwa Inari*. Philadelphia: Lippincott.

———. 2001. [1916]. *The Haunted House: More Samurai Tales of the Tokugawa*. London: Kegan Paul.

Deguchi, Midori. 1985. "One Hundred Demons and One Hundred Supernatural Tales." In *Japanese Ghosts and Demons: Art of the Supernatural*. Edited by Stephen Addiss. New York: George Braziller, 15–24.

Demiéville, Paul. 1937. "Byō." In *Hōbōgirin, Fasc. 3*. Paris: Librairie d'amérique et d'Orient, 224–70.

———. 1985. *Buddhism and Healing: Demiéville's Article "Byō" from Hōbōgirin*. Translation by Mark Tatz. Lanham, MD: University Press of America.

De Visser, Marinus Willem. 1908. "The Tengu." *Transactions of the Asiatic Society of Japan* 36,2: 25–99.

———. 1913. *The Dragon in China and Japan*. Amsterdam: Verhandelingen der Koniklijke Akademie van Weteschappen.

———. 1914. *The Bodhisattva Titsang (Jizō) in China and Japan*. Berlin: Oesterheld and Co.

Dosse, François. 1994. *New History in France: The Triumph of the Annales*. Urbana: University of Illinois Press.

Dunn, C. J. 1966. *The Early Japanese Puppet Drama*. London: Luzan and Co.

Duquenne, Robert. 1972. "Sanshakubō Gongen, an Aspect of Fudō Myō-ō." *Transactions of the International Conference of Orientalists in Japan* 17: 119–20.

Dykstra, Yoshiko Kurata. 1978. "Jizō, the Most Merciful: Tales from *Jizō Bosatsu Reigenki*." *Monumenta Nipponica* 33/2: 178–200.

Earns, Lane. 1994. "The Nagasaki Bugyo and the Development of Bureaucratic Rule in Seventeenth-Century Japan." *Asian Culture* 22/2: 63–73.

Ebersole, Gary. 1989. *Ritual Poetry and the Politics of Death in Early Japan*. Princeton: Princeton University Press.

Ebisawa Arimichi. 1955. "Kirishitan bateren tsuihōrei." *Rekishi kyōiku* 3/9: 87–93.

———. 1960. *Christianity in Japan: A Bibliography of Japanese and Chinese Sources (Part 1, 1543–1858)*. Tokyo: International Christian University.

———. 1981. *Kirishitan no dan'atsu to teikō*. Tokyo: Yūzankaku.

Egaku Kyokusui, ed. 1989. *Zenshū no ingō, dōgō, kaimyō jiten*. Tokyo: Kokusho kankōkai.

Eiheijishi Hensan Iinkai, ed. 1982. *Eiheijishi*. 2 vols. Eiheijichō: Daihonzan Eiheiji.

———. 2002. *Eiheiji shiryō zensho 1*. Eiheijichō: Daihonzan Eiheiji.

Eisenhofer-Halim, Hannelore. 1995. *Dōshō (629–700): Leben und Werken eines japanis-*

*chen Buddhisten vor dem Hintergrund der chinesisch-japanischen Beziehungen im 7.
    Jh.* Frankfurt am Maim: Peter Lang.
Elison, George. 1991. *Deus Destroyed: The Image of Christianity in Early Modern
    Japan.* Cambridge: Council on East Asian Studies, Harvard University.
Elisonas, Jurgis. 2000. "The Jesuits, the Devil, and Pollution in Japan." *Bulletin of Por-
    tuguese Japanese Studies* 1: 3–27.
El-Tom, Abdullahi Osman. 1985. "Drinking the Koran: The Meaning of the Koranic
    Verses in Berti Erasure." *Africa* 55/4: 414–31.
Endō Hiroaki. 1981. "Zenshū no chihō hatten: Sado chihō o chūshin to shite." *Ko-
    mazawa daigaku shigaku ronshū* 11: 34–53.
———. 1986. "Chūsei makki no sōran to Sōtōshū jiin no dōkō: Kita, higashi Shinano
    chihō o chūshin to shite." *Chihōshi kenkyū* 201: 44–56.
———. 1987. "Minami Izu ni okeru Kakusōha no tenkai: Daibaiji o chūshin o shite."
    Shūgaku kenkyū 29: 151–56.
———. 1988. "Mikawa no kuni Ryūkeiin rinjūsei to chiiki shakai: 'shidōchō' bunseki o
    chūshin to shite." *Shūgaku kenkyū* 30: 156–61.
———. 1988. "Saijōjizō 'saijō zenji rintōchō' ni tsuite." *Shūgaku kenkyū* 31: 191–96.
———. 1989. "Sengoku daimyō Takedashi no Sōtōshū tōsei to Saijōji rinjū mondai."
    Komazawa daigaku shigaku ronshū 19: 52–61.
———. 1991. "Rinjū jiin ni okeru jūji ninmei hōhō ni tsuite." *Shūgaku kenkyū* 33:
    239–44.
Endō Jun. 1998. "'The Shinto Funeral Movement' in Early Modern and Modern Japan."
    Translation by Norman Havens. *Nihon bunka kenkyūsho kiyō* 82: 1–31.
Endō Kazuko. 1993. *Toyama no kusuri uri.* Tokyo: Simul shuppansha.
Enomoto [Shōshi] Chika. 1986. "Yamagataken Murayama chihō no jigoku-e to etoki."
    Etoki kenkyū 4: 16–32.
———. 1994. "Morinji to bunbuku kagama." *Ōtsuma joshi daigaku kiyō* 26: 135–57.
Faure, Bernard. 1991. *The Rhetoric of Immediacy: A Cultural Critique of Chan/Zen
    Buddhism.* Princeton: Princeton University Press.
———. 1993. *Chan Insights and Oversights.* Princeton: Princeton University Press.
———. 1995. "Quand l'habit fait le moine: The Symbolism of the Kāsāya in Sōtō Zen."
    Cahiers d'Extrême-Asie 8: 335–69.
———. 1996. *Visions of Power: Imagining Medieval Japanese Buddhism.* Princeton:
    Princeton University Press.
———. 1997. *The Will to Orthodoxy: A Critical Genealogy of Northern Chan Bud-
    dhism.* Stanford: Stanford University Press.
———. 1998. *The Red Thread: Buddhist Approaches to Sexuality.* Princeton: Princeton
    University Press.
———. 2003. *The Power of Denial: Buddhism, Purity, and Gender.* Princeton: Princeton
    University Press.
Filliozat, Jean. 1934. "La médicine indienne et l'expansion bouddhique en Extrême-
    Orient." *Journal Asiatique* 224: 301–11.
Finckh, Elisabeth. 1978. *Foundations of Tibetan Medicine.* Vol. 1. London: Watkins.
Fister, Patricia. 1985. "*Tengu*, the Mountain Goblin." In *Japanese Ghosts and Demons: Art
    of the Supernatural.* Edited by Stephen Addiss. New York: George Braziller, 103–28.
———. 2000. "Creating Devotional Art with Body Fragments: The Buddhist Nun Bunchi
    and Her Father, Emperor Gomizuno-o." *Japanese Journal of Religious Studies* 27/3–4:
    213–38.
Formanek, Susanne. 1993. "Pilgrimage in the Edo Period: Forerunner of Medieval Do-
    mestic Pilgrimage? The Example of the Pilgrimage to Mt. Tateyama." In *The Culture
    of Japan as Seen through Its Leisure.* Edited by Sepp Linhart and Sabine Frühstück. Al-
    bany: State University of New York Press, 165–94.
Foulk, T. Griffith. 1987. "The "Ch'an School" and Its Place in the Buddhist Monastic
    Tradition." Ph.D. dissertation, University of Michigan.

Fowler, Sherry. 1997. "In Search of the Dragon: Mt. Murō's Sacred Topography." *Japanese Journal of Religious Studies* 24/1–2: 145–62.

Fujii Manabu and Sakurai Keiyū, eds. 1988. *Nanzenji monjo, gekan*. Kyoto: Nanzenji shūmu honsho.

Fujii Masao and Itō Yuishin. 1997. *Sōsai bukkyō: Sono rekishi to gendaiteki kadai*. Tokyo: Jōdoshū sōgō kenkyūsho.

Fujikawa Yū. 1980. *Fujikawa Yū cho sakushū 3*. Kyoto: Shibunkaku shuppan.

Fujiki Atsunori. 1988. "Honji matsuji keisei no ichi kōsatsu: Dairenji to Taiunji no baai." *Niigata Kōnan kōkō kenkyū shūroku* 16: 1–16.

———. 1992. "Sado no kuni ni okeru Sōtōshū Tsūgenha no kyōsen tenkai ni tsuite." *Niigata Kōnan kōkō kenkyū shūroku* 20: 1–23.

Fujita Teikō. 1996. *Kinsei Shugendō no chiikiteki tenkai*. Tokyo: Iwata shoin.

Fujiyoshi Jikai. 1979. "Suzuki Shōsan to kirisutokyō." *Zen bunka kenkyūsho kiyō* 11: 127–47; rpt. in *Suzuki Shōsan no Zen*. Kyoto: Zen bunka kenkyūsho, 1984, 181–202.

———. 1984. *Suzuki Shōsan no Zen*. Kyoto: Zen bunka kenkyūsho.

Fukuda Ajio. 1976. "Kinsei jidan seido no seiritsu to fukudanka." *Shakai denshō kenkyū* 5: 32–49.

———. 1992. "Kinsei jidan seido to fukudanka." In *Bukkyō minzokugaku taikei 7: Tera to chiiki shakai*. Edited by Togawa Anshō. Tokyo: Meichō shuppan, 49–66.

Furuta Shōkin. 1956. *Kinsei no Zensha tachi*. Kyoto: Heirakuji shoten.

Futaba Kenkō, ed. 1980–81. *Nihon bukkyōshi kenkyū: Kokka to bukkyō, kinsei, kindaihen*. 2 vols. Kyoto: Nagata bunshōdō.

———. 1990. *Nihon bukkyōshi chū*. Kyoto: Nagata bunshōdō.

———. 1990. *Shiryō Nihon bukkyōshi kenkyū chū: Ōtomi seiken kara kinsei*. Kyoto: Nagata bunshōdō.

Galassi, Francesco L. 1992. "Buying a Passport to Heaven: Usury, Restitution, and the Merchants of Medieval Genoa." *Religion* 4: 313–26.

Girard, Fréderic. 2002. "Discours bouddhiques face au christianisme." In *Repenser l'ordre, repenser l'héritage: Paysage intellectuel du Japon (XVIIe–XIXe siècles)*. Edited by Fréderic Girard, Annick Horiuchi, and Mieko Macé. Geneva: Librairie Droz, 167–207.

Glassman, Hank. 1999. "*Mokuren no sōshi*: The Tale of Mokuren." *Buddhist Literature* 1: 120–61.

———. 2001. "The Religious Construction of Motherhood in Medieval Japan." Ph.D. dissertation, Stanford University, 2001.

———. 2002. "The Nude Jizō at Denkōji: Notes on Women's Salvation in Kamakura Buddhism." In *Engendering Faith: Women and Buddhism in Pre-Modern Japan*. Edited by Barbara Ruch. Ann Arbor: Center for Japanese Studies, University of Michigan, 383–413.

———. 2004. "At the Crossroads of Birth and Death: The Blood-Pool Hell and Post-mortem Fetal Extraction." In *Death Rituals and the Afterlife in Japanese Buddhism*. Edited by Mariko Walter and Jacqueline Stone. Honolulu: University of Hawai'i Press.

Gonoi Takashi. 1983. *Tokugawa shoki Kirishitanshi kenkyū*. Tokyo: Yoshikawa kōbunkan.

———. 1995. "Keichō jūkyūnen shōgatsu no Kyoto ni okeru Kirisutokyō hakugai ni kansuru ichi kōsatsu: Shoki bakusei to Kirisutokyō." In *Kinsei shakai to shūkyō*. Edited by Fujino Tamotsu. Tokyo: Yūzankaku, 385–420.

Goodwin, Janet. 1989. "Shooing the Dead to Paradise." *Japanese Journal of Religious Studies* 16/1: 63–80.

Gosen Shishi Hensan Iinkai, ed. 1997. *Gosen shishi: Shiryō 3, kinsei 2*. Gosen, Niigata: Gosenshi.

Grapard, Allan G. 1982. "Flying Mountains and Walkers of Emptiness: Toward a Definition of Sacred Space in Japanese Religions." *History of Religions* 21/3: 195–221.

———. 1984. "Japan's Cultural Revolution: The Separation of Shinto and Buddhist Divinities in Meiji (*shimbutsu bunri*) and a Case Study: Tōnomine." *History of Religions* 23/3: 240–65.

———. 1986. "Lotus in the Mountain, Mountain in the Lotus: *Rokugō Kaizan Nimmon Daibosatsu Hongi.*" *Monumenta Nipponica* 41/1: 21–50.

———. 1990. "Preface: Ritual and Power." *Journal of Ritual Studies* 4/ 2: 1–4.

———. 1993. "The Textualized Mountain—Enmountained Text: The Lotus Sutra in Kunisaki." In *The Lotus Sutra in Japanese Culture.* Edited by George Tanabe and Willa Tanabe. Honolulu: University of Hawai'i Press, 159–90.

———. 1994. "Geosophia, Geognosis, and Geopiety: Orders of Significance in Japanese Representations of Space." In *NowHere: Space, Time, and Modernity.* Edited by Roger Friedland and Deirdre Boden. Berkeley: University of California Press, 372–401.

———. 1998. "Geotyping Sacred Space: The Case of Mount Hiko in Japan." In *Sacred Space: Shrine, City, Land.* Edited by Benjamin Kedar and Zwi Werblowsky. New York: New York University Press, 215–49.

Gregory, Peter. 1999. "The Vitality of Buddhism in the Sung." In *Buddhism in the Sung.* Edited by Peter Gregory and Daniel Getz. Honolulu: University of Hawai'i Press, 1–20.

Groemer, Gerald. 2000. "A Short History of *Gannin*: Popular Religious Performers in Tokugawa Japan." *Japanese Journal of Religious Studies* 27/2: 41–72.

———. 2001. "The Creation of the Edo Outcaste Order." *Journal of Japanese Studies* 27/2: 263–94.

Gross, Lawrence. 1998. "Manzan Dōhaku and the Transmission of the Teaching." Ph.D. dissertation, Stanford University.

Grotenhuis, Elizabeth ten. 1999. *Japanese Mandalas: Representations of Sacred Geography.* Honolulu: University of Hawai'i Press.

Haga Noboru. 1970. *Sōgi no rekishi.* Tokyo: Yūzankaku.

Hagiwara Tatsuo. 1970. "Tone chūryū chihō ni okeru Sōtōshū no hatten." *Ibaraki kenshi kenkyū* 17: 23–32.

———. 1980. "Ansei yonenban Ketsubonkyō engi (Abikoshi Shōsenji shozō)." *Shiryō to denshō* 1: 20–22.

———. 1980. "Kumano bikuni no seitai." In *Nihon minzoku fūdoron.* Edited by Chiba Tokuji. Tokyo: Kōbundō, 269–82.

———. 1983. *Miko to bukkyōshi.* Tokyo: Yoshikawa kōbunkan.

———. 1985. "Chomei Zenshū jiin no nazo to sono kaimei: Shimousa Sōneiji, Shimotsuke Daichūji no baai." In *Dōgen zenji to Sōtōshū.* Edited by Kawamura Kōdō and Ishikawa Rikizan. Tokyo: Yoshikawa kōbunkan, 250–68.

———. 1985. "Kumano bikuni to etoki." In *Nihon no koten bungaku 3: Issatsu no kōza, Etoki.* Tokyo: Yūseidō, 57–67.

———. 1998. "Kumano bikuni no shimei." In *Kumano sanzan shinkō jiten.* Edited by Katō Takahisa. Tokyo: Ebisu kōshō shuppan kabushiki gaisha, 296–309.

Hakone Chōritsu Kyōdo Shiryōkan, ed. 1997. "*Tōji no michi*" *kankei shiryō chōsa hōkokusho.* Hakone: Hakone chōritsu kyōdo shiryōkan.

Hall, David. 1989. *Worlds of Wonder, Days of Judgement: Popular Religious Belief in Early New England.* New York: Alfred A. Knopf.

———, ed. 1997. *Lived Religion in America: Toward a History of Practice.* Princeton: Princeton University Press.

Hanuki Masai. 1962. "Tōmon Zensō to shinjin kedo no setsuwa." *Komazawa shigaku* 10: 44–51; rpt. in *Chūsei Zenrin seiritsushi no kenkyū.* Tokyo: Yoshikawa kōbunkan, 1993: 335–40.

———. 1968. "Chūsei Aizuryō no Zenshū shoha to sono dan'otsu." *Komazawa shigaku* 15: 18–36.

———. 1974. "Zenshū no chihō hatten to kyūbukkyō." *Chihōshi kenkyū* 130: 17–19.

———. 1993. *Chūsei Zenrin seiritsushi no kenkyū.* Tokyo: Yoshikawa kōbunkan.

————. 1994. "Chūsei, kinsei ni okeru Sōtōshū no hatten to bōshō." *Kyōka kenshū* 37: 31–44.

Hara Jun'ichirō. 1998. "Ōyama, Fuji, Enoshima." *Chihōshi kenkyū* 274: 24–28.

Harada Kōdō. 1988. "Sōjiji goin rinjū seido kō." *KDBK* 46: 48–78.

Harada Masatoshi. 1998. *Nihon chūsei no Zenshū to shakai*. Tokyo: Yoshikawa kōbunkan.

Hardacre, Helen. 1994. "Conflict between Shugendō and the New Religions of Bakumatsu Japan." *Japanese Journal of Religious Studies* 21/2–3: 137–67.

————. 1997. *Marketing the Menacing Fetus in Japan*. Berkeley: University of California Press.

————. 2001. "Sources for the Study of Religion and Society in the Late Edo Period." *Japanese Journal of Religious Studies* 28,3–4: 227–60.

————. 2002. *Religion and Society in Nineteenth-Century Japan: A Study of the Southern Kanto Region, Using Late Edo and Early Meiji Gazetteers*. Ann Arbor: Center for Japanese Studies, University of Michigan.

Hareyama Shun'ei. 2001. "Jukai nyūi ni tsuite." *Shūgaku kenkyū kiyō* 14: 127–46.

Harrison, Elizabeth. 1992. "Encountering Amida: Jōdo Shinshū Sermons in Eighteenth-Century Japan." Ph.D. dissertation, University of Chicago.

Hasebe Hachirō. 2002. "Sōden ni miru 'densetsu' no igi: 'Eihei kaisan genzenji gyōjō denmonki' o megutte." In *Dōgen zenji kenkyū ronshū: Dōgen zenji nanahyaku gojukai daionkinen shuppan*. Eiheijichō: Daihonzan Eiheiji daionki kyoku, 538–64.

Hasegawa Masatoshi. 1980. *Kinsei nenbutsusha shūdan no kōdō to shisō: Jōdoshū no baai*. Tokyo: Hyōronsha.

————. 1985. *Kinsei Jōdoshū no shinkō to kyōka*. Tokyo: Keisuisha; rpt. Tokyo: Hokushindō, 1988.

Hasegawa Shunpō. 1997. *Gennō Zenji to Jōzaiin*. Fukushima: Jōzaiin.

Haskel, Peter. 1984. *Bankei Zen: Translations from the Record of Bankei*. New York: Grove Weidenfeld Press.

————. 2001. *Letting Go: The Story of Zen Master Tōsui (Tōsui oshō densan)*. Honolulu: University of Hawai'i Press.

Haskel, Peter, and Ryūichi Abe. 1996. *Great Fool: Zen Master Ryōkan—Poems, Letters, and Other Writings*. Honolulu: University of Hawai'i Press.

Hatanaka Toshiyuki. 1992. *"Kawata" to heijin: Kinsei mibun shakairon*. Kyoto: Kamogawa shuppan.

Hattori Toshirō. 1978. *Edo jidai igakushi no kenkyū*. Tokyo: Yoshikawa kōbunkan.

————. 1982. *Shaka no igaku*. Nagoya: Reimei shobō.

Hayashi Hisayoshi. 1997. *Bukkyō ni miru sabetsu no kongen: Sendara, etori hōshi no gongen*. Tokyo: Akashi shoten.

Hayashi Jun. 1994. "Kinsei no sōkai ni kansuru ichi kōsatsu: Sō to zoku no shiten kara." *Nihon bukkyō gakkai nenpō* 59: 265–82.

Hayashi Masahiko. 1984. "Kumano bikuni no etoki." In *Zōho Nihon no etoki: Shiryō to kenkyū*. Tokyo: Miyai shoten, 126–46.

————. 1990. "Etoki suru Kumano bikuni." In *Imēji ridingu sōso: Kaiga no hakken*. Tokyo: Heibonsha, 143–52.

————. 2000. *Etoki no tōzen*. Tokyo: Kasama shoin.

————. 2003. "Bukkyō setsuwaga to etoki: 'Dōjōji engi emaki' no tenkai." *Komazawa daigaku bukkyō bungaku kenkyū* 6: 35–59.

Heine, Steven. 1994. "Sōtō Zen and the Inari Cult: Symbiotic and Exorcistic Trends in Buddhist-Folk Religious Amalgamations." *Pacific World* 10: 75–101.

___. 1999. *Shifting Shape, Shaping Text: Philosophy and Folklore in the Fox Kōan*. Honolulu: University of Hawai'i Press.

Higuchi Seitarō. 1975. "Chūsei ni okeru kitō to iryō." *Nihon ishigaku zasshi* 21/3: 224–36.

Hirano Eiji. 1998. "Fujikō, Ōyamakō no junpai to yūzan." *Chihōshi kenkyū* 274: 29–32.

Hiranuma Yoshirō. 1957. *Kinsei jiin monzenmachi no kenkyū*. Tokyo: Waseda daigaku shuppansha.

Hiraoka Jōkai. 1988. *Nihon jiinshi no kenkyū: Chūsei, kinseihen*. Tokyo: Yoshikawa kōbunkan.

Hiratsukashi Hakubutsukan Shishi Hensangakari, ed. 1993. *Hiratsukashishi 12: Betsuhen minzoku*. Hiratsuka: Hiratsuka.

Hirose Fumihiko. 1998. "Kinsei Higashi Mikawa ni okeru ryōshu to tera to mura: Mikawa no kuni Yanagun Nakaurimura, Sōtōshū Jikōji o jirei to shite." *Komazawa daigaku shigaku ronshū* 28: 73–84.

Hirose Nobuko. 1992. *Immovable Wisdom: The Art of Zen Strategy, The Teachings of Takuan Soho*. Shaftesbury, UK: Element.

Hirose Ryōkō. 1974. "Keizan zenji ni hajimaru Sōtōshū rinjūsei ni tsuite." *Shūgaku kenkyū* 16: 93–98.

———. 1974. "Sōtōshū chihō tenkai ni kansuru ichi kōsatsu: Daichi to Higo no kuni Kikuchishi no baai." *Komazawa shigaku* 21: 38–59.

———. 1976. "Chūsei rinka zenrin no jūji hōhō: Noto Yōkōji rinjūsei no seiritsu to tenkai." *Komazawa shigaku ronshū* 6: 53–71.

———. 1976. "Sōtō Zensō no chihō katsudō: Tōtōmi no kuni ni okeru Shōdō Kōsei no katsudō o chūshin to shite." In *Chihō bunka no dentō to kōzō*. Edited by Chihōshi kenkyū kyōgikai. Tokyo: Yūzankaku, 133–64.

———. 1977. "Chūsei Zen'in no unei to keizai katsudō: Owari no kuni Chitagun Kenkon'in shozō 'ichimaigami utsushi' no bunseki o chūshin to shite." *Komazawa shigaku* 24: 72–91.

———. 1977. "Chūsei Zensō to jukai-e: Aichiken Chitagun Kenkon'inzō 'Kechimyakushū' 'shōshichō' no bunseki o chūshin to shite." In *Minzoku shigaku no hōhō*. Tokyo: Yūzankaku, 305–59; rpt. in *Zenshū chihō tenkaishi no kenkyū*. Tokyo: Yoshikawa kōbunkan, 1988, 422–81.

———. 1978. "Kinsei Sōtōshū ni okeru rokusho secchi ni tsuite." *SKKK* 10: 195–212.

———. 1979. "Chihō zenrin no jūji seido ni kansuru ichi kōsatsu: Tōtōmi Daitōin no rinjūsei." *SKKK* 11: 269–84.

———. 1979. "Eiheiji jūji seido ni kansuru ichi kōsatsu: Shusse, zuisse no mondai o chūshin ni." *Shūgaku kenkyū* 21: 126–32.

———. 1979. "Kinsei Sōtōshū no rokusho setchi to sono keikō." *IBK* 27/2: 369–71.

———. 1979. "Kinsei Sōtōshū sōroku jiin no seiritsu katei: Tōtōmi Kasuisai no baai." In *Kinsei bukkyō no shomondai*. Edited by Tamamuro Fumio and Ōkuwa Hitoshi. Tokyo: Yūzankaku, 85–110.

———. 1979. "Sentai jizōson zō." *Sanshō* (May): 14–15.

———. 1979. "Zenshū no kyōdan unei to rinjūsei: Kaga Budaji, Echizen Ryūtakuji no baai." *Zenshū no shomondai*. Edited by Furuta Shōkin. Tokyo: Yūzankaku, 279–326.

———. 1981. "'Kakochō' kara mita kinsei no Sueyoshimura." In *Hachijōjima Sueyoshichiku bunkazai chōsa hōkoku*. Edited by Kyōikuchō. Tokyo: Kyōikuchō, 121–39.

———. 1982. "Chihō hatten ni tomonau Sōtōshū monpa no taiō." *Shūgaku kenkyū* 24: 161–66.

———. 1983. "Shūkyō to bunka: Yūki no tera to minshū." In *Yūkishishi 5: Kinsei tsūshihen*. Yūki, Ibaraki: Yūkishishi hensanshitsu, 529–639.

———. 1983. "Sōtō Zen sō ni okeru shinjin kedo, akurei chin'atsu." *IBK* 31/2: 233–36; rpt. in *Zenshū chihō tenkaishi no kenkyū*. Tokyo: Yoshikawa kōbunkan, 1988: 415–21, and in *Zen to sono rekishi*. Edited by Ishikawa Rikizan and Hirose Ryōkō. Tokyo: Perikansha, 1999: 275–84.

———. 1983. "Yūki no tera to minshū." In *Yūkishishi 5: Kinsei tsūshi hen*. Yūki: Yūkishishi, 529–639.

————. 1985. "Chū-Kinsei ni okeru Sōtō zensō no kōsatsu: Tōtōmi Daitōin no rinjūsei." *Shūkyō kenkyū* 27: 337–69.

————. 1985. "Chūsei kōki ni okeru zensō zenji to chiiki shakai: Tōkai Kantō chihō no Sōtōshū o chūshin to shite." In *Dōgen zenji to Sōtōshū*. Edited by Kawamura Kōdō and Ishikawa Rikizan. Tokyo: Yoshikawa kōbunkan, 214–49.

————. 1985. "Honmatsu seido no seiritsu to tenkai: Sōtōshū." *Rekishi kōron* 111/2: 54–60.

————. 1987. "Mōoka chihō no jisha." In *Mōokashishi 6*. Mōokashi: Mōokashi, 643–773.

————. 1988. *Zenshū chihō tenkaishi no kenkyū*. Tokyo: Yoshikawa kōbunkan.

————. 1988. "Kita Kantō no gekokujō to Sōtōshū jiin: Yūkishi Tagayashi to Utsunomiyashi Hagashi no baai." *Komazawa shigaku* 39–40: 5–18.

————, with Endō Hiroaki. 1993. "Isobe Anzenji, Mizuumi Fushun'in to Sōtō zenshū no chihō tenkai." In *Sōwa no jiin 2*. Sōwa: Sōwachō kyōiku iinkai, 1–39.

————. 1993. "Sōtōshū kyōdan soshiki no kakuritsu to bakufu no shūkyō tōsei." In *Dōgen shisō no ayumi 3: Edo jidai*. Edited by Sōtōshū Shūgaku Kenkyūsho. Tokyo: Yoshikawa kōbunkan, 248–90.

————. 1995. "Nihon Sōtōshū no chū, kinsei ni okeru jukai to kaimyō." In *Kaimyō no imi to kinō*. Edited by Sōtōshū Gendai Kyōgaku Center. Tokyo: Sōtōshū gendai kyōgaku center, 59–81.

————. ed. 1997. *Jikōjishi*. Aichi: Jikōji.

————. 1997. "Mura no jiin to murabito no kaimyō." In *Shōen to mura o aruku*. Edited by Fujiki Hisashi and Arano Yasunori. Tokyo: Azekura shobō, 393–424.

————. 1997–98. "Sōtōshū no tenkai to chiiki shakai." *Chōryū* (1) 559: 20–28; (2) 560: 26–30; (3) 561: 25–30; (4) 562: 25–31; (5) 563: 25–31; (6) 564: 25–28; (7) 565: 25–32; (8) 566: 25–29; (9) 567: 21–26; (10) 568: 20–29; (11) 569: 27–32.

————. 2002. "Chū-kinsei ni okeru Kinoshita Dōshōan to Sōtōshū kyōdan." In *Dōgen zenji kenkyū ronshū: Dōgen zenji nanahyaku gojukai daionkinen shuppan*. Eiheijichō: Daihonzan Eiheiji daionki kyoku, 565–616.

Hiruma Hisashi. 1973. "Edo no kaichō, Edo kaichō nenpyō." In *Edo chōnin no kenkyū 2*. Edited by Nishiyama Matsunosuke. Tokyo: Yoshikawa kōbunkan, 273–548.

————. 1980. *Edo no kaichō*. Tokyo: Yoshikawa kōbunkan.

Hiruta Genshirō. 1985. *Hayariyamai to kitsune-tsuki: Kinsei shomin no iryō jijō*. Tokyo: Misuzu shobō.

Honda Hideo. 1983. "Meijiki no Sekimotojuku to Saijōji (3)." *Daiyū* 27: 21–24.

Honganji Kikan Undō Honbu Jimukyoku. 1997. *Hōmyō, kakochō*. Kyoto: Honganji shuppan.

Horiguchi Hideki. 1992. "Gunmaken jiin meisaichō sakuin." *Sōbun* 9: 53–106.

Hoshino Gentei. 1972. "Satsumahan no Shinshū kinsei to Honganji no dōkō." *Shinshū kenkyū* 17: 16–25.

————. 1980. "Satsumahan no shoki Shinshū kinsei seisaku." In *Bukkyō no rekishi to bunka*. Edited by Bukkyō Shigakkai. Kyoto: Dōhōsha shuppan, 757–84.

————. 1984. "Satsumahan no kenchiku shihai to Shinshū kinseisaku." *Shinshū kenkyū* 28: 1–16.

Hou, Ching-lang. 1975. *Monnaies d'offrande et la notion de trésorerie dans la religion chinoise*. Paris: Institut des Hautes Études Chinoises, Collège de France.

Hōzawa Naohide. 2000. "Kinsei." In *Nihon bukkyō no kenkyū hō*. Edited by Nihon Bukkyō Kenkyūkai. Kyoto: Hōzōkan, 47–61.

Hozumi Nobushige. 1903. *Goningumi seido*. Tokyo: Yūhikaku shobō.

Hsing Yun. 2002. *Sutra of the Medicine Buddha with an Introduction, Comments and Prayers*. Hacienda Heights, CA: Buddha's Light Publishing.

Hur, Nam-Lin. 2000. *Prayer and Play in Late Tokugawa Japan: Asakusa Sensōji and Edo Society*. Cambridge: East Asian Monographs 185, Harvard University Asia Center.

————. forthcoming. *Death and Social Order in Tokugawa Japan: Buddhism, Anti-Christianity, and the Danka System.* Cambridge: Harvard University Asia Center.

Ichimura Shōhei, 1994. *Zen Master Keizan's Monastic Regulations.* Tsurumi: Daihonzan Sōjiji.

Ifune Manzen. 1972. *Kyōdo Zenshūshi: Jushū (Machino, Yanagida-udetsu o fukumu) jiin no seiritsu o chūshin ni.* Tamasu: Seisui bunko.

Iishiro Kazuko. 1985. "Matsudo daigongen to Matsudōkō: Shinai ni okeru nyoninkō no hensen katei o tōshite." *Abikoshishi kenkyū* 9: 173–99.

Iizuka Daiten. 1999. "Chūsei Sōtōshū ni okeru kirigami no sōden ni tsuite." *Shūgaku kenkyū* 41: 175–80.

Ikegami Songi. 1979. "Kinsei Nichiren kyōdan no honmatsu kankei." In *Kinsei Bukkyō no shomondai.* Edited by Tamamuro Fumio and Ōkuwa Hitoshi. Tokyo: Yūzankaku, 47–63.

Imaeda Aishin. 1961. "Nihon bukkyō no chiiki hatten: Zenshū." *Bukkyō shigaku kenkyū* 9/3–4: 2–15.

Imamura Michio. 1983. *Nihon no minkan iryō.* Tokyo: Kōbundō.

Imatani Akira and Takano Toshihiko, ed. 1998. *Chūkinsei no shūkyō to kokka.* Tokyo: Iwata shoin.

Inobe Shigeo. 1928. *Fuji no shinkō.* Tokyo: Kokin shoin; rpt. Tokyo: Heibonsha, 1983.

Ishida Mizumaro. 1995. *Nyobon: Hijiri no sei.* Tokyo: Chikuma shobō.

Ishii Ryōsuke. 1995. "Yoshiwara." In *Nyonin sabetsu to kinsei senmin.* Edited by Ishii Ryōsuke and Arai Kōjirō. Tokyo: Akashi shoten, 9–178.

Ishikawa Rikizan. 1981. "Chūsei ni okeru Zenshū kirigami no shiryōteki kachi." *Shūkyō kenkyū* 54/3: 219–20.

————. 1982. "Chūsei Sōtōshū kirigami no denshō ni tsuite." *IBK* 30/2: 742–46.

————. 1983–93. "Chūsei Sōtōshū kirigami no bunrui shiron." (1) *KDBK* 41 (1983): 338–50; (2) *KDBR* 14 (1983): 123–55; (3) *KDBK* 42 (1984): 82–96; (4) *KDBR* 15 (1984): 152–69; (5) *KDBK* 43 (1985): 94–116; (6) *KDBR* 16 (1985): 102–52; (7) *KDBK* 44 (1986): 250–67; (8) *KDBR* 17 (1986): 179–213; (9) *KDBK* 45 (1987): 167–98; (10) *KDBR* 18 (1987): 163–92; (11) *KDBK* 46 (1988): 128–55; (12) *KDBR* 19 (1988): 159–97; (13) *KDBK* 47 (1989): 157–89; (14) *KDBR* 20 (1989): 108–34; (15) *KDBK* 48 (1990): 22–41; (16) *KDBR* 21 (1990): 142–68; (17) *KDBK* 49 (1991): 1–19; (18) *KDBR* 22 (1991): 24–34; (19) *KDBK* 50 (1992): 29–50; (20) *KDBR* 23 (1992): 95–126; (21) *KDBK* 51 (1993): 100–25.

————. 1985. "Chūsei Sōtōshū to reizan shinkō." *IBK* 33/2: 26–31.

————. 1985. "Chūsei Zenshū to shinbutsu shūgō: Toku ni Sōtōshū no chihōteki tenkai to kirigami shiryō o chūshin ni shite." *Nihon bukkyō* 60–61: 41–56.

————. 1985. "Sabetsu kirigami to sabetsu jishō ni tsuite." *Shūgaku kenkyū* 27: 137–42.

————. 1989. "Chūsei Sōtōshū ni okeru jukai girei ni tsuite: Shuju no jukai girei shinansho no hassei to sono shakaiteki kinō." *Bukkyō shigaku kenkyū* 32/3: 60–80.

————. 1991. "'shōbōgenzō' no gōron to 'Denkōroku,' 'shushōgi' no gōron." *Shūgaku kenkyū* 33: 105–12.

————. 1995. "Kirigami denshō to kinsei Sōtōshū: 'Betsubuku,' 'motsugo sasō' kankei kirigami no kinseiteki henyō o megutte." In *Minzoku shūkyō no kōzō to keifu.* Edited by Tamamuro Fumio. Tokyo: Yūzankaku, 298–322.

————. 2000. "The Transmission of *Kirigami* (Secret Initiation Documents): A Sōtō Practice in Medieval Japan." In *The Koan: Text and Context in Zen Buddhism.* Edited by Steve Heine and Dale Wright. Translated by Seishū Kawahashi. Oxford: Oxford University Press, 233–43.

————. 2001. *Zenshū sōden shiryō no kenkyū.* 2 vols. Kyoto: Hōzōkan.

Itabashi Kuritsu Bijutsukan, ed. 2001. *Ano yo no jōkei.* Tokyo: Itabashi kuritsu bijutsukan.

Itasaka Yōko, ed. 1987. *Edo onsen kikō.* Tokyo: Heibonsha.

Itō Atsushi. 2002. *Nihon no sarayashiki densetsu.* Fukuoka: Kaichōsha.

Itō Dōgaku, Chishō Misawa, and Shōei Watanabe. 1986. *Dōryōson teito gojun junshakuki*. Minami Ashigara: Daiyūzan Saijōji.

Itō Kanji. 1991. "Sosen sūhai to ie." In *Sorei shinkō*. Edited by Akata Mitsuo. Tokyo: Yūzankaku, 371–86.

Itō Katsumi. 1993. "Toshi to Zenshū jiin." *Shinagawa rekishikan kiyō* 8: 51–92.

Itō, Lucy S. 1952. "Kō: Japanese Confraternities." *Monumenta Nipponica* 8: 411–15.

Itō Yoshihisa. 2001. "Sōtōshū kyōdan ni okeru sōsaishi: Keizan zenji no shūhen made." *Shūgaku kenkyū kiyō* 14: 219–32.

Itō Yūshin. 1997. "Bukkyō to sōsai: Hitotsu no Nihon bukkyōron." In *Sōsai bukkyō: Sono rekishi to gendaiteki kadai*. Edited by Fujii Masao and Itō Yuishin. Tokyo: Jōdoshū sōgō kenkyūsho, 3–22.

Iwamoto Issaku. 1997. "Daiyūzan no sugibayashi." *Shidan Ashigara* 35: 72–79.

Iwanaga Shōsei et al. 2003. " 'Nihon tōjō rentōroku' no kenkyū (1)." *KDZN* 15: 145–204.

Iwasaka Michiko and Barre Toelken. 1994. *Ghosts and the Japanese: Cultural Experience in Japanese Death Legends*. Logan: Utah State University Press.

Iwasaki Sōjun. 1974. " 'Dōryōgū Tokyo kaichō sankeizu' ni tsuite." *Shidan Ashigara* 12: 10–12.

———. 1993. "Daiyūzan Saijōji rinjūsei ni tsuite (1)." *Daiyū* 55: 11–16.

Iwaya Kyōju. 1988. "Buraku jiinsei ni tsuite no ichi kōsatsu: Harima no kuni Shinshū kyōdan o chūshin ni." *Dōwa kyōiku ronkyū* 10: 128–51.

Jaffe, Richard. 2001. *Neither Monk nor Layman: Clerical Marriage in Modern Japanese Buddhism*. Princeton: Princeton University Press.

Jannetta, Ann Bowman. 1987. *Epidemics and Mortality in Early Modern Japan*. Princeton: Princeton University Press.

———. 1992. "Famine Mortality in Nineteenth-Century Japan: The Evidence from a Temple Register." *Population Studies* 46: 427–43.

———. 2001. "Disease Dissemination in the Early Modern World: Connecting East and West." In *Higashi to nishi no iryō bunka*. Edited by Yoshida Tadashi and Yasuaki Fukuse. Kyoto: Shibunkaku shuppan, 3–17.

Jiin Honmatsuchō Kenkyūkai, ed. 1981. *Edo bakufu jiin honmatsuchō shūsei*. 3 vols. Tokyo: Yūzankaku.

Jordan, Brenda. 1985. "*Yūrei*: Tales of Female Ghosts." In *Japanese Ghosts and Demons: Art of the Supernatural*. Edited by Stephen Addiss. New York: George Braziller, 25–48.

Kagamishima Hiroyuki. 1937. "Sekkyōbushi ni okeru Dōgen zenji denki no kyakushoku: Eiheiji kaisanki ni tsuite." *Dōgen* 4/2: 15–17; 4/3: 10–13.

Kagamishima Sōjun, ed. 1980. [1944]. *Enkyōdo Sōtōshū jiin honmatsuchō*. Tsurumi: Daihonzan Sōjiji; rpt. Tokyo: Meicho fukyūkai.

Kageyama Gyōo, ed. 1956. *Nichirenshū Fuju Fuseha no kenkyū*. Kyoto: Heirakuji shoten.

Kaji Nobuyuki. 1994. *Chinmoku no shūkyō: Jukyō*. Tokyo: Chikuma shoten.

Kamii Fumiaki. 1997. "Jōdoshū sōgishiki no hensen." In *Sōsai bukkyō: Sono rekishi to gendaiteki kadai*. Edited by Fujii Masao and Itō Yuishin. Tokyo: Jōdoshū sōgō kenkyūsho, 51–95.

Kamstra, J. H. 1988. "Jizō on the Verge of Life and Death: The Bodhisattva-God of Japan's Buddhism of the Dead." In *Funerary Symbols and Religion*. Edited by J. H. Kamstra et al. Kampen: J. H. Kok, 73–88.

Kanno Yōsuke. 2002. "Kinsei no sōryo, shugen to mura shakai." *Komazawa daigaku shigaku ronshū* 32: 65–78.

Kanzaki Akitoshi. 1970. "Ryōshu to nōmin: Kenchichō to ninbetsuchō." In *Kinsei kyōdoshi kenkyūhō: Kyōdoshi kenkyū kōza 4*. Edited by Furushima Toshio et al. Tokyo: Akakura shoten, 113–62.

Kasahara Kazuo. 1978. *Kinsei ōjōden no sekai: Seiji kenryoku to shūkyō to minshū.* Tokyo: Kyōikusha.

———, ed. 2001. *A History of Japanese Religions.* Tokyo: Kōsei Publishing Co.

Kashiwahara Yūsen. 1971. *Kinsei shomin bukkyō no kenkyū.* Kyoto: Hōzōkan.

———. 1996. *Shinshūshi bukkyōshi no kenkyū 2: Kinsei.* Kyoto: Heirakuji.

Kashiwahara Yūsen and Fujii Manabu. 1973. *Kinsei bukkyō no shisō.* Tokyo: Zoku Nihon shisō taikei 5, Iwanami shoten.

Kasuisai Shiryōshū Hensan Iinkai, ed. 1989–98. *Kasuisai shiryōshū.* 5 vols. Kyoto: Shibunkaku shuppan.

Katayama Shūken. 1973. "Suzuki Shōsan no chosaku oyobi jūishū ni okeru ichi kōsatsu to Shimabarashi toshokanzō 'Ha Kirishitan' no shōkai." *SKKK* 5: 128–29.

Katsurai Kazuo. 1976. "Kama no gara ni kansuru kinpi: Taiji bunri no koshū nōto." *Tosa minzoku* 30: 1–3; rpt. in *Sōsō bosei kenkyū shūsei Vol. 1: Sōhō.* Tokyo: Meicho shuppan, 1979, 291–95.

Katz, Paul R. 1995. *Demon Hordes and Burning Boats: The Cult of Marshal Wen in Late Imperial Chekiang.* Albany: State University of New York Press.

Kawaguchi Kyōko. 1961. "Kirishitan korobi shōmon." *Kumamoto shigaku* 19/20: 39–69.

Kawakami Mitsuyo. 1988. "Two Views of Spirits as Seen in the Bon Observances of the Shima Region." *Japanese Journal of Religious Studies* 15/2–3: 121–30.

Kawatō Masashi. 2002. *Nihon no yume shinkō.* Machida: Tamagawa daigaku shuppanbu.

Kawamura Kōdō. 1975. *Shohan taikō Eihei kaisan Dōgen zenji gyōjō Kenzeiki.* Tokyo: Taishukan shoten.

Kelly, William W. 1994. "Incendiary Actions: Fires and Firefighting in the Shogun's Capital and the People's City." In *Edo and Paris: Urban Life and the State in the Early Modern Era.* Edited by James McClain, John Merriman, and Ugawa Kaoru. Ithaca: Cornell University Press, 310–31.

Ketelaar, James. 1990. *Of Heretics and Martyrs in Meiji Japan: Buddhism and Its Persecution.* Princeton: Princeton University Press.

Kieschnick, John. 1997. *The Eminent Monk: Buddhist Ideals in Medieval Chinese Hagiography.* Honolulu: Kuroda Institute Studies in East Asian Buddhism 10, University of Hawai'i Press.

———. 2000. "Blood Writing in Chinese Buddhism." *Journal of the International Association of Buddhist Studies* 23/2: 177–94.

———. 2003. *The Impact of Buddhism on Chinese Material Culture.* Princeton: Princeton University Press.

Kikuchi Takeshi. 1978. "Kinsei bukkyō tōsei no ichi kenkyū: Ihōgi hatto no jittai to sono haikei." *Nihon rekishi* 365: 66–88.

Kimura Shungen and Takenaka Chitai. 1998. *Zenshū no darani.* Tokyo: Daitō shuppansha.

King, Winston. 1986. *Death was His Kōan: The Samurai Zen of Suzuki Shōsan.* Berkeley: Asian Humanities Press.

Kinoshita Futoshi. 1998. "Mortality Crises in the Tokugawa Period: A View from the *Shūmon Aratame-Chō* in Northeastern Japan." *Nichibunken Japan Review* (1998): 53–72.

Kinoshita Jūzō. 1981. "Dōshōan ni tsuite." *Sanshō* 457 (September): 64–67.

———. 1988. "Dōshōan to Kagoshima Shimazuke ni tsuite." *Sanshō* 535: 88–93.

Kirino Kōgaku. 2001. "Shūmon no sōsō to shinkō: Dōgen zenji ni okeru sōsōkan o megutte." *Shūgaku kenkyū kiyō* 14: 177–91.

Kitagawa Toyouji. 1984. "Dewa no kuni Murayamagun Yoshikawamura shūshi ninbetsuchō ni yoru kazokushi no kenkyū: Anāru gakuha narabi ni Kenburiji sukūru no shosetsu o joron to shite." *Tōyō daigaku shakaigaku kiyō* 21: 217–42.

Kitamura Gyōon. 1989. *Kinsei kaichō no kenkyū.* Tokyo: Meicho shuppan.

Kizu Yuzuru. 1995. "Sabetsu kaimyō ni zange." *Buraku kaihō* 398: 84–89.

Klein, Susan B. 1995. "Women as Serpent: The Demonic Feminine in the Noh Play *Dōjōji.*" In *Religious Reflections on the Human Body.* Edited by Jane Marie Law. Bloomington: Indiana University Press, 100–136.

————. 2002. *Allegories of Desire: Esoteric Literary Commentaries of Medieval Japan.* Harvard-Yenching Institute Monograph Series 55. Cambridge: Harvard University Asia Center.

Kobayashi Daiji. 1987. *Sabetsu kaimyō no rekishi.* Tokyo: Yūzankaku shuppan.

Kobayashi Masahiro. 1991. *Shūmon mondai o kangaeru: Danka seido to sōzoku no kankei.* Tokyo: Daisan bunmei.

Kobayashi Yutaka, ed. 1987. *Shuzenji no rekishi.* Shuzenji: Nagakura shoten.

Kodama Satoru. 1976. *Kinsei Shinshū no tenkai katei: Nishi Nihon o chūshin to shite.* Tokyo: Yoshikawa kōbunkan.

Kodate Chūzō. 1968. "Tsugaru Sōtōshūshi josetsu." *Hirosaki daigaku kokushi kenkyū* 52: 1–14.

Kōdate Naomi. 1988. "Chi no ike jigoku no esō o meguru oboegaki: Kyūsaisha to shite no Nyoirin Kannon no mondai o chūshin ni." *Etoki kenkyū* 6: 53–76; rpt. in *Jigoku no sekai.* Edited by Sakamoto Kaname. Tokyo: Keisuisha, 1990, 667–90.

————. 1989. "Shiryō shōkai 'Ketsubonkyō wage': Kinseiki Jōdoshū ni okeru Ketsubonkyō shinkō." *Bukkyō minzoku kenkyū* 6: 59–91.

————. 1990. "'Gikyō' Ketsubonkyō o meguru shinkō no shosō." *Kokubungaku kaishaku to kanshō* 55/8: 42–51.

————. 1991. "'Ketsubonkyō' to nyonin kyūsai: 'Chi no ike jigoku no katari' o chūshin to shite." *Kokubungaku kaishaku to kanshō* 56/5: 124–28.

————. 1997. "Ketsubonkyō shinkō reijō to shite no Tateyama." *Sangaku shugen* 20: 75–84.

Kōdate Naomi with Makino Kazuo, 1996. "Ketsubonkyō no juyō to tenkai." In *Onna to otoko no jikū 3.* Edited by Okano Haruko. Tokyo: Nihon joseishi saikō 6, bekkan 1, Fujiwara shoten, 81–115.

Kodera, James. 1980. *Dōgen's Formative Years in China: An Historical Study and Annotated Translation of the "Hōkyō-ki."* London: Routledge & Kegan Paul.

Komaru Toshio, ed. 1996. "'Hakone yokutōki'." *Kyōdo Kanagawa* 36: 37–45.

Kōmoto Mitsugi. 1980. "Jiin to danka no sōshiki." In *Kōza Nihon no minzoku shūkyō 5: Minzoku shūkyō to shakai.* Edited by Gorai Shigeru et al. Tokyo: Kōbundō, 100–23.

Kouamé, Nathalie. 2000. *Initiation à la Paléographie Japonaise: à travers les manuscrits du pèlerinage de Shikoku.* Paris: Langues Mondes L'asiathèque.

————. 2001. *Pèlerinage et société dans le Japon des Tokugawa: Le pèlerinage de Shikoku entre 1598–1868.* Paris: École Française d'Extrême-Orient.

Kudō Eishō. 1988. "Sabetsu no ronri kōzō: Sōtōshū sabetsu kirigami ni okeru gō, rinne, busshō shisō ni tsuite." *Shūgaku kenkyū* 30: 131–36.

————. 1997. "Raibyōsha sabetsu ni ideologii kōzō: Sabetsu ideologii hihan e no kōsō." *Shūgaku kenkyū* 39: 300–305.

————. 1998. "Sendara sabetsu no ideologii kōzō." *Shūgaku kenkyū* 40: 267–72.

Kumagai Chūkō. 1978. *Eiheiji nenpyō.* Tokyo: Rekishi toshosha.

————. 1987. "Dōshōan to Eiheiji." *Sanshō* 524: 38.

————. 1997. "Kinoshita Dōshō ni tsuite: 'Korefusa Kōki' tōjō no jigenin Dōshō kara." *Shūgaku kenkyū* 39: 139–44.

Kumagai Tōzen, ed. 1967. *Osorezan Honbō Entsūjishi.* Aomori: Entsūji.

Kumamoto Einin. 1988. "Ryōan Emyō no Saijōji kaisō ni kansuru ichi kōsatsu." *Shūkyō kenkyū* 61/9: 199–200.

————. 1989. "Dōryōson to Daiyūzan Saijōji ni kansuru rekishiteki ichi kōsatsu." *Shūkyō kenkyū* 62/4: 306–8.

————. 1990. "Ryōan Emyō to sono monka ni tsuite." *Shukyo kenkyu* 63/4: 196–97.

————. 2002. "Dōgen to Tokiyori o meguru nidai no kabuki." *KDBR* 33: 211–20.

Kurachi Katsunao. 1975. "Suzuki Shōsan no shisō: Bakuhansei seiritsuki no shihai shisō ni tsuite no hitotsu no kokoromi." *Nihonshi kenkyū* 155: 24–49.

Kuriyama Taion. 1965. *Sōjijishi*. Yokohama: Daihonzan Sōjiji.

Kyōka Kenshūjo, ed. 1985. *Shūmon sōsai no tokushitsu o saguru*. Kyoto: Dōhōsha shuppan.

LaFleur, William R. 1983. *The Karma of Words: Buddhism and the Literary Arts in Medieval Japan*. Berkeley: University of California Press.

———. 1989. "Hungry Ghosts and Hungry People: Somacity and Rationality in Medieval Japan." In *Fragments for a History of the Human Body, Part One*. Edited by Michael Feher. New York: Urzone, 271–303.

Laidlaw, Ian. 2001. "The Origins and Future of the Burakumin." M.A. thesis, University of Otago.

Lalou, Marcelle. 1938. "Le culte des Nāgas et la thérapeutique." *Journal Asiatique* 226: 1–19.

Le Goff, Jacques. 1988. *Your Money or Your Life: Economy and Religion in the Middle Ages*. New York: Zone Books.

Liscutin, Nicola. 2000. "Mapping the Sacred Body: Shinto Versus Popular Beliefs at Mt. Iwaki in Tsugaru." In *Shinto in History: Ways of the Kami*. Edited by John Breen and Mark Teeuwen. Honolulu: University of Hawai'i Press, 186–204.

Lishka, Dennis. 1976. "Buddhist Wisdom and Its Expression as Art: The Dharma of the Zen Master Takuan." Ph.D. dissertation, University of Wisconsin.

———. 1978. "Zen and the Creative Process: The 'Kendō-Zen' Thought of the Rinzai Master Takuan." *Japanese Journal of Religious Studies* 5/2–3: 139–58.

Liyanaratne, Jinadasa. 1991. "Sinhalese Medical Manuscripts in Paris." In *Medical Literature from India, Sri Lanka and Tibet*. Edited by G. Jan Meulenbeld. Leiden: E. J. Brill, 73–90.

———. 1992. "Sri Lankan Medical Manuscripts in the Bodleian Library, Oxford." *Journal of the European Ayurvedic Society* 2: 36–40.

———. 1995. "Buddhism and Traditional Medicine in Sri Lanka." *The Pacific World* 11: 124–42.

McDannell, Colleen. 1995. *Material Christianity: Religion and Popular Christianity in America*. New Haven: Yale University Press.

Macé, Mieko. 1992. "Evolution de la médecine japonaise face au modèle chinois: Des origines jusqu'au milieu du XVIIIe siècle, L'autonomie par la synthèse." *Cipango: Cahiers d'études japonaises* 1: 111–60.

———. 1994. "L'anatomie occidentale et l'expérience clinique dans la médecine japonaise du XVIe au XVIIIe siècle." In *Nombres, astres, plantes et viscères*. Edited by I. Ang and P. Will. Paris: Mémoires de l'institut des Hautes Etudes Chinoises 35, Collège de France, 135–75.

———. 1994. "Otsuki Gentaku (1757–1827) et la médecine chinoise." In *Mélanges offerts à René Sieffert à l'occasion de son soixante-dixième anniversaire*. Paris: Institut national des langues et civilisations orientales/Centre d'études japonaises, 397–418.

———. 1997. "La médecine de Hoashi Banri (1778–1852): Recherche d'une médecine universelle par un naturaliste encyclopédiste de la première moitié du XIXe siècle." In *Le vase de béryl: Études sur le Japon et la Chine en hommage à Bernard Frank*. Edited by Jacqueline Pigeot and Hartmut Rotermund. Arles: Éditions Philippe Picquier, 405–15.

———. 1998. "Le chinois classique comme moyen d'accès à la modernité: La réception des concepts médicaux occidentaux dans le Japon des XVIIIe et XIXe siècles." *Daruma* 4: 79–103.

———. 1998. "La pensée médicale de l'époque d'Edo et la modernité." In *Tradition et modernité: Quelques aspects du Japon d'Edo et de Meiji*. Edited by S. Murakami-Giroux and C. Séguy. Strasbourg: Université Marc Bloch-Strasbourg, 83–109.

———. 1999. "Japanese Medicine and Modernity in the First Half of the 19th Century: A Case in Point, Hoashi Banri." In *Current Perspectives in the History of Science in*

East Asia. Edited by Kim Yung Sik and Francesca Bray. Seoul: Seoul National University Press, 504–16.

———. 2002. "Takano Chōei (1804–1850): Un savant pris au piège de son temps." In *Repenser l'ordre, repenser l'héritage: Paysage intellectuel du Japon (XVIIe–XIXe siècles)*. Edited by Fréderic Girard, Annick Horiuchi, Mieko Macé. Geneva: Librairie Droz, 449–95.

Machida Shiritsu Hakubutsukan, ed. 1991. *Goō hōin: Inori to chikai no jufu*. Machida: Machida shiritsu hakubutsukan.

McMullin, Neil. 1985. *Buddhism and the State in Sixteenth-Century Japan*. Princeton: Princeton University Press.

MacRae, John R. 1986. *The Northern School and the Formation of Early Ch'an Buddhism*. Honolulu: University of Hawai'i Press.

———. 2003. *Seeing through Zen: Encounter, Transformation, and Genealogy in Chinese Chan Buddhism*. Berkeley: University of California Press.

Maeda Hiromi. 1999. "Ikeda Mitsumasa's Shrine Reform during the Kanbun Period (1661–1672)." Paper presented at November American Academy of Religion meeting, Boston.

———. 2002. "Imperial Authority and Local Shrines: Yoshida Shinto and Its Influence on the Development of Local Shrines." *Japanese Journal of Religious Studies* 29/3–4: 325–58.

———. 2003. "Imperial Authority and Local Shrines: The Yoshida House and the Creation of a Countrywide Shinto Institution in Early Modern Japan." Ph.D. dissertation, Harvard University.

Mahinda, Wetera. 1997. "Medical Practice of Buddhist Monks: A Historical Analysis of Attitudes and Problems." In *Recent Researches in Buddhist Studies: Essays in Honour of Professor Y. Karunadasa*. Edited by Kuala Lumpur Dhammajoti et al. Colombo: Y. Karunadasa Felicitation Committee, 454–65.

Mamoru Takada. 1999. *Onna to hebi*. Tokyo: Chikuma shobō.

Manabe Kōsai. 1960. *Jizō bosatsu no kenkyū*. Kyoto: Sanmitsudō shoten.

Manabe Shunshō. 1994. "Hell of the Bloody Pond and the Rebirth of Women in the Paradise." *Indogaku bukkyōgaku kenkyū* 43/1: 34–38.

Marcure, Kenneth. 1985. "The *Danka* System." *Monumenta Nipponica* 40/1: 39–67.

Matsuda Bunyū. 1982. "Daiyūzan Saijōji no rekishi." *Shūkyō to gendai* 4/5: 30–36.

———. 1984. *Daiyūzan to gokaisansama: Ryōan Emyō zenji no ashiato o tazunete*. Minami Ashigara: Daiyūzan Saijōji.

———. 1995. "Shūmon ni okeru kaimyō juyō no hon'i: Bosatsukai to shite no jukai." In *Kaimyō no imi to kinō*. Edited by Sōtōshū Gendai Kyōgaku Center. Tokyo: Sōtōshū gendai kyōgaku center, 88–92.

Matsuda Shigeo. 1988. *Kirishitan tōrō no shinkō*. Tokyo: Kōbunsha.

Matsumoto Kōichi. 1995. "Kaimyō shinkō no rekishi to mondaiten." In *Kaimyō no imi to kinō*. Edited by Sōtōshū Gendai Kyōgaku Center. Tokyo: Sōtōshū gendai kyōgaku center, 7–14.

Matsune Taka. 1992. "Jōhōsarenakatta sabetsu hōmyō." *Buraku kaihō* 347: 28–36.

Matsuoka Hideaki. 1989. "Waga kuni ni okeru Ketsubonkyō shinkō ni tsuite no ikkōsatsu." *Tokyo daigaku shūkyōgaku nenpō* 6: 85–100; rpt. in *Nihon joseishi ronshū 5: Josei to shūkyō*. Edited by Sōgō joseishi kenkyūkai. Tokyo: Yoshikawa kōbunkan, 1998, pp. 257–79.

Matsuura Shūkō. 1969. *Zenke no sōhō to tsuizen kuyō no kenkyū*. Tokyo: Sankibō busshorin.

———. 1985. *Sonshuku sōhō no kenkyū*. Tokyo: Sankibō busshorin.

Matsuyama Zenshō. 1961. "Tōhoku chihō ni okeru Sōtōshū kyōdan seiritsu no tokushusei: Shōbōji, Eitokuji o chūshin to shite." *Nihon bukkyō* 10: 38–54.

Matsuzaki Kenzō. 1979. "Mawari Jizō no shokeitai: Higashi Nihon no mawari Jizō o chūshin ni." *Nihon bukkyō* 48: 19–37.

Mega Atsuko. 1995. *Hanka no naka no onnatachi: Okayamahan no kiroku kara.* Tokyo: Heibonsha.

Mertz, John. 1996. "Close Encounters of the First Kind: Jippensha Ikku, Kanagaki Robun, and the Literary Construction of National Identity." *Asian Cultural Studies* 22 (1996): 43–58.

Michel, Wolfgang. 2001. "On the Reception of Western Medicine in Seventeenth Century Japan." In *Higashi to nishi no iryō bunka.* Edited by Yoshida Tadashi and Yasuaki Fukuse. Kyoto: Shibunkaku shuppan, 3–17.

Minakata Kumakusu. 1931–32. "Haramifu no shigai yori taiji o hikihanasu koto." *Kyōdo kenkyū* 5/4: 245–46.

Minami Ashigarashi, ed. 1990. *Minami Ashigara shishi betsuhen (8): Jisha, bunkazai, Saijōji rinjūchō.* Minami Ashigara: Minami Ashigarashi.

———. 1999. *Minami Ashigara shishi (6, tsūshihen 1).* Minami Ashigara: Minami Ashigarashi.

Minegishi Shūsai. 1974. "Chūsei Sōtōshū kyōdan no chihō denpa to sono juyōsō." *Kyōka kenshū* 17: 79–85.

Misawa Chishō. 1982. "Daiyūzan Saijōji no bunkazai." *Shūkyō to gendai* 4/5: 42–47.

———. 1991. "Daiyūzan Saijōji to itoku jintsū Dōryō daisatta." *Shidan Ashigara* 29: 8–10.

Mita Genshō. 1975. *Kirishitan denshō.* Tokyo: Hōbunkan shuppan.

Miura Toshiaki. 1983. *Kinsei jisha meimokukin no shiteki kenkyū.* Tokyo: Yoshikawa kōbunkan.

Miyahara Ichirō. 1997. "Kinsei wabishōmon no kōzō to seishitsu: Chichibu Ōnomura no jirei kara." *Kokugakuin daigaku daigakuin kiyō* 29: 305–21.

Miyake Hitoshi. 1997. "Tsuizen kuyō no etoki: Tōzanha Shugen no chiiki teichaku." *Keiō gijuku daigakuin shakaikagaku kenkyūka kiyō* 36: 65–68.

———. 2001. *Shugendō: Essays on the Structure of Japanese Folk Religion.* Ann Arbor: Center for Japanese Studies, University of Michigan.

Miyao Shigeo, ed. 1933. *Kobanashi nido no memie 8.* Tokyo: Kobanashi hanpukai.

Miyashita Hidehiko. 1998. "Tōhoku chihō ni okeru chūsei Sōtō kyōdan no tenkai no ichi danmen: Fukushimaken sesshōseki setsuwa o chūshin to shite." *Aichi gakuin daigaku bunkenkai kiyō* 9: 75–83.

Miyazaki Eishū. 1959. *Kinsei Fuju Fuseha no kenkyū.* Kyoto: Heirakuji shoten.

———. 1969. *Fuju fuseha no genryū to tenkai.* Kyoto: Heirakuji shoten.

———, ed. 1978. *Hokekyō kenkyū 7: Kinsei Hokke bukkyō no tenkai.* Kyoto: Heirakuji shoten.

Miyazaki Fumiko. 2002. "Reijō Osorezan no tanjō." *Kan: Rekishi, kankyō, bunmei* 8: 356–79.

Miyazaki Fumiko with Duncan Williams. 2001. "The Intersection of the Local and Translocal at a Sacred Site: The Case of Osorezan in Tokugawa Japan." *Japanese Journal of Religious Studies* 28/3–4: 399–440.

Mizuno Hakuryū. 1975. "Bihoku chiiki ni okeru Sōtōshū kyōdan no keisei to tenkai." *Tōkai bukkyō* 20.

———. 1983. "Owari ni okeru Sōtōshū kyōdan no keisei ni tsuite." *Shūgaku kenkyū* 25: 107–13.

Moerman, D. Max. 1999. "Localizing Paradise: Kumano Pilgrimage in Medieval Japan." Ph.D. dissertation, Stanford University.

———. 2004. *Localizing Paradise: Kumano Pilgrimage and the Religious Landscape of Premodern Japan.* Cambridge: Harvard University Asia Center.

Mogami Takayoshi. [1960]. 1979. "Muenbotoke ni tsuite." In *Sōsō bosei kenkyū shūsei 3.* Edited by Takeda Chōshū. Tokyo: Meicho shuppan, 1979, 386–93.

Mohr, Michel. 1994. "Zen Buddhism during the Tokugawa Period: The Challenge to Go beyond Sectarian Consciousness." *Japanese Journal of Religious Studies* 21, 4: 341–72.

———. 1997. *Traité sur l'inépuisable lampe du Zen: Tōrei et sa vision de l'éveil.* 2 vols. Bruxelles: Institute Belge des Hautes Études Chinoises, 1997.

———. 2002. "L'Héritage contesté de Dokuan Genkō: Tradition et conflits dans le bouddhisme Zen du XVIIe siècle." In *Repenser l'ordre, repenser l'héritage: Paysage intellectuel du Japon (XVIIe–XIXe siècles).* Edited by Fréderic Girard, Annick Horiuchi, Mieko Macé. Geneva: Librairie Droz, 209–63.

Momozono Keishin. 1954. "Sappan ni okeru shūmon tefuda aratame no jisshi kaisū ni tsuite." *Kadai shigaku* 2: 27–33.

Monier-Williams, Monier. [1899]. 1999. *Sanskrit-English Dictionary.* New Delhi: Munshivam Manoharlal.

Monma Sachio. 1986. "Shūmon ni okeru sabetsu jishō." *Shūgaku kenkyū* 28: 97–106.

Mori Keizō, ed. 1977. *Kinsei Zenrin genkōroku.* Tokyo: Nihon zusho sentā.

Morimoto Kazuhiko. 2002. "Fukudanka kara ikka ichiji e: Dewa no kuni Murayamagun Yamaiemura no jirei." In *Mizoku girei no sekai.* Edited by Mori Takao. Osaka: Seibundō shuppan, 250–69.

Morimoto Sangai. 1960. "Ryōō." *Zen bunka* 18: 45–50.

Morioka Kiyomi. 1981. *Shinshū kyōdan ni okeru 'ie' seido.* Tokyo: Sōbunsha.

Murai Sanae. 1995. "Bakuhansei seiritsuki ni okeru haiya katsudō: Zensō o chūshin ni." In *Kinsei shakai to shūkyō.* Edited by Fujino Tamotsu. Tokyo: Yūzankaku, 457–87.

Murakami Tadashi. 1969. "Higo no kuni Amakusa ni okeru tenryō no seiritsu katci: Daikan Suzuki Shigenari, Shigetoshi o chūshin ni." *Komazawa joshi tanki daigaku kenkyū kiyō* 3: 25–40.

Murayama Shūichi. 1996. *Tenjin goryō shinkō.* Tokyo: Hanawa shobō.

Muromine Bai'itsu. 1965. *Sōjijishi.* Yokohama: Daihonzan Sōjiji.

Nagahara Keiji. 1979. "Medieval Origins of the Eta-Hinin." *Journal of Japanese Studies* 5,2: 385–403.

Nagamitsu Norikazu and Tsumaga Junko, ed. 1978. *Nichirenshū Fuju Fuseha dokushi nenpyō.* Tokyo: Kaimei shoin.

Nagata, Mary. 1999. "Why Did You Change Your Name? Name Changing Patterns and the Life Course in Early Modern Japan." *The History of the Family: An International Quarterly* 4,3: 315–38.

Nagata, Mary, and Chiyo Yonemura. 1998. "Continuity, Solidarity, Family and Enterprise: What Is an IE?" In *House and Stem Family in Eurasian Perspective.* Edited by Antoinette Fauve-Chamoux and Emiko Ochiai. France: Proceedings of the Twelfth International Economic History Congress, 193–214.

Nagata Mizu. 2002. "Transitions in Attitudes toward Women in the Buddhist Canon: The Three Obligations, the Five Obstructions, and the Eight Rules of Reverence." In *Japanese Women and Buddhism.* Edited by Barbara Ruch. Translated by Paul Watt. Ann Arbor: Center for Japanese Studies, University of Michigan, 279–96.

Nakagawa Sugane. 1999. "Inari Worship in Early Modern Osaka." In *Osaka: The Merchant's Capital of Early Modern Japan.* Edited by James McClain and Osamu Wakita. Ithaca: Cornell University Press, 180–212.

Nakajima Keiko. 1992. "Senryūji no mawari Jizō." In *Minkan no Jizō shinkō.* Edited by Ōshima Tatehiko. Tokyo: Keisuisha, 121–78.

Nakamichi Hirochika. 1986. "Continuity and Change: Funeral Customs in Modern Japan." *Japanese Journal of Religious Studies* 13/2–3: 177–92.

Nakamura, Ellen. 2000. "Takano Choei and his Country Friends: A Receptive History of Rangaku." Ph.D. dissertation, Australian National University.

Nakamura Gashun. 1987. "Jūsanbutsu shinkō no denpa ni tsuite: Kyoto Seiganji Jūsanbutsudō o chūshin to shite." *Mikage shigaku* 12: 45–65.

Nakamura Hajime and Ichio Kasahara, eds. 1972. *Ajia bukkyōshi Nihonhen 7: Edo bukkyō, taisei bukkyō to chika shinkō.* Tokyo: Kōsei shuppansha.

Nakamura Kaoru. 1993. "Bukkyō to rai (hansen byō) (3)." *Dōhō bukkyō* 28: 73–140.

Nakano Jūsai. 1987. "Shūmon fukyōjō ni okeru sabetsu jishō 1: Sei sabetsu 'Ketsubonkyō' ni tsuite." *Kyōka kenshū* 30: 283–90.

———. 1993. "Shūmon fukyōjo ni okeru sabetsu jishō (8): Shūseijō ni miru sabetsu to sono mondaiten." *Kyōka kenshū* 36: 120–29.

———. 1998. "'ashiki gōron' no kokufuku: Hansenbyō ni okeru kakuri to danzetsu." *Shūgaku kenkyū* 40: 267–72.

Nakano Keijirō. 1964. "Ōmorishi no sūbutsu seisaku to sono bukkyō bunka." *Shidan Ashigara* 2: 36–44.

Nakano Takeshi. 1995. *Ryaku engi shūsei 1.* Tokyo: Renseisha.

Nakano Tōzen. 1969. "Kōsōden ni okeru shomin geinō no eikyō: Sekkyōbon 'Echizen no kuni Eiheiji kaisanki' ni tsuite." *Shūgaku kenkyū* 11: 61–66.

———. 1999. "Sekkyōbushi 'Echizen no kuni Eiheiji kaisanki' o tōshite mita Dōgen zenji shinkō." *Kyōka kenshū* 43: 45–51.

Nakano Tōzen and Shun'ei Yoshida, eds. 1998. *Akiba shinkō.* Tokyo: Yūzankaku.

Nakano Yūshin [Yūko]. 1993–94. "Sōtōshū ni okeru Ketsubonkyō shinkō." (1) *Shūgaku kenkyū* 35: 269–74; (2) *Sōtōshū shūgaku kenkyūsho kiyō* 7: 115–38.

Nakao Ryōshin. 1998. "Zenmon no sōgi to kaimyō juyō." *Nihon bukkyō gakkai nenpō* 63: 135–48.

Nakaseko Shōdō. 1997. *Dōgen zenjiden kenkyū zoku.* Tokyo: Kokusho kankōkai.

Nakayama Tarō. 1928. *Nihon minzokugaku.* Tokyo: Ōkayama shoten.

Namihira Emiko. 1988. "Ijō shisha no sōhō to shūzoku." In *Bukkyō minzokugaku taikei 4: Sosen saishi to sōbo.* Edited by Fujii Masao. Tokyo: Meicho shuppan, 141–60.

Nanba Tsuneo and Katsuko Komatsu, eds. 2000. *Bukkyō igaku no michi o saguru.* Osaka: Tōhō shuppan.

Nara Yasuaki [Kōmei]. 1988. *May the Deceased Get Enlightenment! An Aspect of the Enculturation of Buddhism in Japan.* Tokyo: Jōchi daigaku Ajia bunka kenkyūsho; rpt. *Buddhist-Christian Studies* 15 (1995): 19–42.

Narikawa Mineo. 1995. "Zenshū no sōsai girei." *Aichi gakuin daigaku Zen kenkyūsho kiyō* 24: 121–66.

Neary, Ian. 1989. *Political Protest and Social Control in Prewar Japan: The Origins of Buraku Liberation.* Manchester: Manchester University Press.

Nei Kiyoshi. 1980. "Toyama baiyaku to shugenja ni tsuite." *IBK* 28/2: 116–17.

———. 1983. "Kirishitan denrai to Arima, Shimabara chihō no jiin." *Nihon rekishi* 427: 72–78.

Ng, Wai-ming. 2000. *The I Ching in Tokugawa Thought and Culture.* Honolulu: University of Hawai'i Press/Association for Asian Studies.

Nichirenshū Jinken Mondai Taisaku Kaigi, ed. 1992. *Sabetsu kaimyō to wa.* Tokyo: Nichirenshū shūmuin.

Nihon Bukkyō Kenkyūkai, ed. 1981. *Zusetsu Nihon bukkyōshi 3: Kinsei.* Kyoto: Hōzōkan.

———. 1995. *Nihon no bukkyō 4: Kinsei, kindai to bukkyō.* Kyoto: Hōzōkan.

———. 2000. *Nihon bukkyō no kenkyū hō.* Kyoto: Hōzōkan.

Nihonyanagi Kenji. 1997. "Nihon mikkyō igaku to yakubutsugaku." In *Rekishi no naka no yamai to igaku.* Edited by Yamada Keiji and Shigehisa Kuriyama. Kyoto: Shibunkaku shuppan, 545–66.

Nishida Kōzō. 1991. "Myōdō Jōe: Shi no wakare." *Edo jidai bungakushi* 8: 11–45.

Nishida Shin'in. 1989. "Sabetsu mondai kara nani ga towareteiru no ka: Zen'aku ingaron no mondaisei ni tsuite no joron." *Shinshū Ōtaniha kyōgaku kenkyūsho kyōka kenkyū* 99: 100–58.

Nishigai Kenji. 1984. *Kinsei yugyō hijiri no kenkyū: Mokujiki kanshō o chūshin to shite.* Tokyo: San'ichi shobō.

———. 1997. *Minshu shūkyō no inori to sugata: Maneki.* Tokyo: Gyōsei.

———. 1998. "Nariwai no ba to shite no dōjadō: Nishi Sagami o chūshin ni shite." *Chihōshi kenkyū* 274: 49–52.

Nishiki Kōichi. 1989. "Kinsei Kantō ni okeru 'chōri' jidan kankei." *Chihōshi kenkyū* 219: 26–40.

———. 1989. "Kinsei Kantō no 'chōri' to dannadera: Sabetsu no rekishiteki ichizuke o mezashite." *Buraku mondai kenkyū* 98: 43–63.

Noguchi Takenori. [1966] 1979. "Fukudankasei to fūfubetsu, oyakobetsu bosei: Nihon no shinzoku kenkyū no ichi shikaku." In *Sōsō bosei kenkyū shūsei 4*. Edited by Mogami Takayoshi. Tokyo: Meichō shuppan, 1979, 375–403.

———. 1980. "Han dankasei." In *Kōza Nihon no minzoku shūkyō 5: Minzoku shūkyō to shakai*. Edited by Gorai Shigeru et al. Tokyo: Kōbundō, 124–37.

Nosco, Peter. 1996. "Keeping the Faith: *Bakuhan* Policy towards Religions in Seventeenth-Century Japan." In *Religion in Japan: Arrows to Heaven and Earth*. Edited by Peter Kornicki and Ian McMullen. Cambridge: Cambridge University Press, 136–55.

Numata Shishi Hensan Iinkai. 1998. "Kashōzan no minzoku shinkō." In *Numatashi shi: minzokuhen*. Edited by Numata Shishi Hensan Iinkai. Numata: Numata shishi hensan iinkai, 973–1012.

Ōbayashi Tarō. 1985. "*Uji* Society and *Ie* Society from Prehistory to Medieval Times." *Journal of Japanese Studies* 11/1: 3–27.

Obelkevich, James. 1979. *Religion and the People from the Middle Ages through the Counter-Reformation: Studies in the History of Popular Religious Beliefs and Practices*. Chapel Hill: University of North Carolina Press.

Oda Susumu. 1989. "Bukkyō to igaku." *Mitsugi to shugyō*. Edited by Yuasa Yasuo. Tokyo: Shunjūsha, 276–319.

Odake Shōkyō. 1998. *Shinshū to sōgi: Dōhō undō no shiten kara*. Kyoto: Honganji shuppan.

Oikawa Jun, ed. 1983. *Hanamaki no densetsu*. Tokyo: Kokusho kankōkai.

Oinuma Seiji. 1990. "Daiyūzan meiboku no matsu." *Shidan Ashigara* 28: 27–36.

Ōishi Manabu. 1994. "Kinsei Ōbakushū jiin to chiiki: Musashi no kuni Tamagun Naganumamura o rei ni." *Inagishi kenkyū* 56: 1–17.

———. 1996. *Kyōhō kaikaku no chiiki seisaku*. Tokyo: Yoshikawa kōbunkan.

Okumoto Takehiro. 1986. "Kinsei zenki no jiin fukkō undō: Suzuki Shōsan o chūshin to shite." *Ryūkoku shidan* 87: 35–56; rpt. in *Nihon joseishi ronshū 5: Josei to shūkyō*. Edited by Sōgō joseishi kenkyūkai. Tokyo: Yoshikawa kōbunkan, 1998, 106–26.

Okumura Hirozumi, ed. 1989. *Shinpen Nihon Jizō jiten*. Tokyo: Murata shoten.

Ōkuwa Hitoshi. 1978. "Kinsei shoki no bukkyō fukkō undō: Suzuki Shōsan to sono shūhen." In *Nihon ni okeru kokka to shūkyō*. Edited by Shimode Sekiyo Hakase Kanreki Kinenkai. Tokyo: Daizō shuppan, 219–46.

———. 1979. *Jidan no shisō*. Tokyo: Kyōikusha.

———. 1979. "Bakuhansei bukkyō no keisei: Suzuki Shōsan to sono shūhen." *Ronshū Nihonjin no seikatsu to shinkō*. Edited by Ōtani Daigaku Kokushi Gakkai. Kyoto: Dōhōsha shuppan, 765–800.

———. 1979. "Bakuhansei kokka no bukkyō tōsei: Shinji kinshirei o megutte." In *Kinsei Bukkyō no shomondai*. Edited by Tamamuro Fumio and Ōkuwa Hitoshi. Tokyo: Yūzankaku, 3–22.

———, ed. 1984. *Sessō Sōsai: Zen to kokka to kirishitan*. Kyoto: Dōhōsha shuppan.

———. 1986. "Kinsei shoki bukkyō shisōshi ni okeru shinshōron: Sessō Sōsai 'Zenkyō Tōron' o megutte." In *Ronshū Nihon bukkyōshi: Edo jidai*. Edited by Tamamuro Fumio. Tokyo: Yūzankaku shuppan, 157–78.

———. 1995. "Jidan seido no seiritsu katei." In *Kinsei shakai to shūkyō*. Edited by Fujino Tamotsu. Tokyo: Yūzankaku, 189–228.

———. 2003. *Nihon bukkyō no kinsei*. Kyoto: Hōzōkan.

Ōno Ichirō. 1998. "Seichi no settoka to shinkō no sōgō kanren." *Chihōshi kenkyū* 274: 33–37.

Ōno Shinkō. 1976. "Shitsunai denpō no hōe to dō sahōchū no kesa no atsukai kata ni tsuite." *Shūgaku kenkyū* 18: 91–96.

Ooms, Herman. 1976. "A Structural Analysis of Japanese Ancestral Rites and Beliefs." In *Ancestors*. Edited by William Newell. The Hague: Mouton, 61–90.

———. 1985. *Tokugawa Ideology: Early Constructs, 1570–1680*. Princeton: Princeton University Press.

———. 1986. "'Primeval Chaos' and 'Mental Void' in Early Tokugawa Ideology: Fujiwara Seika, Suzuki Shōsan, and Yamazaki Ansai." *Japanese Journal of Religious Studies* 13/4: 245–60.

———. 1996. *Tokugawa Village Practice: Class, Status, Power, Law.* Berkeley: University of California Press.

Ōsaka Kōshō, ed. 1996. *Akitaken Sōtōshū jiden taiyō.* Akita: Mumyōsha shuppan.

———. 1999. *Akitaken Sōtōshū hen'nenshi.* Akita: Mumyōsha shuppan.

Ōshima Tatehiko. 1984. "Yuo Daimyōjin." In *Edo shomin no tera: Kaizōjishi.* Edited by Samura Ryūei and Kugai Shōkō. Tokyo: Kaizōji, 89–99.

———, ed. 1992. *Minkan no Jizō shinkō.* Tokyo: Keisuisha.

———. 1999. "Koyasu jinja to koyasukō: Chibashi Hanamigawaku Hatachō." *Seikō minzoku* 169: 24–29.

———, et al., eds. 2002–03. *Jūyonkanbon Jizō bosatsu reigenki.* Tokyo: Miyai shobō. 2 vols.

Ōwa Iwao. 1997. *Tengu to tennō.* Tokyo: Hakusuisha.

Ōyagi Kogaku. 1992. *Zenpōji engi kankei kōshō.* Tsuruoka: Zenpōji.

Ozaki Masayoshi. 1994–95. "Segaki-e ni kansuru ichi kōsatsu." (2) *IBK* 43/1: 131–34; (3) *SKK* 26: 91–104.

———. 1996–97. "Sōtōshū sōsai girei to Onmyōdō." (1) *IBK* 45/1: 202–5; (2) *SKK* 28: 219–38.

Ozaki, Norman. 1979. "Conceptual Changes in Japanese Medicine during the Tokugawa Period." Ph.D. dissertation, University of California, San Francisco.

Ozaki Shōzen. 1994. "Kaimyō no yakuwari ni tsuite." *SKK* 25: 91–106.

———. 1995. "Kaimyō no sabetsusei no kaishō no tame ni." In *Kaimyō no imi to kinō.* Edited by Sōtōshū Gendai Kyōgaku Center. Tokyo: Sōtōshū gendai kyōgaku center, 23–29.

Ozawa Yūichi. 1998. "Daiyūzan sandō no kōhi to nijūhashuku." *Shidan Ashigara* 2: 10–19.

Pagès, Léon. 1869. *Histoire de la religion chrétienne au Japon depuis 1598 jusqu'à 1651.* Paris, n.p.

Parker, Joseph. 1999. *Zen Buddhist Landscape Arts of Early Muromachi Japan (1336–1573).* Albany: State University of New York Press.

Payne, Richard. 1999. "Shingon Services for the Dead." In *Religions of Japan in Practice.* Edited by George J. Tanabe. Princeton: Princeton University Press, 159–65.

Peschard-Erlih, Erika. 1991. *Les mondes infernaux et les peintures des six voies dans le Japon bouddhique.* Paris: Institut national des langues et civilisations orientales Paris 3.

Philippi, Donald L., trans. 1959. *Kojiki: Translated with an Introduction and Notes.* Tokyo: The Institute for Japanese Culture and Classics, Kokugakuin University.

Picone, Mary. 1983. "Lineaments of Ungratified Desire, Rebirth in Snake Form in Japanese Popular Religion." *Res* 5: 105–14.

Rambelli, Fabio. 2002. "Secret Buddhas: The Limits of Buddhist Representation." *Monumenta Nipponica* 57/3: 271–307.

Reader, Ian. 1983. "Contemporary Thought in Sōtō Zen Buddhism: An Investigation of the Publications and Teachings of the Sect in the Light of Their Cultural and Historical Context." Ph.D. dissertation, University of Leeds.

————. 1989. "Images of Sōtō Zen: Buddhism as a Religion of the Family in Contemporary Japan." *Scottish Journal of Religious Studies* 10/1: 5–21.

Reader, Ian, and George Tanabe. 1998. *Practically Religious: Worldly Benefits and the Common Religion of Japan.* Honolulu: University of Hawai'i Press.

Reider, Noriko Tsunoda. 1999. "'Chrysanthemum Tryst': Remaking a Chinese Ghost Story in Japan." *Sino-Japanese Studies* 12/1: 33–46.

————. 2001. "The Emergence of *Kaidan-shū*: The Collection of Tales of the Strange and Mysterious in the Edo Period." *Asian Folklore Studies* 60/1: 79–100.

Riggs, David. 2002. "The Rekindling of a Tradition: Menzan Zuihō and the Reform of Japanese Sōtō Zen in the Tokugawa Era." Ph.D. dissertation, University of California, Los Angeles.

Rotermund, Hartmut O. 1968. *Die Yamabushi: aspekte ihres Glaubens, Lebens und ihrer sozialen Funktion im japanischen Mittelalter.* Hamburg: Hamburgisches Museum fur Völkerkunde.

————. 1973. *Majinai-uta: Grundlagen, Inhalte und Formelemente japanischer magischer Geschichte des 17–20 Jahrhunderts.* Tokyo: Deutsche Gesellschaft fur Natur und Volkerkunde Ostasiens; rpt. Hamburg: OAG, 1975.

————. 1983. *Pèlerinage aux neuf sommets: Carnet de route d'un religieux itinérant dans le Japon du XIXe siècle.* Paris: Centre National de la Recherche Scientifique.

————. 1991. *Hōsōgami ou la petite vérole aisément: Matériaux pour l'étude des épidémies dans le Japon des XVIIIe, XIXe siècles.* Paris: Maisonneuve & Larose.

————. 1995. *Hōsōgami: Edo jidai no yamai o meguru minkan shinkō no kenkyū.* Tokyo: Iwanami shoten.

————. 1995. "Krankheitsbilder in Krankheits-Bildern: Zu den sozial-historischen Bezügen der Darstellungen der Masern (*Hashika-e*)." In *Buch und Bild als gesellschaftliche Kommunikationsmittel in Japan einst und jetzt.* Edited by Susanne Formanek and Sepp Linhart. Druck: Literas, 107–38.

————. 2001. "Demonic Affliction or Contagious Disease? Changing Perceptions of Smallpox in the Late Edo Period." Translated by Royall Tyler. *Japanese Journal of Religious Studies* 28/3–4: 373–98.

Ruch, Barbara A. 1990. "The Other Side of Culture in Medieval Japan." In *Cambridge History of Japan.* Vol. 3: *Medieval Japan.* Edited by Kozo Yamamura. Cambridge: Cambridge University Press, 500–543.

————. 1992. "Coping with Death: Paradigms of Heaven and Hell and the Six Realms in Early Literature and Painting." *Flowing Traces: Buddhism and the Literary and Visual Arts of Japan.* Edited by James Sanford, Masatoshi Nagatomi, and William LaFleur. Princeton: Princeton University Press, 93–130.

————. 2002. "Woman to Woman: *Kumano bikuni* Proslytizers in Medieval and Early Modern Japan." In *Japanese Women and Buddhism.* Edited by Barbara Ruch. Ann Arbor: Center for Japanese Studies, University of Michigan, 537–80.

Ruppert, Brian O. 2002. "Buddhist Rain-making in Early Japan: The Dragon King and the Ritual Careers of Esoteric Monks." *History of Religions* 42/2: 143–74.

Saitō Manabu. 1988. "'Buraku sabetsu to Jōdo shinshū' kenkyū kōsō nōto." *Dōwa kyōiku ronkyū* 10: 152–66.

Sakai, Robert K., et al., trans. 1975. *The Status System and Social Organization of Satsuma: A Translation of the "Shūmon Tefuda Aratame Jōmoku."* Honolulu: University of Hawai'i Press.

Sakauchi Tatsuo. 1974. "Sōtōshū ni okeru mikkyō no juyō." *Shūgaku kenkyū* 16: 35–40.

Sakurai Tokutarō. 1997. "Fukudankasei seiritsu no kiban: Dannadera to sokusaidera." *Shūkyō kenkyū* 70,4: 290–91.

————. 1988. *Kō shūdan no kenkyū.* Tokyo: Sakurai Tokutarō chosakushū 1, Yoshikawa kōbunkan.

Samel, Gerti. 2001. *Tibetan Medicine: A Practical and Inspirational Guide to Diagnosis, Treating and Healing the Buddhist Way*. London: Little, Brown.

Sanford, James H. 1997. "Wind, Waters, Stupas, Mandalas: Fetal Buddhahood in Shingon." *Japanese Journal of Religious Studies* 24/1–2: 1–38.

Sasaki Kōkan. 1993. "'Hotoke shinkō' no seikaku kō: Shūkyō jinruigakuteki shiten kara." *Bunka (Komazawa daigaku)* 16: 29–44.

——. 1995. "Kaimyō no shūkyō: Shakaiteki imi ni tsuite." In *Kaimyō no imi to kinō*. Edited by Sōtōshū Gendai Kyōgaku Center. Tokyo: Sōtōshū gendai kyōgaku center, 15–22.

——. 1998. "'*Hotoke* Belief' and the Anthropology of Religion." Translated by Norman Havens. *Nihon bunka kenkyūsho kiyō* 81: 39–59.

Sasao Tetsuo. 1968. *Kinsei Akita no Rinzai Zen*. Akita: Daihizenji.

——. 1971. *Akitaken Sōtōshū kyōdanshi*. Akita: Daihizenji (rpt. as *Akitaken ni okeru Sōtōshūshi no kenkyū*, 1978).

——. 1972. *Kinsei Akita no tōjō zensō*. Akita: Daihizenji.

Satō Eishin. 1980. "Sado ni okeru jiin no rekishiteki tenkai ni tsuite: Toku ni tōmon jiin o chūshin to shite." *KDBN* 14: 150–53.

Satō Etsujō. 1985. "Owari nanbu chiiki ni okeru Sōtō Zen no tenkai ni tsuite." *Shūkyō kenkyū* 68/4: 216–17.

——. 1987. "Ise chihō ni okeru Sōtōshū no tenkai (2)." *Shūkyō kenkyū* 60/4: 336–37.

——. 1989. "Seihoku chiiki ni okeru bukkyō shoshū no tenkai ni tsuite: Sōtōshū o chūshin to shite." *Shūkyō kenkyū* 62/4: 372–73.

——. 1990. "Owari hokubu chiiki ni okeru Sōtō Zen no tenkai." *Shūgaku kenkyū* 32: 211–16.

——. 1991. "Mikawa chiiki ni okeru Sōtōshū no tenkai (1)." *Shūgaku kenkyū* 33: 245–50.

——. 1997. "Satsuma ni okeru Sōtōshū: Shimazushi to no kankei ni tsuite." *Shūkyō kenkyū* 70/4: 261–62.

Satō Shōshi. 1990–91. "Shūmon sōsai girei no hensen 1–2." *Kyōka kenshū* 33: 46–62; 34: 39–53.

——. 1991. "Tōmon ni okeru zaike sōhō." *Shūkyō kenkyū* 64/4: 328–30.

Satō Shunkō. 1987. "'Chinju Hakusan' kō (jō)." *SKK* 19: 114–24.

——. 1986–88. "Sōtōshū kyōdan ni okeru 'Hakusan shinkō' juyōshi no mondai." *Shūgaku kenkyū* (1) 28: 148–51; (2) 29: 157–60; (3) 30: 168–71.

——. 1988. "'Hakusan' no isō: Sōtōshū kyōdanshi kenkyū no ichi shikō." *KDBR* 19: 343–59.

——. 1992–93. "Kinsei sonraku shakai ni okeru Shugen to Sōtōshū jiin." *Shūgaku kenkyū* (1) 34: 237–41; (2) 35: 238–43.

——. 1994. "'sesshū' no shiten kara miru Shugen jiin to Sōtōshū jiin: Kinsei kindai, Akitahan Hinai chihō ni okeru jirei hōkoku." *Kyōka kenshū* 37: 263–68.

——. 1994–95. "Kinsei Sōtō Zensō no seiu girei." *Shūgaku kenkyū* (1) 36: 205–10; (2) 37: 233–38.

——. 1996. "Kinsei Shugenja no shinkō ni miru Zen to Shintō." *Shūgaku kenkyū* 38: 234–39.

——. 1998. "Kinsei Zenshū to Taishiryū Shintō: Kugihonji Taiseikyō to Sōtōshū Tokuō Ryōkō no shūhen." *IBK* 47/1: 173–76.

——. 1999. "Tokuō Ryōkō no Shintō shisō." *Shūgaku kenkyū* 41: 211–16.

Sawada, Janine. 1993. *Confucian Values and Popular Zen: Sekimon Shingaku in Eighteenth-Century Japan*. Honolulu: University of Hawai'i Press.

——. 1994. "Religious Conflict in Bakumatsu Japan: Zen Master Imakita Kōsen and Confucian Scholar Higashi Takusha." *Japanese Journal of Religious Studies* 21/2–3: 211–30.

————. 2002. "Tokugawa Religious History: Studies in Western Languages." *Early Modern Japan* 10/1: 39–64.

————. 2002. "Bibliography: Religion and Thought in Early Modern Japan." *Early Modern Japan* 10/1: 72–85.

Sawayama Mikako. 1997. "Sendaihan ryōnai akago yōiku shihō to kanren shiryō: Higashiyama chihō o chūshin ni." In *Kinsei Nihon mabiki kankō shiryō shūsei*. Edited by Ōta Motoko. Tokyo: Tōsui shobō, 33–127.

Schafer, Edward H. 1956. "The Development of Bathing Customs in Ancient and Medieval China and the History of the Floriate Clear Palace." *Journal of the American Oriental Society* 76: 57–82.

Schopen, Gregory. 1997. *Bones, Stones, and Buddhist Monks: Collected Papers on the Archaeology, Epigraphy, and Texts of Monastic Buddhism in India*. Honolulu: University of Hawai'i Press.

————. 2004. *Buddhist Monks and Business Matters: Some More Papers on Monastic Buddhism in India*. Honolulu: University of Hawai'i Press.

Schüffner, Rudolf. 1938. *Die Fünferschaft als Grundlage der Staats- und Gemeindeverwaltung und des sozialen Friedens in Japan zur Zeit der Taikwa-Reform und in der Tokugawa-Periode*. Leipzig: Harrassowitz.

Schwaller, Dieter. 1988. "Der Text Mukai Nanshin der Japanischen Zen-Mönchs Chōon Dōkai." *Asiatische Studien/Etudes Asiatiques* 42: 107–119.

————. 1989. *Der Japanische Ōbaku-Mönch Tetsugen Dōkō: Leben, Denken, Schriften*. Bern: Peter Lang.

————. 1996. *Unreiner Zen? Zwei Texte des Ōbaku-Mönchs Chōon Dōkai (1628–1695)*. Bern: Peter Lang.

Sebes, Joseph S. 1979. "Christian Influences on the Shimabara Rebellion, 1637–1638." *Annals of the Jesuit Historical Society* 48: 136–48.

Seidel, Anna. 1978. "Buying One's Way to Heaven: The Celestial Treasury in Chinese Religions." *History of Religions* 17,3–4: 419–31.

————. 1992–93. "Mountains and Hells: Religious Geography in Japanese Mandara Paintings." *Studies in Central and East Asian Religions* 5–6: 122–33.

————. 1996–97. "Descante aux enfers et rédemption des femmes dans le Bouddhisme populaire Japonaise: le pèlerinage du Mont Tateyama." *Cahiers d'Extrême-Asie* 9: 1–14.

Seigle, Cecilia Segawa. 1993. *Yoshiwara: The Glittering World of the Japanese Courtesan*. Honolulu: University of Hawai'i Press.

Seki Tadao. 1986. "Shōsenji no bunkazai, shikō." *Abikoshishi kenkyū* 10: 93–115.

Sekiya Sōhei. 1980. "Meisatsu Daiyūzan no keiiki." *Shidan Ashigara* 18: 4–8.

Sengupta, Sudha. 1989. "Early Buddhism in Japan and the First Indian Priest." In *Amalā Prajñā: Aspects of Buddhist Studies, Professor P. V. Bapat Felicitation*. Edited by N. H. Samtani. Delhi: Sri Satgun Publications, 423–30.

Sengupta, Sukumar. 1989. "Medical Data in the Milindapañha." In *Dr. B. M. Narua Birth Centenary Commemoration Volume*. Calcutta: Bengal Buddhist Association, 111–17.

Seo, Audrey. 1997. "Painting-Calligraphy Interactions in the Zen Art of Hakuin Ekaku (1685–1768)." Ph.D. dissertation, University of Kansas.

Setagayaku Kuritsu Kyōdo Shiryōkan, ed. 1992. *Shaji sankei to daisankō*. Tokyo: Setagayaku kyōdo shiryōkan.

Sharf, Robert. 2001. *Coming to Terms with Chinese Buddhism: A Reading of the Treasure Store Treatise*. Honolulu: University of Hawai'i Press.

Sharma, Arvind. 1989. "The Relation between Disease and Karma in the Milindapañha." In *Amalā Prajñā: Aspects of Buddhist Studies, Professor P. V. Bapat Felicitation*. Edited by N. H. Samtani. Delhi: Sri Satgun Publications, 139–49.

Shaw, R.D.M. 1963. *The Embossed Tea Kettle: Orate Gama and Other Works of Hakuin Zenji*. London: George Allen and Unwin.
Shibata Minoru. 1968. "Kinsei no sezoku shugi to bukkyō." *Bukkyō shigaku* 14/1: 1–15.
Shibatsuji Shunroku, ed. 1979. *Ryūō no Jishōji*. Ryūōchō: Saitō kōgyō.
Shidan Ashigara. 1994. "Kongōsui." *Shidan Ashigara* 32: 92–93.
Shiga Myōgen. 1987–88. "Daiyūzan Saijōji no kaisō engi ni tsuite." *SKK* (1) 19: 104–13; (2) 20: 21–35.
Shiina Hiroo. 1979. "Tokuō Ryōkō to Shimousa Shōsenji." *Abikoshishi kenkyū* 4: 548–62.
Shiina Kōyū, ed. 1983. *Tentokuzan Ryūsenin*. Chiba: Ryūsenin.
———. 1995. "Edoki Zenkairon no tenkai." In *Kaimyō no imi to kinō*. Edited by Sōtōshū Gendai Kyōgaku Center. Tokyo: Sōtōshū gendai kyōgaku center, 82–87.
———. 1995. "Nihon Sōtōshū ni okeru kaimyō (chūsei)." In *Kaimyō no imi to kinō*. Edited by Sōtōshū Gendai Kyōgaku Center. Tokyo: Sōtōshū gendai kyōgaku center, 54–58.
Shimada Hiromi. 1991. *Kaimyō: Naze shigo ni namae o kaeru no ka*. Kyoto: Hōzōkan.
Shimazu Norifumi. 1991. "Kumano shinkō to Nachidaki hōin." In *Goō hōin: Inori to chikai no jufu*. Edited by Machida Shiritsu Hakubutsukan. Machida: Machida shiritsu hakubutsukan, 120–24.
———. 1998. "Kumano goō hōin: Inori no gofu." In *Kumano sanzan shinkō jiten*. Edited by Katō Takahisa. Tokyo: Ebisu kōshō shuppan kabushiki gaisha, 260–75.
Shimizu Hirokazu. 1995. "Bateren tsuihōrei no happu o megutte." In *Kinsei shakai to shūkyō*. Edited by Fujino Tamotsu. Tokyo: Yūzankaku, 359–84.
Shin Kumamotoshishi hensan iinkai, ed. 1996. *Shin Kumamotoshishi: Shiryōhen 3, kinsei 1*. Kumamoto: Kumamotoshi.
Shioiri Shinichi. 1985. "Honmatsu seido no seiritsu to tenkai: Tendaishū." *Rekishi kōron* 111/2: 31–37.
Shiroyama Daiken. 1994. "Hōshōji kakochō sabetsu kisai e no tori kumi." *Buraku kaihō kenkyū* 1: 21–27.
Shōji Chika. 1986. "Yamagataken Murayama chihō no jigokue to etoki." *Etoki kenkyū* 4: 16–32.
Shūkyō to Gendai Henshūbu. 1982. "Daiyūzan o sasaeru Dōryōson no kō." *Shūkyō to gendai* 4,5: 58–63.
Smith, George. 1861. *Ten Weeks in Japan*. London: Longman, Green, Longman, and Roberts.
Smith, Robert J. 1974. *Ancestor Worship in Contemporary Japan*. Stanford: Stanford University Press.
Smyers, Karen A. 1998. *The Fox and the Jewel: Shared and Private Meanings in Contemporary Japanese Inari Worship*. Honolulu: University of Hawai'i Press.
Somada Yoshio. 1981. "Kinsei zenki no jiin gyōsei." *Nihonshi kenkyū* 223: 95–123.
Sōtōshū Dendōbu Eidōka, ed. 1992. *Jinken kara mita baikaryū eisanka*. Tokyo: Sōtōshū shūmuchō.
Sōtōshū Jinken Yōgo Suishin Honbu, ed. 1987. *"Ashiki gōron" kokufuku no tame ni*. Tokyo: Shūkyō to sabetsu booklet 7, Sōtōshū shūmuchō.
———. 1988. *"Zenmon shōsōkun" o yomu*. Tokyo: Shūkyō to sabetsu booklet 8, Sōtōshū shūmuchō.
———. 1993. *"Gō" ni tsuite: Dōgen zenji no ningenkan to buraku kaihō*. Tokyo: Shūkyō to sabetsu booklet 9, Sōtōshū shūmuchō.
Sōtōshū Kinsei Sōden Shūsei Hensan Iinkai, ed. 1986. *Sōtōshū kinsei sōden shūsei*. Tokyo: Sōtōshū shūmuchō.
Sōtōshū Shūhō Chōsa Iinkai, ed. 1992. "Shūhō chōsa iinkai chōsa mokuroku oyobi kaidai: Shōsenji." *Sōtō shūhō* 628 (1992): 410–11.
Sōtōshū Shūmuchō. 1981. "Sōtōshū ni taisuru buraku kaihō dōmei no kakunin kyūdankai keika hōkoku." *Sōtō shūhō* 551: 354–60.

————. 1983. "Buraku kaihō dōmei no mōshiire ni taisuru Sōtōshū no kaitōsho." *Sōtō shūhō* 573: 1–52.

————. 1991. "'Gō' ron ni tsuite: Dōgen Zenji no jinkenkan to buraku kaihō." *Genshoku kenkyū* 12: 6–82.

————. 1994. *"Sabetsu kaimyō" no kaisei ni tsuite.* Tokyo: Sōtōshū Shūmuchō.

————. 1995. *Sōtōshū shūsei sōgō chōsa hōkokusho.* Tokyo: Sōtōshū shūmuchō.

Soymié, Michel. 1965. "Ketsubonkyō no shiryōteki kenkyū." In *Dōkyō kenkyū 1.* Edited by Michel Soymié and Iriya Yoshitaka. Tokyo: Shōshinsha, 109–66.

Stablein, William George. 1978. "A Descriptive Analysis of the Content of Nepalese Buddhist *Pūjās* as a Medical-Cultural System with References to Tibetan Parallels." In *Himalayan Anthropology.* Edited by James Fisher. The Hague: Mouton, 529–37.

Stefánsson, Halldór. 1995. "On Structural Duality in Japanese Conceptions of Death: Collective Forms of Death Rituals in Morimachi." In *Ceremony and Ritual in Japan: Religious Practices in an Industrialized Society.* Edited by Jan van Bremen and D. P. Martinez. London: Routledge, 83–107.

Strickmann, Michel. 2002. *Chinese Magical Medicine.* Edited by Bernard Faure. Stanford: Stanford University Press.

Sugimoto Shunryū. 1982. [1956]. *Tōjō shitsunai kirigami sanwa kenkyū narabi hiroku.* Tokyo: Sōtōshū shūmuchō.

Suwa Gijun. 1984. "Chūgoku bukkyō ni okeru keni kinzetsu no shisō no tenkai to zasetsu." *Aichi gakuin daigaku bungakubu kiyō* 14: 167–85.

Suzuki Akira. 1991. *Edo no myōyaku.* Tokyo: Iwasaki bijutsusha.

————. 1999. *Denshōyaku no jiten: Gama no abura kara yakuyōshū made.* Tokyo: Tokyodō shuppan.

Suzuki Hikaru. 2000. *The Price of Death: The Funeral Industry in Contemporary Japan.* Stanford: Stanford University Press.

Suzuki Iwayumi. 1981. "'shisha kuyō' no ichi kōsatsu: 'Mori kuyō' o megutte." *Shūkyō kenkyū* 64,3: 289–91.

———. 1996. "'Mori kuyō' no jiin gyōjika." *Shūkyō kenkyū* 69/4: 258–59.

Suzuki Kazuo. 1998. *Edo, mōhitotsu no fūkei: Ōedo jisha hanjōki.* Tokyo: Yomiuri shinbunsha.

Suzuki Masakata. 2002. *Nyonin kinsei.* Tokyo: Yoshikawa kōbunkan.

Suzuki Taizan. 1942. *Zenshū no chihō hatten.* Tokyo: Azebō shobō; rpt. Tokyo: Yoshikawa kōbunkan, 1983.

————. 1976. "'Obuse gata' ni kansuru Hirose Ryōkō kun no hanron o shashi gigi no ichi ni oyobu: Hanron ni taisuru hanron." *Shūgaku kenkyū* 18: 9–14.

————. 1978. "Mikawa ni okeru Sōtō Zen no tenkai." *Rekishi techō* 6/7.

————. 1982. *Kasuisai shiten: Chūtō chihō Bukkyō kyōdanshi kō, Fukuroishishi no ikkan to shite.* Fukuroi: Kasuisai.

————. 1993. *Sōtōshū no chiikiteki tenkai.* Kyoto: Shibunkaku shuppan.

Suzuki Yoshiaki. 1996. *Kinsei bukkyō to kange: Bakuen katsudō to chiiki shakai no kenkyū.* Tokyo: Iwata shoin.

Tagami Taishū. 1992. *Bukkyō to sei sabetsu.* Tokyo: Tokyo shoseki.

Taii Yukiko. 1994. "Okiku." In *Nihon fushigi kaku-u denshō jinbutsu dokuhon.* Edited by Miyazaki Miyu. Tokyo: Shinjinbutsu ōraisha, 210–11.

Taira Masayuki. 2001. "Tabous et alimentation carnées dans l'histoire du Japon." In *Identités, marges, méditations: Regards croisés sur la société japonaise.* Edited by Jean-Pierre Berthron, Anne Bouchy, and Pierre Souyri. Translated by Pierre Souyri. Paris: École Française d'Extrême-Orient, 165–82.

Takada, Mamoru. 1999. *Onna to hebi.* Tokyo: Chikuma shobō.

Takahashi Masato, ed. 1986. *Shinshū no bukkyō jiin 3: Zenshū.* Matsumoto: Kyōdo shuppansha.

Takahashi Mitsugi. 1983. "'Jizō bosatsu reigenki' seiritsu no ichi haikei." In *Jizō shinkō.* Edited by Tokutarō Sakurai. Tokyo: Minshu shukyōshi sōsho 10, Yūzankaku, 33–44.

Takahashi Zenryū. 1980. "Honmatsu seiritsu to Tokugawa bakufu no shūkyō seisaku ni tsuite." In _Enkyōdo Sōtōshū jiin honmatsuchō_. Edited by Kagamishima Sōjun. Tokyo: Meicho fukyūkai, 1–16.

Takano Toshihiko. 1989. _Kinsei Nihon no kokka kenryoku to shūkyō_. Tokyo: Tokyo daigaku shuppankai.

Takeda Chōshū. 1957. _Sosen sūhai_. Kyoto: Heirakuji shoten.

——. 1971. _Minzoku bukkyō to sosen shinkō_. Tokyo: Tokyo daigaku shuppankai.

——. 1972. _Kinsei sonraku no shaji to shinbutsu shūgō_. Kyoto: Hōzōkan.

Takei Shōgu. 1978. "Akihasan no shinkō." In _Fuji, Ontake to chūbu reizan_. Edited by Suzuki Shōei. Tokyo: Meicho shuppan, 202–18.

Takemi Momoko. 1976. "Ketsubonkyō no keifu to sono shinkō." _Bukkyō minzoku kenkyū_ 3: 1–9.

——. 1981. "Nihon ni okeru Ketsubonkyō shinkō ni tsuite." _Nihon bukkyō_ 41: 37–49.

——. 1983. "'Menstruation Sutra' Belief in Japan." _Japanese Journal of Religious Studies_ 10/2–3: 229–46 (Translated by W. Michael Kelsey).

Takemura Makio. 1981. "Sōdai seido no hensen ni tsuite." _Shūkyōhō kenkyū_ 2: 79–105.

Takemura Satoru. 1964. _Kirishitan ibutsu no kenkyū_. Tokyo: Kaibunsha shuppan.

Takenuki Genshō. 1976. "Tanba Sonobehan ni okeru Sōtōshū kyōdan no hatten." _Hanazono daigaku kenkyū kiyō_ 7: 121–59.

——. 1978. "'Daitokuji matsujichō' ni tsuite." _Zen bunka kenkyū kiyō_ 10: 171–98.

——. 1979. "Kinsei ni okeru Daitokuji kyōdan: Enkyō no matsujichō o chūshin to shite." In _Kinsei bukkyō no shomondai_. Edited by Tamamuro Fumio and Ōkuwa Hitoshi. Tokyo: Yūzankaku, 145–75.

——. 1980. "Honmatsu kankei no keisei ni tsuite: Zenshū o sozai to shite." _Kinsei bukkyō_ 4/4: 21–27.

——. 1986. "Kinsei gozanha kyōdan: Tenmei, Kan'ei jiin honmatsuchō o chūshin ni shite." In _Ronshū Nihon bukkyōshi: Edo jidai_. Edited by Tamamuro Fumio. Tokyo: Yūzankaku shuppan, 271–304.

——. 1990. _Kinsei Ōbakushū matsujichō shūsei_. Tokyo: Yūzankaku shuppan.

——. 1990. "Ōbakushū no kenkyū: Matsujichō to sore ni miru kyōdan." _Hanazono daigaku kenkyū kiyō_ 21: 34–52.

Takeuchi Kenjō. 1987. "Ise chihō ni okeru Sōtōshū no tenkai (1)." _Shūkyō kenkyū_ 60/4: 335–36.

Takeuchi Kōdō. 2003. "Keizan zenji monka no sōgikan." _Shūgaku kenkyū_ 45: 133–38.

Takeuchi Makoto. 1994. "Festivals and Fights: The Law and the People of Edo." In _Edo and Paris: Urban Life and the State in the Early Modern Era_. Edited by James McClain, John Merriman, and Ugawa Kaoru. Ithaca: Cornell University Press, 384–406.

Takeuchi Michio. 1980–82. "Echigo ni okeru Sōtōshū kyōdan no tenkai ni tsuite." (1) _Niigata kenshi kenkyū_ 7: 1–23; (2) _Shūgaku kenkyū_ 24: 7–13.

——. 1987. "Chūsei Echigo no Zenshū kyōdan no tenkai ni tsuite." _Shūgaku kenkyū_ 29: 113–20.

——. 1989. "Chihō Zenshūshi no kenkyū: Echigo Tsumaari chihō o chūshin ni shite." _Zen kenkyūsho kiyō_ 27: 1–22.

——. 1998. _Echigo Zenshūshi no kenkyū_. Tokyo: Takashi shoin.

Tamamuro Fumio. 1968. "Sōsai kara kitō e: Kinsei bukkyō ni okeru taiwa naiyō no henka." In _Fukyōsha to minshū to no taiwa_. Edited by Nihon Shūkyōshi Kenkyūkai. Kyōtō: Hōzōkan, 128–35.

——. 1974. "Kan'ei no shoshū matsujichō ni tsuite." In _Nihon ni okeru seiji to shūkyō_. Edited by Kasahara Kazuo. Tokyo: Yoshikawa kōbunkan, 101–30.

——. 1981. "Jiin honmatsuchō no seikaku to mondaiten." In _Edo bakufu jiin honmatsuchō shūsei_. Edited by Jiin Honmatsuchō Kenkyūkai. Tokyo: Yūzankaku, 5–26.

——. 1985–86. _Edoki no shūkyō tōsei_. 2 vols. Tokyo: Sōtōshū shūmuchō.

——. 1985b. "Danka seido no seiritsu." _Rekishi kōron_ 2: 115–22.

——. 1986. _Ronshū Nihon bukkyōshi 7: Edo jidai_. Tokyo: Yūzankaku.

————. 1986. "Bakuhan taisei to bukkyō: Kirishitan danatsu to danka seido no tenkai." In *Ronshū Nihon bukkyōshi: Edo jidai.* Edited by Tamamuro Fumio. Tokyo: Yūzankaku shuppan, 1–42.

————. 1987. *Nihon bukkyōshi: Kinsei.* Tokyo: Yoshikawa kōbunkan.

————. 1992. "'Enmei jizō inkō riyakuki' ni tsuite." *Meiji daigaku kyōiku ronshū* 243: 141–63.

————. 1993. "Sōtōshū to Shintō to no kōshō: 'shinpen Sagami no kuni fudokikō' o chūshin to shite." In *Dōgen shisō no ayumi 3: Edo jidai.* Edited by Sōtōshū shūgaku kenkyūsho. Tokyo: Yoshikawa kōbunkan, 224–47.

————. 1994. "Edo jidai ni okeru chokkyo shie, ten'e no tenkai." *Sōtōshū jinken yōgo suishin honbu kiyō* 1: 133–67.

————. 1995. "Danka seido no tenkai katei: Sagami no kuni Ashigarakamigun Chitsushimamura shūmon ninbetsuchō no bunseki." In *Kinsei shakai to shūkyō.* Edited by Fujino Tamotsu. Tokyo: Yūzankaku, 171–88.

————. 1995. "'Dōshōan Monjo' ni tsuite." *Sanshō* (1) 622: 19–25; (2) 623: 20–28; (3) 624: 26–39.

————, ed. 1996. *Nihon bukkyō no rekishi: Edo jidai.* Tokyo: Kōsei shuppansha.

————. 1996. "Okayamahan no jisha seiri seisaku ni tsuite." *Meiji daigaku jinbun kagaku kenkyūsho kiyō* 40: 364–82.

————. 1997. "Kirishitan kinsei to terauke seido." In *Le vase de béryl: Études sur le Japon et la Chine en hommage à Bernard Frank.* Edited by Jacqueline Pigeot and Hartmut Rotermund. Arles, France: Éditions Philippe Picquier, 581–606.

————. 1997. "On the Suppression of Buddhism." In *New Directions in the Study of Meiji Japan.* Edited by Helen Hardacre and Adam Kern. Translated by Adam Kern. Leiden: E. J. Brill, 499–505.

————. 1999. *Edo jidai no Sōtōshū no tenkai.* Tokyo: Sōtōshū booklet shūkyō to sabetsu 11, Sōtōshū shūmuchō.

————. 1999. *Sōshiki to danka.* Tokyo: Yoshikawa kōbunkan.

————. 1999. "Edo jidai no jibyō shūkyō: 'togenuki Jizō' o chūshin to shite." *Kumamoto igakkaishi* 72/2–3: 190–99.

————. 1999. "Nihon ni okeru minzoku shinkō: Togenuki Jizō shinkō." In *Rekishi no naka no minshū bunka.* Edited by Meiji Daigaku Jinbun Kagaku Kenkyūsho. Tokyo: Meiji daigaku kōkai bunka kōza, Kazama shobō, 5–64.

————. 2000. "Togenuki Jizō to byōki." In *Kurashi no naka no sukui.* Edited by Nihon Fūzokushi Gakkai. Tokyo: Tsukubanekai, 72–108.

————. 2001. "Danka seido no seiritsu to tenkai." *Kanagawa chiikishi kenkyū* 19: 1–31.

————. 2001. "Local Society and the Temple-Parishioner Relationship within the *Bakufu*'s Governance Structure." Translated by Holly Sanders. *Japanese Journal of Religious Studies* 28/3–4: 260–92.

Tamamuro Fumio with Ōkuwa Hitoshi, ed. 1971. *Edo bakufu no shūkyō tōsei.* Tokyo: Hyōronsha.

Tamamuro Fumio et al., eds. 1977–79. *Yugyō nikkan.* 3 vols. Tokyo: Kadokawa shoten.

————. 1978–80. *Kinsei ōjōden shūsei.* 3 vols. Tokyo: Yamakawa shuppansha.

————. 1982. *Zenkoku Jishū shiryō shozai mokuroku.* Tokyo: Daigaku kyōikusha.

————. 1982. "Sōtōshū to danka seido." In *Shūkyō shūdan no ashita e no kadai: Sōtōshū shūsei jittai chōsa hōkokusho.* Edited by Odawara Rinin. Tokyo: Sōtōshū shūmuchō, 304–14.

————. 1979. *Kinsei bukkyō no shomondai.* Tokyo: Yūzankaku.

Tamamuro Taijō. 1963. *Sōshiki bukkyō.* Tokyo: Daihōrinkaku.

————, ed. 1967. *Nihon bukkyōshi 3: Kinsei kindaihen.* Kyoto: Hōzōkan.

Tanaka Hisao. 1965. "Kobaka: Sono sōsei ni shimaru ichi ni shite." *Minzoku* 29: 14–24; rpt. in *Sōsō bosei kenkyū shūsei 1.* Edited by Doi Takuji and Satō Yoneshi. Tokyo: Meicho shuppan, 1979, 314–30.

————. 1978. *Sosen saishi no kenkyū*. Tokyo: Kōbundō.

Tanaka Masaaki. 1980. "'ichimantai inzō Jizōson kan'ōki' (gen Sugamo Jizō) ni tsuite." *Bukkyō minzoku kenkyū* 5: 41–48.

————. 1992. "'ichimantai inzō Jizō kan'ōki' no koto domo." In *Minkan no Jizō shinkō*. Edited by Ōshima Tatehiko. Tokyo: Keisuisha, 109–20.

Tanaka Sen'ichi. 1992. "Sōshū Ōyamakō no oshi to danka." In *Ōyama shinkō*. Edited by Tamamuro Fumio. Tokyo: Yūzankaku, 63–90.

Tanaka Takako. 1996. *Sei naru onna: Saigū, Megami, Chūjōhime*. Kyoto: Jinbun shoin.

Tanaka Yōhei. 2001. "Kinsei ni okeru shugen jiin no kaidan to kitō jidan kankei." *Fūzoku shigaku* 16: 18–31.

Tanigawa Zenryū, ed. 1993. *Sōtōshū Fukudasan Tokuunji*. Matsumoto: Tokuunji.

Tatsukawa Shōji. 1979. *Kinsei byōsōshi: Edo jidai no byōki to iryō*. Tokyo: Heibonsha.

————. 1993. *Byōki o iyasu chiisa na kamigami*. Tokyo: Heibonsha.

Teiser, Stephen F. 1988. *The Ghost Festival in Medieval China*. Princeton: Princeton University Press.

————. 1994. *The Scripture on the Ten Kings and the Making of Purgatory in Medieval Chinese Buddhism*. Honolulu: University of Hawai'i Press.

Terabayashi Shun. 1998. *Kyūsai no hito: Kosetsu, Ninshō*. Tokyo: Tōyō keizai shinpōsha.

Till, Barry, and Paula Swart. 1997. "Elegance and Spirituality of Japanese Kesa." *Arts of Asia* 27/4: 51–63.

Tōdai Shiryō Hensanjo, ed. 1968–69. *Dai Nihon kinsei shiryō: Shoshū matsujichō*. 2 vols. Tokyo: Tokyo daigaku shuppankai.

Tokieda Tsutomu. 1984. "Chūsei Tōgoku ni okeru Ketsubonkyō shinkō no yōsō: Kusatsu Shiranesan o chūshin to shite." *Shinano* 36/8: 28–45.

————. 1984. "Sekibutsu to Ketsubonkyō shinkō: Ōyama sanroku Minoge no Jizōson o megutte." *Nihon no sekibutsu* 32: 27–33.

Tokoro Rikiyo. 1989. "Uirō uri kō." In *Sengokuki shokunin no keifu: Sugiyama Hiroshi hakase tsuitō ronshū*. Edited by Tokoro Rikiyo and Nagahara Keiji. Tokyo: Kadokawa shoten, 323–37.

Tokushōji Gojikai, ed. 1994. *Tokushōji engi to jihō*. Niigata: Tokushōji.

Tomonaga Kenzō. 1989. "Gendai no buraku mondai." In *Buraku kahōshi: Netsu to hikari*. Edited by Buraku Mondai Kenkyūsho. Osaka: Buraku mondai kenkyūsho, 154–312.

Toyoda Takeshi. 1938. *Nihon shūkyō seidoshi no kenkyū*. Tokyo: Kōseikaku.

Tsuji Zennosuke. 1953–55. *Nihon bukkyōshi 8–10*. Tokyo: Iwanami shoten.

————. 1955. *Nihon bukkyōshi 4*. Tokyo: Iwanami shoten.

Tsukada Akinobu. 1977. "Rentai no Kōshakushū: Kinsei shōdō setsuwa no ichikōbō." *Bungaku ronsō* 52: 76–93.

Tsunoda Tairyū. 2001. "Sōtōshū ni okeru sōsai no shūgiteki igizuke." *Shūgaku kenkyū kiyō* 14: 119–25.

Tsuruoka Tokio, ed. 1982. *Jippensha Ikku "Hakone, enoshima, Kamakura dōchūki."* Tokyo: Senshūsha.

Tsutsumi Kunihiko. 1993. "Kosodate yūreitan no genzō: Sōtōshū sōsō girei o tegakari to shite." *Kyoto Seika daigaku kiyō* 4: 244–56; rpt. in *Setsuwa: Sukui to shite no shi*. Edited by Setsuwa Denshō Gakkai. Tokyo: Kanrin shobō, 1994, 117–42; rpt. as "Kosodate yūreitan no genfūkei." In *Kinsei setsuwa to zensō*. Osaka: Izumi shoin, 1999, 133–52.

————. 1993. "Tōmon Zensō to shinrei saido setsuwa: Wakasa Kōyōji no engi o chūshin." *Denshō bungaku kenkyū* 41: 25–45.

————. 1993. "Zensō no hōriki: Sōtōshū kanyo no higuruma setsuwa to kinsei kidan bungei." *Setsuwa bungaku kenkyū* 28: 53–73.

————. 1996. *Kinsei Bukkyō setsuwa no kenkyū: Shōdō to bungei*. Tokyo: Kanrin shobō.

————. 1996. "Dōgen eden no seiritsu." In *Shūso kōsōeden (etoki) shū*. Edited by

Watanabe Shōgo and Masahiko Hayashi. Tokyo: Denshō bungaku shiryō shūsei 15, Miyai shoten, 281–340.

———. 1999. *Kinsei setsuwa to zensō*. Osaka: Izumi shoin.

———. 1999. "Ano yo no shōkohin: Kinsei setsuwa no naka no katasode yūreitan." *Setsuwa denshōgaku* 7: 131–46.

———. 1999. "'Dōgen eden' to etoki." *Kokubungaku kaishaku to kanshō* 64/12: 151–63.

Tyler, Royall. 1977. *Selected Writings of Suzuki Shōsan*. Ithaca: China-Japan Program, Cornell University.

———. 1984. "The Tokugawa Peace and Popular Religion: Suzuki Shōsan, Kakugyō Tōbutsu, and Jikigyō Miroku." In *Confucianism and Tokugawa Culture*. Edited by Peter Nosco. Princeton: Princeton University Press, 92–119.

———, trans. 2001. *The Tale of Genji*. New York: Viking.

Udaka Ryōtetsu. ed. 1979. *Edo Jōdoshū jiin shiryō shūsei*. Tokyo: Daitō shuppansha.

———. 1982. "Jōdoshū no furegashira seido ni tsuite: Toku ni Shinano no kuni o chūshin to shite." *IBK* 31/1: 236–39.

———. 1983. "Shoshū Edo furegashira seiritsu nenji kō." *Taishō daigaku kenkyū kiyō* 68: 59–87.

———. 1987. *Edo bakufu no bukkyō kyōdan tōsei*. Tokyo: Tōyō bunka.

———. 1987b. *Tokugawa Ieyasu to Kantō bukkyō kyōdan*. Tokyo: Tōyō bunka.

Ueba Akio. 1985. "Honmatsu seido no seiritsu to tenkai: Jōdo Shinshū." *Rekishi kōron* 111/2: 49–54.

———. 1999. *Kinsei Shinshū kyōdan to toshi jiin*. Kyoto: Hōzōkan.

Ueda Junichi. 1986. "Chūsei chihō Zen'in no hatten ni kansuru ichi kōsatsu: Satsuma Noda Kan'ōji no baai." *Shien* 123.

———. 1995. "Zenshū ni okeru isō to iryō no mondai ni tsuite." *Zengaku kenkyū* 73: 81–100.

Uemura Takayoshi. 1982. "Hiradohan ni okeru jiin seisaku to tōmon jiin." *Shūgaku kenkyū* 24: 135–40.

Ujiie Mikito. 1997. *Fugimitsū: Kinjirareta ai no Edo*. Tokyo: Kōdansha.

Usami Hideki. 1997. "Kinsei Yakuho no 'shōhyō, Shōgoken' hogo." *Shiga daigaku keizaigakubu fuzoku shiryōkan* 30: 83–107.

Vaporis, Constantine. 1994. *Breaking Barriers: Travel and the State in Early Modern Japan*. Cambridge: Council on East Asian Studies, Harvard University Press.

Vargas-O'Brian, Ivette. 2002. "The Life of dGe slong ma dPalmo: The Experience of a Leper, the Founder of a Fasting Ritual, a Transmitter of Buddhist Teachings on Suffering and Renunciation in Tibetan Religious History." *Journal of the International Association of Buddhist Studies* 24/2: 157–86.

Vesey, Alexander M. 2001. "Entering the Temple: Priests, Peasants, and Village Contention in Tokugawa Japan." *Japanese Journal of Religious Studies* 28/3–4: 293–328.

———. 2002. "The Buddhist Clergy and Village Society in Early Modern Japan." Ph.D. dissertation, Princeton University.

Wada Kenju. 1959. "Sagami heiya ni okeru Sōtōshū no hatten ni tsuite." *Komazawa daigaku shūkyō shakai kenkyūshohō* 4: 2–13.

———. 1970. "Bukkyō shūzoku ni arawareta kazu no kōsatsu: Kuyō shūzoku o chūshin to shite." *KDBK* 28: 31–45.

———. 1973. "Sagami ni okeru bukkyō kyōdan seiritsu hatten ni kansuru kōsatsu." *KDBK* 31: 69–87; *KDBR* 4: 1–15.

———. 1981. "Bukkyō sōsō jibutsu no hatten hikaku kō." *KDBK* 39: 21–35.

Waddell, Norman A. 1984. *The Unborn: The Life and Teaching of Zen Master Bankei, 1622–1693*. San Francisco: North Point Press.

———. 1994. *The Essential Teachings of Zen Master Hakuin: A Translation of the Sokkō-roku Kaien-fusetsu*. Boston: Shambhala Publications.

————. 1996. *Zen Words from the Heart: Hakuin's Commentary on the Heart Sutra*. Boston: Shambhala Publications.

————. 1999. *Wild Ivy: The Spiritual Autobiography of Zen Master Hakuin*. Boston: Shambhala Publications.

Wakabayashi Haruko. 1995. "Tengu: Images of the Buddhist Concepts of Evil in Medieval Japan." Ph.D. dissertation, Princeton University.

————. 2002. "The Dharma for Sovereigns and Warriors: Onjō-ji's Claim for Legitimacy in *Tengu zōshi*." *Japanese Journal of Religious Studies* 29/1–2: 35–66.

Wakatsuki Shōgo. 1971. "Edo jidai no sōryo no daraku ni tsuite: Sono shorei." *KDBR* 2: 5–19.

Wakita Haruko. 1995. "Women and the Creation of the *Ie* in Japan: An Overview from the Medieval Period to the Present." *U.S.-Japan Women's Journal English Supplement* 4: 83–105.

————. 1999. "The Formation of the *Ie* and Medieval Myth: The *Shintōshū*, Nō Theatre, and Picture Scrolls of Temple Origins." In *Gender and Japanese History*. Vol. 1. Edited by Wakita Haruko, Anne Bouchy, and Ueno Chizuko. Translated by Micah Auberback. Osaka: Osaka University Press, 53–85.

Wallace, Vesna A. 1995. "Buddhist Tantric Medicine in the *Kālacakratantra*." *The Pacific World* 11: 155–74.

Walter, Mariko. 2004. "Structure of the Japanese Buddhist Funeral." In *Death Rituals and the Afterlife in Japanese Buddhism*. Edited by Mariko Walter and Jacqueline Stone. Honolulu: University of Hawai'i Press.

Wang-Toutain, Françoise. 1997. *Le bodhisattva Kṣitigarbha en Chine du Ve au XIIIe siècle*. Paris: Presses de l'École Française d'Extrême Orient.

Wang Xiuwen. 2000. "Momo no densetsushi." *Nihon kenkyū* 20: 125–72.

Watanabe Kōshō. 1960. "Sōtōshū kyōdan no kinseiteki hatten: Bakufu seido to no kanren ni oite." *Hōsei shigaku* 13.

————. 1963. "Kinsei Sōtō kyōdan no keisei katei: Denpō kuji o chūshin to shite." *IBK* 11/1: 166–67.

————. 1965. "Kinsei jiin no sōroku kikō to deiri no kenkyū: Ōshū chiiki no Sōtōshū rokusho no bunseki." *Komazawa daigaku shūkyō shakai kenkyūshohō* 7: 16–24.

————. 1967. "Sōtōshū kyōdan no chihō sōroku to daimyō no tenpō: Ōshū Miharuyō ni okeru rokusho sōron." *Hōsei shigaku* 19: 65–73.

Watanabe Masao. 1979. *Miura hantō no nōmin seikatsu*. Kanagawa Pref.: Rōkkō shōkai.

Watanabe Shōei. 1980. "Zen to kitō, sono kankei ni tsuite." *Shūkyō kenkyū* 55/3: 204–5.

————. 1981. "Zenshū to minshū ni tsuite: Daiyūzan Saijōji no baai." *SKKK* 13: 166–84.

————. 1981–82. "Daiyūzan Saijōji ni okeru shūkyōteki keitai ni tsuite." *Shūkyō kenkyū* (1) 64/3: 293–95; (2) 65/3: 185–86.

————. 1982. "Saijōji no nenju gyōji no ichi shiten." *Shūkyō to gendai* 4/5: 51–57.

————. 1982–83. "Zenshū jiin to minshū ni tsuite (2): Nenmatsu nenshi no Saijōji o chūshin ni; (3) Daiyūzan Saijōji no kōchū keisei ni tsuite." (2) *SKKK* 14: 82–106; (3) *SKK* 15: 51–74.

————. 1985. "Mori kuyō to Zenshū jiin ni tsuite no ichishiten." *Shūkyō kenkyū* 68,4: 210–11.

————. 1986. "Edo kara Meiji made no kaichō." In *Dōryōson teito gojunshakuki*. Edited by Itō Dōgaku et al. Minami Ashigara: Daiyūzan Saijōji, 83–164.

————. 1986. " 'Mori kuyō' ni okeru Zenshū jiin no ichi." *SKKK* 17: 134–48.

————. 1986. "Zenshū jiin no kaichō ni tsuite: Daiyūzan Saijōji no baai." *SKKK* 18: 114–24.

————. 1986. "Zenshū jiin to tengu shinkō to ichi rei: Kashōzan to Numata matsuri no baai." *Shūkyō kenkyū* 69,4: 305–6.

————. 1987. "Zenshū jiin to Akiba shinkō to shomin: Akibadera no himatsuri o chūshin ni." *Shūkyō kenkyū* 60/4: 333–35.

————. 1989. "Zenshū jiin no kitō to kōmoto ni tsuite." *Shūkyō kenkyū* 62/4: 305–6.

————. 1990. "Akiba shinkō to Akiba sanjakubō no nanajūgozen ni tsuite." *Shūkyō kenkyū* 63/4: 254–56.

————. 1995. "Zenshū kitō jiin to shomin no sesshoku ni tsuite." *Shūkyō kenkyū* 68/4: 371–73.

————. 1996. "Akiba shinkō ni okeru shinkō taishō no ichirei ni tsuite." *Shūkyō kenkyū* 69/4: 306–7.

————. 1998. "Akiba shinkō to daisankō no genjō ni tsuite." *Shūkyō kenkyū* 71/4: 399–401.

————. 1999. "Minzoku shūkyō kara mita Akiba shinkō no ichi." *Shūkyō kenkyū* 72/4: 323–24.

————. 2001. "Minzoku bukkyō to shite no Akiba shinkō to zenshū jiin ni tsuite." *Shukyō kenkyū* 74/4: 353–54.

Watanabe Shōgo. 1989. *Tsuizen kūyō no hotokesama: Jūsanbutsu shinkō.* Tokyo: Keisuisha.

————. 1995. *Chūseishi no minshū shōdō bungei.* Tokyo: Iwata shoin.

Watanabe Takeo. 1983. "Mukashi no Dōryōkōson mōde to kosandō." *Shidan Ashigara* 21: 5–12.

Watari Kōichi. 1986. "Kinsei Jizō setsuwashū to Jizō engi: Jūyonkanbon 'Jizō bosatsu reigenki' no baai." *Musashino bungaku* 33: 14–18.

————. 1987. "Jōe to kinsei Jizō setsuwashū: 'Enmei Jizō bosatsukyō jikidanshō' no haikei." *Setsuwa bungaku kenkyū* 22: 1–9.

————. 1989. "'Jizō bosatsu riyakushū' no sekai: Jōkyō, Genroku jidai no minkan Jizō shinkō." *Bukkyō minzoku kenkyū* 6: 39–58.

————. 1991. "'Jizō bosatsu rijōki' ni tsuite." *Meiji daigaku kyōyō ronshū* 242: 39–59.

————. 1993. "'Jizō bosatsu mujukyō' ni tsuite." *Meiji daigaku kyōyō ronshū* 257: 235–62.

————. 1999. "Osanaki mōjatachi no sekai: 'sai no kawara' no zuzō o megutte." In *"Sei to shi" no zuzōgaku.* Edited by Meiji Daigaku Jinbun Kagaku Kenkyūsho. Tokyo: Kazama shobō, 197–243.

Waters, Virginia Skord. 1997. "Sex, Lies, and the Illustrated Scroll: The *Dōjōji Engi Emaki.*" *Monumenta Nipponica* 57/1: 59–84.

Watt, Paul B. 1978. "The Life and Thought of Jiun Sonja (1718–1804)." Ph.D. dissertation, Columbia University.

————. 1984. "Jiun Sonja (1718–1804): A Response to Confucianism within the Context of Buddhist Reform." In *Confucianism and Tokugawa Culture.* Edited by Peter Nosco. Princeton: Princeton University Press, 188–214.

Wigmore, John Henry, ed. 1969. *Law and Justice in Tokugawa Japan: Materials for the History of Japanese Law and Justice under the Tokugawa Shogunate, 1603–1867.* Tokyo: Kokusai bunka shinkōkai.

Williams, Duncan. 1998. "Temples, Pharmacies, Traveling Salesmen, and Pilgrims: Buddhist Production and Distribution of Medicine in Edo Japan." *Supplement to the Japanese Religions Bulletin,* New Series 23 (Februrary): 20–29.

————. 1998. "The Monastery, Popular Rituals, and the Zen Master: New Histories of Medieval Japanese Zen Buddhism." *Critical Review of Books in Religion,* 255–64.

————. 1999. "Arai to iyashi no bunka: Bukkyō to onsen." In *Nihon de mitsuketa takaramono.* Edited by Imanishi Shōko. Tokyo: Kōdansha, 59–70.

————. 2000. "Representations of Zen: A Social and Institutional History of Sōtō Zen Buddhism in Edo Japan." Ph.D. dissertation, Harvard University.

————. 2004. "Funerary Zen: Sōtō Zen Death Management in Tokugawa Japan." In

Death Rituals and the Afterlife in Japanese Buddhism. Edited by Jacqueline Stone and Mariko Walter. Honolulu: University of Hawai'i Press.

———. 2003. "How Dōshō's Medicine Saved Dōgen: Medicine, Dōshō'an, and Edo-Period Dōgen Biographies." In *Chan Buddhism in Ritual Context*. Edited by Bernard Faure. London: Routledge Curzon Press, 266–88.

———. 2003. "Nihon bukkyō ni okeru seisui: Shingonshū no keisusutadī." In *The Proceedings of the Fourth Symposium on Global Perspectives in Japanese Studies: Encountering Japanese Studies Abroad*. Tokyo: Ochanomizu University, 219–25.

———. 2004. "Religion in Early Modern Japan." In *Nanzan Guidebook for the Study of Japanese Religions*. Edited by Paul Swanson et al. Nanzan: Nanzan Institute for Religion and Culture.

———. 2004. "The Cult of Doryō Daigongen and Saijōji: A Sōtō Zen Prayer Temple in Early Modern Japan." In *Title TBA*. Edited by Carl Bielefeldt. Stanford: Stanford University Press.

———. 2004. "The Healing Jizō Bodhisattva in Tokugawa Japan: The 1822 *Enmei Jizō-son inkō riyakuki.*" *Monumenta Nipponica*, forthcoming.

Williams, Duncan, and Barbara Ambros, eds. 2001. *Local Religion in Tokugawa History*. Nanzan: Japanese Journal of Religious Studies Special Issue 28/3–4, Nanzan Institute for Religion and Culture.

Williams, Duncan, et al., ed. 2004. "Saijō rinjū dainikkan ni tsuite." *Minzoku bukkyō kenkyūkai kiyō* 2.

Yamada Keiji and Shigehisa Kuriyama, eds. 1997. *Rekishi no naka no yamai to igaku*. Kyoto: Shibunkaku shuppan.

Yamaguchi Yaichirō. 1953. "Shitai bunri maisō jiken: Ninpu sōsō girei." *Minkan denshō* 17/5: 50–52.

Yamamoto Mitsumasa. 1973. "Sōshū Yagurazawa ōkan ni tsuite." *Kanagawa kenshi kenkyū* 19: 46–56.

Yamamoto Naotomo. 1981–82. "Kinsei buraku jiin no seiritsu ni tsuite." *Kyoto burakushi kenkyūsho kiyō* (1) 1: 80–126; (2) 2: 34–62.

Yamamoto Seiki. 1979. "Kinsei Sōtōshū no honmatsu seido ni tsuite." In *Kinsei Bukkyō no shomondai*. Edited by Tamamuro Fumio and Ōkuwa Hitoshi. Tokyo: Yūzankaku, 65–84; rpt. in *Dōgen zenji to Sōtōshū*. Eidted by Kawamura Kōdō and Ishikawa Rikizan. Tokyo: Yoshikawa kōbunkan, 1985, 269–90.

———. 1980. "Kan'ei no shoshū honmatsuchō (Sōtōshū) ni tsuite." *Nihon Bukkyō* 50–51: 50–77.

———. 1988. "Shoki Zenshū jiin no seikaku ni tsuite: Kōzuke no kuni Chōrakuji o chūshin ni." In *Nihon shūkyōshi ronsan*. Edited by Shimode Sekiyo. Tokyo: Ōfūsha, 192–215.

Yamamoto Shun'ichi. 1993. *Nihon raishi*. Tokyo: Tokyo daigaku shuppankai.

Yamaoka Ryūkō. 1979. "Bukkyō jiin ni okeru shūkyōteki fukugō no ichi keitai: Daiyūzan Saijōji no jirei." *SKKK* 11: 157–68.

———. 1982. "Daiyūzan Saijōji no kō no ichi kōsatsu." *Shūkyō kenkyū* 65/3: 184–85.

———. 1987. "Jiin engi ni mirareru tengu denshō no motif to sono imi." *Komazawa daigaku shūkyōgaku ronshū* 13: 65–75.

Yamatoshi, ed. 1983. *Yamatoshishi 2: Tsushihen kinsei*. Yamato: Yamatoshi.

Yanagita Kunio. 1969. "Senzo no hanashi." In *Teibon Yanagita Kunio 10*. Tokyo: Chikuma shobō, 1–152.

———. 1969. [1931] "Sōei no enkaku shiryō." In *Teibon Yanagita Kunio 15*. Tokyo: Chikuma shobō, 521–52.

———. 1975. [1929] *Sōsō shūzoku goi*. Tokyo: Kokusho kankōkai.

Yasutaka Teruoka. 1989. "The Pleasure Quarters and Tokugawa Culture." In *18th Century Japan: Culture and Society*. Edited by C. Andrew Gerstle. London: Allen and Unwin, 3–32.

Yiengsprukswan, Mimi. 1996. "The Visual Ideology of Buddhist Sculpture in the Late

Heian Period as Configured by Epidemic and Disease." In *Bukkyō bijutsu kenkyū ni okeru zuzō to yōshiki.* Tokyo: 14th International Taniguchi Symposium, Kokusai kōryū bijutsushi kenkyūkai, 69–80.

Yifa. 1996. "The Rules of Purity for the Chan Monastery: An Annotated Translation and Study of the *Chanyuan qinggui*." Ph.D. dissertation, Yale University.

———. 2002. *The Origins of Buddhist Monastic Codes in China. An Annotated Translation and Study of the Chanyuan Qinggui.* Honolulu: University of Hawai'i Press.

Yokoi Noriaki. 1999. "'sesshōseki' densetsu kō: Shūkyō jinruigaku no hōhō to shiza kara." *KDBR* 30: 291–309.

———. 2000. "Gennō oshō no densetsu to onsen." *Zen no kaze* 21: 68–71.

———. 2000. "Zendera no densetsu to onsen no bunka." *Sōtōshū kenkyūin kenkyū kiyō* 30: 145–56.

Yokozeki Ryōin, ed. 1938. *Edo jidai tōmon seiyō.* Tokyo: Bukkyōsha.

Yonemoto, Marcia. 2003. *Mapping Early Modern Japan: Space, Place, and Culture in the Tokugawa Period (1603–1868).* Berkeley: University of California Press.

Yoshida Dōkō. 1998. "Den Jakushitsu Kenkō 'Fukuan Jukai no Enyu' kō: 'shinjin kedo' to 'jukai jōbutsu' ni tsuite." *IBK* 47/1: 167–72.

Yoshida Kasuhiko. 2002. "The Enlightenment of the Dragon King's Daughter in *The Lotus Sutra*." In *Japanese Women and Buddhism.* Edited by Barbara Ruch. Translated by Margaret Childs. Ann Arbor: Center for Japanese Studies, University of Michigan, 297–324.

Yoshida Shun'ei. 1992–95. "Sōtōshū ni okeru Akiba shinkō." *Shūgaku kenkyū* (1) 34: 242–47; (2) 35: 244–50; (3) 36: 211–16; (4) 37: 239–44.

———. 1996. "Minkan shinkō no kyōkagakuteki ichi kōsatsu: Akibakō no chōsa jirei kara." *Kyōka kenshū* 39: 194–200.

Yoshida Tadashi and Yasuaki Fukuse, eds. 2001. *Higashi to nishi no iryō bunka.* Kyoto: Shibunkaku shuppan.

Yoshida Yoshiyuki. 1989. "Ryūnyo no jōbutsu." In *Shiriizu, Josei to bukkyō 2: Sukui to oshie.* Edited by Ōsumi Kazuo and Nishiguchi Junko. Tokyo: Heibonsha, 45–91.

Yoshimura Toyū. 1980. "Kinsei shoki Kumamotohan ni okeru Kirishitan kisei no tenkai." *Shigaku kenkyū* 149: 1–25.

Yoshioka Shin. 1994. *Edo no kigusuriya.* Tokyo: Seiabō.

———. 1998. *Kinsei Nihon yakugyōshi kenkyū.* Tokyo: Yakuji nippōsha.

Yuasa Takashi. 1988. "Edo ni okeru kinseiteki kaichō no tenkai." *Shikan* 99: 87–98.

———. 1996. "Edo no kaichōfuda." *Kokuritsu rekishi minzoku hakubutsukan kenkyū hōkoku* 67: 197–224.

Yuji Sogen. 1995. "Shūtenchū no 'sendara' ni taisuru gendaigo yaku ya chūki no mondai ni tsuite." *Shūgaku kenkyū* 37: 292–97.

Zenshū Chihōshi Chōsakai, ed. 1978–98. *Zenshū chihōshi chōsakai nenpō.* 5 vols. Tokyo: Zenshū chihōshi chōsakai.

Zen Nihon Bukkyōkai, ed. 1987. *Sabetsu mondai to gōron ni tsuite.* Tokyo: Zen Nihon bukkyōkai.

Zwilling, Leonard. 1980. "On Bhaisajyaguru and His Cult." In *Studies in the History of Buddhism.* Edited by A. K. Narain. Delhi: B. R. Publishing Co., 413–21.

Zysk, Kenneth G. 1991. *Asceticism and Healing in Ancient India: Medicine in the Buddhist Monastery.* New York: Oxford University Press.

———. 1995. "New Approaches to the Study of Early Buddhist Medicine: Use of Technical Brāhmanic Sources in Sanskrit for the Interpretation of Pali Medical Texts." *The Pacific World* 11: 143–54.